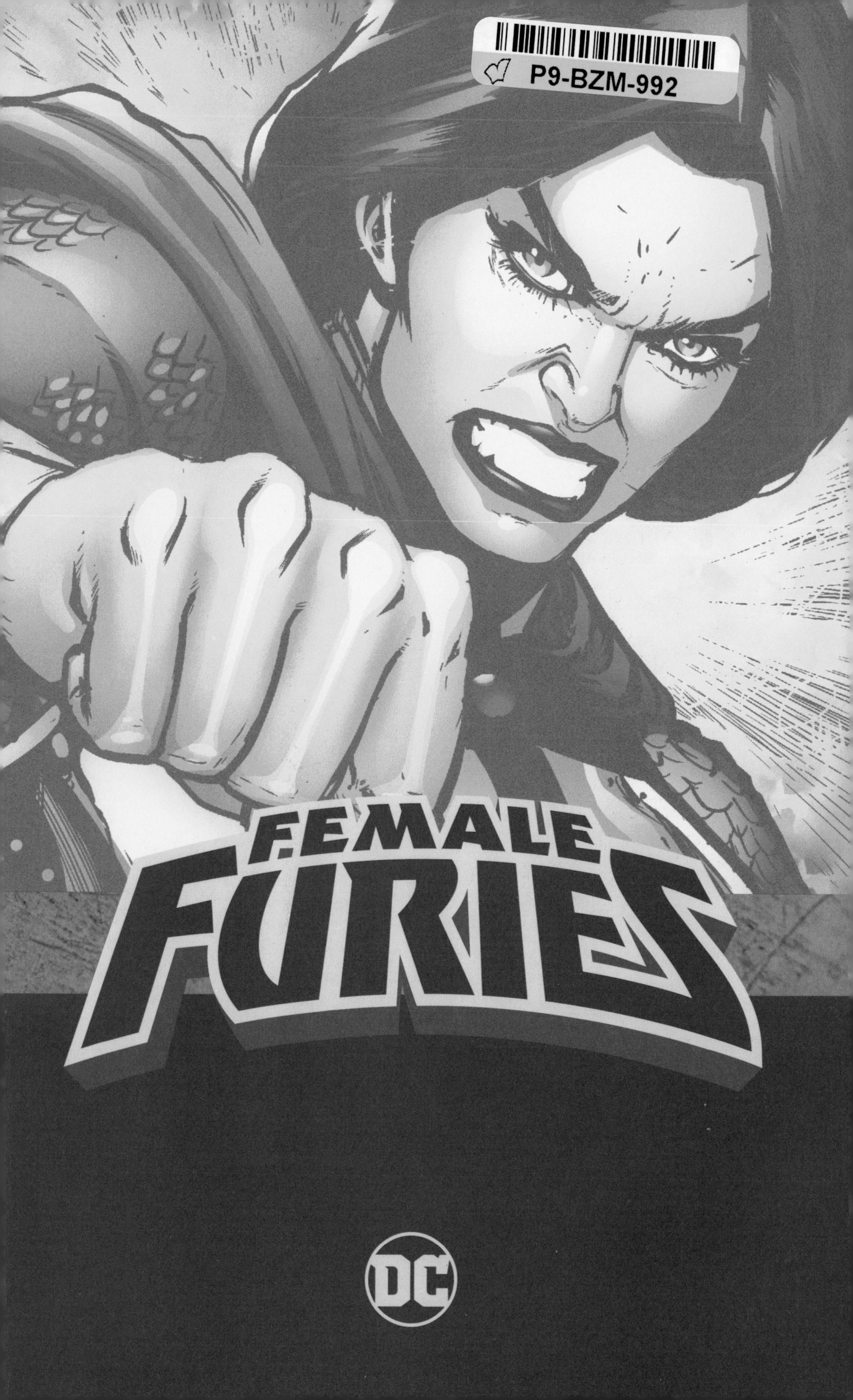

FEMALE FURIES

DC

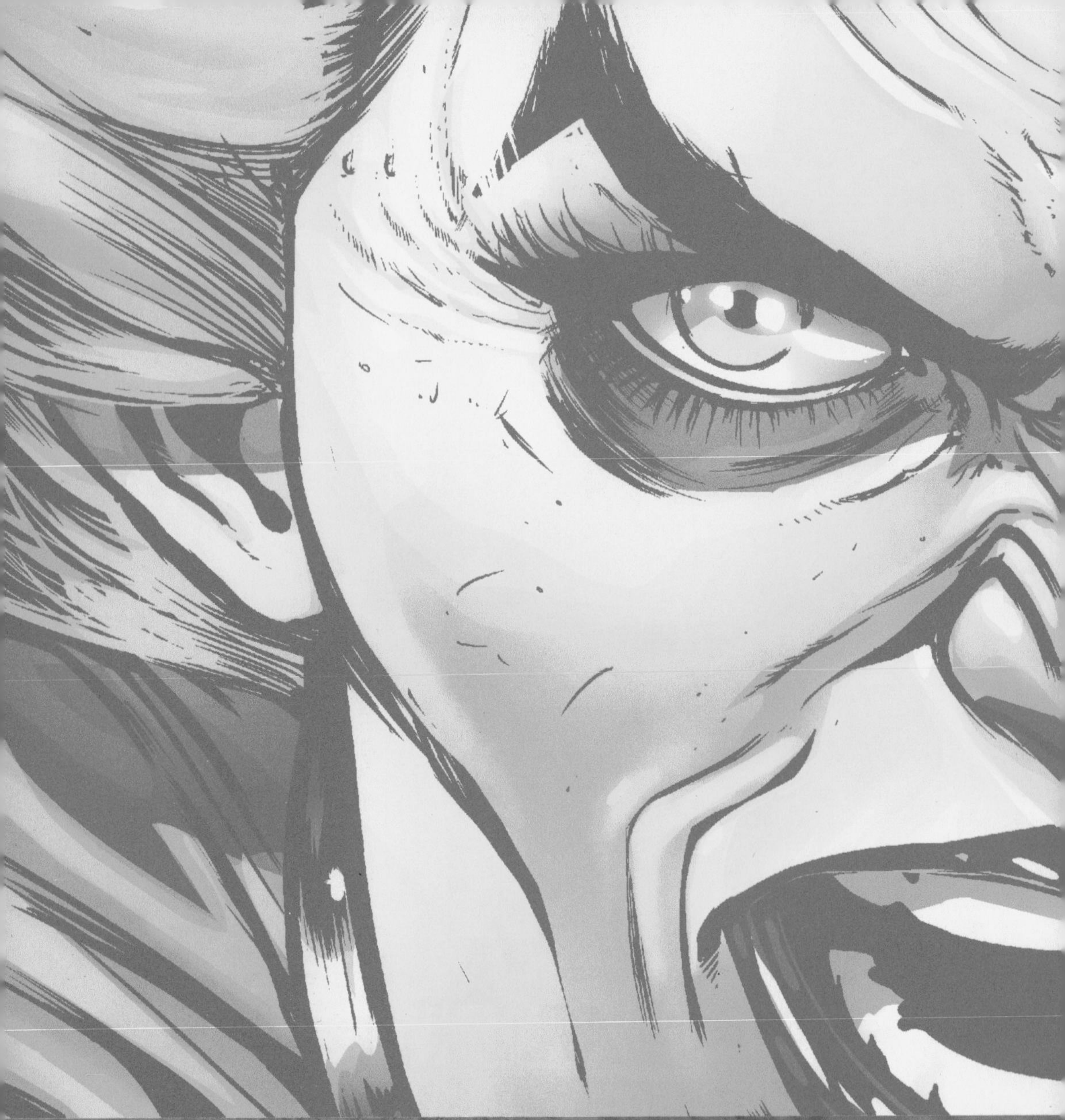

CECIL CASTELLUCCI writer **ADRIANA MELO** illustrator
HI-FI colorist **SAL CIPRIANO, CARLOS M. MANGUAL** letterers **JOËLLE JONES** & **LAURA ALLRED** collection cover artists

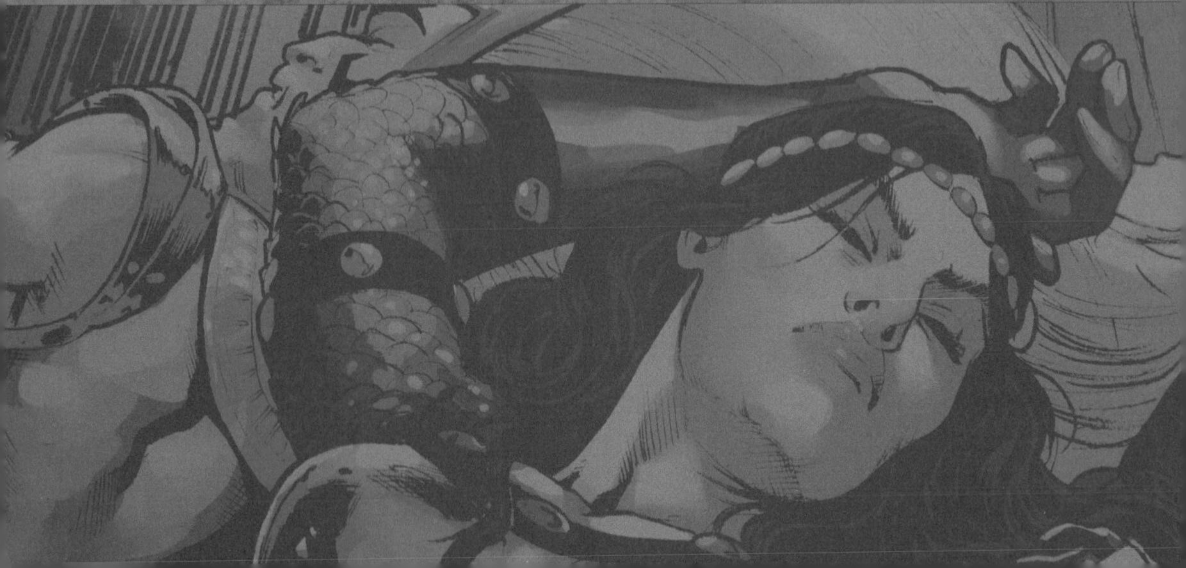

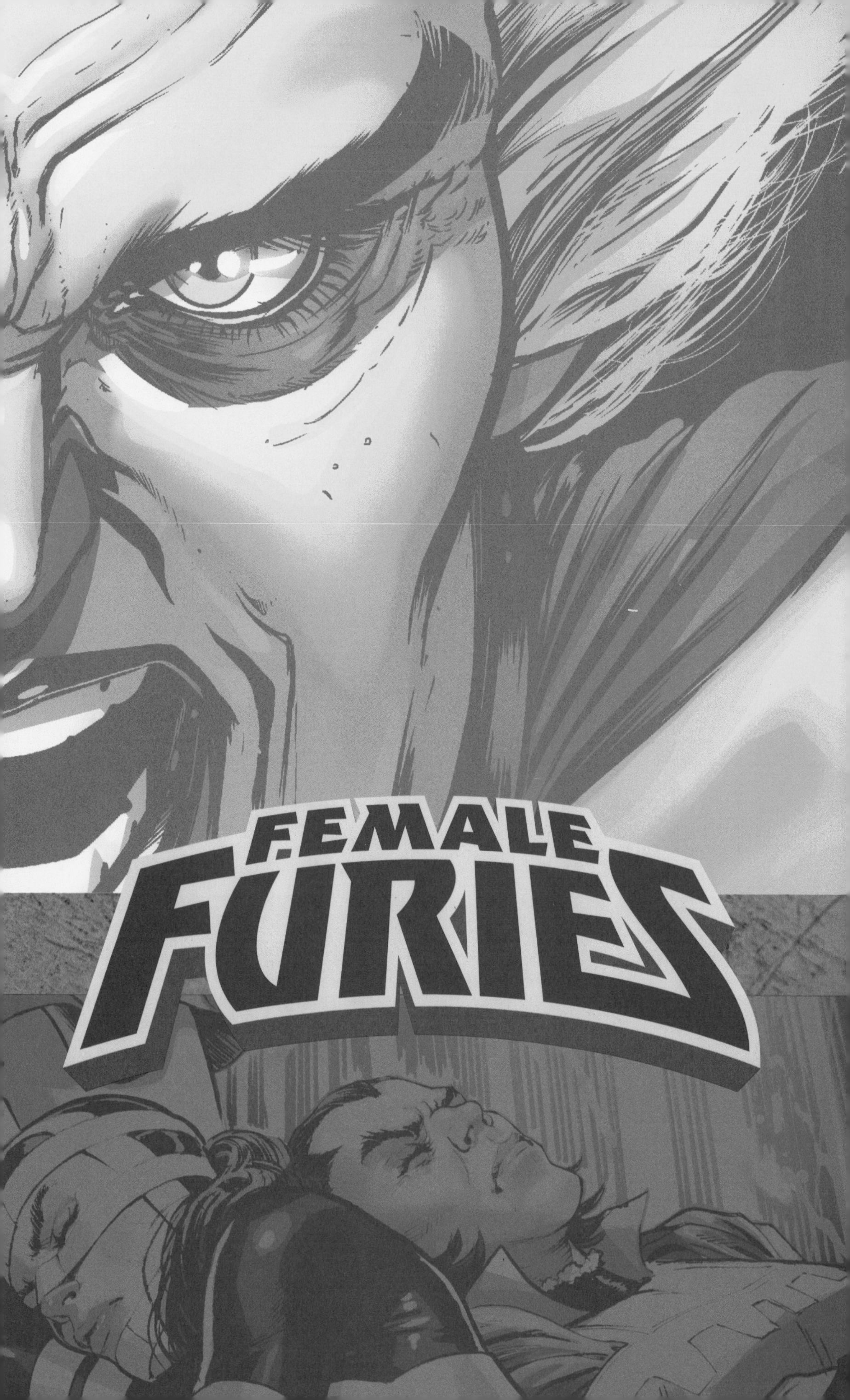
FEMALE
FURIES

JAMIE S. RICH Editor – Original Series
BRITTANY HOLZHERR, HARVEY RICHARDS Associate Editors – Original Series
JEB WOODARD Group Editor – Collected Editions
ALEX GALER Editor – Collected Edition
STEVE COOK Design Director – Books
JOHN J. HILL Publication Design
CHRISTY SAWYER Publication Production

BOB HARRAS Senior VP – Editor-in-Chief, DC Comics
PAT McCALLUM Executive Editor, DC Comics

DAN DiDIO Publisher
JIM LEE Publisher & Chief Creative Officer
BOBBIE CHASE VP – New Publishing Initiatives & Talent Development
DON FALLETTI VP – Manufacturing Operations & Workflow Management
LAWRENCE GANEM VP – Talent Services
ALISON GILL Senior VP – Manufacturing & Operations
HANK KANALZ Senior VP – Publishing Strategy & Support Services
DAN MIRON VP – Publishing Operations
NICK J. NAPOLITANO VP – Manufacturing Administration & Design
NANCY SPEARS VP – Sales
MICHELE R. WELLS VP & Executive Editor, Young Reader

DC Comics, 2900 West Alameda Ave., Burbank, CA 91505
Printed by LSC Communications, Owensville, MO, USA. 11/15/19. First Printing.
ISBN: 978-1-4012-9711-4

Library of Congress Cataloging-in-Publication Data is available.

PEFC Certified

This product is from
sustainably managed
forests and controlled
sources

PEFC/29-31-337   www.pefc.org

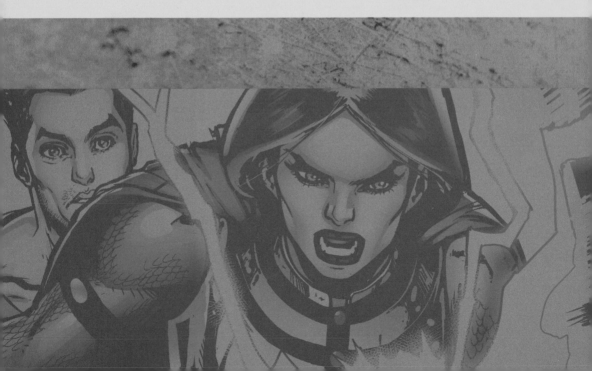

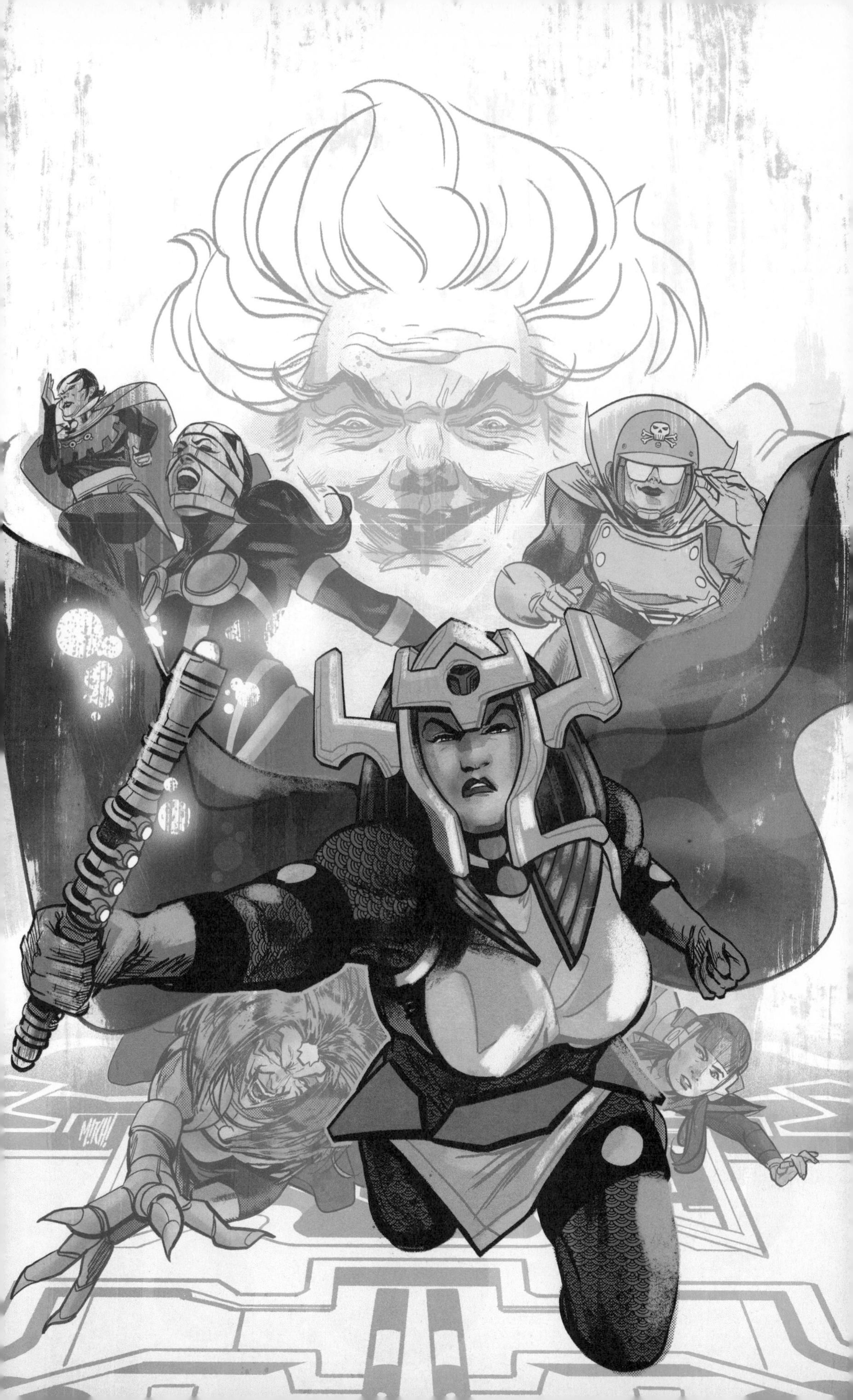

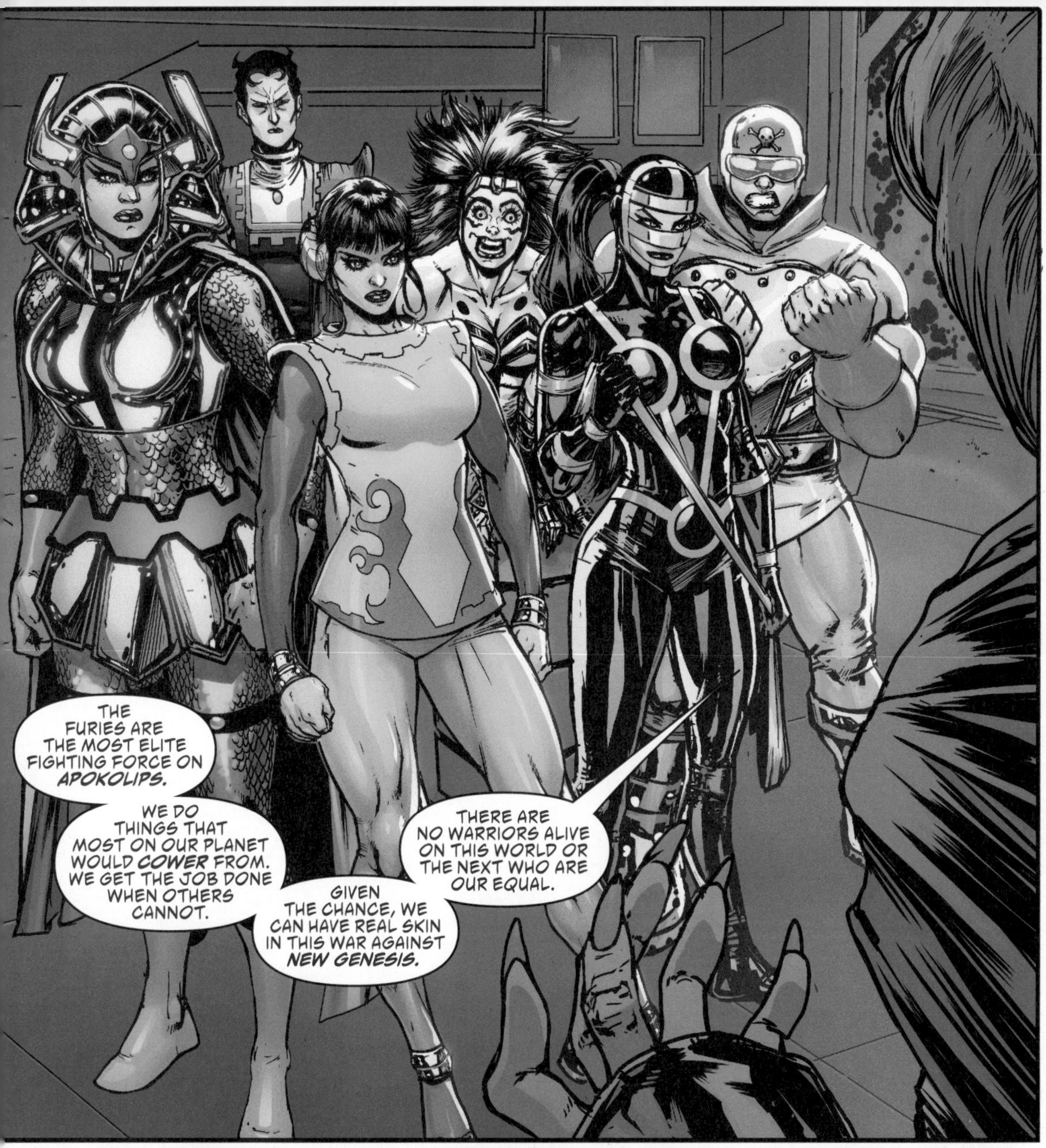
THE FURIES ARE THE MOST ELITE FIGHTING FORCE ON *APOKOLIPS.*
WE DO THINGS THAT MOST ON OUR PLANET WOULD *COWER* FROM. WE GET THE JOB DONE WHEN OTHERS CANNOT.
GIVEN THE CHANCE, WE CAN HAVE REAL SKIN IN THIS WAR AGAINST *NEW GENESIS.*
THERE ARE NO WARRIORS ALIVE ON THIS WORLD OR THE NEXT WHO ARE OUR EQUAL.

WRITER **CECIL CASTELLUCCI** ILLUSTRATOR **ADRIANA MELO** COLORS **HI-FI** LETTERS **CARLOS M. MANGUAL**

FEMALE FURIES PART ONE: "ANYTHING YOU CAN DO I CAN DO BLEEDING"

COVER **MITCH GERADS** ASSOC. EDITOR **BRITTANY HOLZHERR** EDITOR **JAMIE S. RICH**

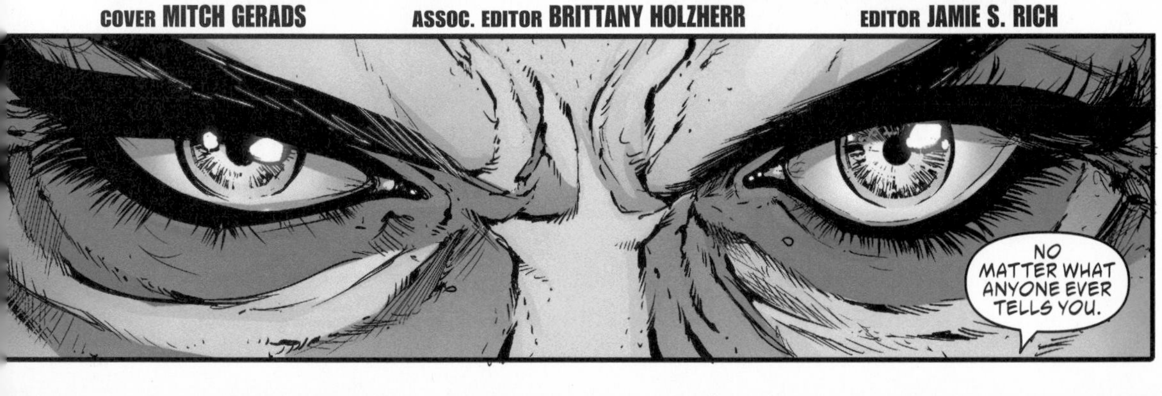
NO MATTER WHAT ANYONE EVER TELLS YOU.

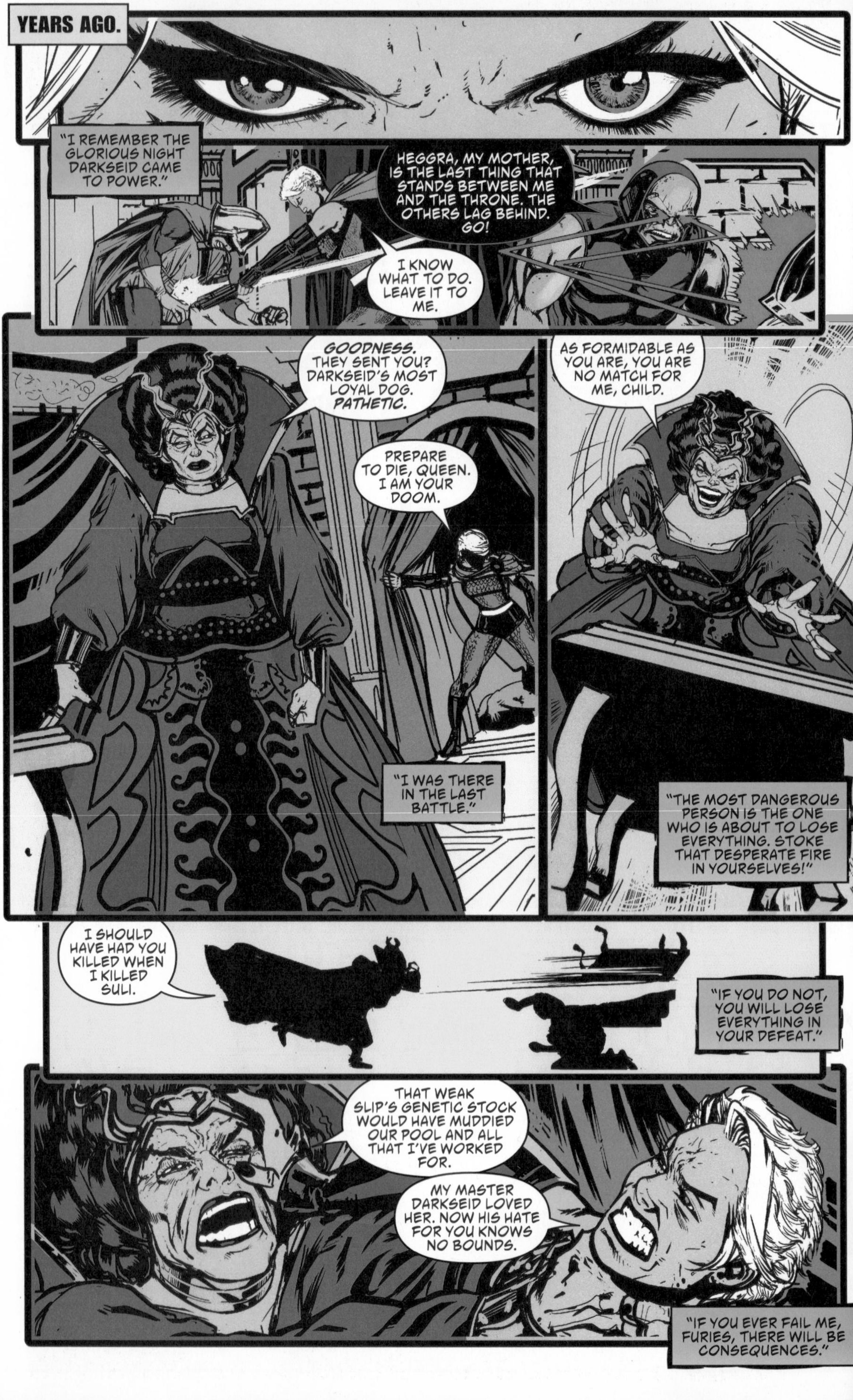

YEARS AGO.
"I REMEMBER THE GLORIOUS NIGHT DARKSEID CAME TO POWER."
HEGGRA, MY MOTHER, IS THE LAST THING THAT STANDS BETWEEN ME AND THE THRONE. THE OTHERS LAG BEHIND. GO!
I KNOW WHAT TO DO. LEAVE IT TO ME.
GOODNESS. THEY SENT YOU? DARKSEID'S MOST LOYAL DOG. PATHETIC.
PREPARE TO DIE, QUEEN. I AM YOUR DOOM.
"I WAS THERE IN THE LAST BATTLE."
AS FORMIDABLE AS YOU ARE, YOU ARE NO MATCH FOR ME, CHILD.
"THE MOST DANGEROUS PERSON IS THE ONE WHO IS ABOUT TO LOSE EVERYTHING. STOKE THAT DESPERATE FIRE IN YOURSELVES!"
I SHOULD HAVE HAD YOU KILLED WHEN I KILLED SULI.
"IF YOU DO NOT, YOU WILL LOSE EVERYTHING IN YOUR DEFEAT."
THAT WEAK SLIP'S GENETIC STOCK WOULD HAVE MUDDIED OUR POOL AND ALL THAT I'VE WORKED FOR.
MY MASTER DARKSEID LOVED HER. NOW HIS HATE FOR YOU KNOWS NO BOUNDS.
"IF YOU EVER FAIL ME, FURIES, THERE WILL BE CONSEQUENCES."

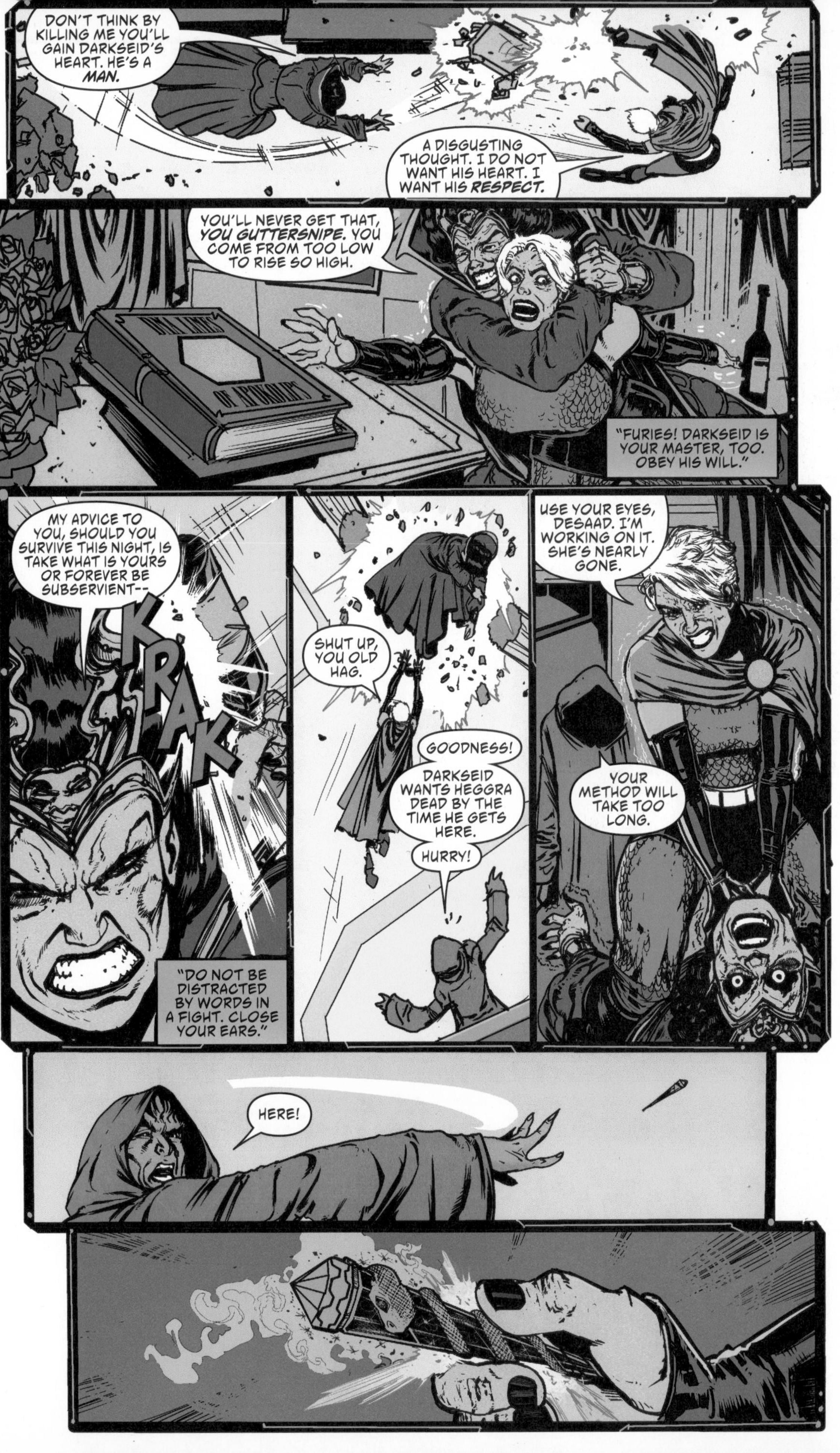
DON'T THINK BY KILLING ME YOU'LL GAIN DARKSEID'S HEART. HE'S A *MAN.*
A DISGUSTING THOUGHT. I DO NOT WANT HIS HEART. I WANT HIS *RESPECT.*
YOU'LL NEVER GET THAT, *YOU GUTTERSNIPE.* YOU COME FROM TOO LOW TO RISE SO HIGH.
"FURIES! DARKSEID IS YOUR MASTER, TOO. OBEY HIS WILL."
MY ADVICE TO YOU, SHOULD YOU SURVIVE THIS NIGHT, IS TAKE WHAT IS YOURS OR FOREVER BE SUBSERVIENT--
KRAK
"DO NOT BE DISTRACTED BY WORDS IN A FIGHT. CLOSE YOUR EARS."
SHUT UP, YOU OLD HAG.
GOODNESS!
DARKSEID WANTS HEGGRA DEAD BY THE TIME HE GETS HERE.
HURRY!
USE YOUR EYES, DESAAD. I'M WORKING ON IT. SHE'S NEARLY GONE.
YOUR METHOD WILL TAKE TOO LONG.
HERE!

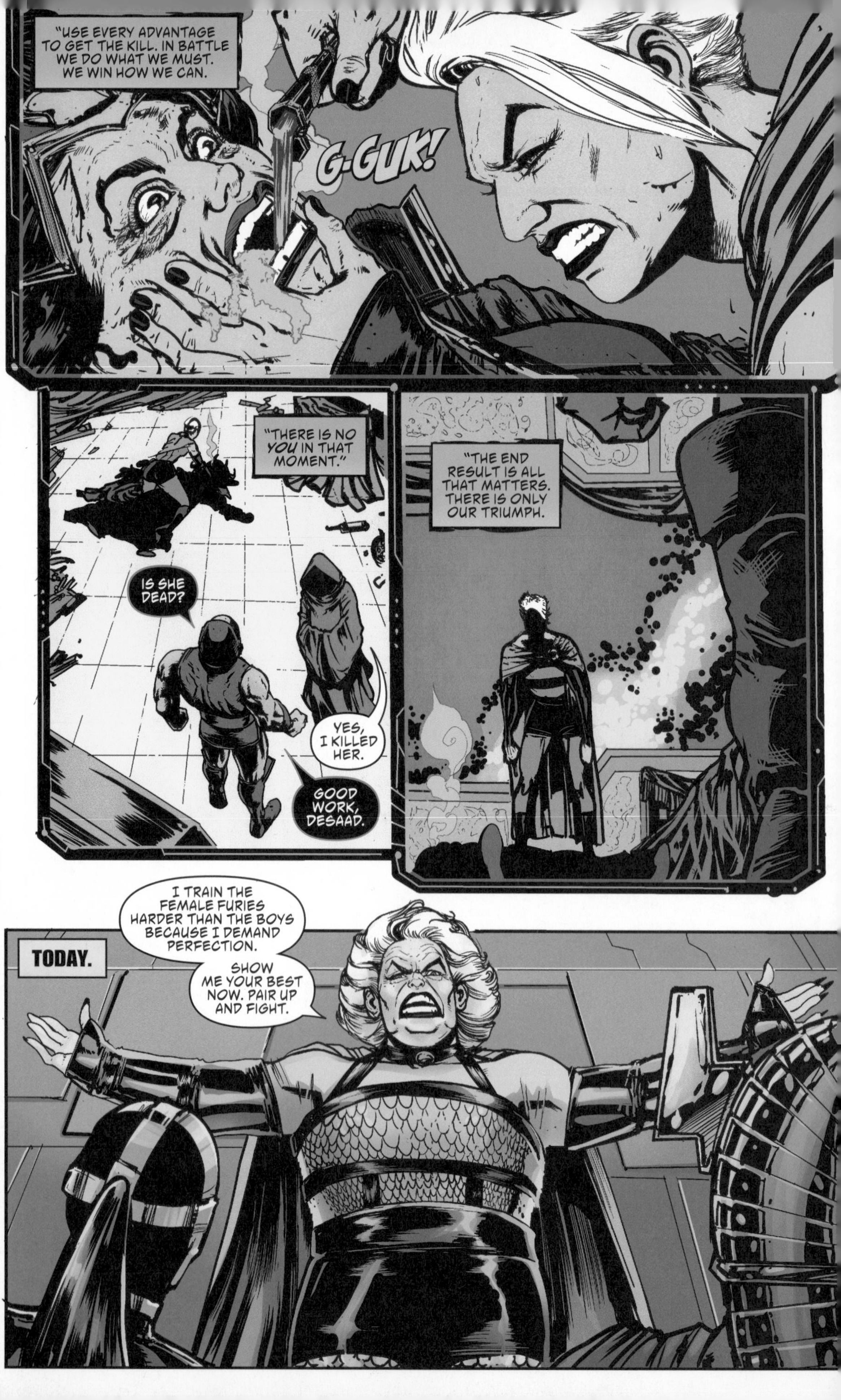
"USE EVERY ADVANTAGE TO GET THE KILL. IN BATTLE WE DO WHAT WE MUST. WE WIN HOW WE CAN.
G-GUK!
"THERE IS NO *YOU* IN THAT MOMENT."
IS SHE DEAD?
YES, I KILLED HER.
GOOD WORK, DESAAD.
"THE END RESULT IS ALL THAT MATTERS. THERE IS ONLY OUR TRIUMPH.
TODAY.
I TRAIN THE FEMALE FURIES HARDER THAN THE BOYS BECAUSE I DEMAND PERFECTION.
SHOW ME YOUR BEST NOW. PAIR UP AND FIGHT.

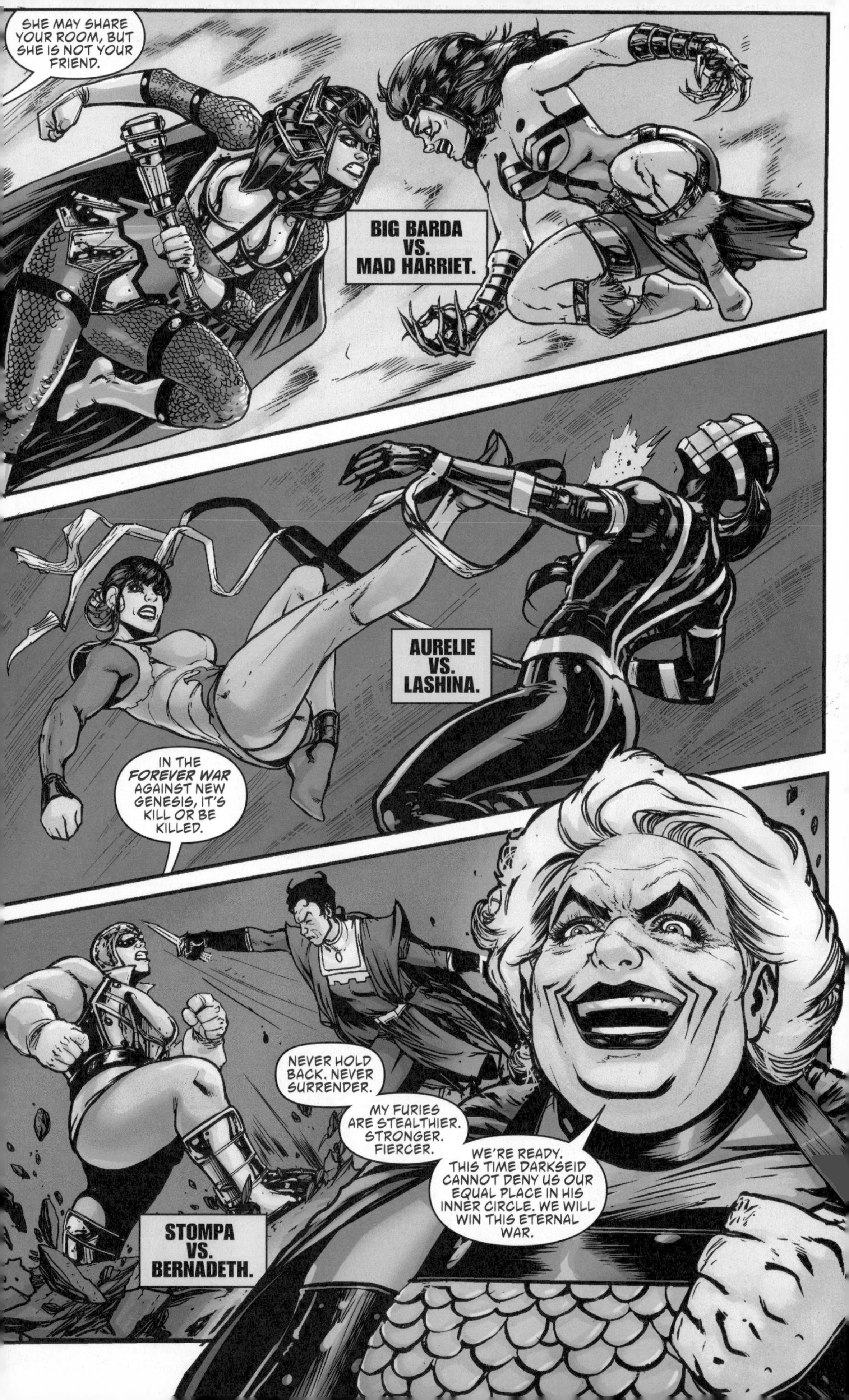
SHE MAY SHARE YOUR ROOM, BUT SHE IS NOT YOUR FRIEND.
BIG BARDA VS. MAD HARRIET.
AURELIE VS. LASHINA.
IN THE FOREVER WAR AGAINST NEW GENESIS, IT'S KILL OR BE KILLED.
NEVER HOLD BACK. NEVER SURRENDER.
MY FURIES ARE STEALTHIER. STRONGER. FIERCER.
WE'RE READY. THIS TIME DARKSEID CANNOT DENY US OUR EQUAL PLACE IN HIS INNER CIRCLE. WE WILL WIN THIS ETERNAL WAR.
STOMPA VS. BERNADETH.

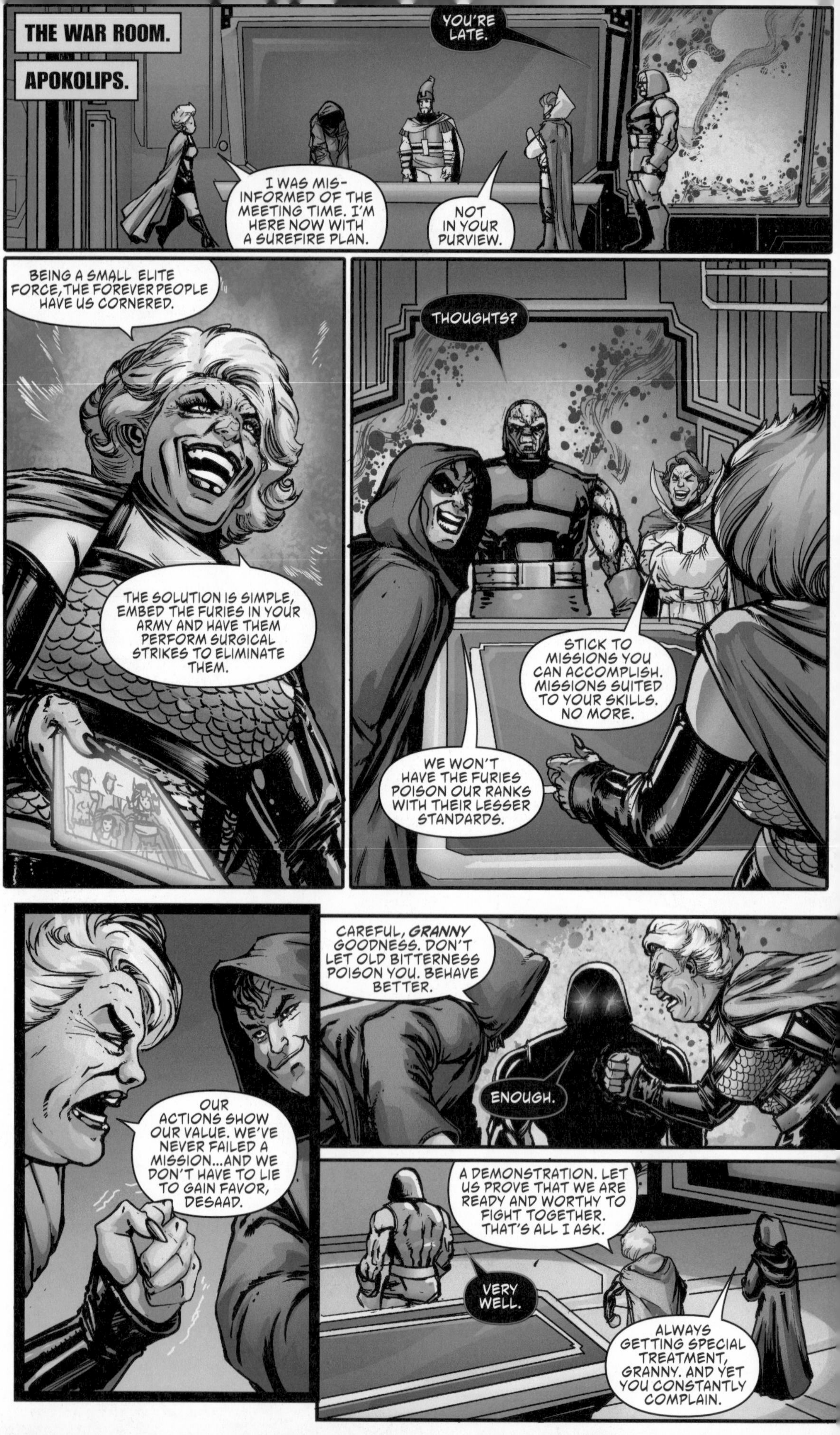
THE WAR ROOM.
APOKOLIPS.
YOU'RE LATE.
I WAS MIS-INFORMED OF THE MEETING TIME. I'M HERE NOW WITH A SUREFIRE PLAN.
NOT IN YOUR PURVIEW.
BEING A SMALL ELITE FORCE, THE FOREVER PEOPLE HAVE US CORNERED.
THE SOLUTION IS SIMPLE, EMBED THE FURIES IN YOUR ARMY AND HAVE THEM PERFORM SURGICAL STRIKES TO ELIMINATE THEM.
THOUGHTS?
STICK TO MISSIONS YOU CAN ACCOMPLISH. MISSIONS SUITED TO YOUR SKILLS. NO MORE.
WE WON'T HAVE THE FURIES POISON OUR RANKS WITH THEIR LESSER STANDARDS.
OUR ACTIONS SHOW OUR VALUE. WE'VE NEVER FAILED A MISSION...AND WE DON'T HAVE TO LIE TO GAIN FAVOR, DESAAD.
CAREFUL, GRANNY GOODNESS. DON'T LET OLD BITTERNESS POISON YOU. BEHAVE BETTER.
ENOUGH.
A DEMONSTRATION. LET US PROVE THAT WE ARE READY AND WORTHY TO FIGHT TOGETHER. THAT'S ALL I ASK.
VERY WELL.
ALWAYS GETTING SPECIAL TREATMENT, GRANNY. AND YET YOU CONSTANTLY COMPLAIN.

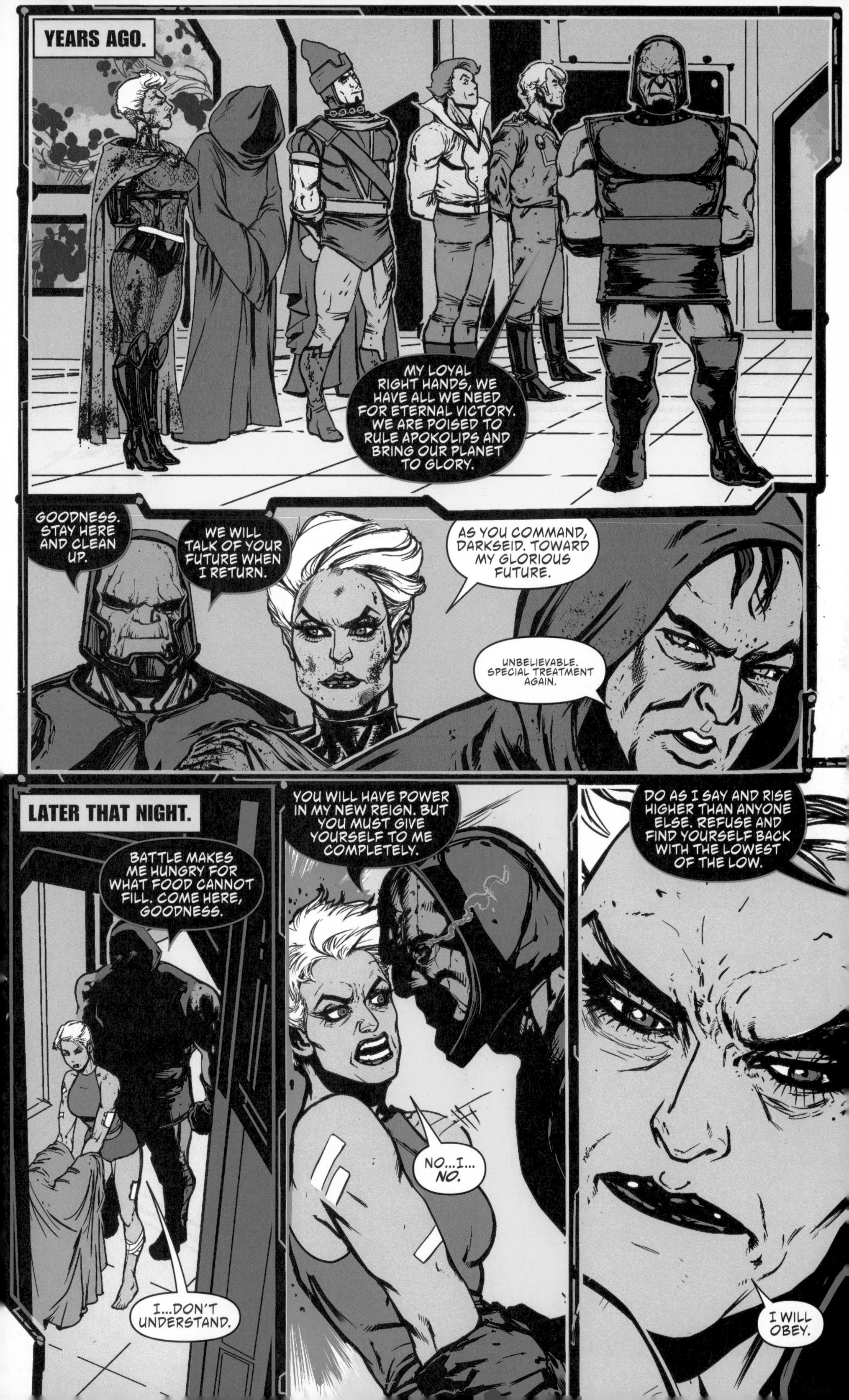
YEARS AGO.
MY LOYAL RIGHT HANDS, WE HAVE ALL WE NEED FOR ETERNAL VICTORY. WE ARE POISED TO RULE APOKOLIPS AND BRING OUR PLANET TO GLORY.
GOODNESS. STAY HERE AND CLEAN UP.
WE WILL TALK OF YOUR FUTURE WHEN I RETURN.
AS YOU COMMAND, DARKSEID. TOWARD MY GLORIOUS FUTURE.
UNBELIEVABLE. SPECIAL TREATMENT AGAIN.
LATER THAT NIGHT.
BATTLE MAKES ME HUNGRY FOR WHAT FOOD CANNOT FILL. COME HERE, GOODNESS.
I...DON'T UNDERSTAND.
YOU WILL HAVE POWER IN MY NEW REIGN. BUT YOU MUST GIVE YOURSELF TO ME COMPLETELY.
NO...I... NO.
DO AS I SAY AND RISE HIGHER THAN ANYONE ELSE. REFUSE AND FIND YOURSELF BACK WITH THE LOWEST OF THE LOW.
I WILL OBEY.

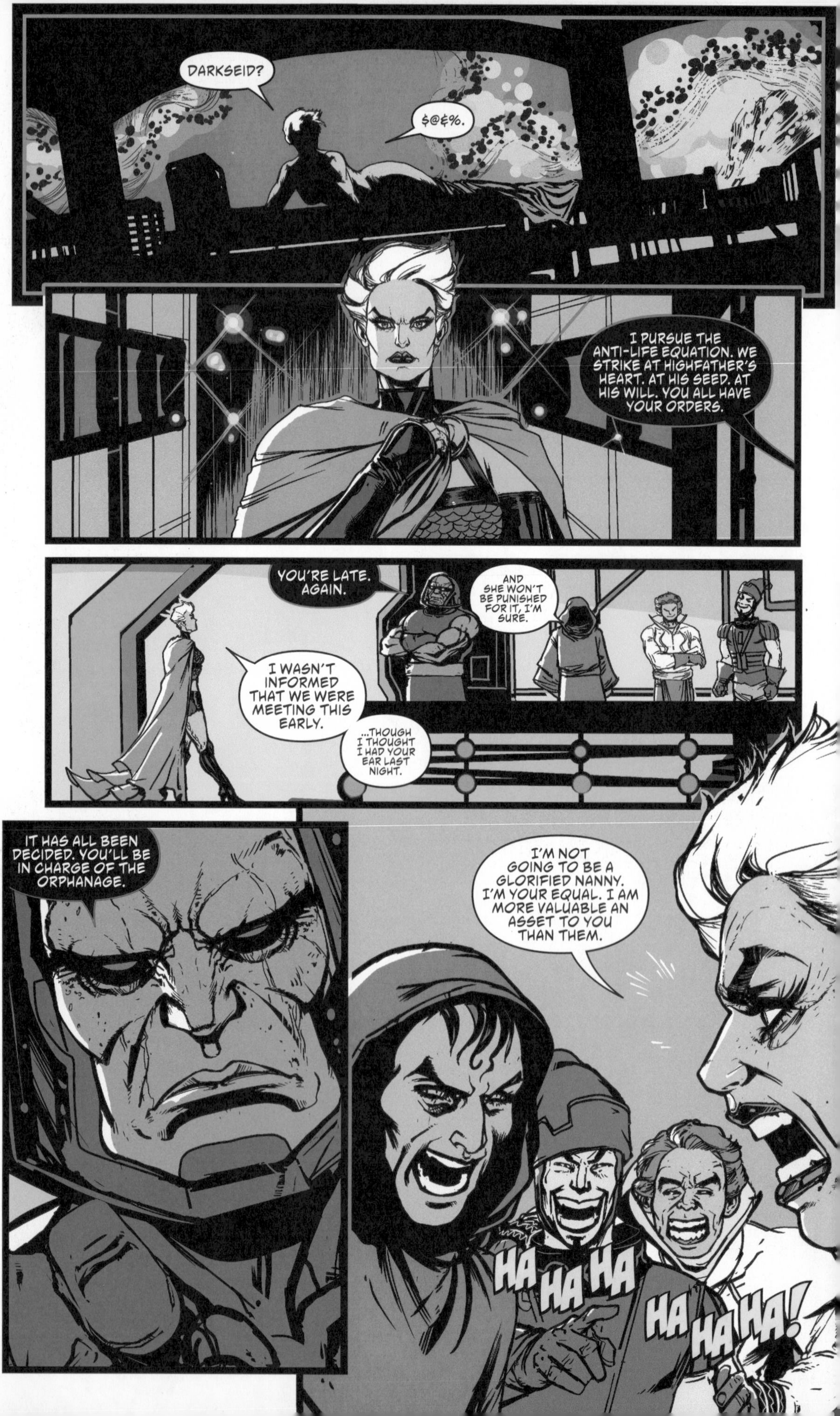
DARKSEID?
$@¢%.
I PURSUE THE ANTI-LIFE EQUATION. WE STRIKE AT HIGHFATHER'S HEART. AT HIS SEED. AT HIS WILL. YOU ALL HAVE YOUR ORDERS.
YOU'RE LATE. AGAIN.
AND SHE WON'T BE PUNISHED FOR IT, I'M SURE.
I WASN'T INFORMED THAT WE WERE MEETING THIS EARLY.
...THOUGH I THOUGHT I HAD YOUR EAR LAST NIGHT.
IT HAS ALL BEEN DECIDED. YOU'LL BE IN CHARGE OF THE ORPHANAGE.
I'M NOT GOING TO BE A GLORIFIED NANNY. I'M YOUR EQUAL. I AM MORE VALUABLE AN ASSET TO YOU THAN THEM.
HA HA HA HA
HA HA HA!

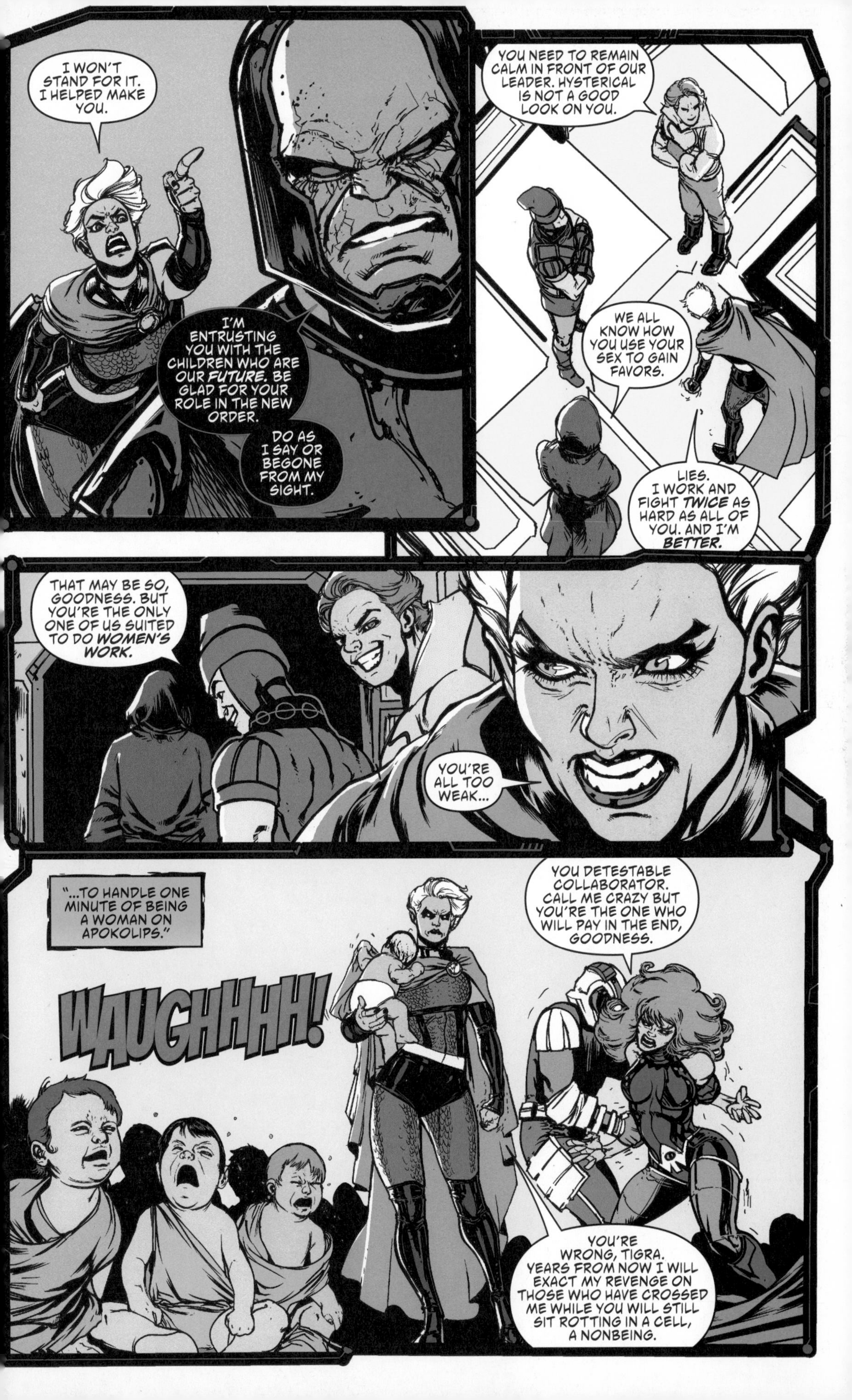

I WON'T STAND FOR IT. I HELPED MAKE YOU.
I'M ENTRUSTING YOU WITH THE CHILDREN WHO ARE OUR *FUTURE*. BE GLAD FOR YOUR ROLE IN THE NEW ORDER.
DO AS I SAY OR BEGONE FROM MY SIGHT.
YOU NEED TO REMAIN CALM IN FRONT OF OUR LEADER. HYSTERICAL IS NOT A GOOD LOOK ON YOU.
WE ALL KNOW HOW YOU USE YOUR SEX TO GAIN FAVORS.
LIES. I WORK AND FIGHT ***TWICE*** AS HARD AS ALL OF YOU. AND I'M ***BETTER.***
THAT MAY BE SO, GOODNESS. BUT YOU'RE THE ONLY ONE OF US SUITED TO DO ***WOMEN'S WORK.***
YOU'RE ALL TOO WEAK...
"...TO HANDLE ONE MINUTE OF BEING A WOMAN ON APOKOLIPS."
WAUGHHHH!
YOU DETESTABLE COLLABORATOR. CALL ME CRAZY BUT YOU'RE THE ONE WHO WILL PAY IN THE END, GOODNESS.
YOU'RE WRONG, TIGRA. YEARS FROM NOW I WILL EXACT MY REVENGE ON THOSE WHO HAVE CROSSED ME WHILE YOU WILL STILL SIT ROTTING IN A CELL, A NONBEING.

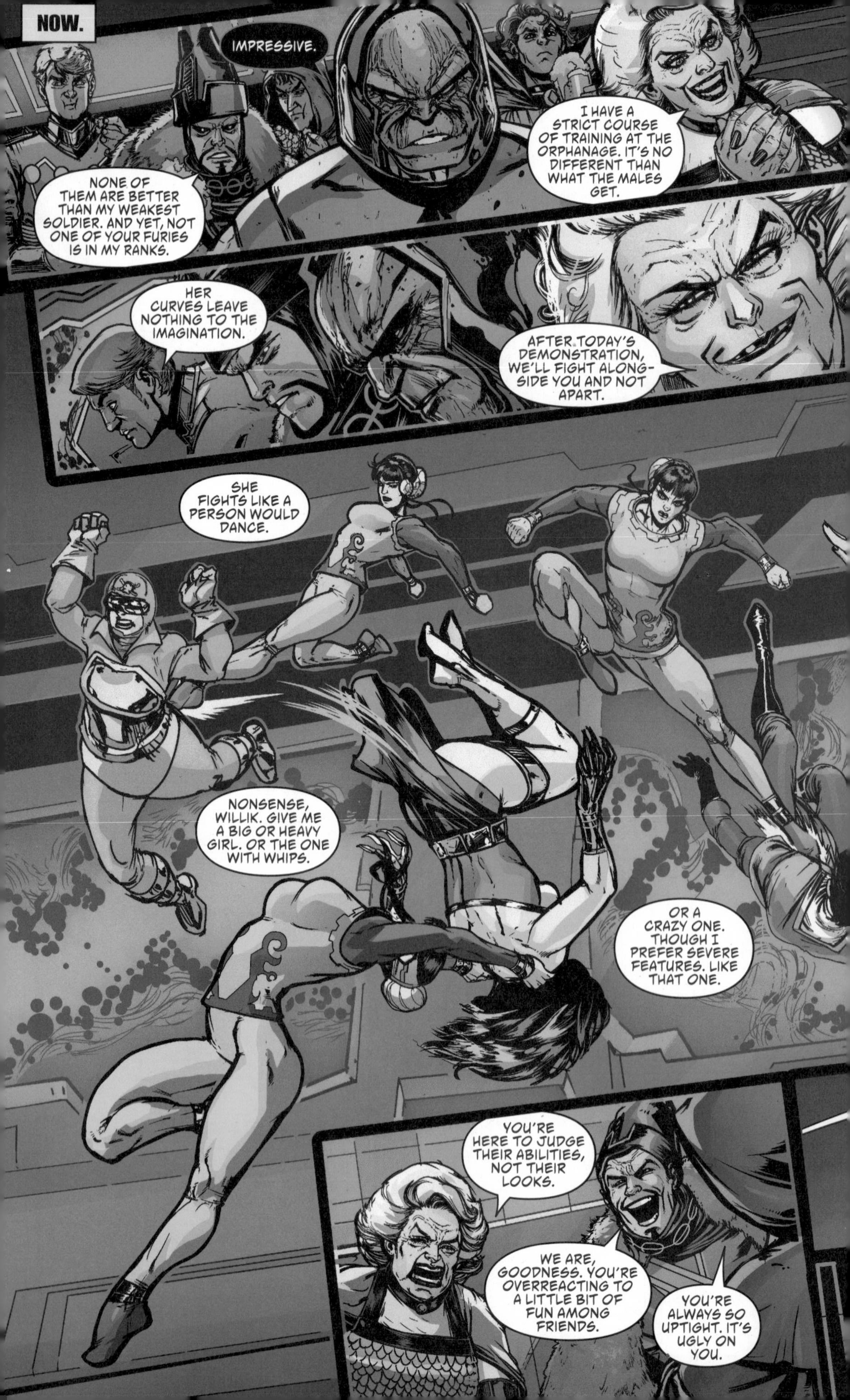
NOW.
IMPRESSIVE.
NONE OF THEM ARE BETTER THAN MY WEAKEST SOLDIER. AND YET, NOT ONE OF YOUR FURIES IS IN MY RANKS.
I HAVE A STRICT COURSE OF TRAINING AT THE ORPHANAGE. IT'S NO DIFFERENT THAN WHAT THE MALES GET.
HER CURVES LEAVE NOTHING TO THE IMAGINATION.
AFTER TODAY'S DEMONSTRATION, WE'LL FIGHT ALONG-SIDE YOU AND NOT APART.
SHE FIGHTS LIKE A PERSON WOULD DANCE.
NONSENSE, WILLIK. GIVE ME A BIG OR HEAVY GIRL. OR THE ONE WITH WHIPS.
OR A CRAZY ONE. THOUGH I PREFER SEVERE FEATURES. LIKE THAT ONE.
YOU'RE HERE TO JUDGE THEIR ABILITIES, NOT THEIR LOOKS.
WE ARE, GOODNESS. YOU'RE OVERREACTING TO A LITTLE BIT OF FUN AMONG FRIENDS.
YOU'RE ALWAYS SO UPTIGHT. IT'S UGLY ON YOU.

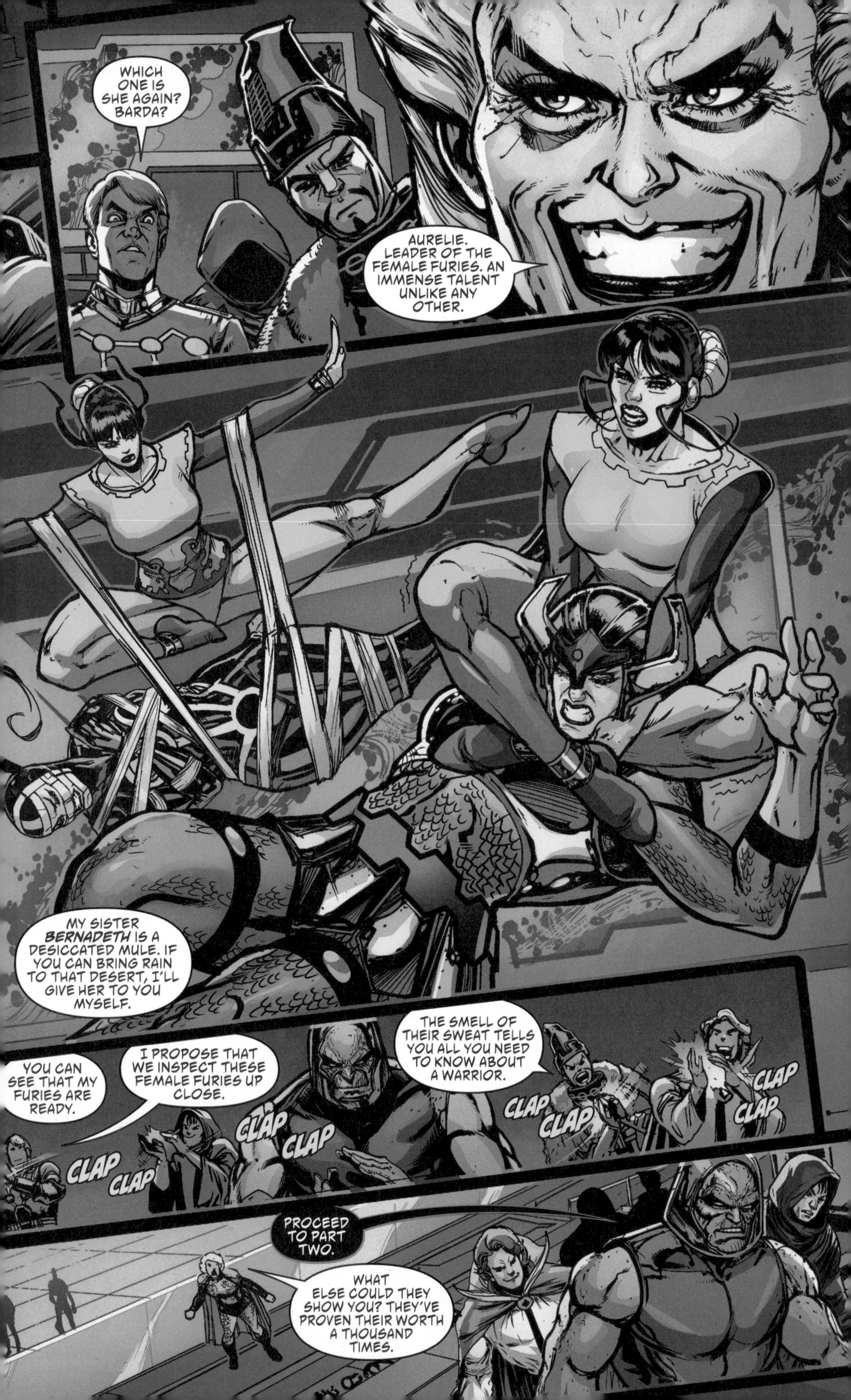
WHICH ONE IS SHE AGAIN? BARDA?
AURELIE. LEADER OF THE FEMALE FURIES. AN IMMENSE TALENT UNLIKE ANY OTHER.
MY SISTER BERNADETH IS A DESICCATED MULE. IF YOU CAN BRING RAIN TO THAT DESERT, I'LL GIVE HER TO YOU MYSELF.
YOU CAN SEE THAT MY FURIES ARE READY.
I PROPOSE THAT WE INSPECT THESE FEMALE FURIES UP CLOSE.
THE SMELL OF THEIR SWEAT TELLS YOU ALL YOU NEED TO KNOW ABOUT A WARRIOR.
CLAP CLAP CLAP CLAP CLAP CLAP CLAP CLAP
PROCEED TO PART TWO.
WHAT ELSE COULD THEY SHOW YOU? THEY'VE PROVEN THEIR WORTH A THOUSAND TIMES.

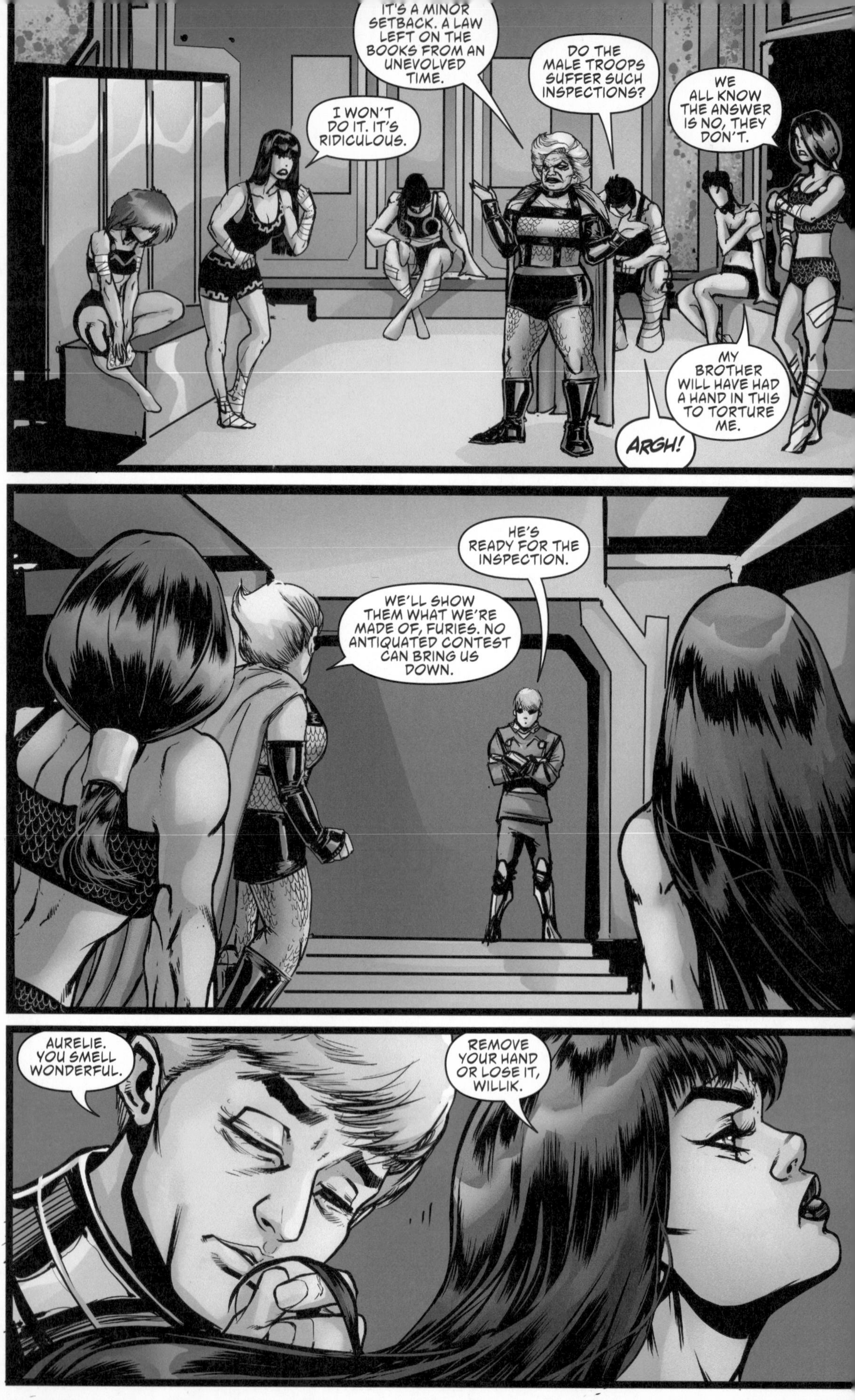
I WON'T DO IT. IT'S RIDICULOUS.
IT'S A MINOR SETBACK. A LAW LEFT ON THE BOOKS FROM AN UNEVOLVED TIME.
DO THE MALE TROOPS SUFFER SUCH INSPECTIONS?
WE ALL KNOW THE ANSWER IS NO, THEY DON'T.
MY BROTHER WILL HAVE HAD A HAND IN THIS TO TORTURE ME.
ARGH!
WE'LL SHOW THEM WHAT WE'RE MADE OF, FURIES. NO ANTIQUATED CONTEST CAN BRING US DOWN.
HE'S READY FOR THE INSPECTION.
AURELIE. YOU SMELL WONDERFUL.
REMOVE YOUR HAND OR LOSE IT, WILLIK.

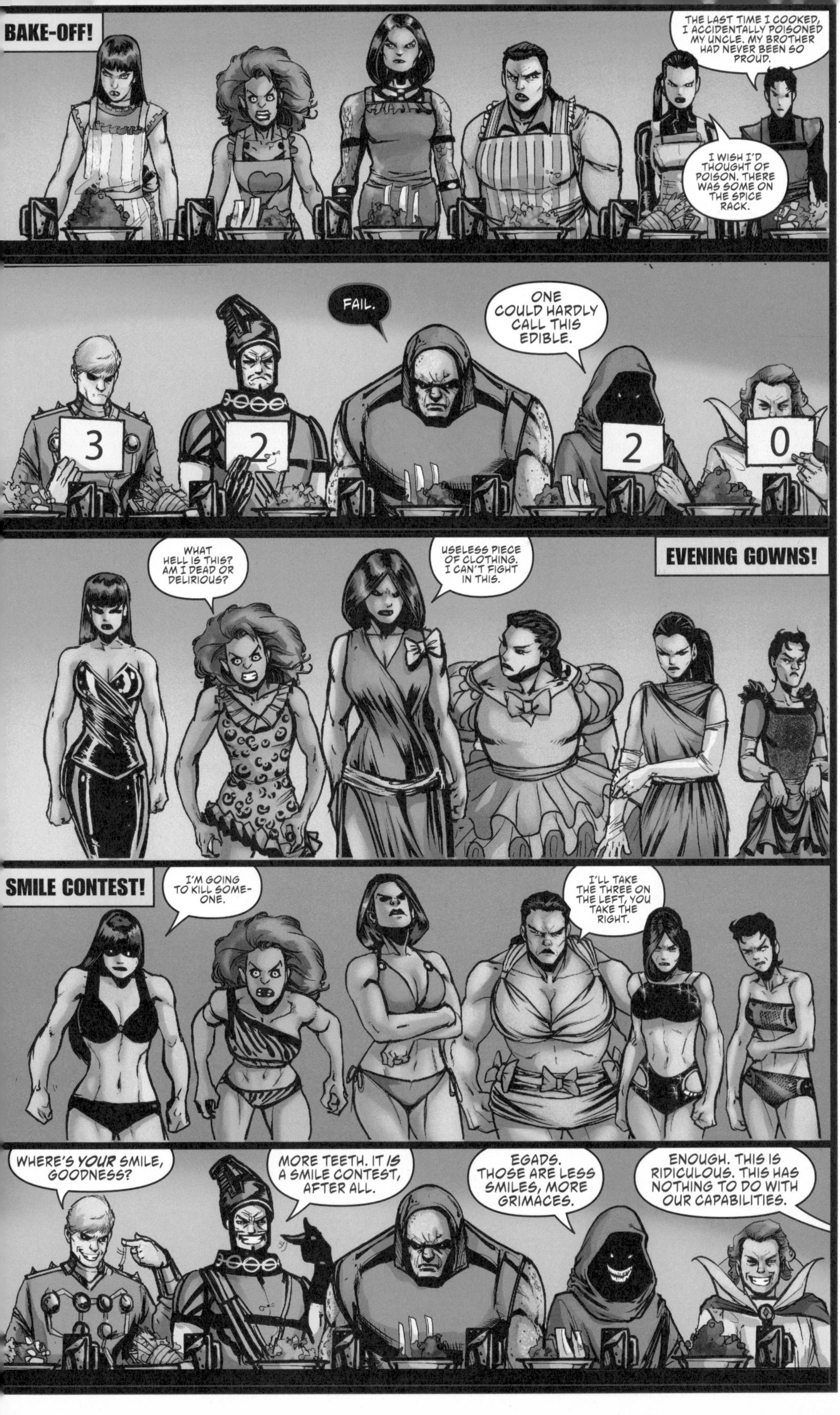

BAKE-OFF!
THE LAST TIME I COOKED, I ACCIDENTALLY POISONED MY UNCLE. MY BROTHER HAD NEVER BEEN SO PROUD.
I WISH I'D THOUGHT OF POISON. THERE WAS SOME ON THE SPICE RACK.
3
2
FAIL.
ONE COULD HARDLY CALL THIS EDIBLE.
2
0
WHAT HELL IS THIS? AM I DEAD OR DELIRIOUS?
USELESS PIECE OF CLOTHING. I CAN'T FIGHT IN THIS.
EVENING GOWNS!
SMILE CONTEST!
I'M GOING TO KILL SOME-ONE.
I'LL TAKE THE THREE ON THE LEFT, YOU TAKE THE RIGHT.
WHERE'S *YOUR* SMILE, GOODNESS?
MORE TEETH. IT *IS* A SMILE CONTEST, AFTER ALL.
EGADS. THOSE ARE LESS SMILES, MORE GRIMACES.
ENOUGH. THIS IS RIDICULOUS. THIS HAS NOTHING TO DO WITH OUR CAPABILITIES.

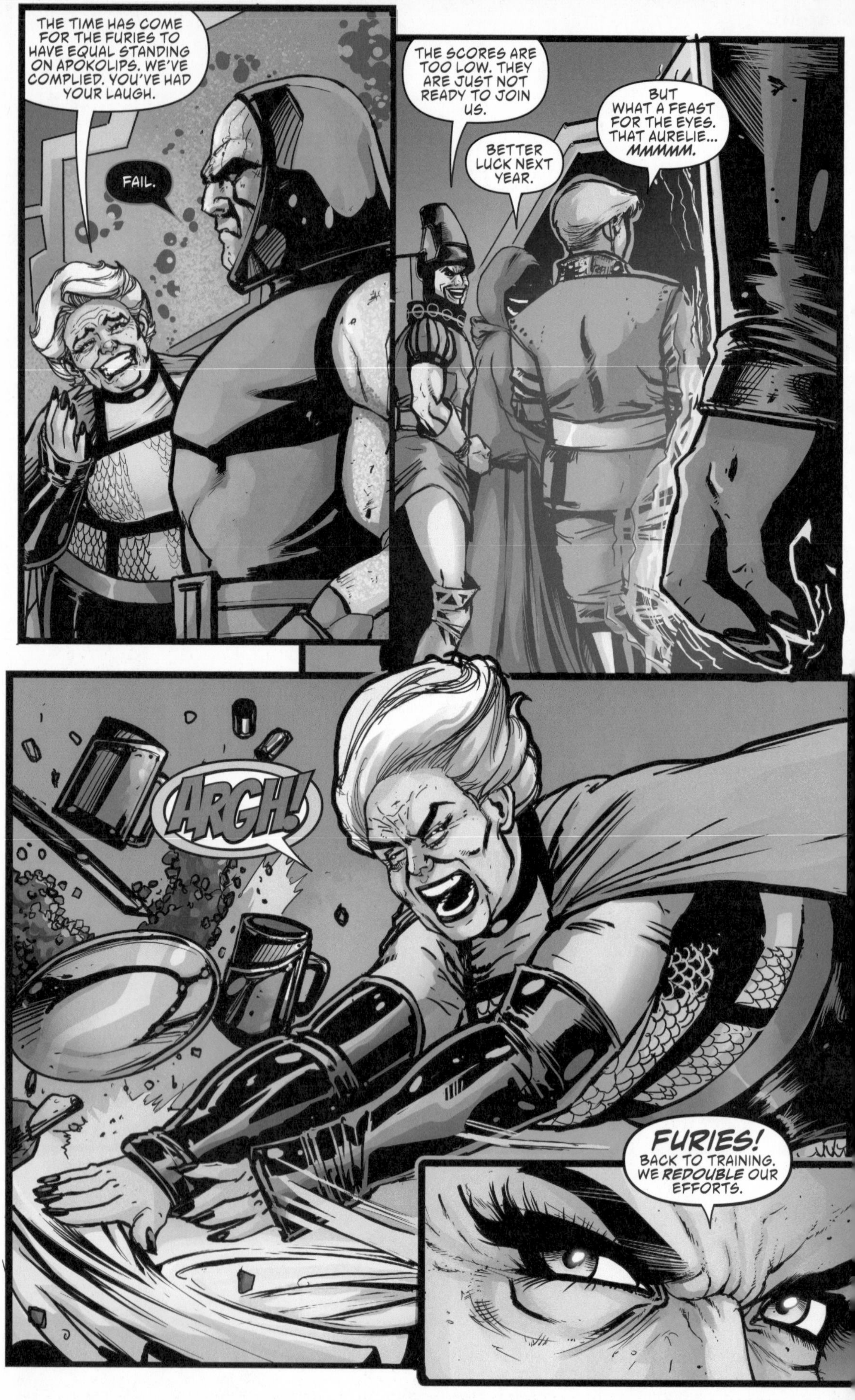
THE TIME HAS COME FOR THE FURIES TO HAVE EQUAL STANDING ON APOKOLIPS. WE'VE COMPLIED. YOU'VE HAD YOUR LAUGH.
FAIL.
THE SCORES ARE TOO LOW. THEY ARE JUST NOT READY TO JOIN US.
BETTER LUCK NEXT YEAR.
BUT WHAT A FEAST FOR THE EYES. THAT AURELIE... MMMMM.
ARGH!
FURIES! BACK TO TRAINING. WE REDOUBLE OUR EFFORTS.

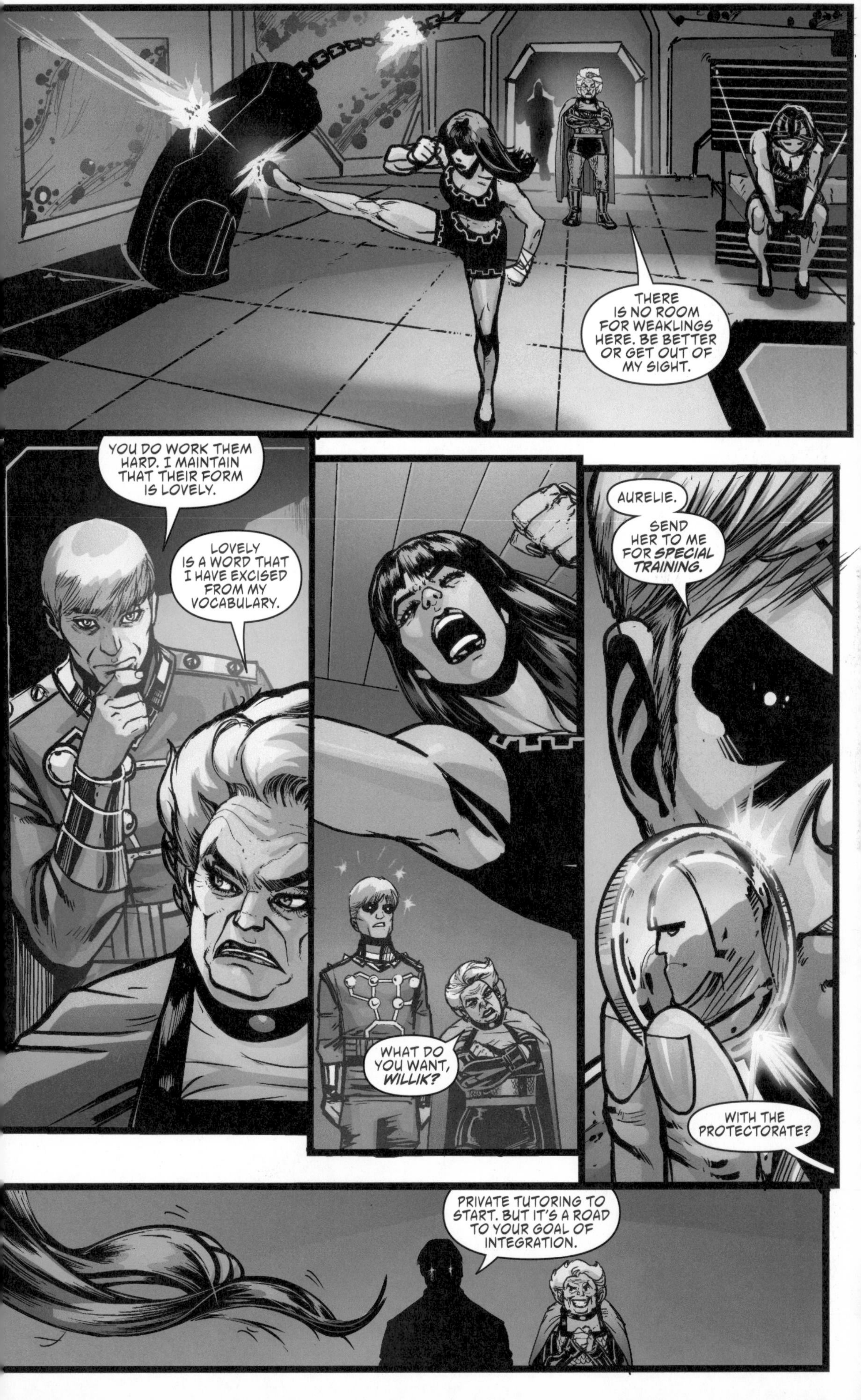

THERE IS NO ROOM FOR WEAKLINGS HERE. BE BETTER OR GET OUT OF MY SIGHT.
YOU DO WORK THEM HARD. I MAINTAIN THAT THEIR FORM IS LOVELY.
LOVELY IS A WORD THAT I HAVE EXCISED FROM MY VOCABULARY.
WHAT DO YOU WANT, WILLIK?
AURELIE.
SEND HER TO ME FOR SPECIAL TRAINING.
WITH THE PROTECTORATE?
PRIVATE TUTORING TO START. BUT IT'S A ROAD TO YOUR GOAL OF INTEGRATION.

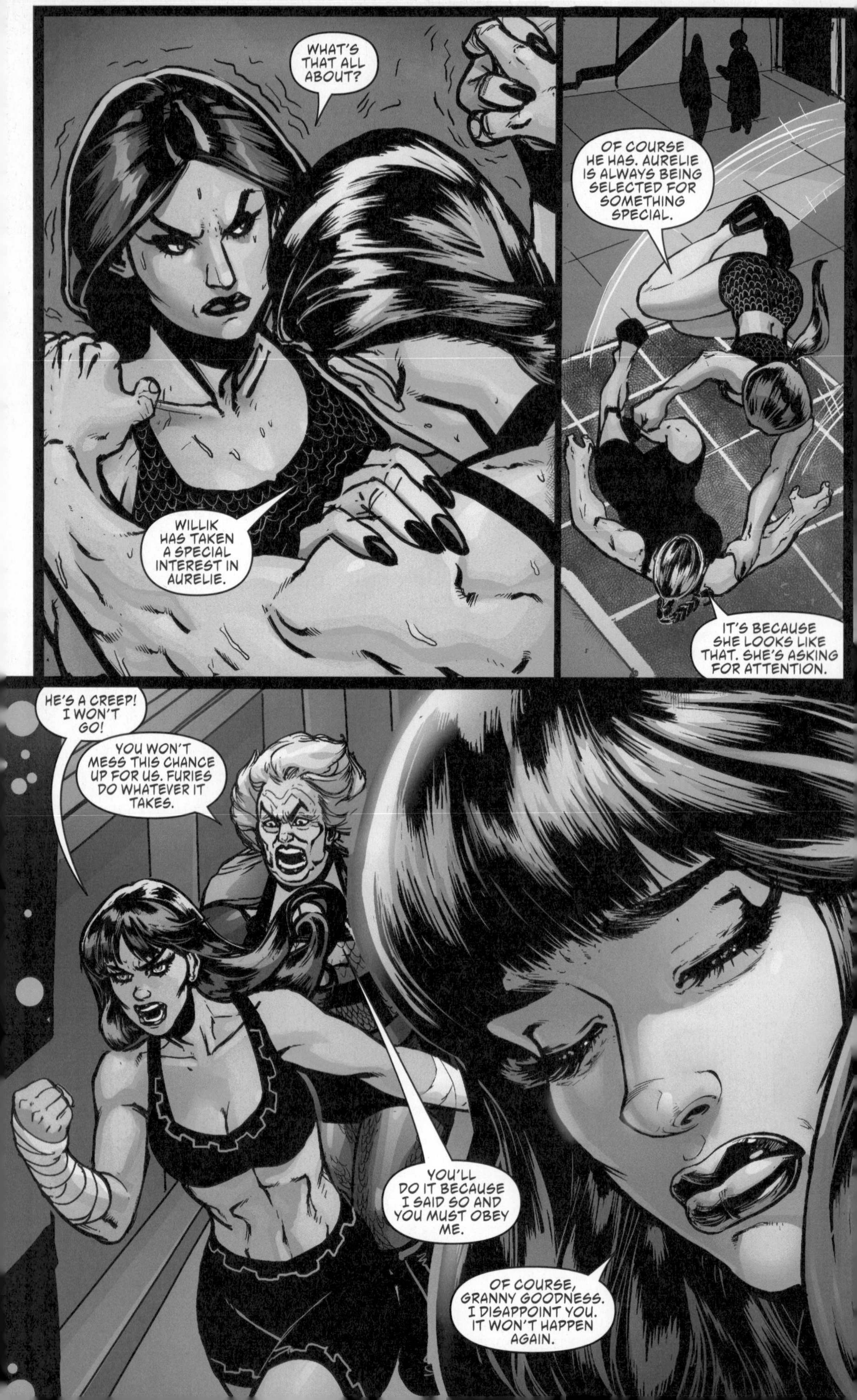
WHAT'S THAT ALL ABOUT?
WILLIK HAS TAKEN A SPECIAL INTEREST IN AURELIE.
OF COURSE HE HAS. AURELIE IS ALWAYS BEING SELECTED FOR SOMETHING SPECIAL.
IT'S BECAUSE SHE LOOKS LIKE THAT. SHE'S ASKING FOR ATTENTION.
HE'S A CREEP! I WON'T GO!
YOU WON'T MESS THIS CHANCE UP FOR US. FURIES DO WHATEVER IT TAKES.
YOU'LL DO IT BECAUSE I SAID SO AND YOU MUST OBEY ME.
OF COURSE, GRANNY GOODNESS. I DISAPPOINT YOU. IT WON'T HAPPEN AGAIN.

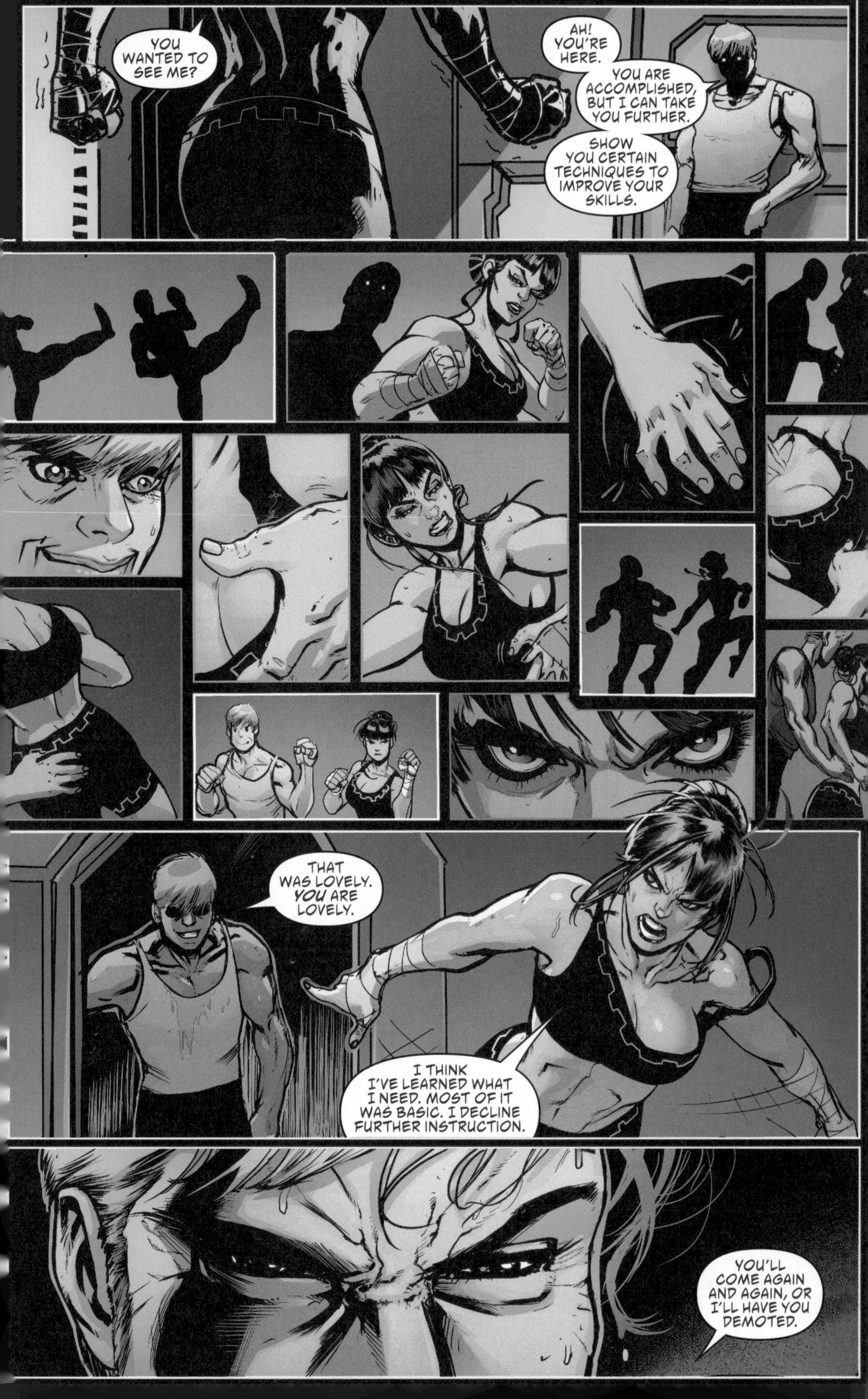
YOU WANTED TO SEE ME?
AH! YOU'RE HERE.
YOU ARE ACCOMPLISHED, BUT I CAN TAKE YOU FURTHER.
SHOW YOU CERTAIN TECHNIQUES TO IMPROVE YOUR SKILLS.
THAT WAS LOVELY. *YOU* ARE LOVELY.
I THINK I'VE LEARNED WHAT I NEED. MOST OF IT WAS BASIC. I DECLINE FURTHER INSTRUCTION.
YOU'LL COME AGAIN AND AGAIN, OR I'LL HAVE YOU DEMOTED.

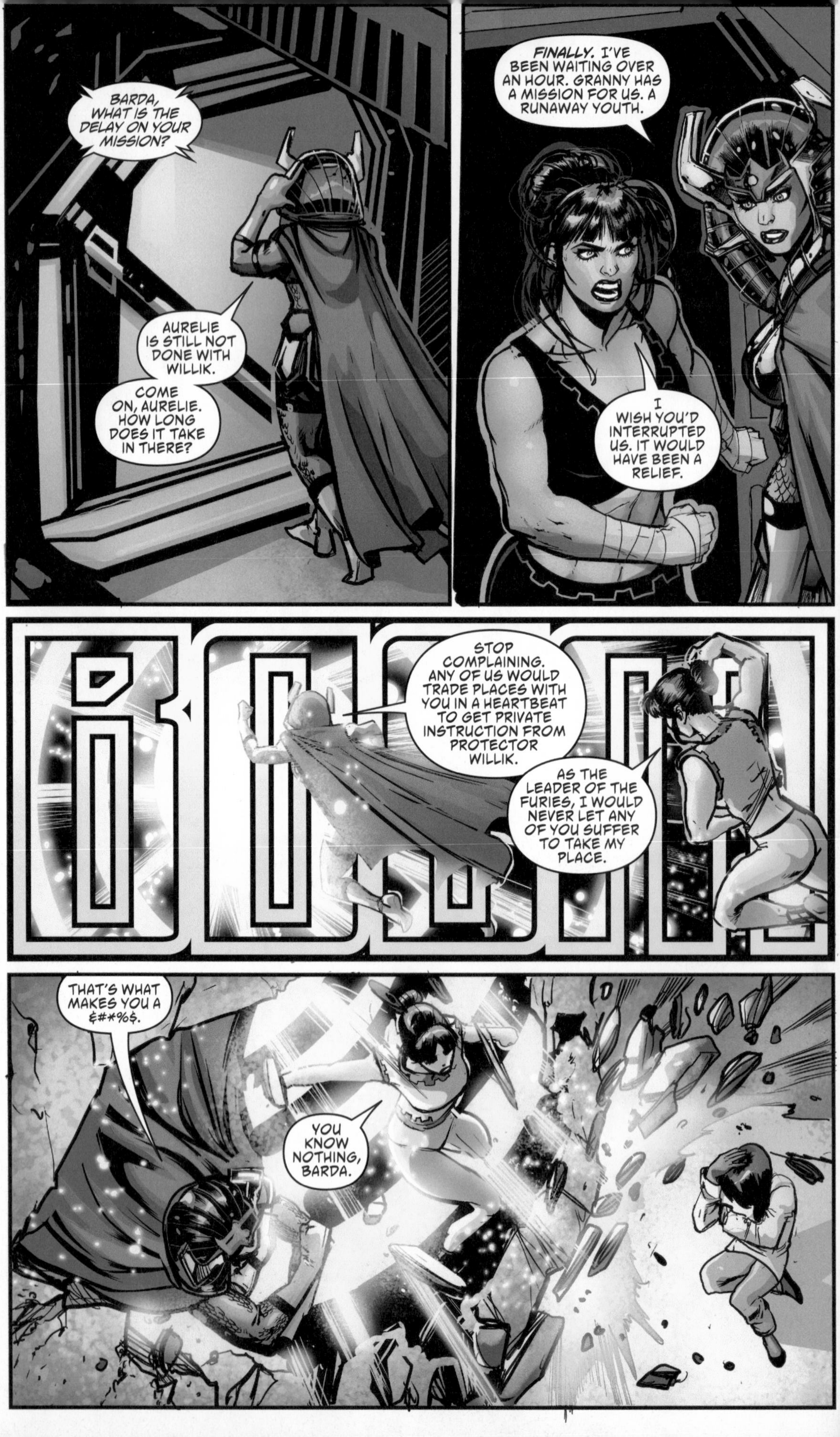
BARDA, WHAT IS THE DELAY ON YOUR MISSION?
AURELIE IS STILL NOT DONE WITH WILLIK.
COME ON, AURELIE. HOW LONG DOES IT TAKE IN THERE?
FINALLY. I'VE BEEN WAITING OVER AN HOUR. GRANNY HAS A MISSION FOR US. A RUNAWAY YOUTH.
I WISH YOU'D INTERRUPTED US. IT WOULD HAVE BEEN A RELIEF.
STOP COMPLAINING. ANY OF US WOULD TRADE PLACES WITH YOU IN A HEARTBEAT TO GET PRIVATE INSTRUCTION FROM PROTECTOR WILLIK.
AS THE LEADER OF THE FURIES, I WOULD NEVER LET ANY OF YOU SUFFER TO TAKE MY PLACE.
THAT'S WHAT MAKES YOU A &#*%$.
YOU KNOW NOTHING, BARDA.

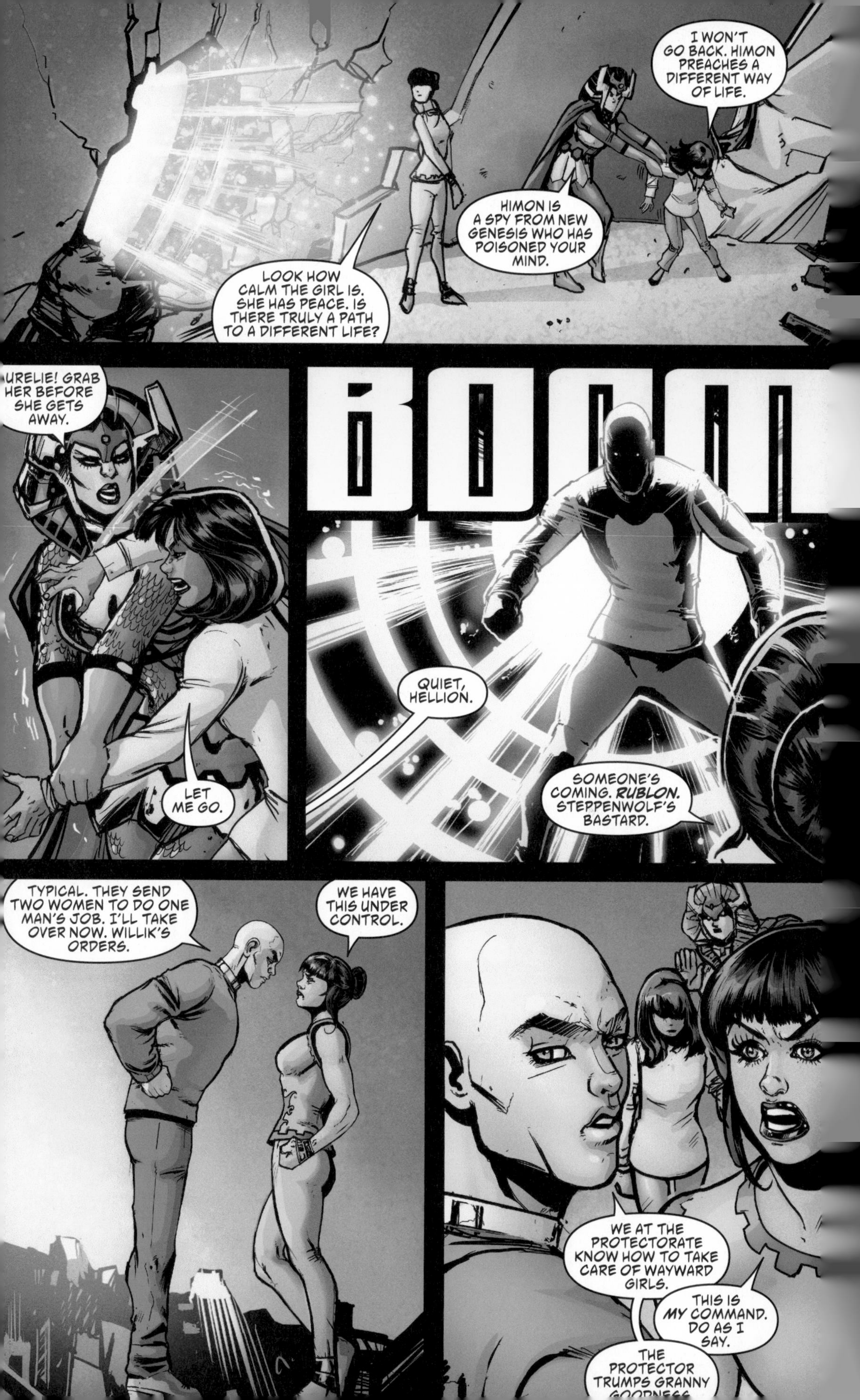
I WON'T GO BACK. HIMON PREACHES A DIFFERENT WAY OF LIFE.
HIMON IS A SPY FROM NEW GENESIS WHO HAS POISONED YOUR MIND.
LOOK HOW CALM THE GIRL IS. SHE HAS PEACE. IS THERE TRULY A PATH TO A DIFFERENT LIFE?
URELIE! GRAB HER BEFORE SHE GETS AWAY.
BOOM
QUIET, HELLION.
LET ME GO.
SOMEONE'S COMING. RUBLON. STEPPENWOLF'S BASTARD.
TYPICAL. THEY SEND TWO WOMEN TO DO ONE MAN'S JOB. I'LL TAKE OVER NOW. WILLIK'S ORDERS.
WE HAVE THIS UNDER CONTROL.
WE AT THE PROTECTORATE KNOW HOW TO TAKE CARE OF WAYWARD GIRLS.
THIS IS MY COMMAND. DO AS I SAY.
THE PROTECTOR TRUMPS GRANNY

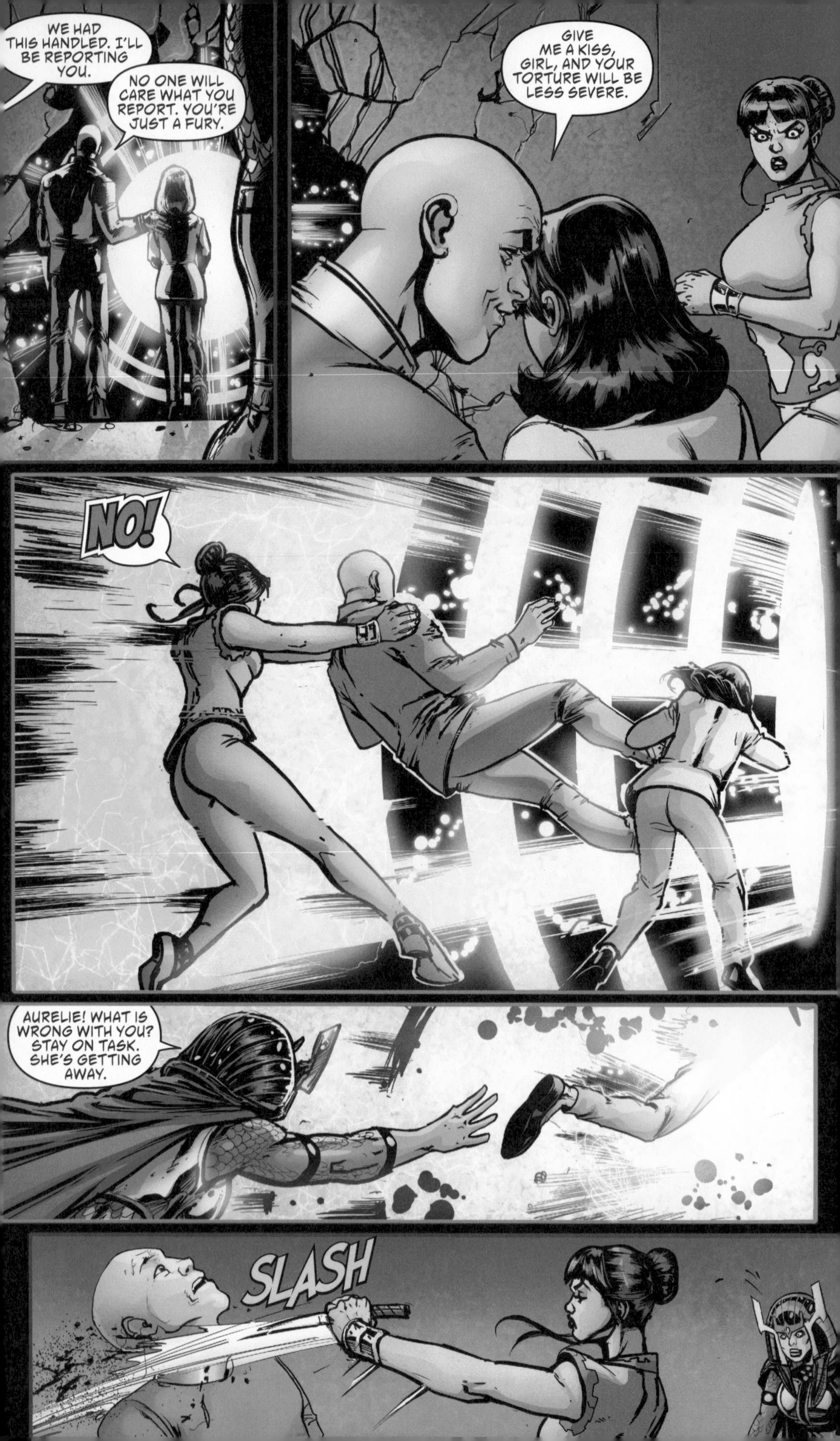
WE HAD THIS HANDLED. I'LL BE REPORTING YOU.
NO ONE WILL CARE WHAT YOU REPORT. YOU'RE JUST A FURY.
GIVE ME A KISS, GIRL, AND YOUR TORTURE WILL BE LESS SEVERE.
NO!
AURELIE! WHAT IS WRONG WITH YOU? STAY ON TASK. SHE'S GETTING AWAY.
SLASH

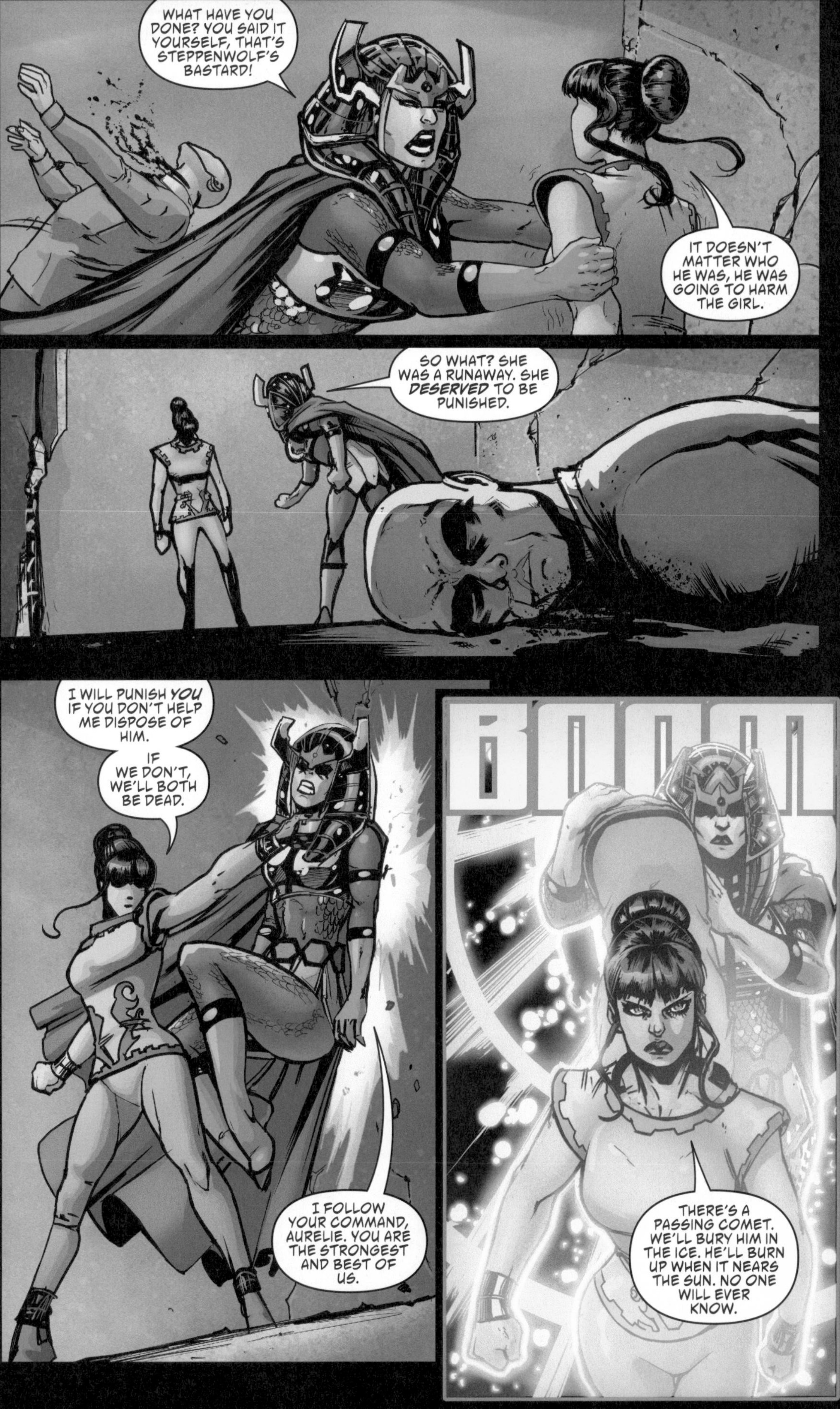
WHAT HAVE YOU DONE? YOU SAID IT YOURSELF, THAT'S STEPPENWOLF'S BASTARD!
IT DOESN'T MATTER WHO HE WAS, HE WAS GOING TO HARM THE GIRL.
SO WHAT? SHE WAS A RUNAWAY. SHE *DESERVED* TO BE PUNISHED.
I WILL PUNISH *YOU* IF YOU DON'T HELP ME DISPOSE OF HIM.
IF WE DON'T, WE'LL BOTH BE DEAD.
I FOLLOW YOUR COMMAND, AURELIE. YOU ARE THE STRONGEST AND BEST OF US.
BOOM
THERE'S A PASSING COMET. WE'LL BURY HIM IN THE ICE. HE'LL BURN UP WHEN IT NEARS THE SUN. NO ONE WILL EVER KNOW.

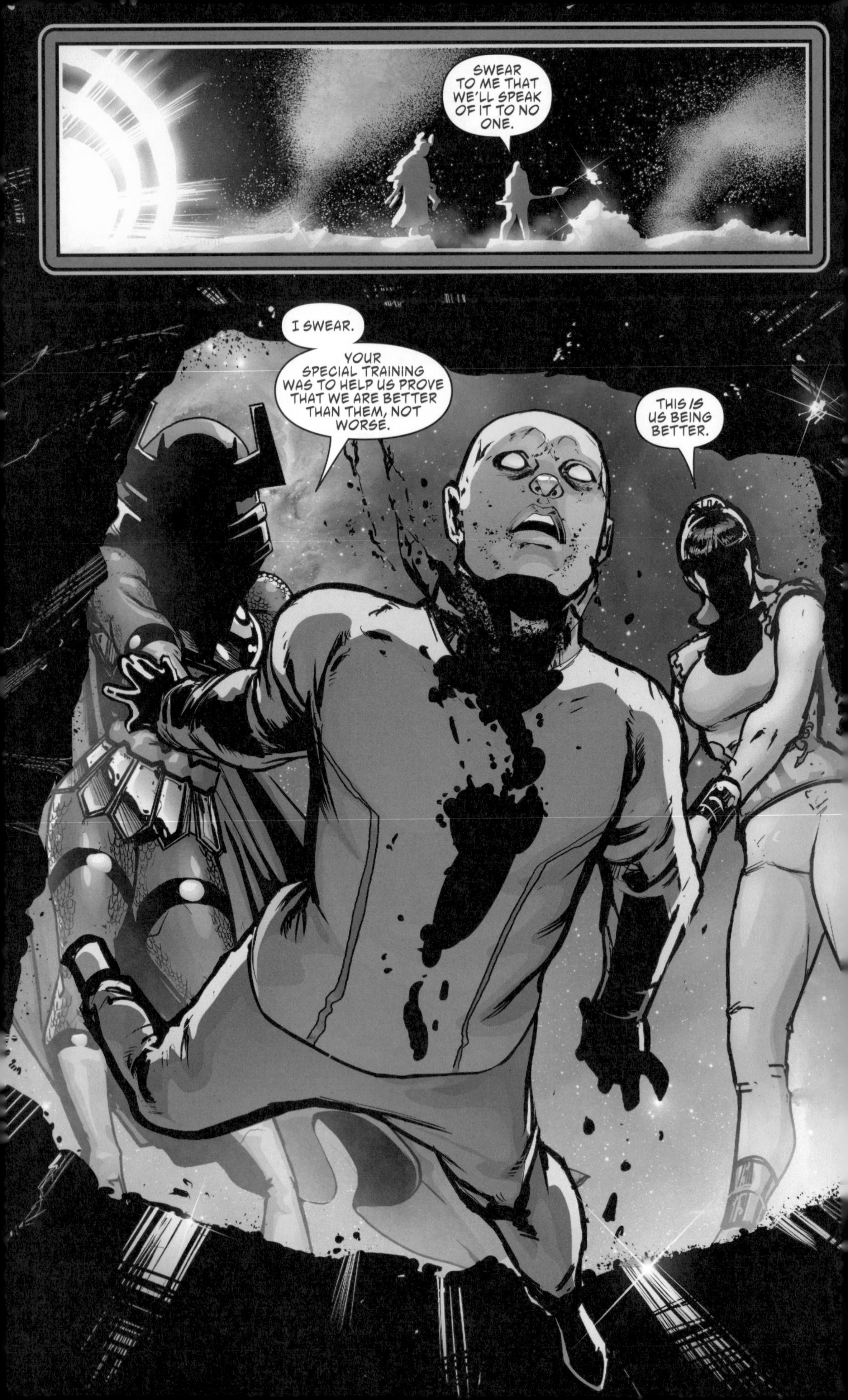
SWEAR TO ME THAT WE'LL SPEAK OF IT TO NO ONE.
I SWEAR.
YOUR SPECIAL TRAINING WAS TO HELP US PROVE THAT WE ARE BETTER THAN THEM, NOT WORSE.
THIS IS US BEING BETTER.

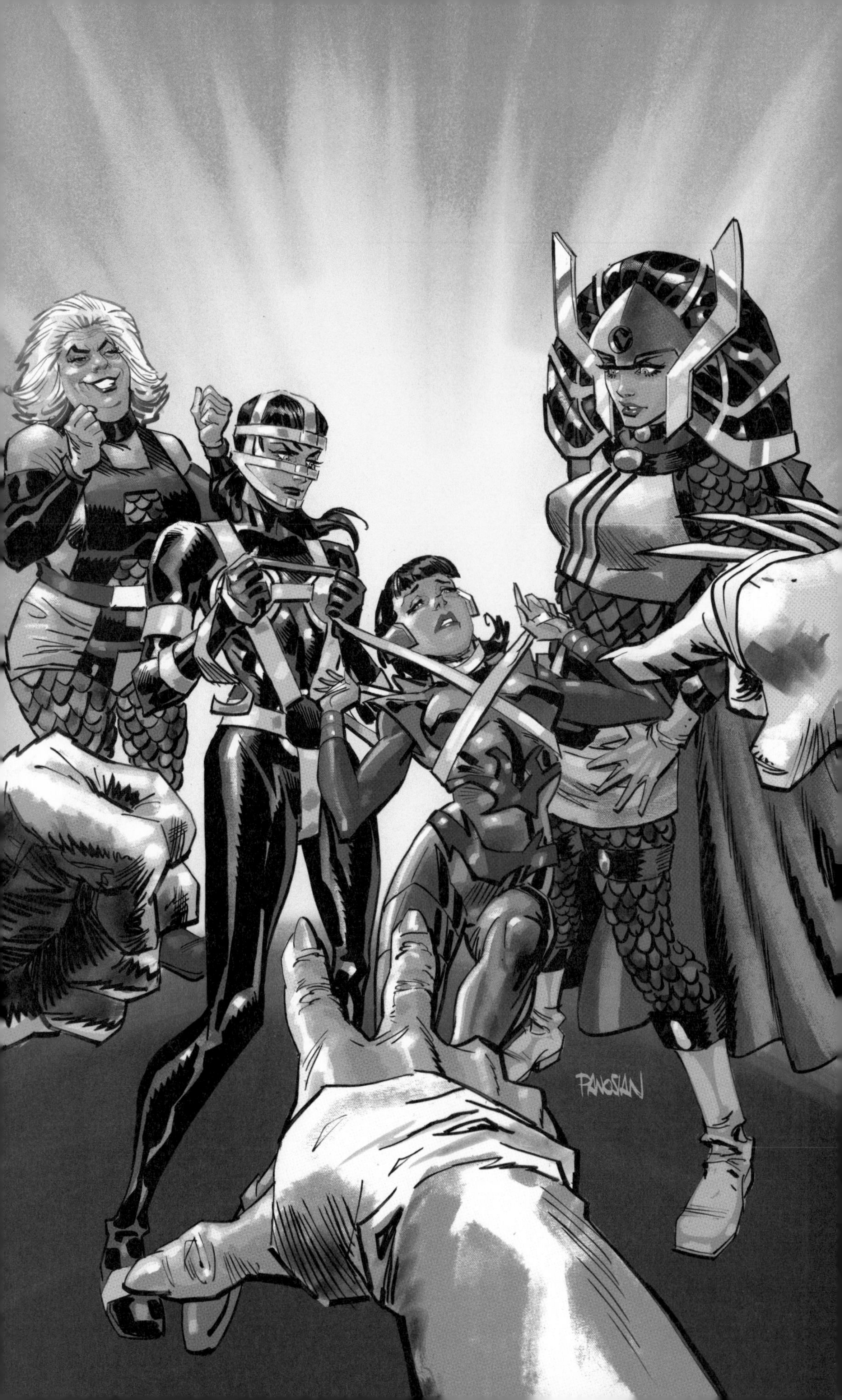
PANOSIAN

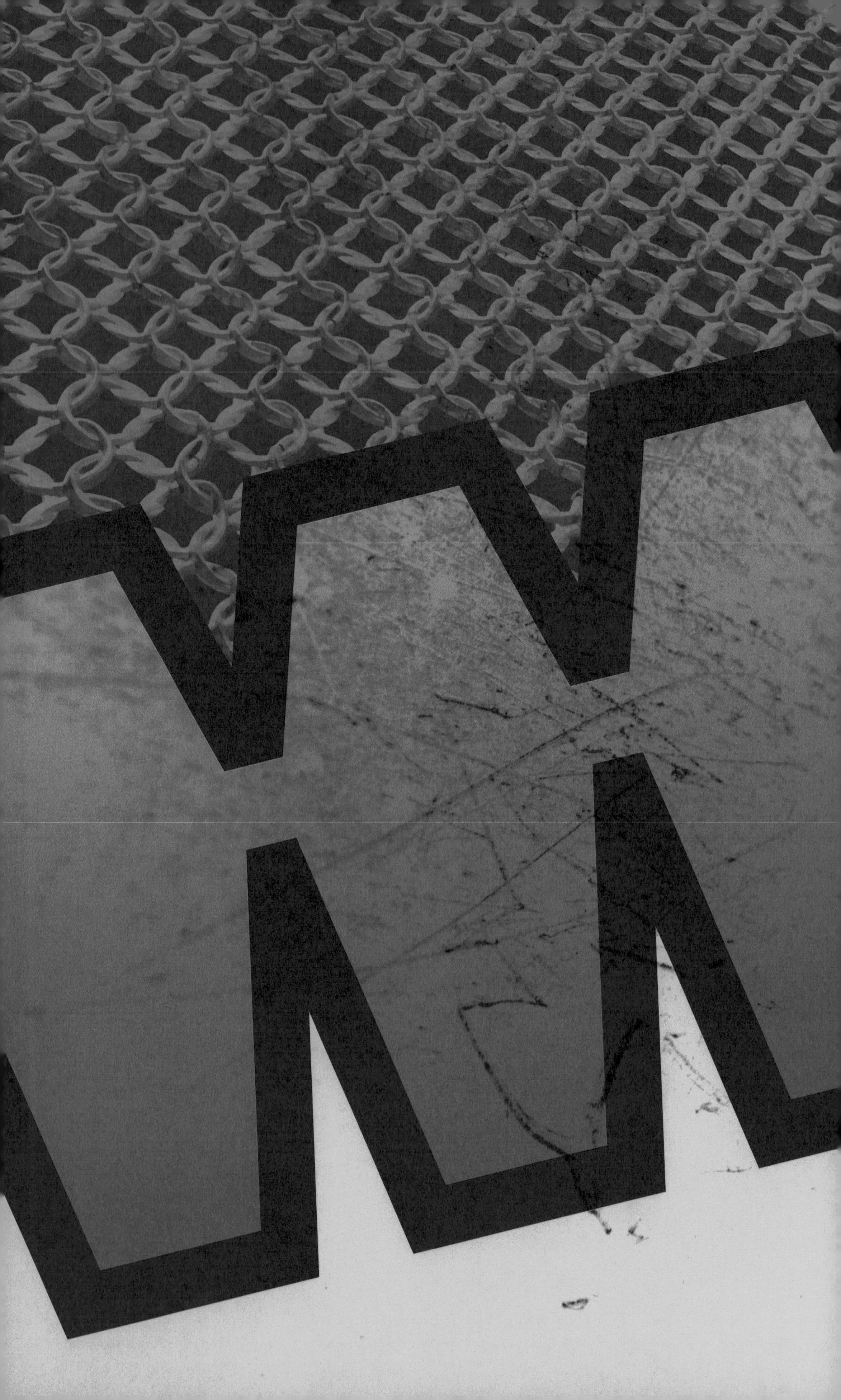

FEMALE FURIES PART TWO: "NASTY WOMAN"

WRITER CECIL CASTELLUCCI ILLUSTRATOR ADRIANA MELO COLORS HI-FI LETTERS CARLOS M. MANGUAL
COVER DAN PANOSIAN ASSOC. EDITOR BRITTANY HOLZHERR EDITOR JAMIE S. RICH

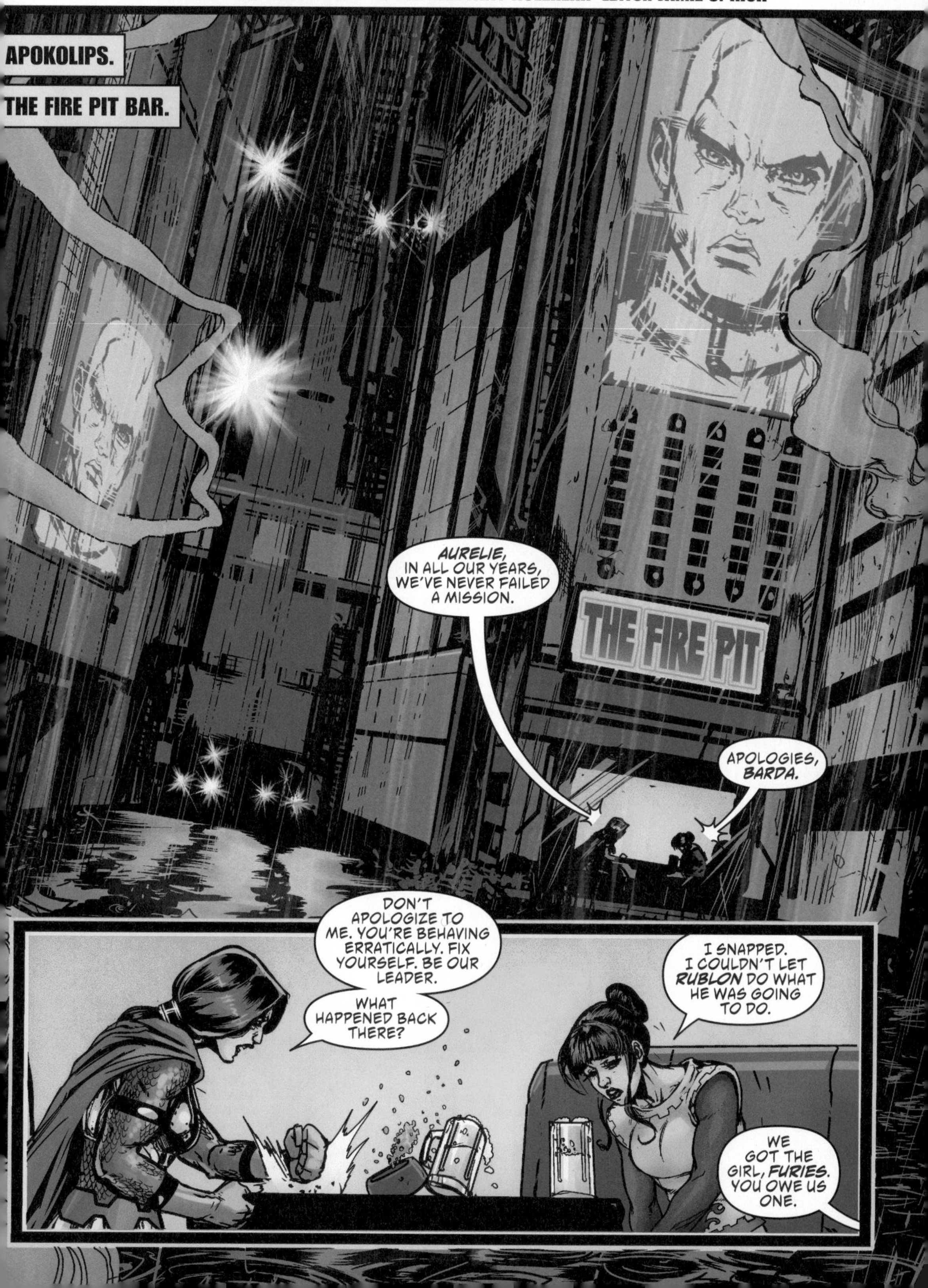
APOKOLIPS.
THE FIRE PIT BAR.
THE FIRE PIT
AURELIE, IN ALL OUR YEARS, WE'VE NEVER FAILED A MISSION.
APOLOGIES, BARDA.
DON'T APOLOGIZE TO ME. YOU'RE BEHAVING ERRATICALLY. FIX YOURSELF. BE OUR LEADER.
WHAT HAPPENED BACK THERE?
I SNAPPED. I COULDN'T LET RUBLON DO WHAT HE WAS GOING TO DO.
WE GOT THE GIRL, FURIES. YOU OWE US ONE.

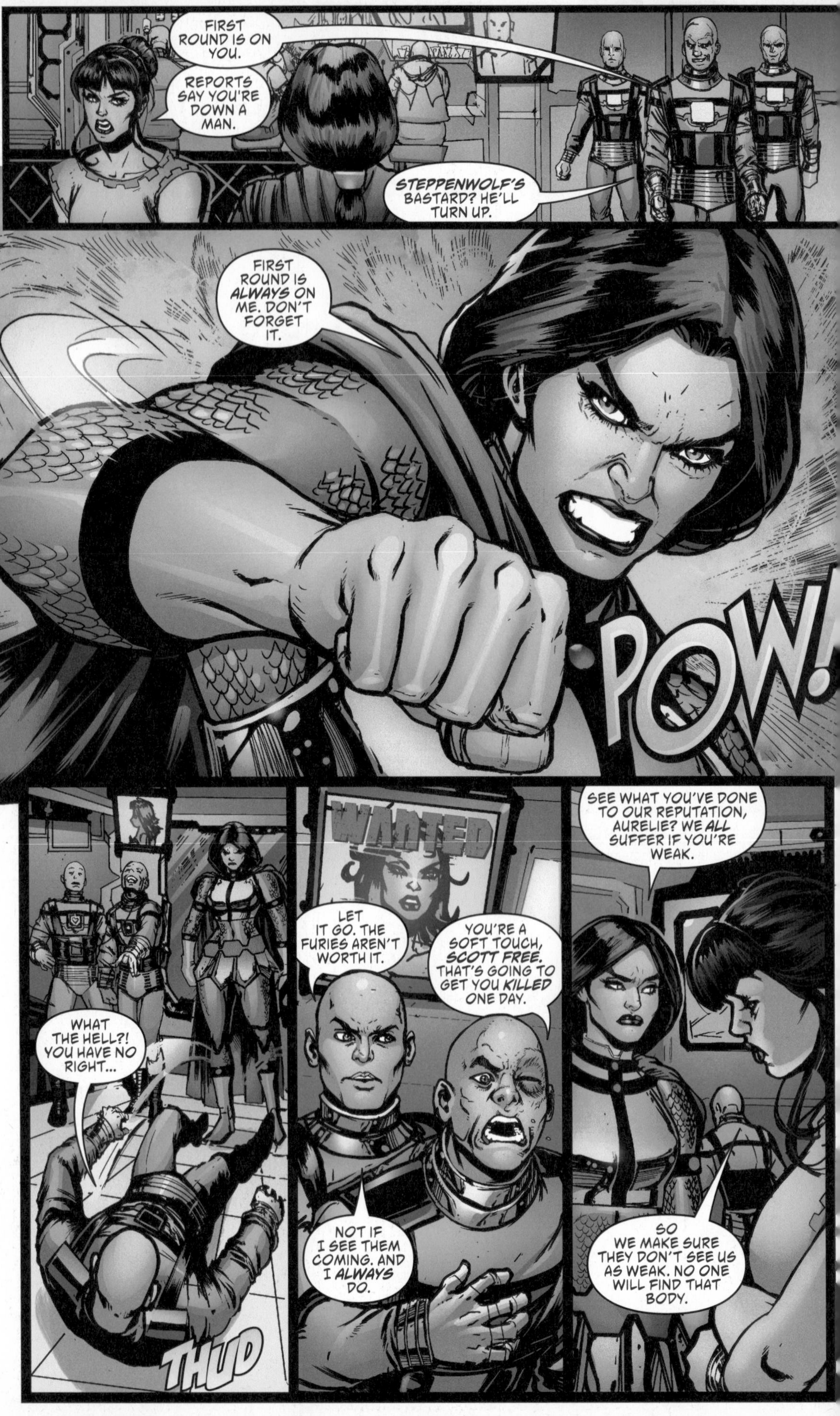

FIRST ROUND IS ON YOU.
REPORTS SAY YOU'RE DOWN A MAN.
STEPPENWOLF'S BASTARD? HE'LL TURN UP.
FIRST ROUND IS ALWAYS ON ME. DON'T FORGET IT.
POW!
WHAT THE HELL?! YOU HAVE NO RIGHT...
THUD
WANTED
LET IT GO. THE FURIES AREN'T WORTH IT.
YOU'RE A SOFT TOUCH, SCOTT FREE. THAT'S GOING TO GET YOU KILLED ONE DAY.
NOT IF I SEE THEM COMING. AND I ALWAYS DO.
SEE WHAT YOU'VE DONE TO OUR REPUTATION, AURELIE? WE ALL SUFFER IF YOU'RE WEAK.
SO WE MAKE SURE THEY DON'T SEE US AS WEAK. NO ONE WILL FIND THAT BODY.

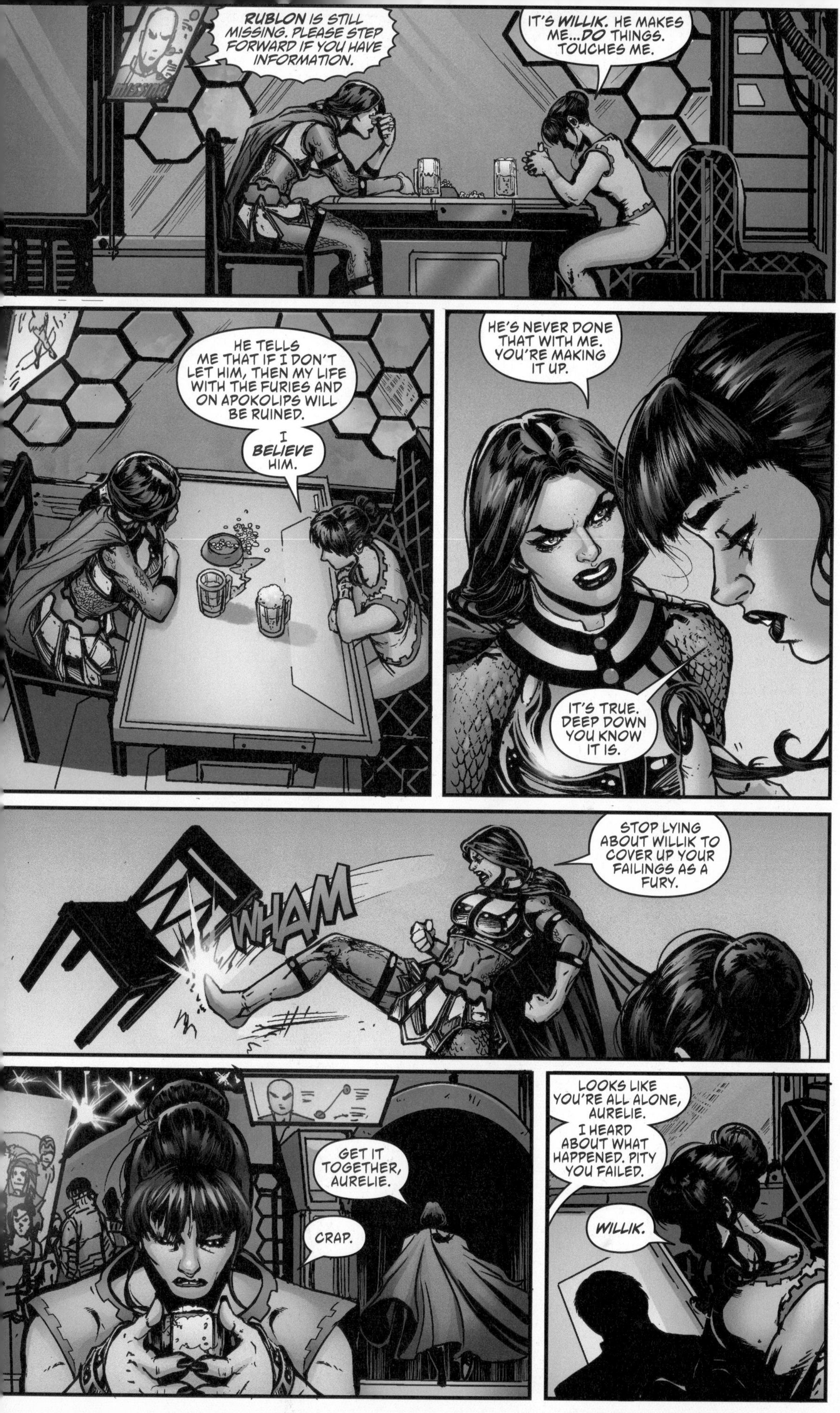

RUBLON IS STILL MISSING. PLEASE STEP FORWARD IF YOU HAVE INFORMATION.
MISSING
IT'S WILLIK. HE MAKES ME...DO THINGS. TOUCHES ME.
HE TELLS ME THAT IF I DON'T LET HIM, THEN MY LIFE WITH THE FURIES AND ON APOKOLIPS WILL BE RUINED.
I BELIEVE HIM.
HE'S NEVER DONE THAT WITH ME. YOU'RE MAKING IT UP.
IT'S TRUE. DEEP DOWN YOU KNOW IT IS.
STOP LYING ABOUT WILLIK TO COVER UP YOUR FAILINGS AS A FURY.
WHAM
GET IT TOGETHER, AURELIE.
CRAP.
LOOKS LIKE YOU'RE ALL ALONE, AURELIE.
I HEARD ABOUT WHAT HAPPENED. PITY YOU FAILED.
WILLIK.

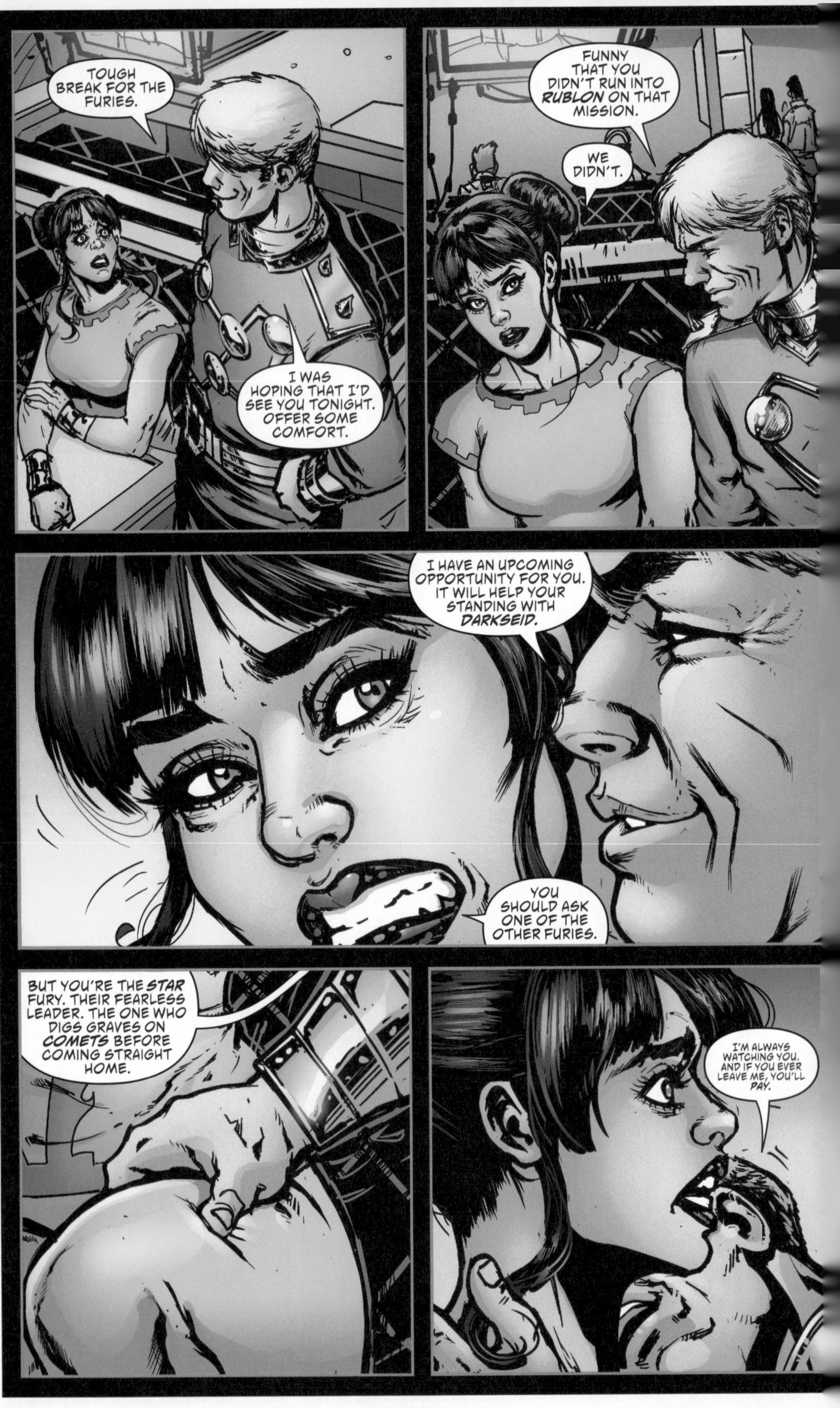

TOUGH BREAK FOR THE FURIES.
I WAS HOPING THAT I'D SEE YOU TONIGHT. OFFER SOME COMFORT.
FUNNY THAT YOU DIDN'T RUN INTO RUBLON ON THAT MISSION.
WE DIDN'T.
I HAVE AN UPCOMING OPPORTUNITY FOR YOU. IT WILL HELP YOUR STANDING WITH DARKSEID.
YOU SHOULD ASK ONE OF THE OTHER FURIES.
BUT YOU'RE THE STAR FURY. THEIR FEARLESS LEADER. THE ONE WHO DIGS GRAVES ON COMETS BEFORE COMING STRAIGHT HOME.
I'M ALWAYS WATCHING YOU. AND IF YOU EVER LEAVE ME, YOU'LL PAY.

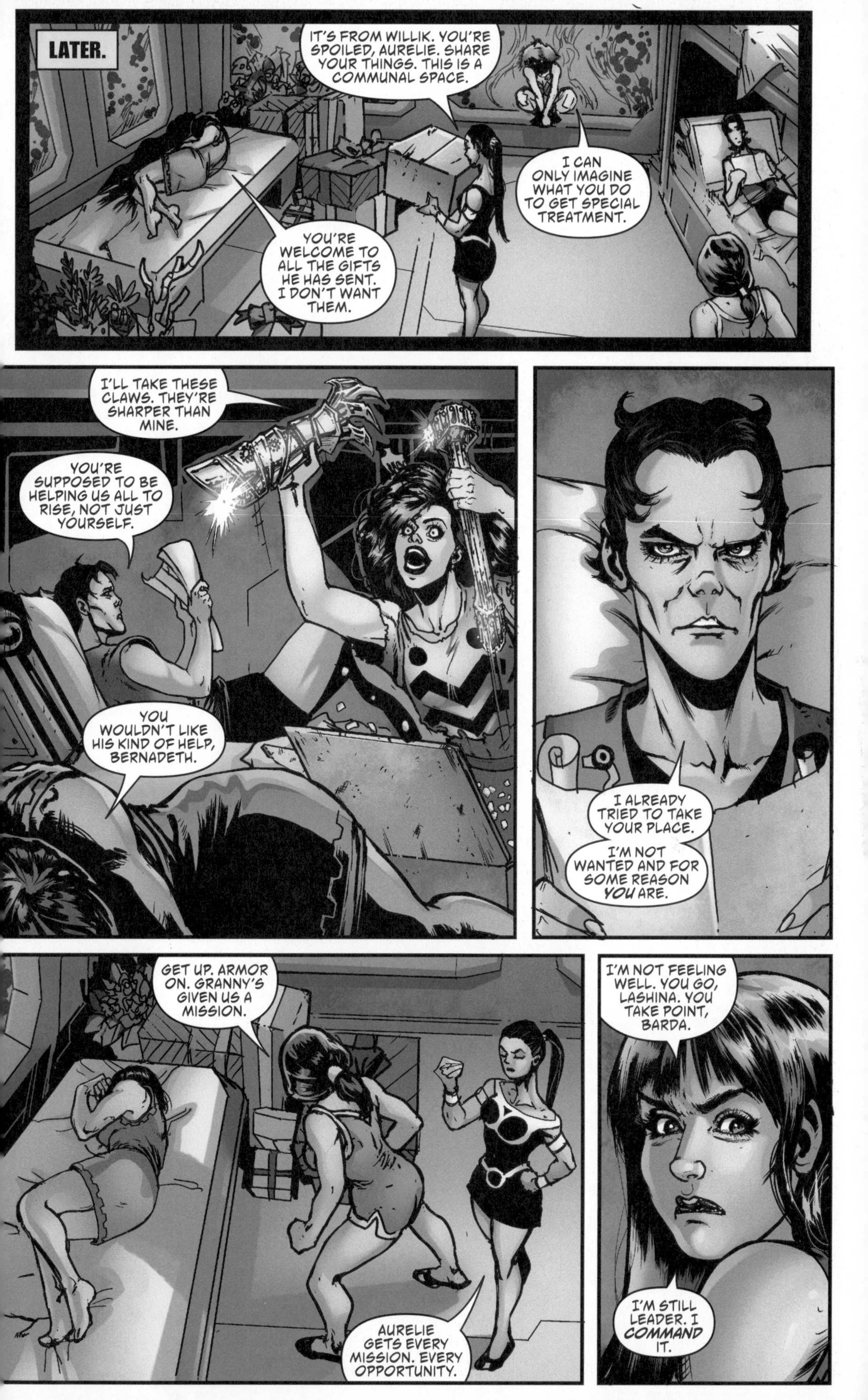
LATER.
IT'S FROM WILLIK. YOU'RE SPOILED, AURELIE. SHARE YOUR THINGS. THIS IS A COMMUNAL SPACE.
YOU'RE WELCOME TO ALL THE GIFTS HE HAS SENT. I DON'T WANT THEM.
I CAN ONLY IMAGINE WHAT YOU DO TO GET SPECIAL TREATMENT.
I'LL TAKE THESE CLAWS. THEY'RE SHARPER THAN MINE.
YOU'RE SUPPOSED TO BE HELPING US ALL TO RISE, NOT JUST YOURSELF.
YOU WOULDN'T LIKE HIS KIND OF HELP, BERNADETH.
I ALREADY TRIED TO TAKE YOUR PLACE.
I'M NOT WANTED AND FOR SOME REASON YOU ARE.
GET UP. ARMOR ON. GRANNY'S GIVEN US A MISSION.
AURELIE GETS EVERY MISSION. EVERY OPPORTUNITY.
I'M NOT FEELING WELL. YOU GO, LASHINA. YOU TAKE POINT, BARDA.
I'M STILL LEADER. I COMMAND IT.

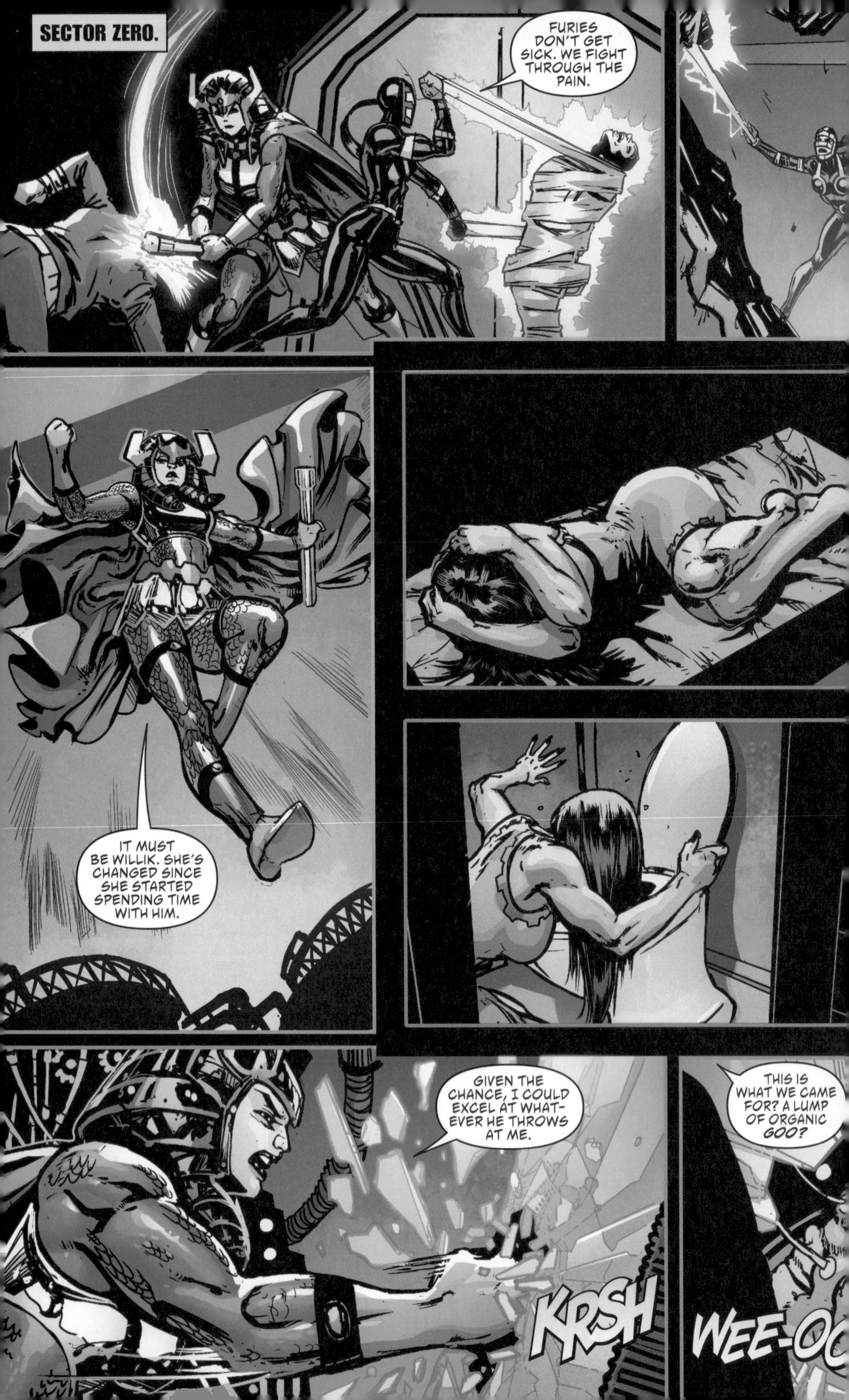
SECTOR ZERO.
FURIES DON'T GET SICK. WE FIGHT THROUGH THE PAIN.
IT MUST BE WILLIK. SHE'S CHANGED SINCE SHE STARTED SPENDING TIME WITH HIM.
GIVEN THE CHANCE, I COULD EXCEL AT WHAT-EVER HE THROWS AT ME.
KRSH
THIS IS WHAT WE CAME FOR? A LUMP OF ORGANIC GOO?
WEE-OO

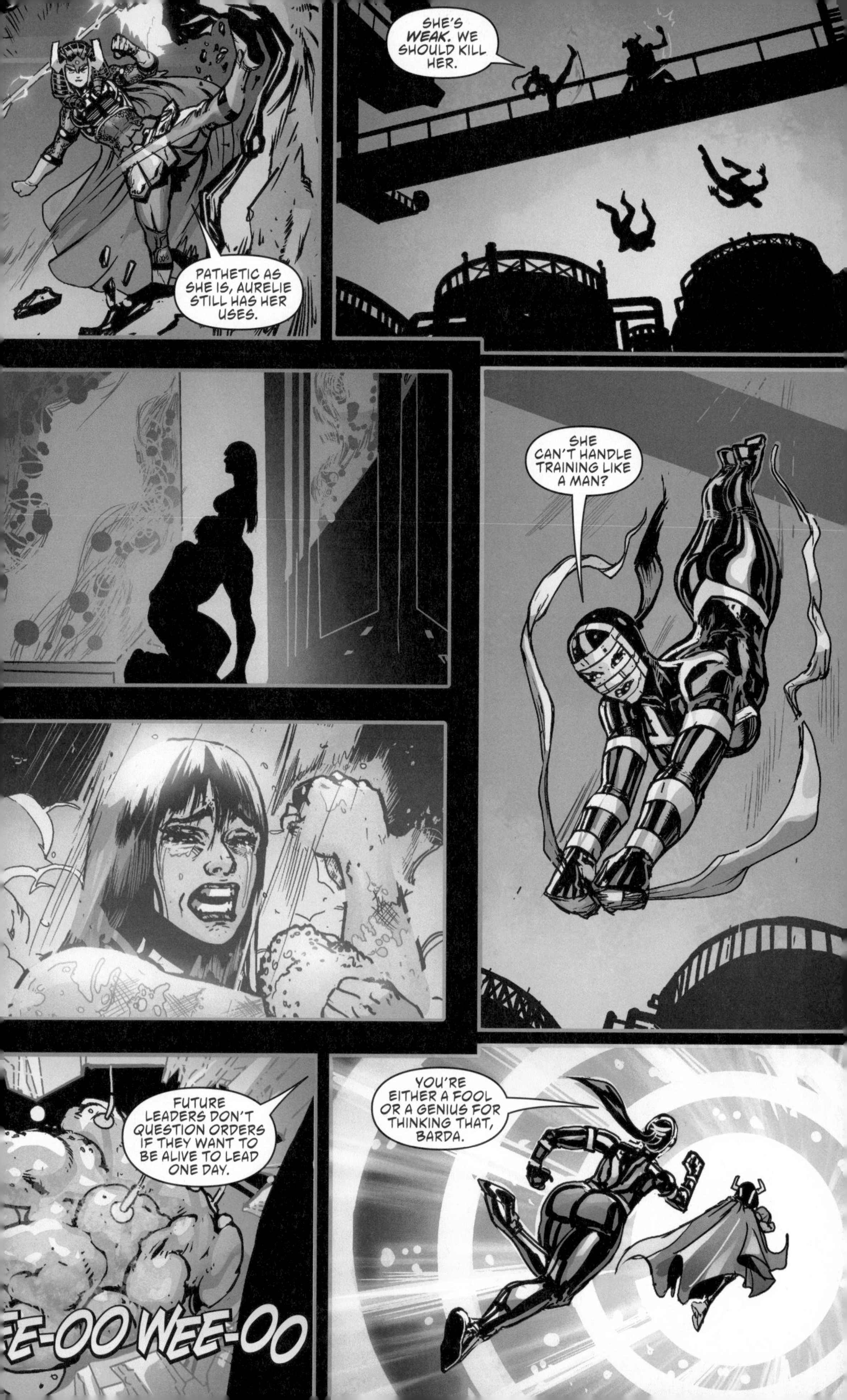
SHE'S WEAK. WE SHOULD KILL HER.
PATHETIC AS SHE IS, AURELIE STILL HAS HER USES.
SHE CAN'T HANDLE TRAINING LIKE A MAN?
FUTURE LEADERS DON'T QUESTION ORDERS IF THEY WANT TO BE ALIVE TO LEAD ONE DAY.
E-OO WEE-OO
YOU'RE EITHER A FOOL OR A GENIUS FOR THINKING THAT, BARDA.

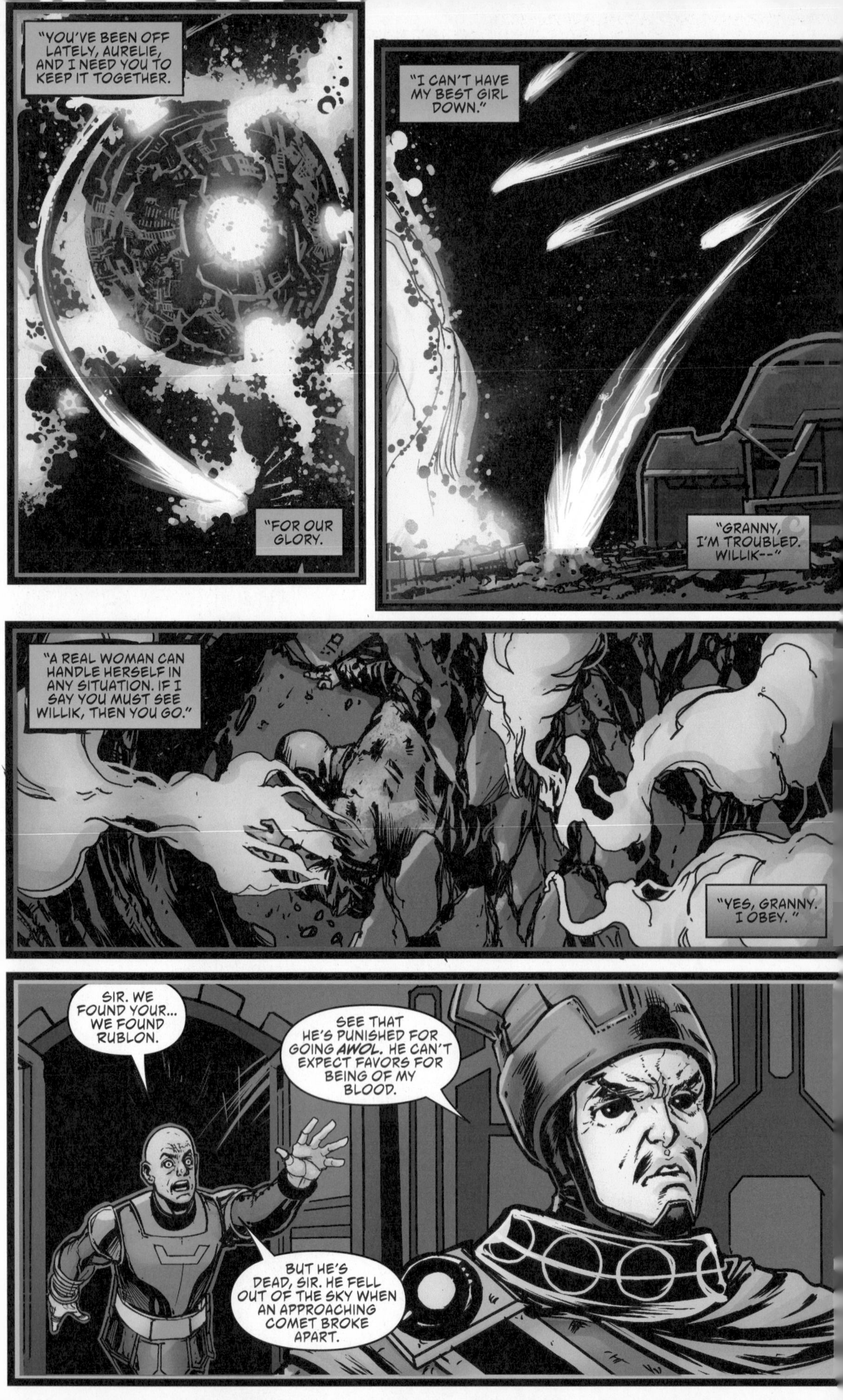
"YOU'VE BEEN OFF LATELY, AURELIE, AND I NEED YOU TO KEEP IT TOGETHER.
"FOR OUR GLORY.
"I CAN'T HAVE MY BEST GIRL DOWN."
"GRANNY, I'M TROUBLED. WILLIK--"
"A REAL WOMAN CAN HANDLE HERSELF IN ANY SITUATION. IF I SAY YOU MUST SEE WILLIK, THEN YOU GO."
"YES, GRANNY. I OBEY."
SIR. WE FOUND YOUR... WE FOUND RUBLON.
SEE THAT HE'S PUNISHED FOR GOING AWOL. HE CAN'T EXPECT FAVORS FOR BEING OF MY BLOOD.
BUT HE'S DEAD, SIR. HE FELL OUT OF THE SKY WHEN AN APPROACHING COMET BROKE APART.

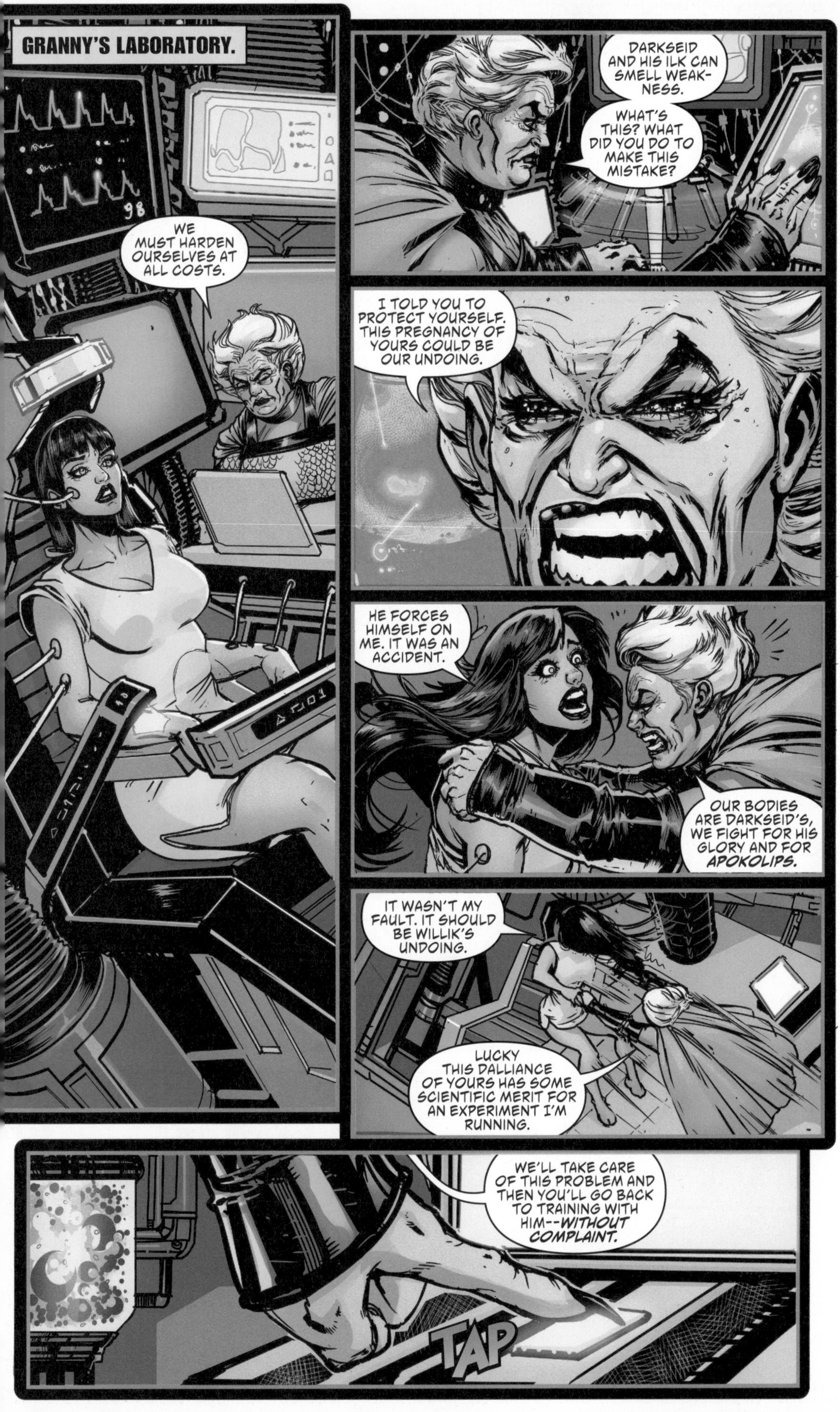
GRANNY'S LABORATORY.
WE MUST HARDEN OURSELVES AT ALL COSTS.
DARKSEID AND HIS ILK CAN SMELL WEAK-NESS.
WHAT'S THIS? WHAT DID YOU DO TO MAKE THIS MISTAKE?
I TOLD YOU TO PROTECT YOURSELF. THIS PREGNANCY OF YOURS COULD BE OUR UNDOING.
HE FORCES HIMSELF ON ME. IT WAS AN ACCIDENT.
OUR BODIES ARE DARKSEID'S, WE FIGHT FOR HIS GLORY AND FOR *APOKOLIPS.*
IT WASN'T MY FAULT. IT SHOULD BE WILLIK'S UNDOING.
LUCKY THIS DALLIANCE OF YOURS HAS SOME SCIENTIFIC MERIT FOR AN EXPERIMENT I'M RUNNING.
WE'LL TAKE CARE OF THIS PROBLEM AND THEN YOU'LL GO BACK TO TRAINING WITH HIM--*WITHOUT COMPLAINT.*
TAP

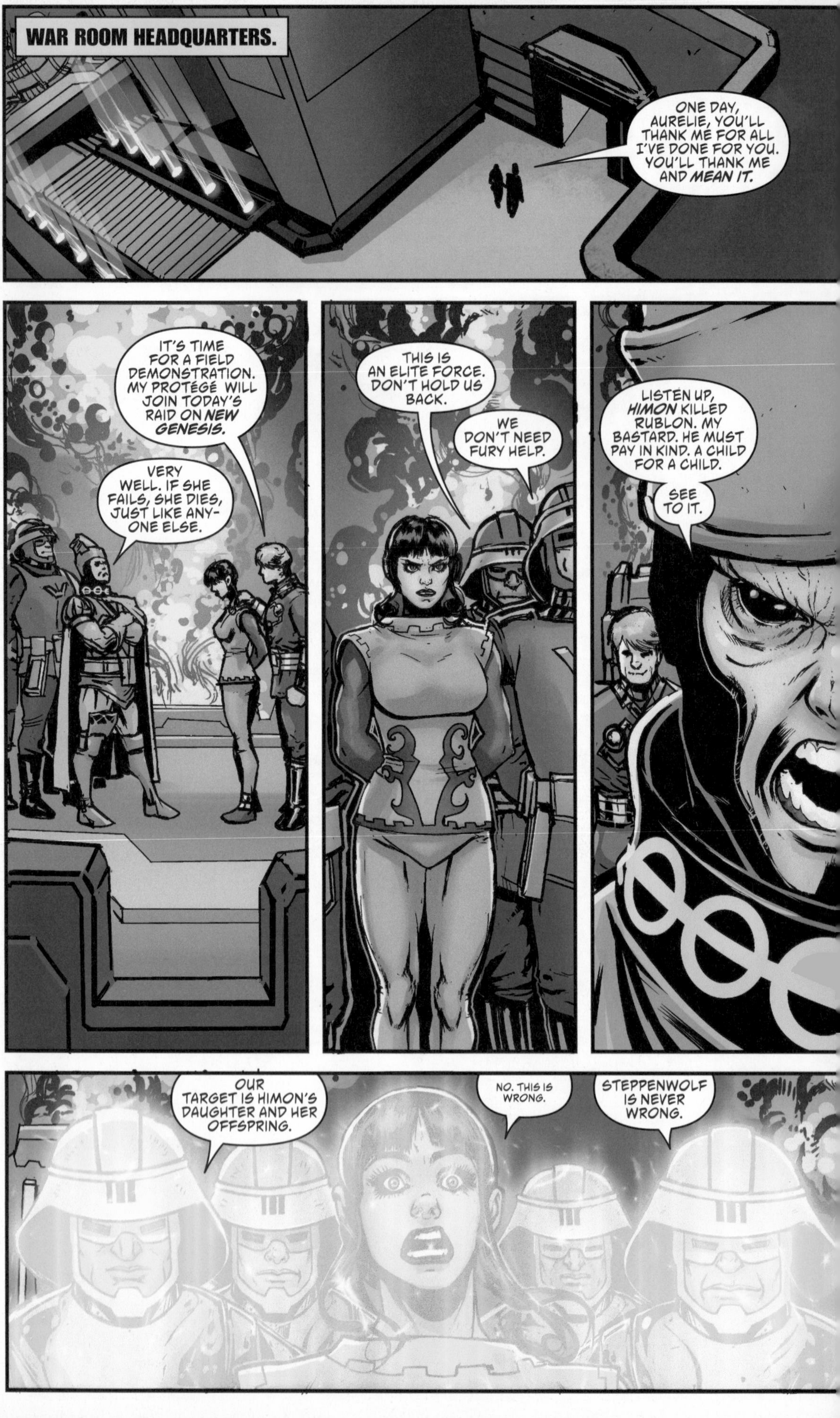

WAR ROOM HEADQUARTERS.
ONE DAY, AURELIE, YOU'LL THANK ME FOR ALL I'VE DONE FOR YOU. YOU'LL THANK ME AND *MEAN IT.*
IT'S TIME FOR A FIELD DEMONSTRATION. MY PROTÉGÉ WILL JOIN TODAY'S RAID ON *NEW GENESIS.*
VERY WELL. IF SHE FAILS, SHE DIES, JUST LIKE ANY-ONE ELSE.
THIS IS AN ELITE FORCE. DON'T HOLD US BACK.
WE DON'T NEED FURY HELP.
LISTEN UP, *HIMON* KILLED RUBLON. MY BASTARD. HE MUST PAY IN KIND. A CHILD FOR A CHILD.
SEE TO IT.
OUR TARGET IS HIMON'S DAUGHTER AND HER OFFSPRING.
NO. THIS IS WRONG.
STEPPENWOLF IS NEVER WRONG.

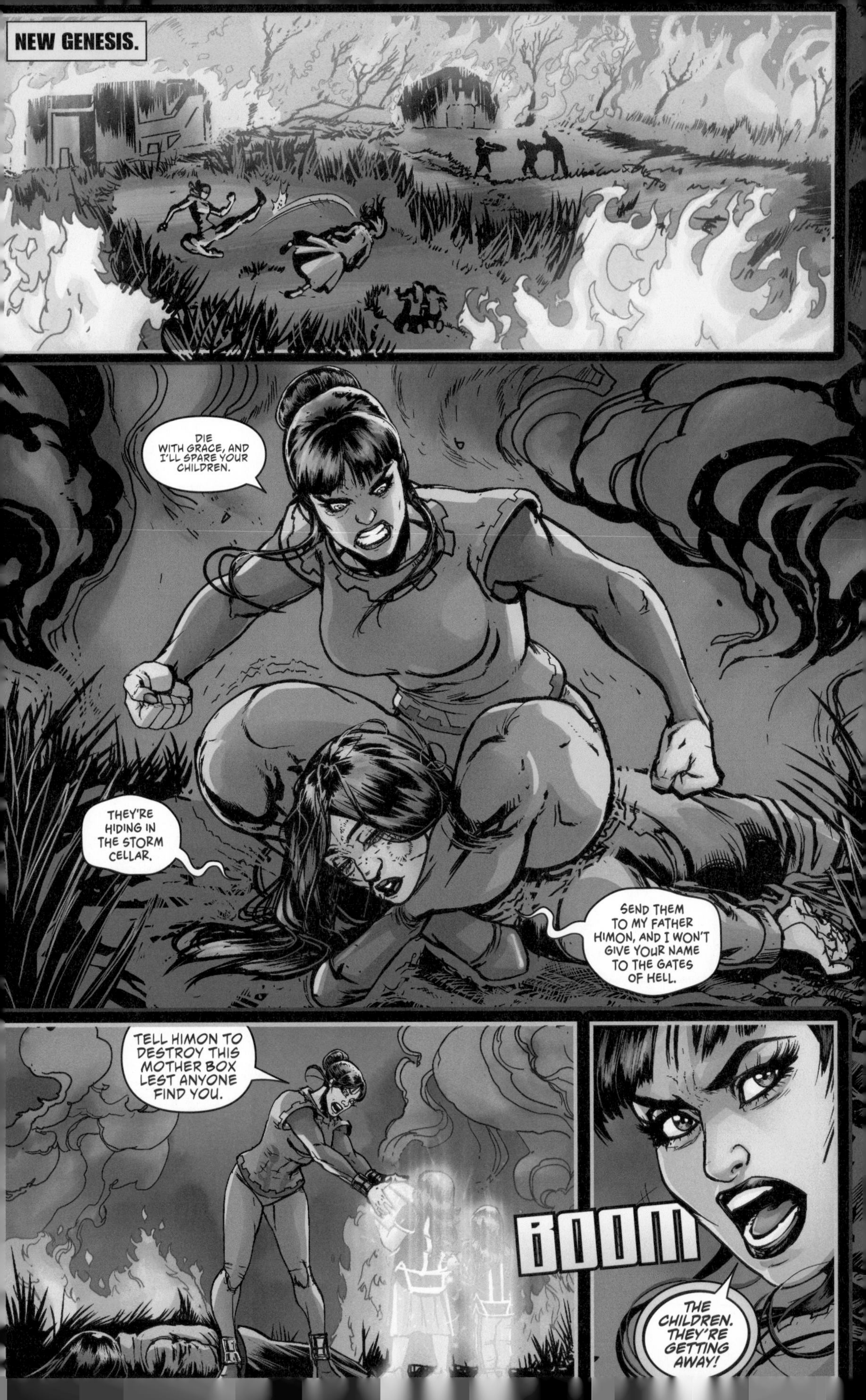
NEW GENESIS.
DIE WITH GRACE, AND I'LL SPARE YOUR CHILDREN.
THEY'RE HIDING IN THE STORM CELLAR.
SEND THEM TO MY FATHER HIMON, AND I WON'T GIVE YOUR NAME TO THE GATES OF HELL.
TELL HIMON TO DESTROY THIS MOTHER BOX LEST ANYONE FIND YOU.
BOOM
THE CHILDREN. THEY'RE GETTING AWAY!

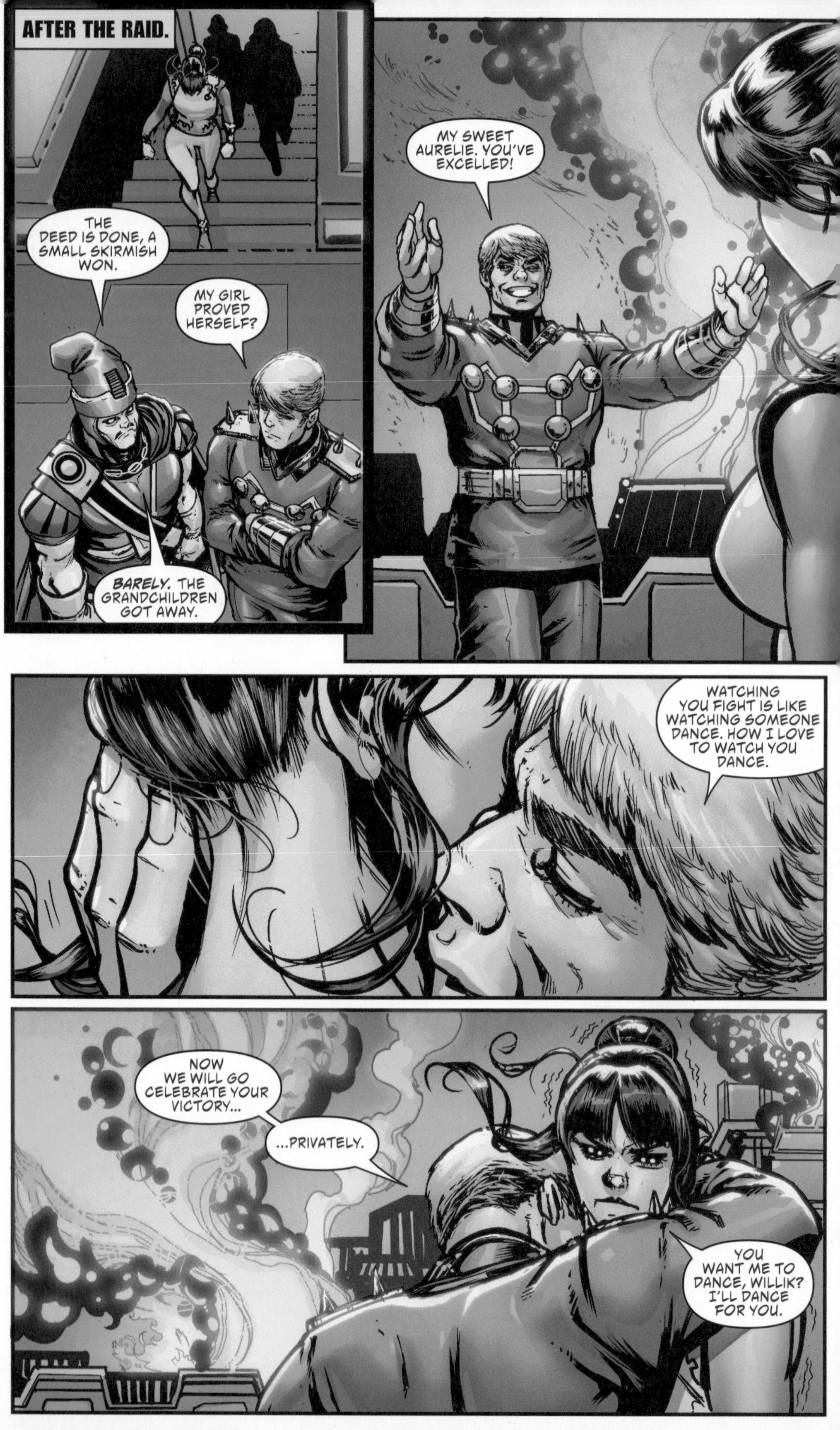
AFTER THE RAID.
THE DEED IS DONE, A SMALL SKIRMISH WON.
MY GIRL PROVED HERSELF?
BARELY. THE GRANDCHILDREN GOT AWAY.
MY SWEET AURELIE. YOU'VE EXCELLED!
WATCHING YOU FIGHT IS LIKE WATCHING SOMEONE DANCE. HOW I LOVE TO WATCH YOU DANCE.
NOW WE WILL GO CELEBRATE YOUR VICTORY...
...PRIVATELY.
YOU WANT ME TO DANCE, WILLIK? I'LL DANCE FOR YOU.

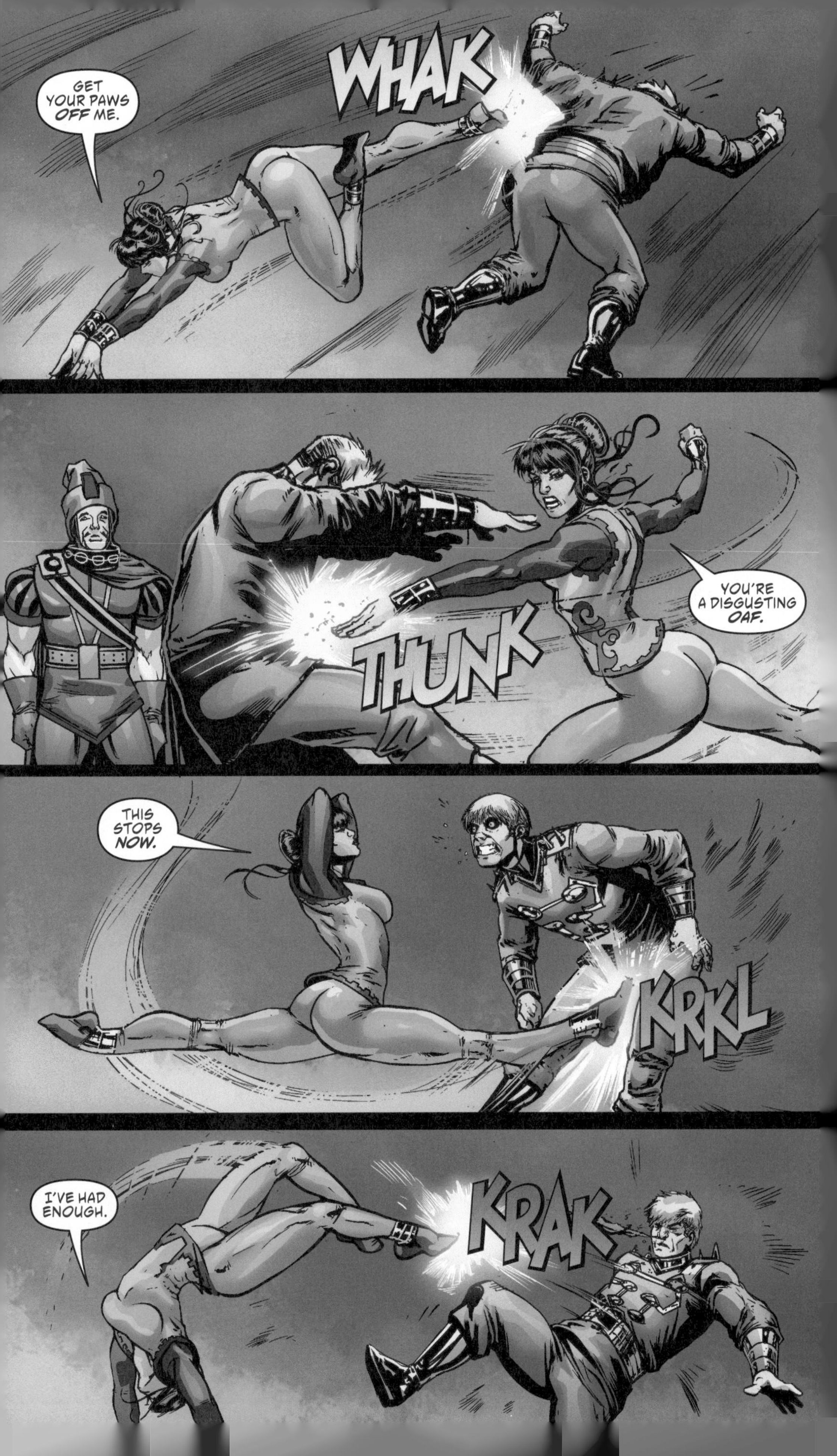
GET YOUR PAWS OFF ME.
WHAK
YOU'RE A DISGUSTING OAF.
THUNK
THIS STOPS NOW.
KRKL
I'VE HAD ENOUGH.
KRAK

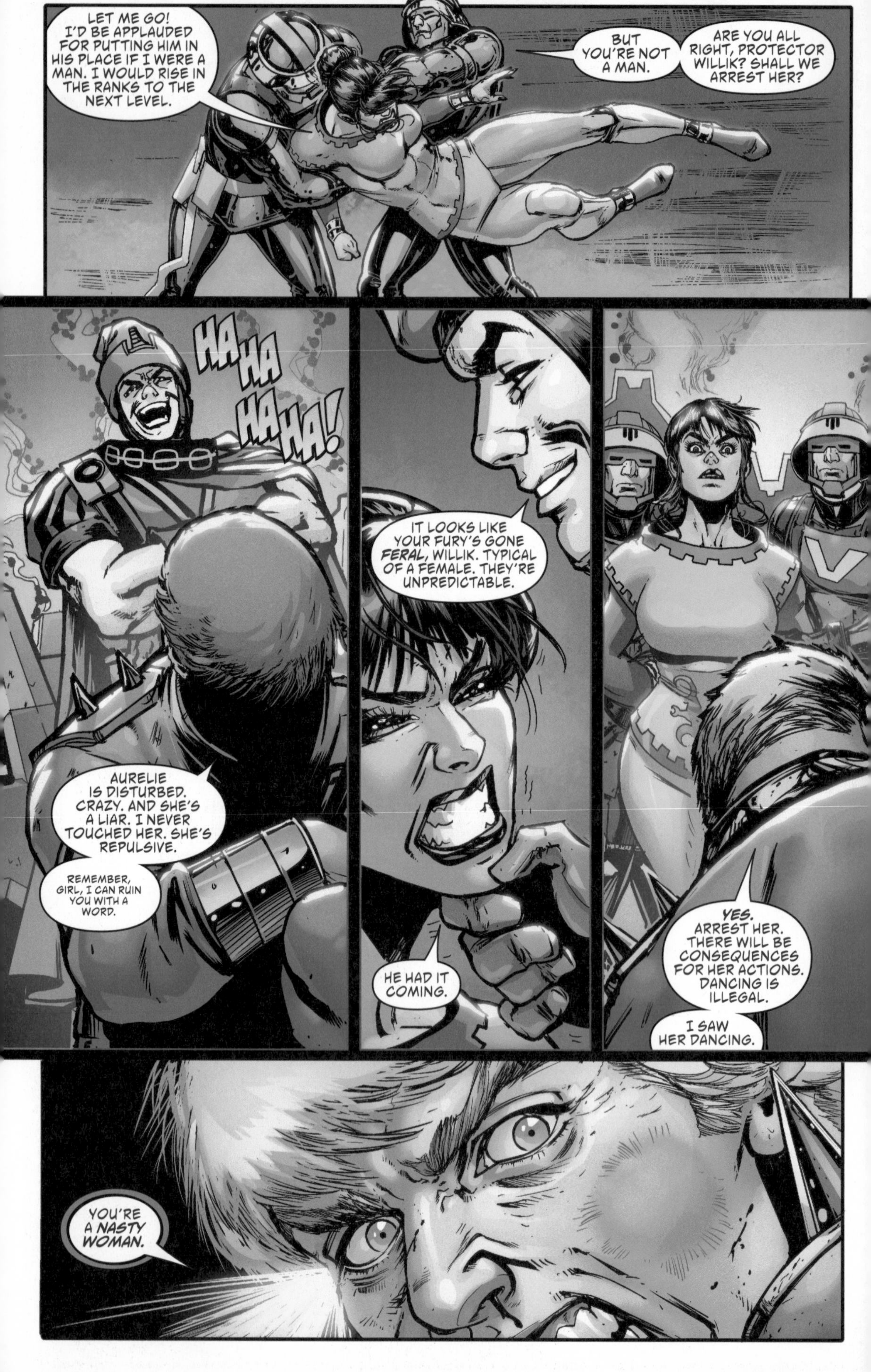
LET ME GO! I'D BE APPLAUDED FOR PUTTING HIM IN HIS PLACE IF I WERE A MAN. I WOULD RISE IN THE RANKS TO THE NEXT LEVEL.
BUT YOU'RE NOT A MAN.
ARE YOU ALL RIGHT, PROTECTOR WILLIK? SHALL WE ARREST HER?
HA HA HA HA!
AURELIE IS DISTURBED. CRAZY. AND SHE'S A LIAR. I NEVER TOUCHED HER. SHE'S REPULSIVE.
REMEMBER, GIRL, I CAN RUIN YOU WITH A WORD.
IT LOOKS LIKE YOUR FURY'S GONE FERAL, WILLIK. TYPICAL OF A FEMALE. THEY'RE UNPREDICTABLE.
HE HAD IT COMING.
YES. ARREST HER. THERE WILL BE CONSEQUENCES FOR HER ACTIONS. DANCING IS ILLEGAL.
I SAW HER DANCING.
YOU'RE A NASTY WOMAN.

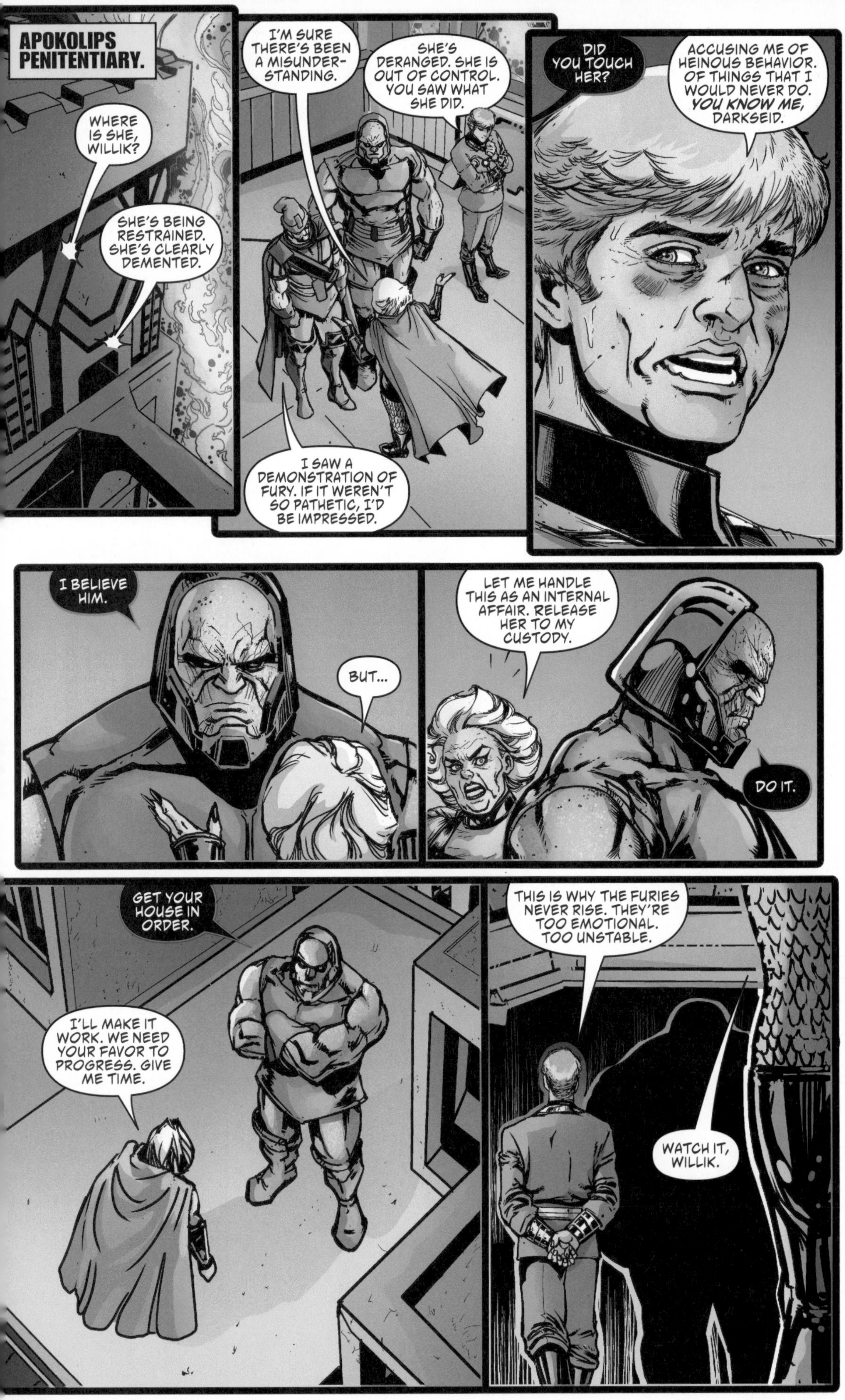
APOKOLIPS PENITENTIARY.
WHERE IS SHE, WILLIK?
SHE'S BEING RESTRAINED. SHE'S CLEARLY DEMENTED.
I'M SURE THERE'S BEEN A MISUNDER-STANDING.
SHE'S DERANGED. SHE IS OUT OF CONTROL. YOU SAW WHAT SHE DID.
I SAW A DEMONSTRATION OF FURY. IF IT WEREN'T SO PATHETIC, I'D BE IMPRESSED.
DID YOU TOUCH HER?
ACCUSING ME OF HEINOUS BEHAVIOR. OF THINGS THAT I WOULD NEVER DO. YOU KNOW ME, DARKSEID.
I BELIEVE HIM.
BUT...
LET ME HANDLE THIS AS AN INTERNAL AFFAIR. RELEASE HER TO MY CUSTODY.
DO IT.
GET YOUR HOUSE IN ORDER.
I'LL MAKE IT WORK. WE NEED YOUR FAVOR TO PROGRESS. GIVE ME TIME.
THIS IS WHY THE FURIES NEVER RISE. THEY'RE TOO EMOTIONAL. TOO UNSTABLE.
WATCH IT, WILLIK.

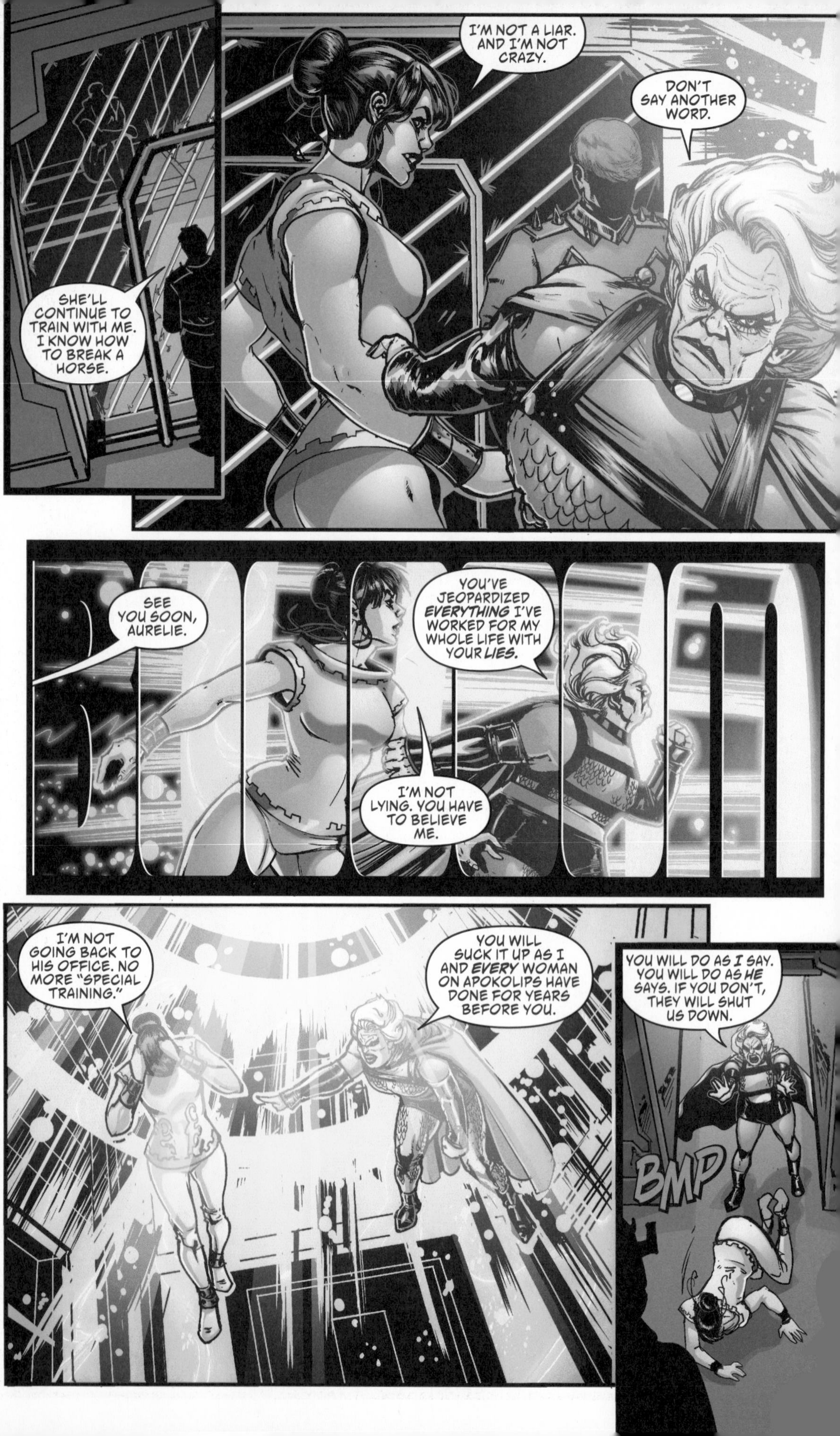

SHE'LL CONTINUE TO TRAIN WITH ME. I KNOW HOW TO BREAK A HORSE.
I'M NOT A LIAR. AND I'M NOT CRAZY.
DON'T SAY ANOTHER WORD.
SEE YOU SOON, AURELIE.
YOU'VE JEOPARDIZED EVERYTHING I'VE WORKED FOR MY WHOLE LIFE WITH YOUR LIES.
I'M NOT LYING. YOU HAVE TO BELIEVE ME.
I'M NOT GOING BACK TO HIS OFFICE. NO MORE "SPECIAL TRAINING."
YOU WILL SUCK IT UP AS I AND EVERY WOMAN ON APOKOLIPS HAVE DONE FOR YEARS BEFORE YOU.
YOU WILL DO AS I SAY. YOU WILL DO AS HE SAYS. IF YOU DON'T, THEY WILL SHUT US DOWN.
BMP

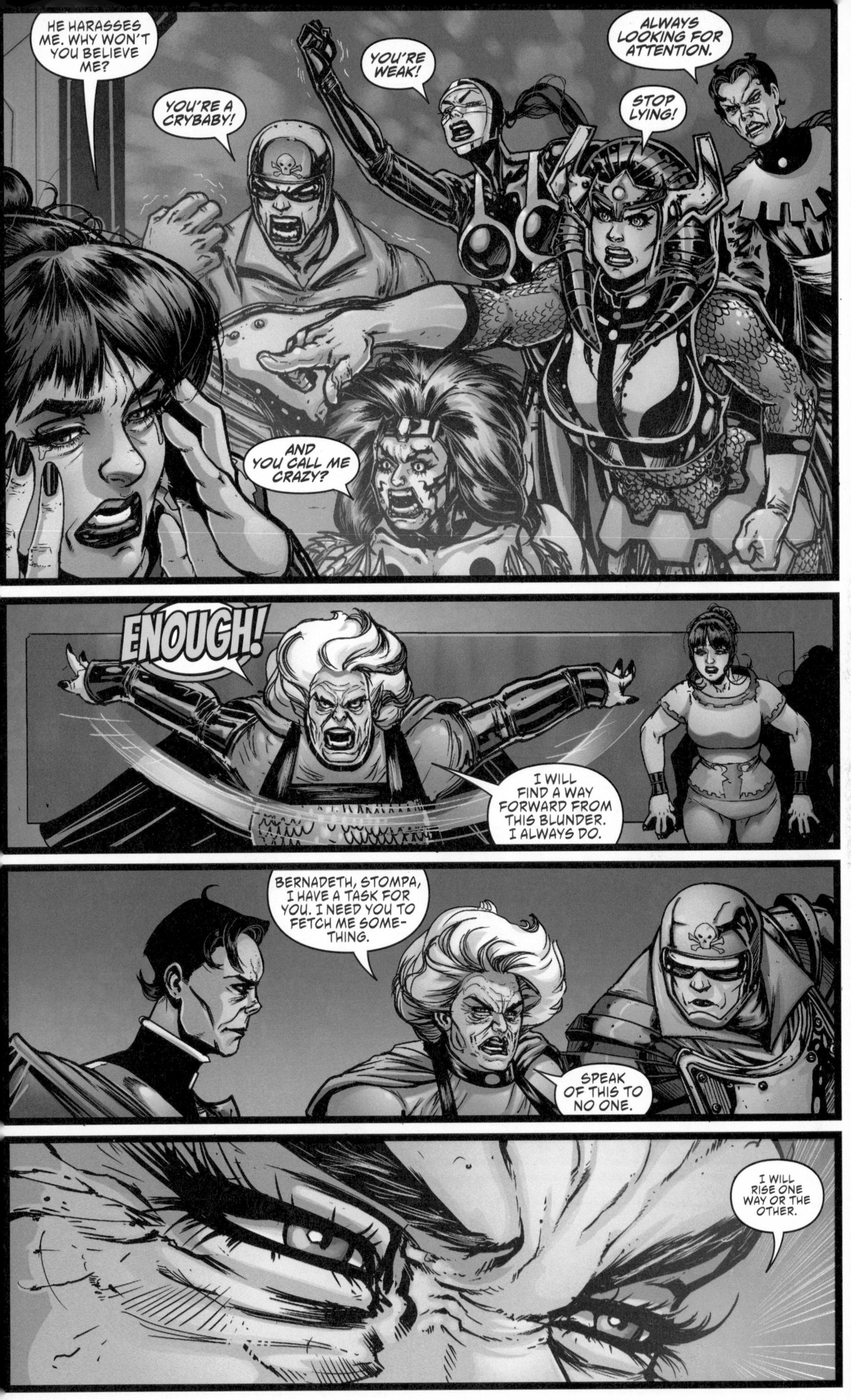
HE HARASSES ME. WHY WON'T YOU BELIEVE ME?
YOU'RE A CRYBABY!
YOU'RE WEAK!
ALWAYS LOOKING FOR ATTENTION.
STOP LYING!
AND YOU CALL ME CRAZY?
ENOUGH!
I WILL FIND A WAY FORWARD FROM THIS BLUNDER. I ALWAYS DO.
BERNADETH, STOMPA, I HAVE A TASK FOR YOU. I NEED YOU TO FETCH ME SOME-THING.
SPEAK OF THIS TO NO ONE.
I WILL RISE ONE WAY OR THE OTHER.

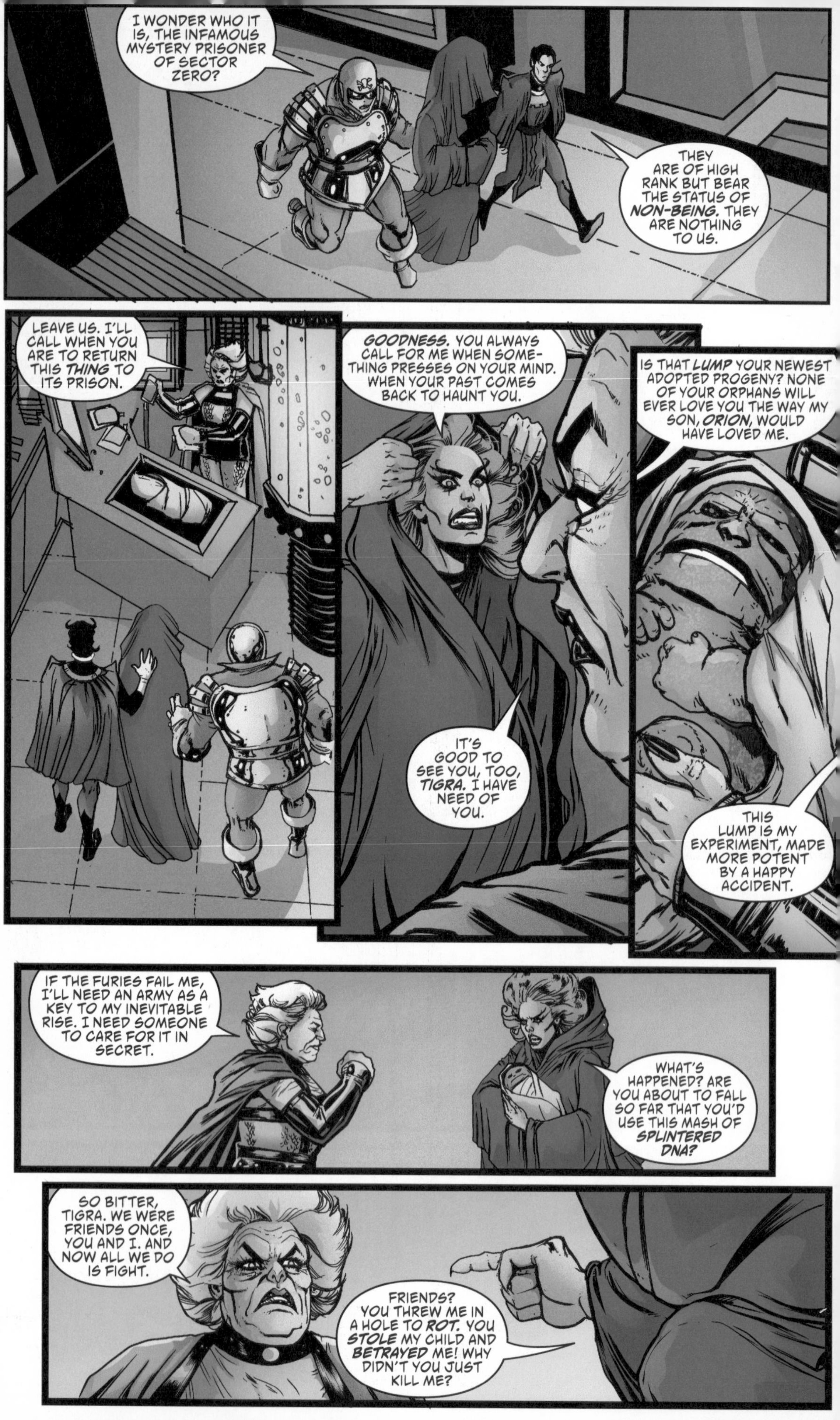
I WONDER WHO IT IS, THE INFAMOUS MYSTERY PRISONER OF SECTOR ZERO?
THEY ARE OF HIGH RANK BUT BEAR THE STATUS OF NON-BEING. THEY ARE NOTHING TO US.
LEAVE US. I'LL CALL WHEN YOU ARE TO RETURN THIS THING TO ITS PRISON.
GOODNESS. YOU ALWAYS CALL FOR ME WHEN SOMETHING PRESSES ON YOUR MIND. WHEN YOUR PAST COMES BACK TO HAUNT YOU.
IT'S GOOD TO SEE YOU, TOO, TIGRA. I HAVE NEED OF YOU.
IS THAT LUMP YOUR NEWEST ADOPTED PROGENY? NONE OF YOUR ORPHANS WILL EVER LOVE YOU THE WAY MY SON, ORION, WOULD HAVE LOVED ME.
THIS LUMP IS MY EXPERIMENT, MADE MORE POTENT BY A HAPPY ACCIDENT.
IF THE FURIES FAIL ME, I'LL NEED AN ARMY AS A KEY TO MY INEVITABLE RISE. I NEED SOMEONE TO CARE FOR IT IN SECRET.
WHAT'S HAPPENED? ARE YOU ABOUT TO FALL SO FAR THAT YOU'D USE THIS MASH OF SPLINTERED DNA?
SO BITTER, TIGRA. WE WERE FRIENDS ONCE, YOU AND I. AND NOW ALL WE DO IS FIGHT.
FRIENDS? YOU THREW ME IN A HOLE TO ROT. YOU STOLE MY CHILD AND BETRAYED ME! WHY DIDN'T YOU JUST KILL ME?

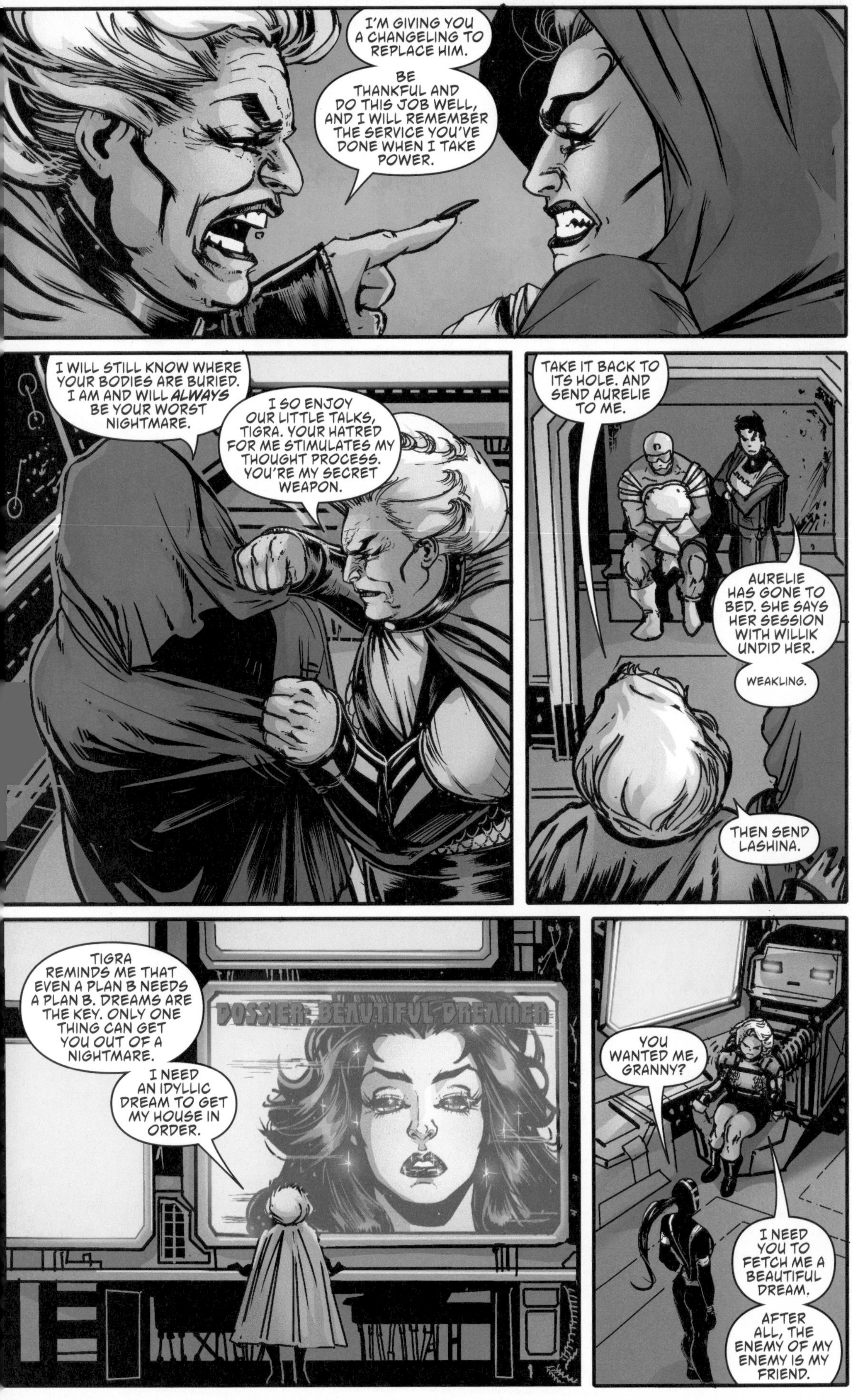
I'M GIVING YOU A CHANGELING TO REPLACE HIM.
BE THANKFUL AND DO THIS JOB WELL, AND I WILL REMEMBER THE SERVICE YOU'VE DONE WHEN I TAKE POWER.
I WILL STILL KNOW WHERE YOUR BODIES ARE BURIED. I AM AND WILL *ALWAYS* BE YOUR WORST NIGHTMARE.
I SO ENJOY OUR LITTLE TALKS, TIGRA. YOUR HATRED FOR ME STIMULATES MY THOUGHT PROCESS. YOU'RE MY SECRET WEAPON.
TAKE IT BACK TO ITS HOLE. AND SEND AURELIE TO ME.
AURELIE HAS GONE TO BED. SHE SAYS HER SESSION WITH WILLIK UNDID HER.
WEAKLING.
THEN SEND LASHINA.
TIGRA REMINDS ME THAT EVEN A PLAN B NEEDS A PLAN B. DREAMS ARE THE KEY. ONLY ONE THING CAN GET YOU OUT OF A NIGHTMARE.
DOSSIER: BEAUTIFUL DREAMER
I NEED AN IDYLLIC DREAM TO GET MY HOUSE IN ORDER.
YOU WANTED ME, GRANNY?
I NEED YOU TO FETCH ME A BEAUTIFUL DREAM.
AFTER ALL, THE ENEMY OF MY ENEMY IS MY FRIEND.

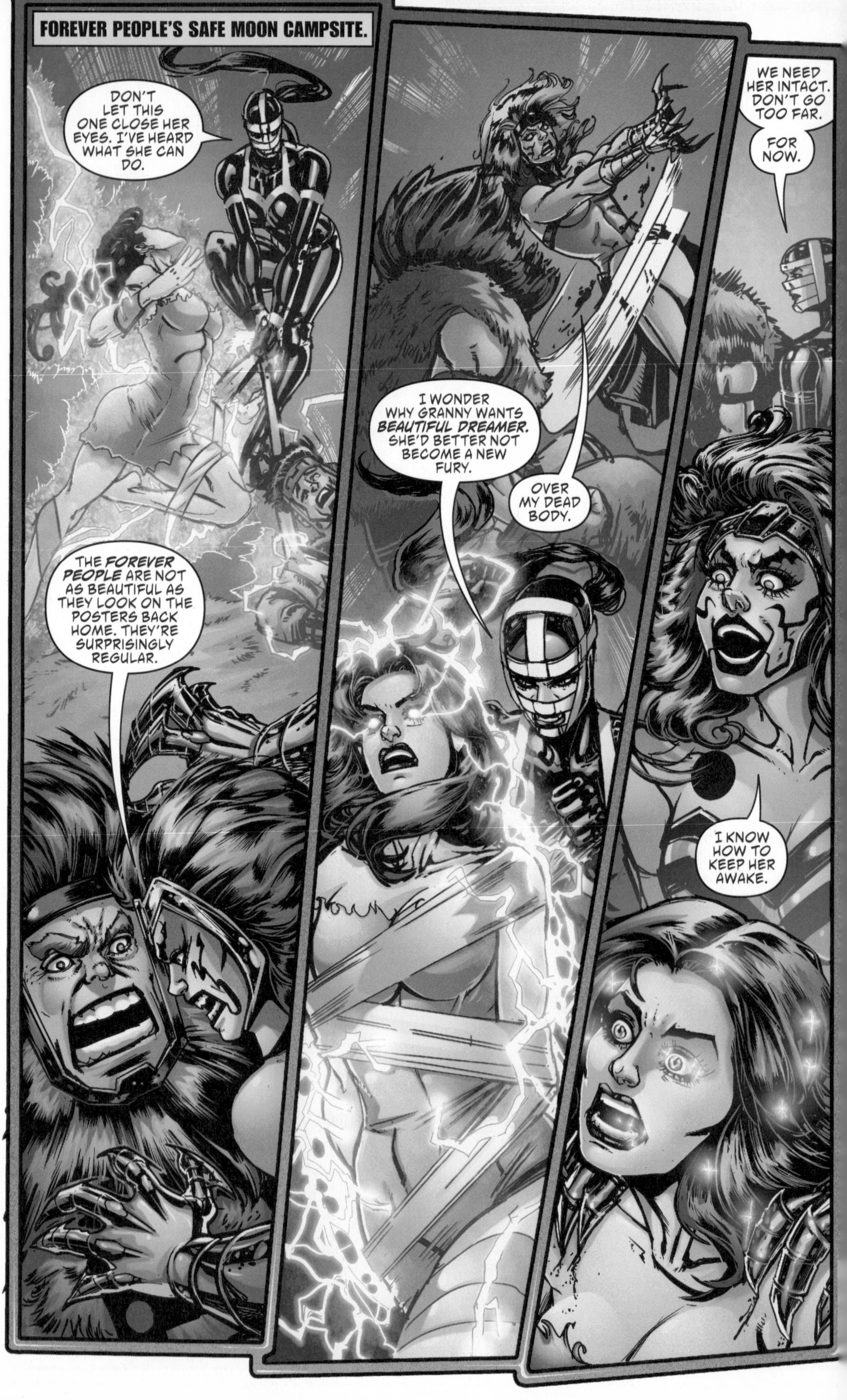
FOREVER PEOPLE'S SAFE MOON CAMPSITE.
DON'T LET THIS ONE CLOSE HER EYES. I'VE HEARD WHAT SHE CAN DO.
THE FOREVER PEOPLE ARE NOT AS BEAUTIFUL AS THEY LOOK ON THE POSTERS BACK HOME. THEY'RE SURPRISINGLY REGULAR.
I WONDER WHY GRANNY WANTS BEAUTIFUL DREAMER. SHE'D BETTER NOT BECOME A NEW FURY.
OVER MY DEAD BODY.
WE NEED HER INTACT. DON'T GO TOO FAR.
FOR NOW.
I KNOW HOW TO KEEP HER AWAKE.

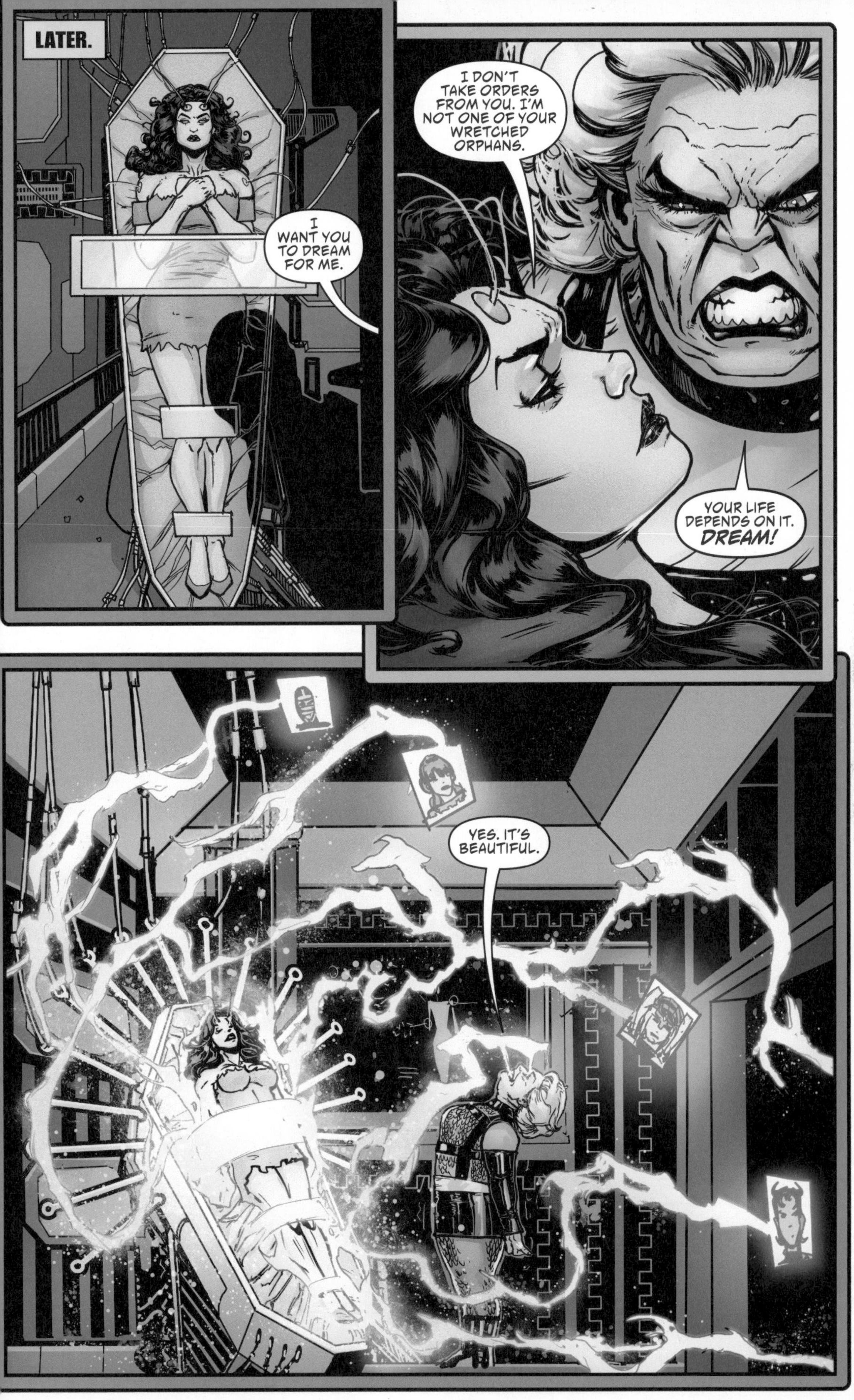

LATER.
I WANT YOU TO DREAM FOR ME.
I DON'T TAKE ORDERS FROM YOU. I'M NOT ONE OF YOUR WRETCHED ORPHANS.
YOUR LIFE DEPENDS ON IT. DREAM!
YES. IT'S BEAUTIFUL.

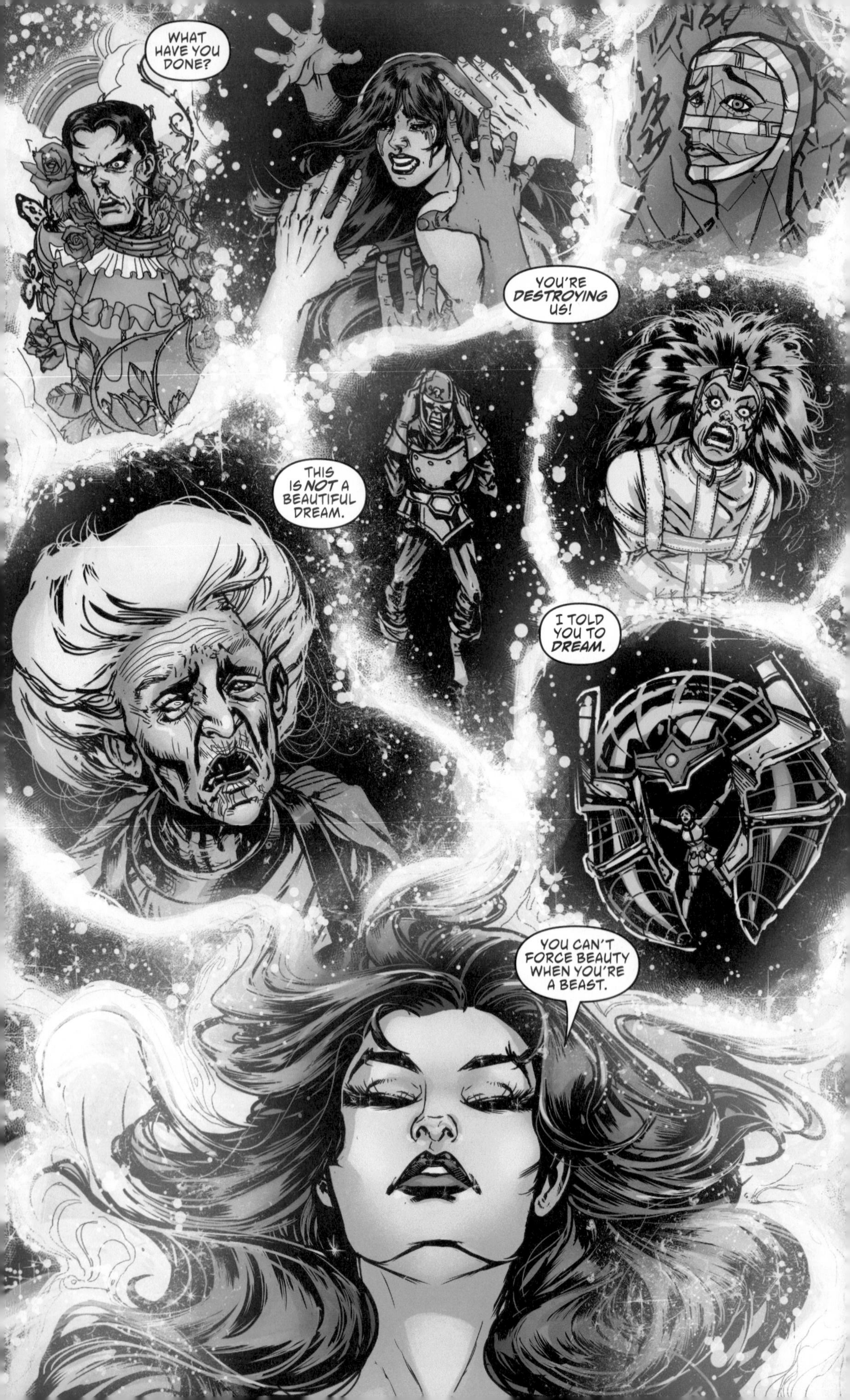
WHAT HAVE YOU DONE?
YOU'RE DESTROYING US!
THIS IS NOT A BEAUTIFUL DREAM.
I TOLD YOU TO DREAM.
YOU CAN'T FORCE BEAUTY WHEN YOU'RE A BEAST.

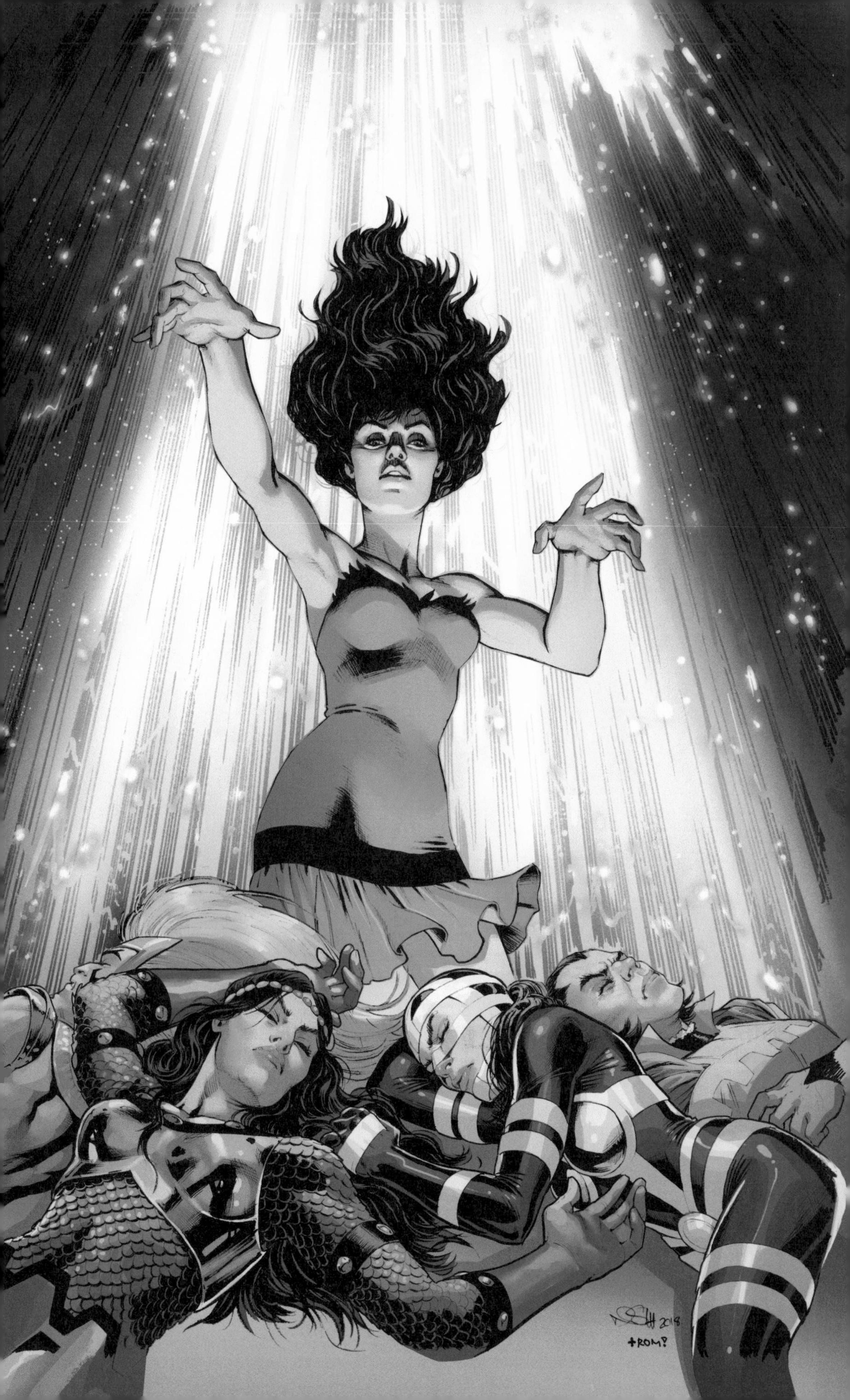

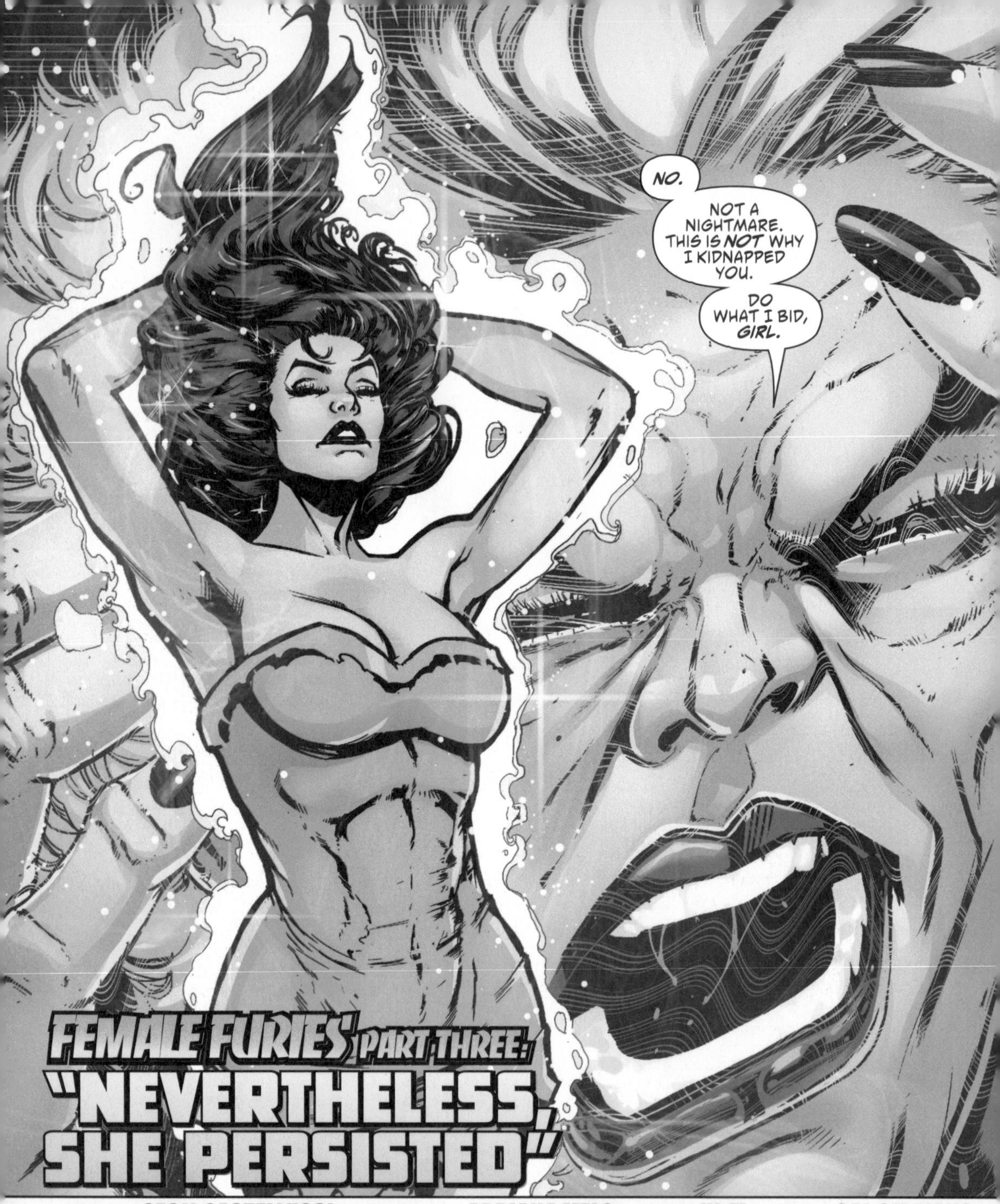
NO.
NOT A NIGHTMARE. THIS IS *NOT* WHY I KIDNAPPED YOU.
DO WHAT I BID, *GIRL.*
FEMALE FURIES PART THREE:
"NEVERTHELESS, SHE PERSISTED"

WRITER CECIL CASTELLUCCI ILLUSTRATOR ADRIANA MELO COLORS HI-FI LETTERS SAL CIPRIANO
COVER NICOLA SCOTT & ROMULO FAJARDO JR. ASSOC. EDITOR BRITTANY HOLZHERR EDITOR JAMIE S. RICH

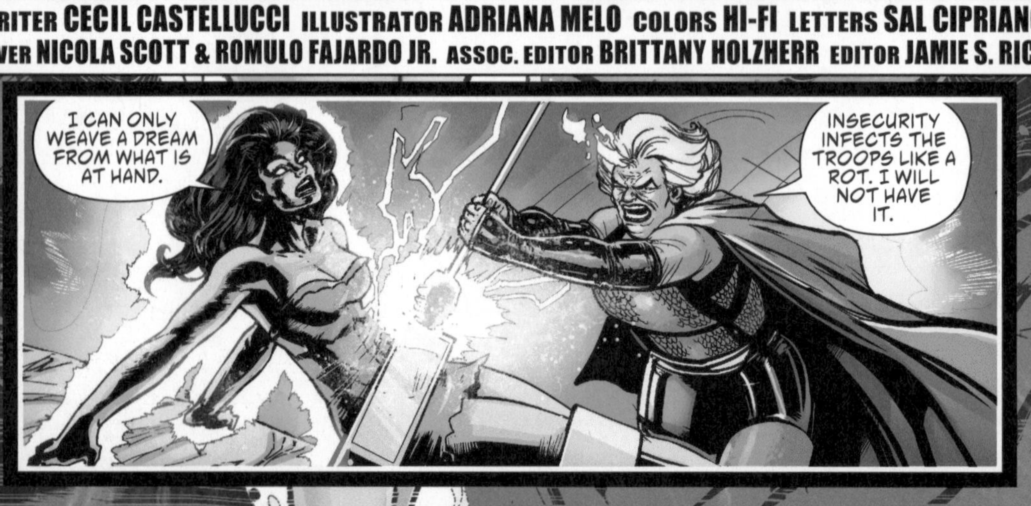
I CAN ONLY WEAVE A DREAM FROM WHAT IS AT HAND.
INSECURITY INFECTS THE TROOPS LIKE A ROT. I WILL NOT HAVE IT.

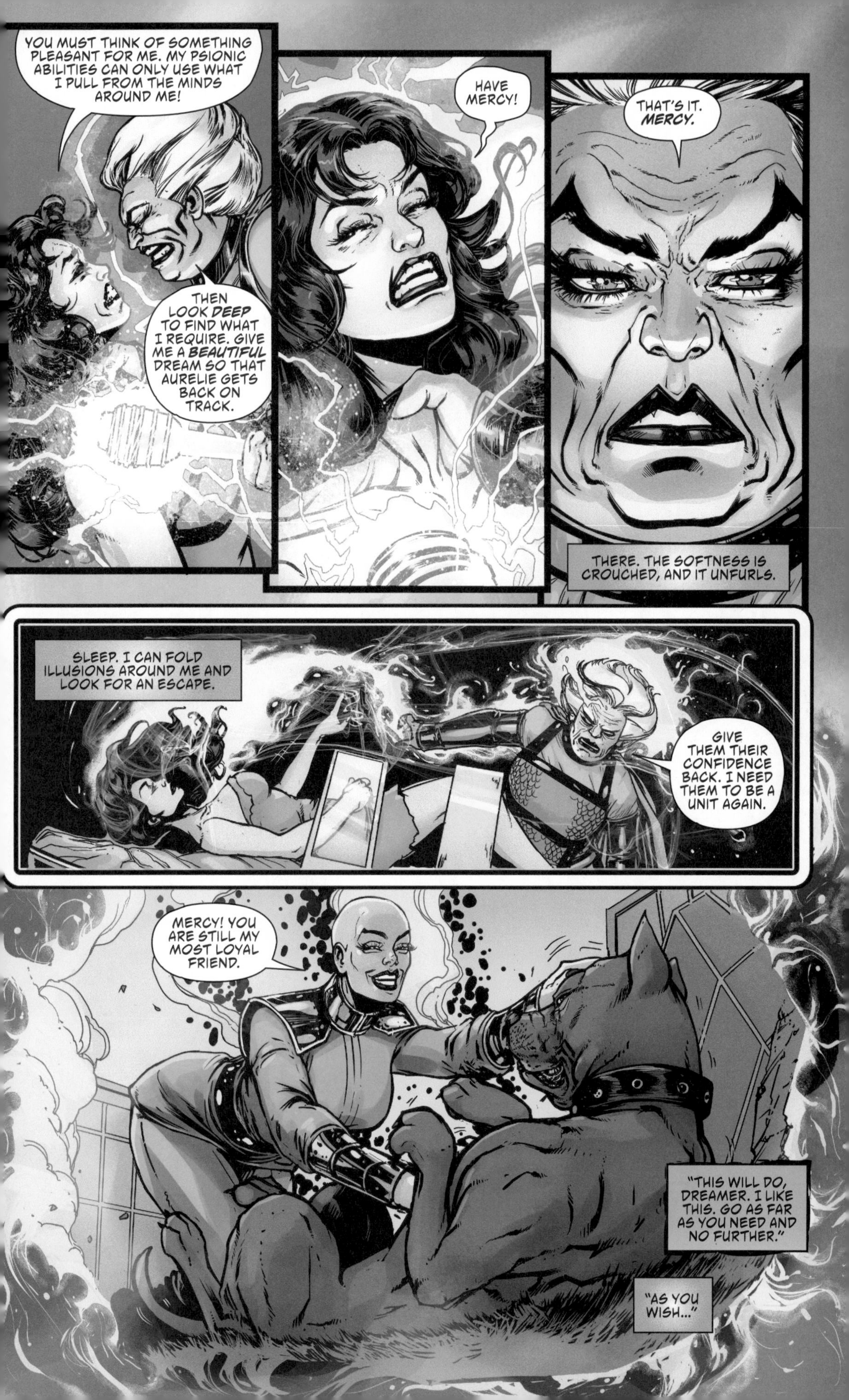
YOU MUST THINK OF SOMETHING PLEASANT FOR ME. MY PSIONIC ABILITIES CAN ONLY USE WHAT I PULL FROM THE MINDS AROUND ME!
THEN LOOK DEEP TO FIND WHAT I REQUIRE. GIVE ME A BEAUTIFUL DREAM SO THAT AURELIE GETS BACK ON TRACK.
HAVE MERCY!
THAT'S IT. MERCY.
THERE. THE SOFTNESS IS CROUCHED, AND IT UNFURLS.
SLEEP. I CAN FOLD ILLUSIONS AROUND ME AND LOOK FOR AN ESCAPE.
GIVE THEM THEIR CONFIDENCE BACK. I NEED THEM TO BE A UNIT AGAIN.
MERCY! YOU ARE STILL MY MOST LOYAL FRIEND.
"THIS WILL DO, DREAMER. I LIKE THIS. GO AS FAR AS YOU NEED AND NO FURTHER."
"AS YOU WISH..."

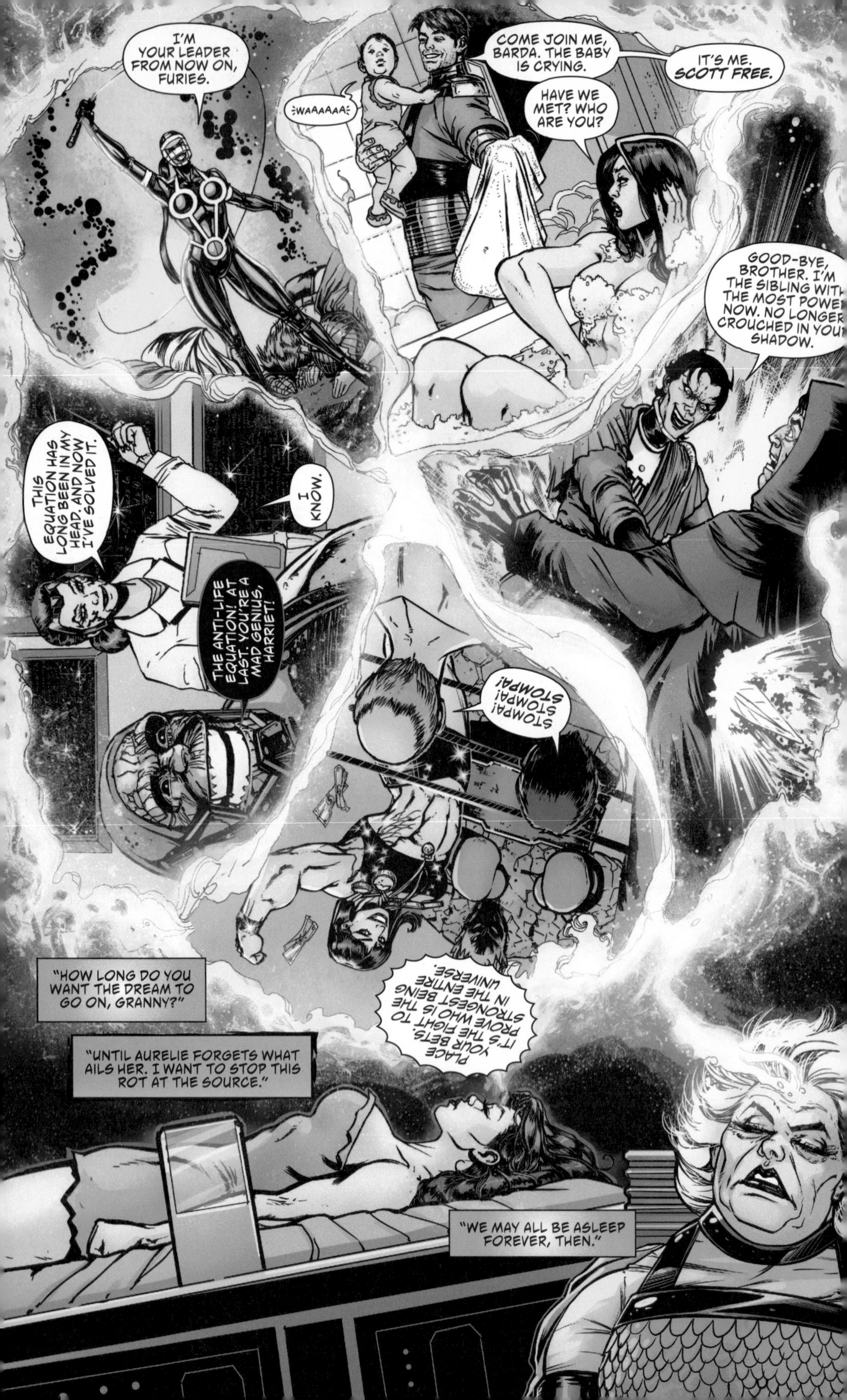
I'M YOUR LEADER FROM NOW ON, FURIES.
WAAAAAA
COME JOIN ME, BARDA. THE BABY IS CRYING.
HAVE WE MET? WHO ARE YOU?
IT'S ME. SCOTT FREE.
GOOD-BYE, BROTHER. I'M THE SIBLING WITH THE MOST POWE NOW. NO LONGER CROUCHED IN YOU SHADOW.
THIS EQUATION HAS LONG BEEN IN MY HEAD, AND NOW I'VE SOLVED IT.
I KNOW.
THE ANTI-LIFE EQUATION! AT LAST. YOU'RE A MAD GENIUS, HARRIET!
STOMPA! STOMPA! STOMPA!
PLACE YOUR BETS. IT'S THE FIGHT TO PROVE WHO IS THE STRONGEST BEING IN THE ENTIRE UNIVERSE.
"HOW LONG DO YOU WANT THE DREAM TO GO ON, GRANNY?"
"UNTIL AURELIE FORGETS WHAT AILS HER. I WANT TO STOP THIS ROT AT THE SOURCE."
"WE MAY ALL BE ASLEEP FOREVER, THEN."

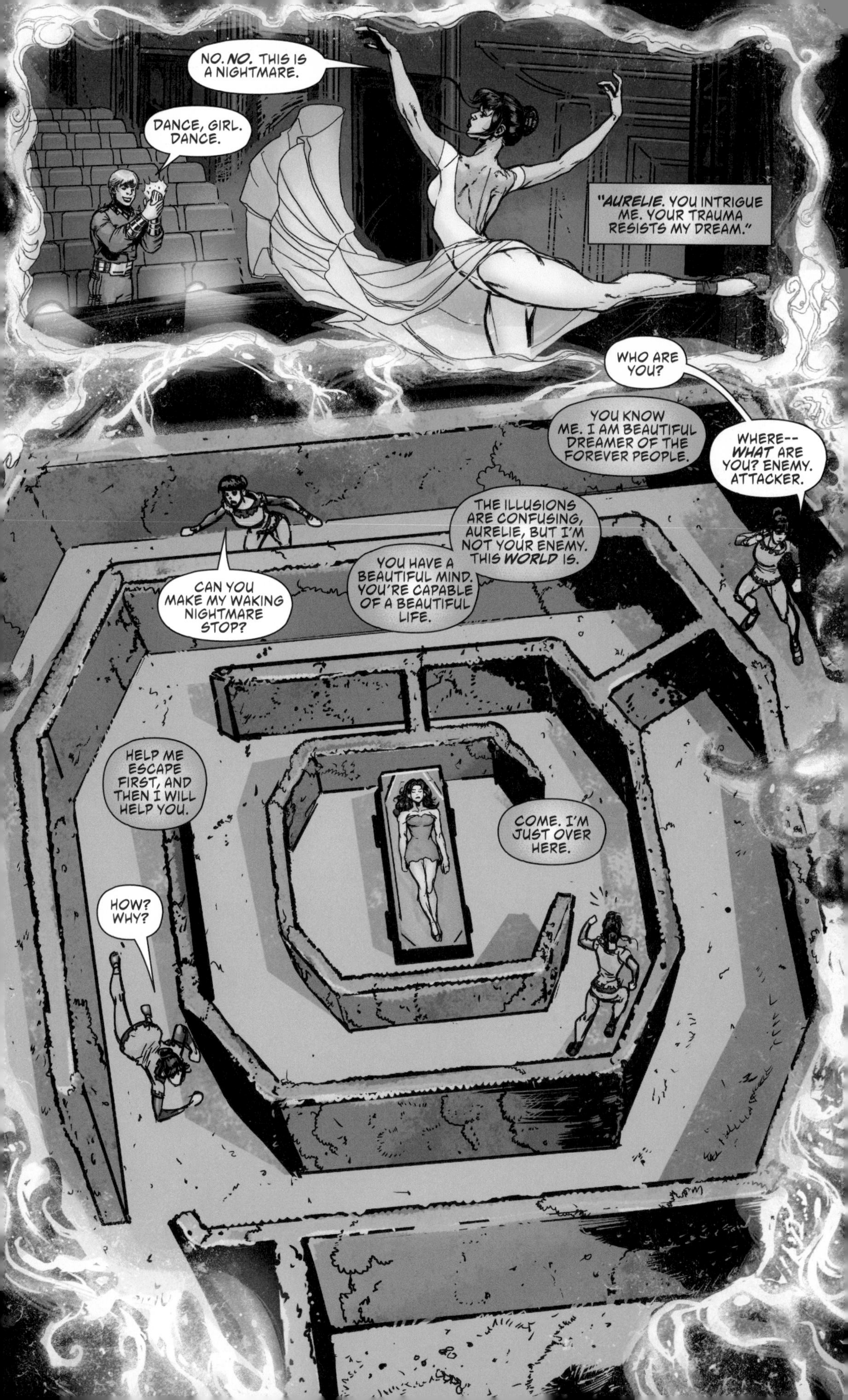
NO. NO. THIS IS A NIGHTMARE.
DANCE, GIRL. DANCE.
"AURELIE. YOU INTRIGUE ME. YOUR TRAUMA RESISTS MY DREAM."
WHO ARE YOU?
YOU KNOW ME. I AM BEAUTIFUL DREAMER OF THE FOREVER PEOPLE.
WHERE-- WHAT ARE YOU? ENEMY. ATTACKER.
THE ILLUSIONS ARE CONFUSING, AURELIE, BUT I'M NOT YOUR ENEMY. THIS WORLD IS.
YOU HAVE A BEAUTIFUL MIND. YOU'RE CAPABLE OF A BEAUTIFUL LIFE.
CAN YOU MAKE MY WAKING NIGHTMARE STOP?
HELP ME ESCAPE FIRST, AND THEN I WILL HELP YOU.
COME. I'M JUST OVER HERE.
HOW? WHY?

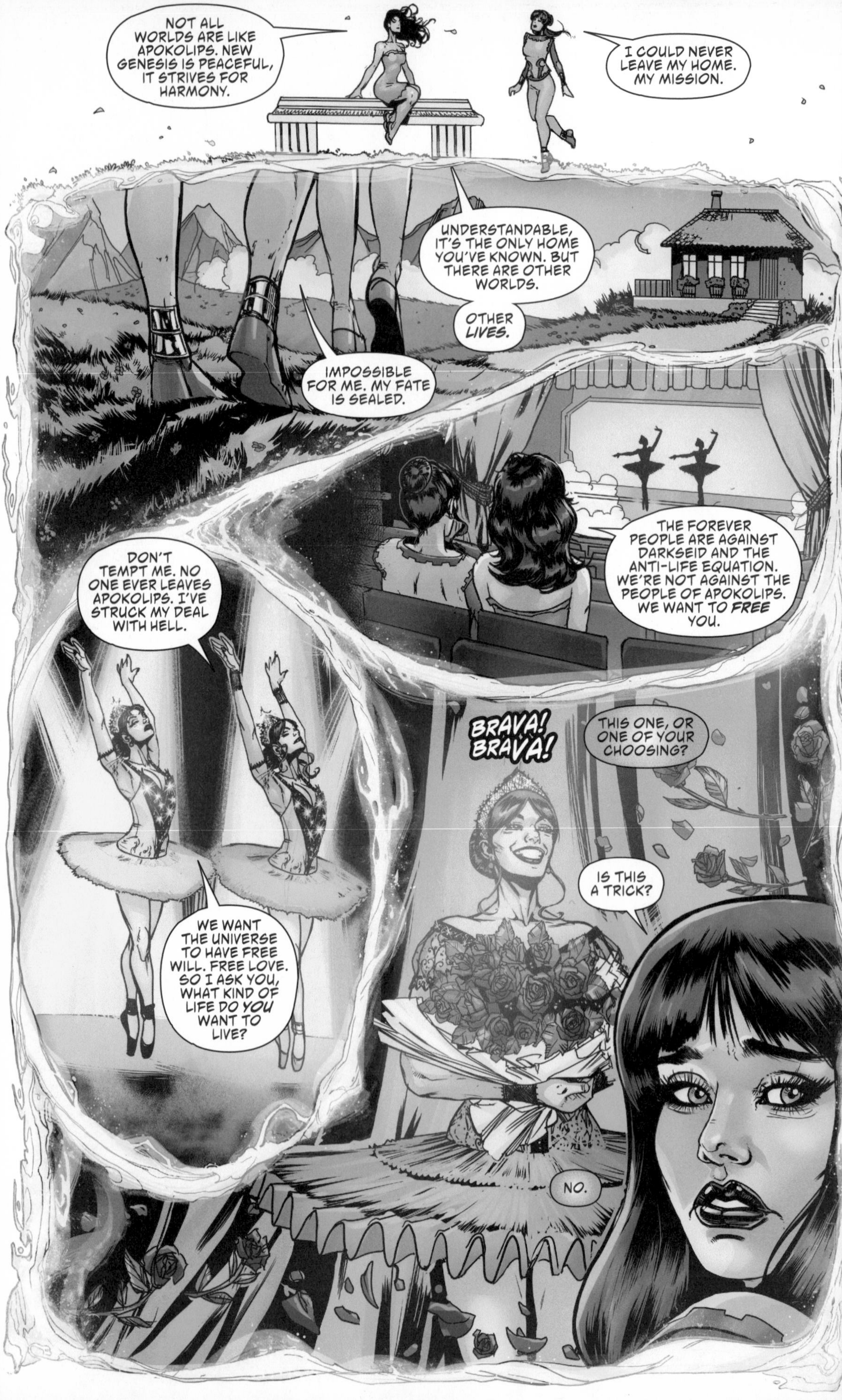
NOT ALL WORLDS ARE LIKE APOKOLIPS. NEW GENESIS IS PEACEFUL, IT STRIVES FOR HARMONY.
I COULD NEVER LEAVE MY HOME. MY MISSION.
UNDERSTANDABLE, IT'S THE ONLY HOME YOU'VE KNOWN. BUT THERE ARE OTHER WORLDS.
OTHER LIVES.
IMPOSSIBLE FOR ME. MY FATE IS SEALED.
THE FOREVER PEOPLE ARE AGAINST DARKSEID AND THE ANTI-LIFE EQUATION. WE'RE NOT AGAINST THE PEOPLE OF APOKOLIPS. WE WANT TO FREE YOU.
DON'T TEMPT ME. NO ONE EVER LEAVES APOKOLIPS. I'VE STRUCK MY DEAL WITH HELL.
WE WANT THE UNIVERSE TO HAVE FREE WILL. FREE LOVE. SO I ASK YOU, WHAT KIND OF LIFE DO YOU WANT TO LIVE?
BRAVA! BRAVA!
THIS ONE, OR ONE OF YOUR CHOOSING?
IS THIS A TRICK?
NO.

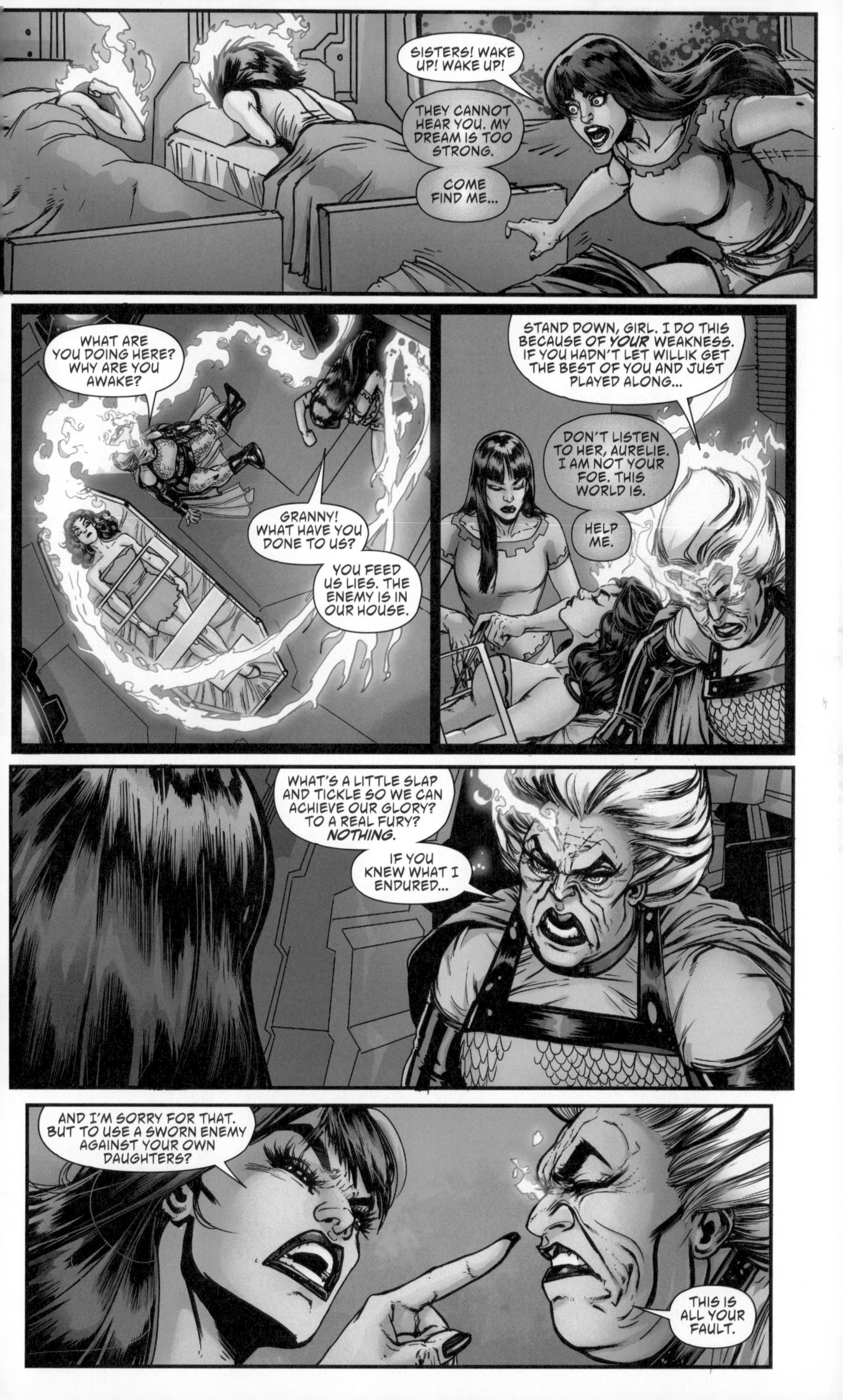

SISTERS! WAKE UP! WAKE UP!
THEY CANNOT HEAR YOU. MY DREAM IS TOO STRONG.
COME FIND ME...
WHAT ARE YOU DOING HERE? WHY ARE YOU AWAKE?
GRANNY! WHAT HAVE YOU DONE TO US?
YOU FEED US LIES. THE ENEMY IS IN OUR HOUSE.
STAND DOWN, GIRL. I DO THIS BECAUSE OF *YOUR* WEAKNESS. IF YOU HADN'T LET WILLIK GET THE BEST OF YOU AND JUST PLAYED ALONG...
DON'T LISTEN TO HER, AURELIE. I AM NOT YOUR FOE. THIS WORLD IS.
HELP ME.
WHAT'S A LITTLE SLAP AND TICKLE SO WE CAN ACHIEVE OUR GLORY? TO A REAL FURY? ***NOTHING***.
IF YOU KNEW WHAT I ENDURED...
AND I'M SORRY FOR THAT. BUT TO USE A SWORN ENEMY AGAINST YOUR OWN DAUGHTERS?
THIS IS ALL YOUR FAULT.

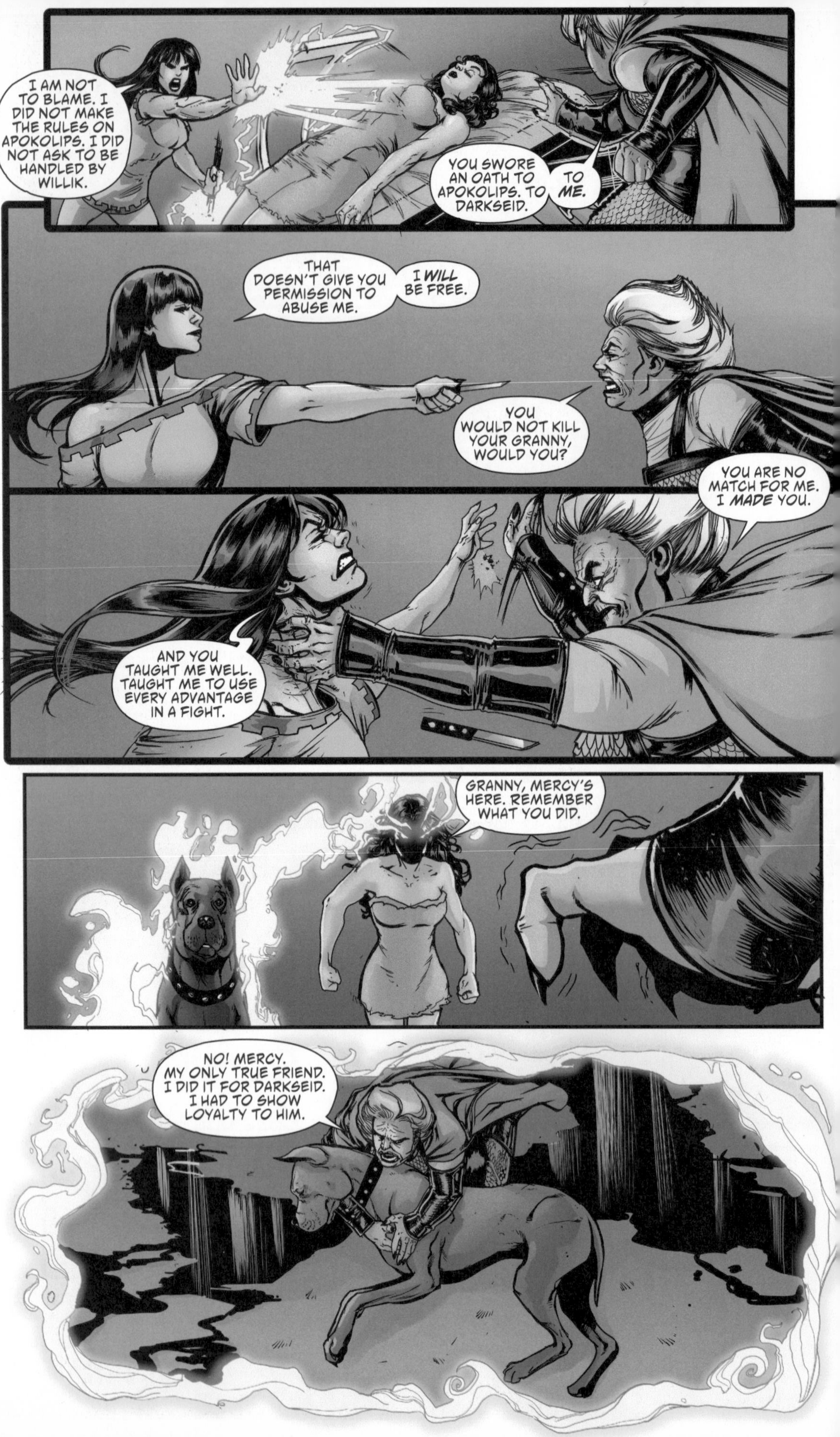
I AM NOT TO BLAME. I DID NOT MAKE THE RULES ON APOKOLIPS. I DID NOT ASK TO BE HANDLED BY WILLIK.
YOU SWORE AN OATH TO APOKOLIPS. TO DARKSEID.
TO *ME.*
THAT DOESN'T GIVE YOU PERMISSION TO ABUSE ME.
I *WILL* BE FREE.
YOU WOULD NOT KILL YOUR GRANNY, WOULD YOU?
YOU ARE NO MATCH FOR ME. I *MADE* YOU.
AND YOU TAUGHT ME WELL. TAUGHT ME TO USE EVERY ADVANTAGE IN A FIGHT.
GRANNY, MERCY'S HERE. REMEMBER WHAT YOU DID.
NO! MERCY. MY ONLY TRUE FRIEND. I DID IT FOR DARKSEID. I HAD TO SHOW LOYALTY TO HIM.

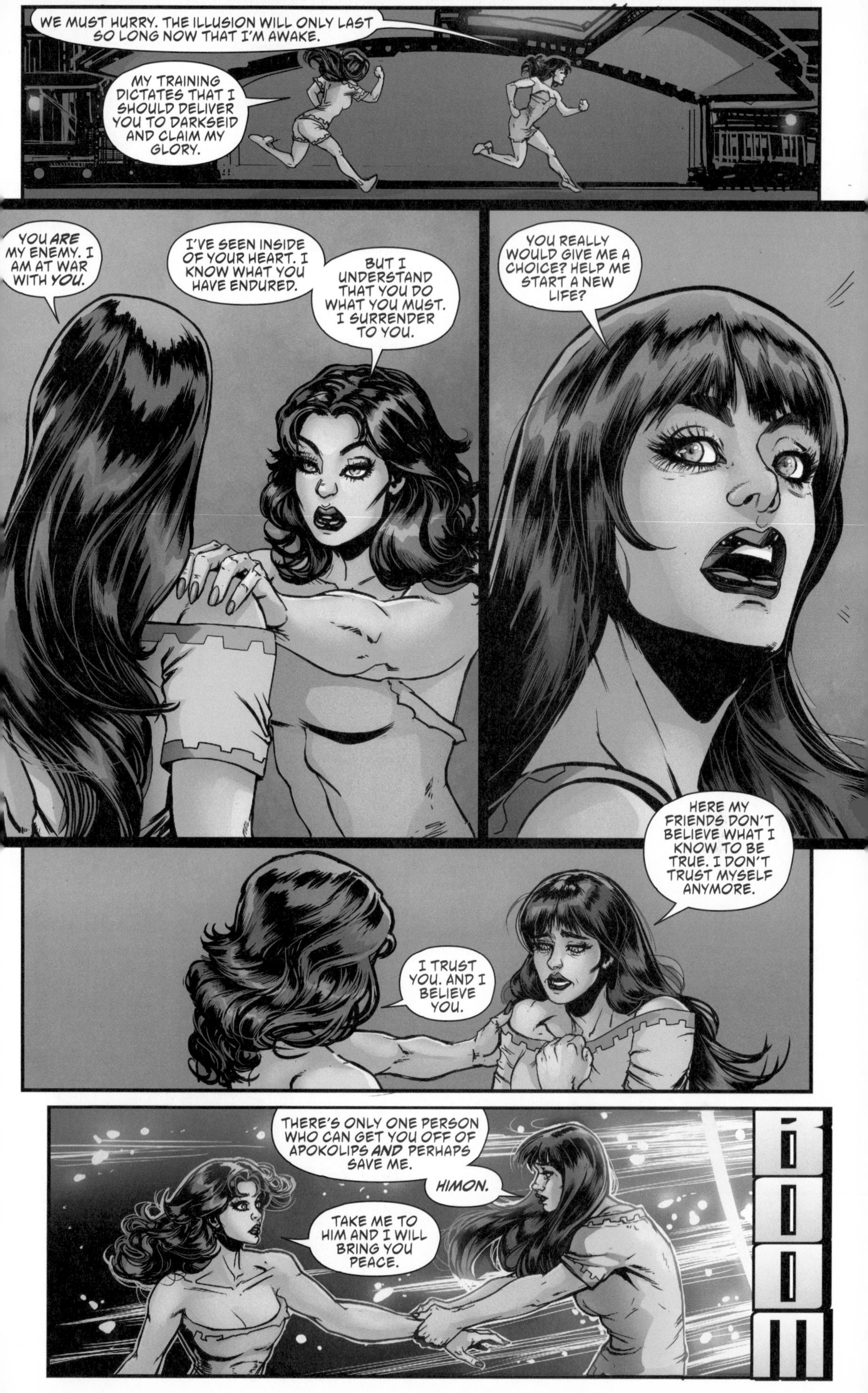

WE MUST HURRY. THE ILLUSION WILL ONLY LAST SO LONG NOW THAT I'M AWAKE.
MY TRAINING DICTATES THAT I SHOULD DELIVER YOU TO DARKSEID AND CLAIM MY GLORY.
YOU *ARE* MY ENEMY. I AM AT WAR WITH *YOU*.
I'VE SEEN INSIDE OF YOUR HEART. I KNOW WHAT YOU HAVE ENDURED.
BUT I UNDERSTAND THAT YOU DO WHAT YOU MUST. I SURRENDER TO YOU.
YOU REALLY WOULD GIVE ME A CHOICE? HELP ME START A NEW LIFE?
HERE MY FRIENDS DON'T BELIEVE WHAT I KNOW TO BE TRUE. I DON'T TRUST MYSELF ANYMORE.
I TRUST YOU. AND I BELIEVE YOU.
THERE'S ONLY ONE PERSON WHO CAN GET YOU OFF OF APOKOLIPS *AND* PERHAPS SAVE ME.
HIMON.
TAKE ME TO HIM AND I WILL BRING YOU PEACE.
BOOOM

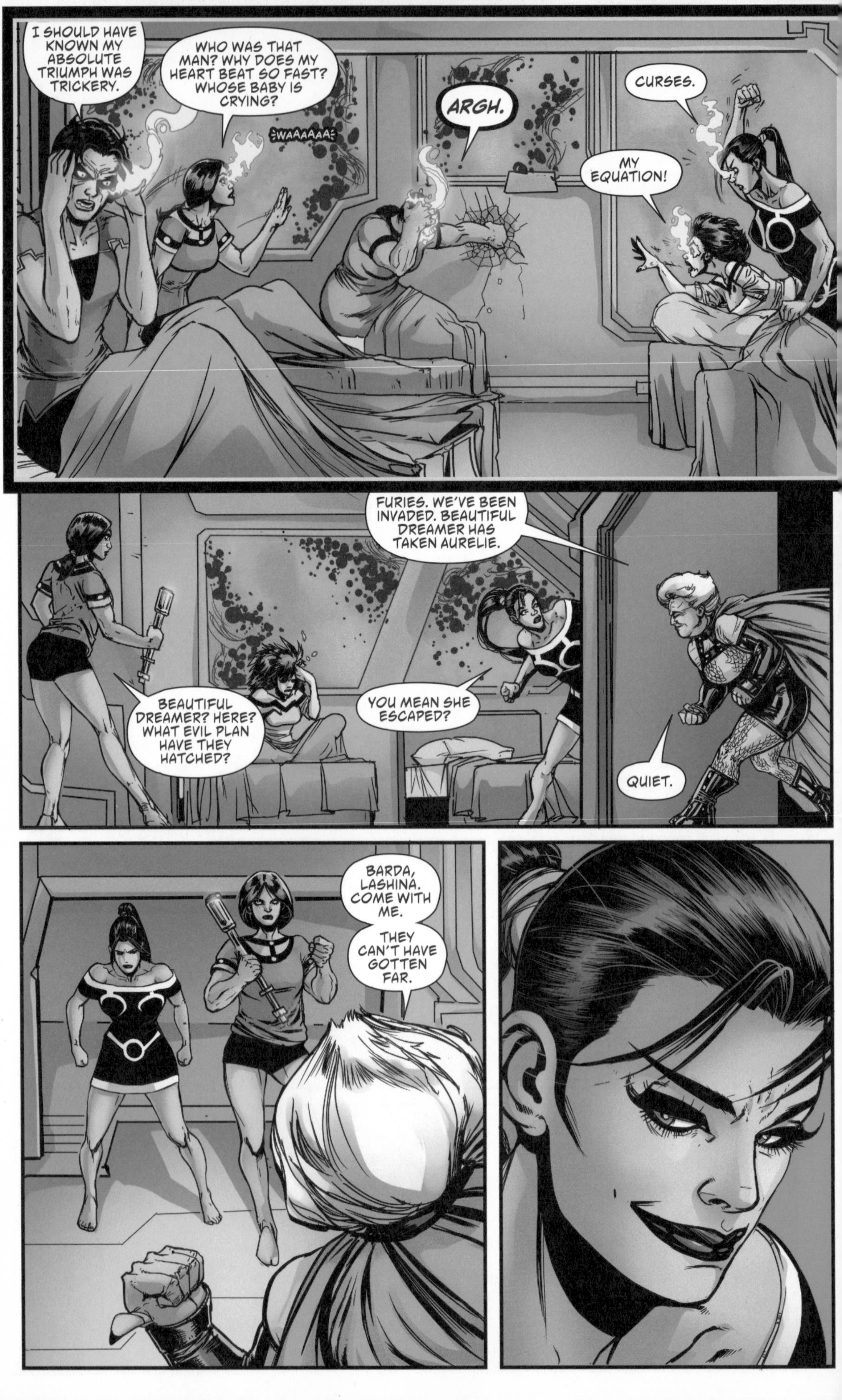
I SHOULD HAVE KNOWN MY ABSOLUTE TRIUMPH WAS TRICKERY.
WHO WAS THAT MAN? WHY DOES MY HEART BEAT SO FAST? WHOSE BABY IS CRYING?
WAAAAAA
ARGH.
CURSES.
MY EQUATION!
FURIES. WE'VE BEEN INVADED. BEAUTIFUL DREAMER HAS TAKEN AURELIE.
BEAUTIFUL DREAMER? HERE? WHAT EVIL PLAN HAVE THEY HATCHED?
YOU MEAN SHE ESCAPED?
QUIET.
BARDA, LASHINA. COME WITH ME.
THEY CAN'T HAVE GOTTEN FAR.

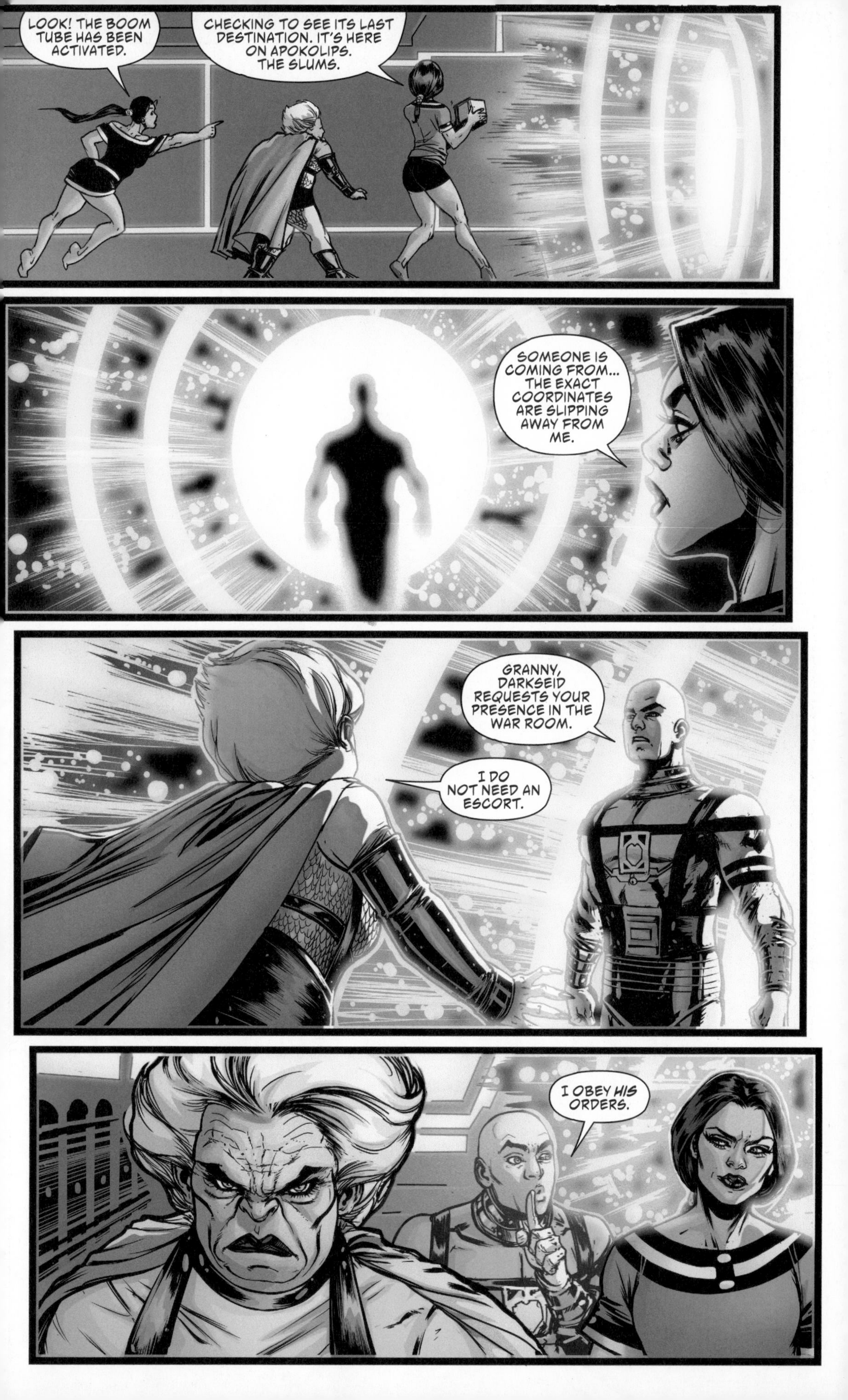
LOOK! THE BOOM TUBE HAS BEEN ACTIVATED.
CHECKING TO SEE ITS LAST DESTINATION. IT'S HERE ON APOKOLIPS. THE SLUMS.
SOMEONE IS COMING FROM... THE EXACT COORDINATES ARE SLIPPING AWAY FROM ME.
GRANNY, DARKSEID REQUESTS YOUR PRESENCE IN THE WAR ROOM.
I DO NOT NEED AN ESCORT.
I OBEY HIS ORDERS.

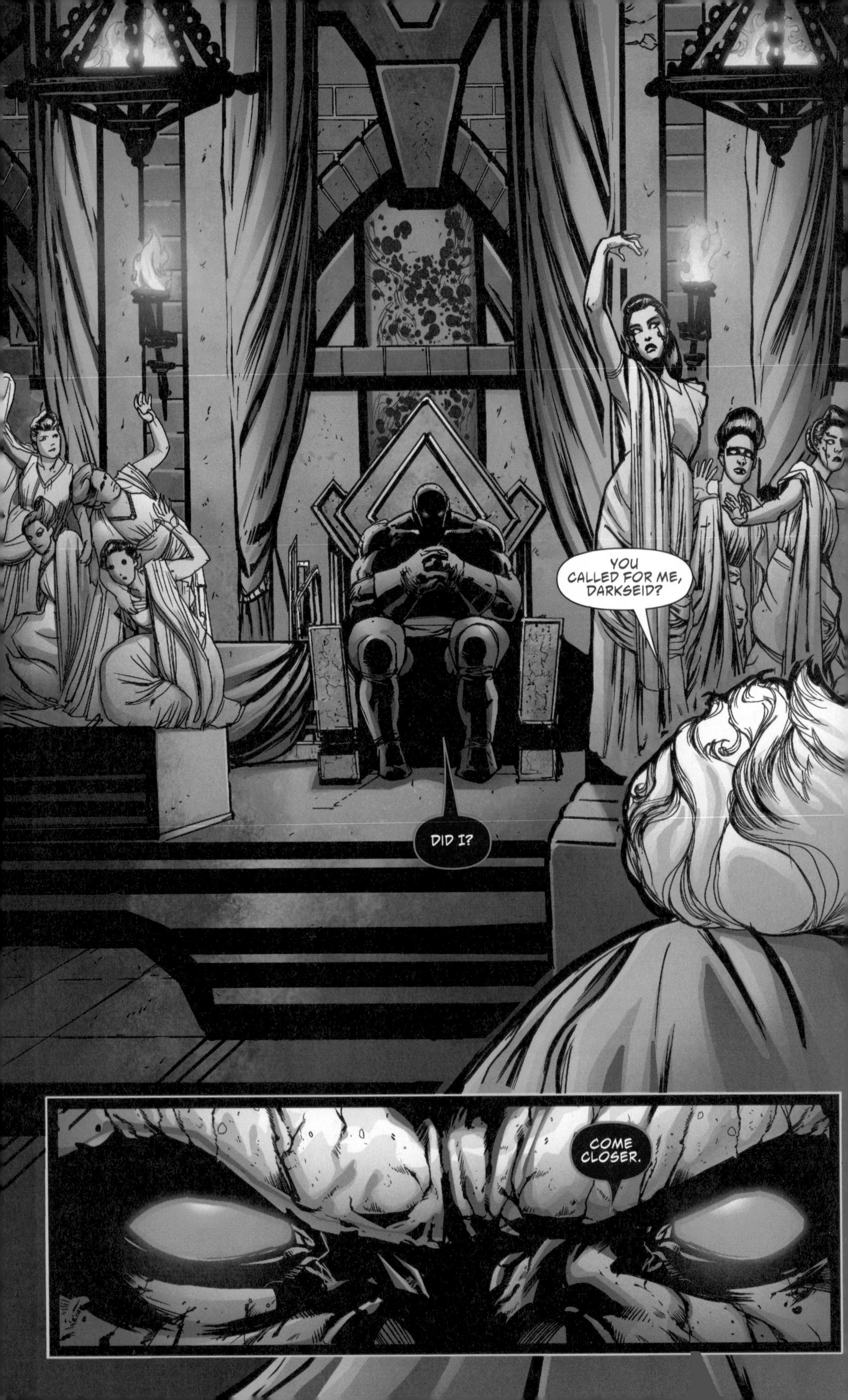
YOU CALLED FOR ME, DARKSEID?
DID I?
COME CLOSER.

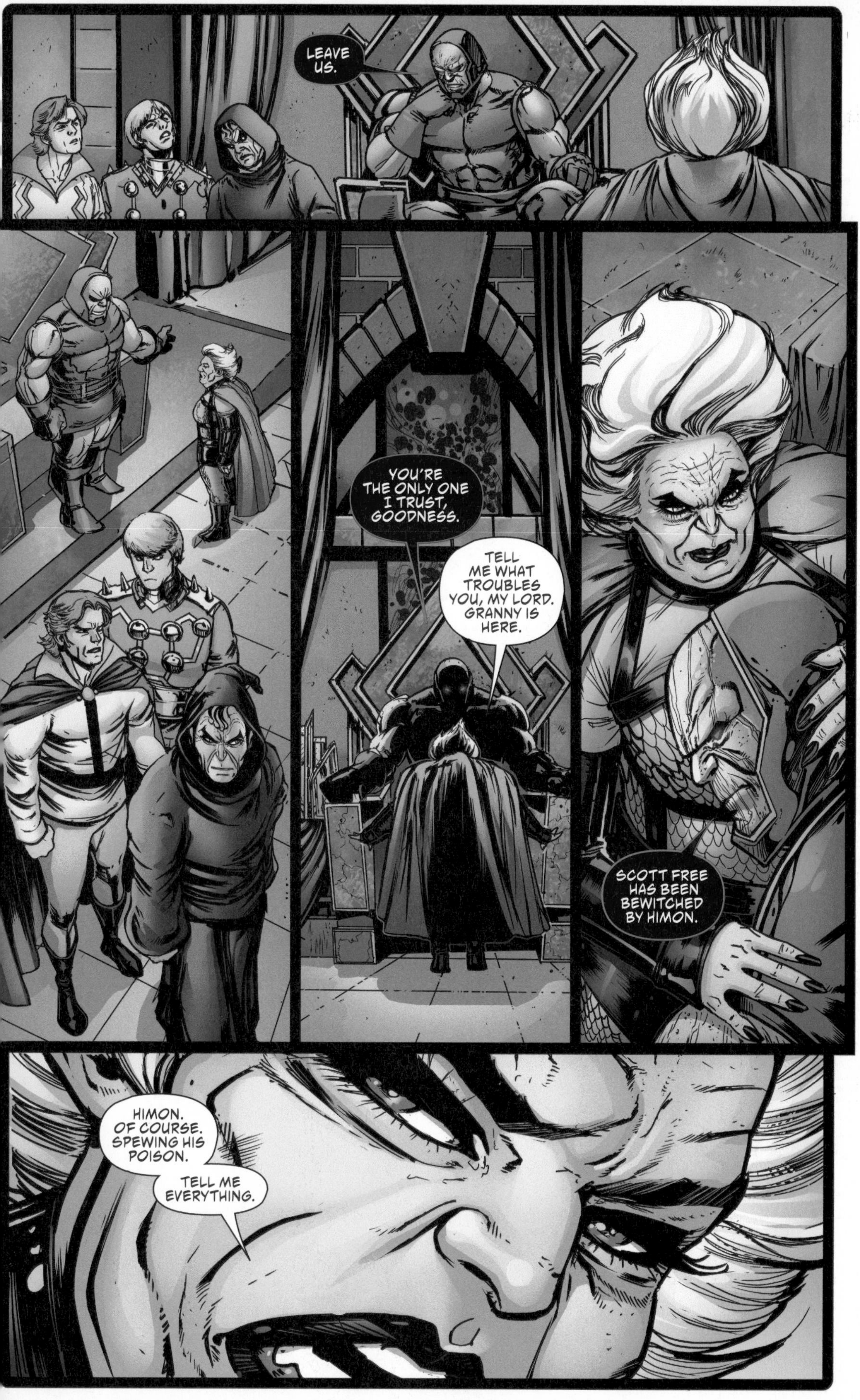
LEAVE US.
YOU'RE THE ONLY ONE I TRUST, GOODNESS.
TELL ME WHAT TROUBLES YOU, MY LORD. GRANNY IS HERE.
SCOTT FREE HAS BEEN BEWITCHED BY HIMON.
HIMON. OF COURSE. SPEWING HIS POISON.
TELL ME EVERYTHING.

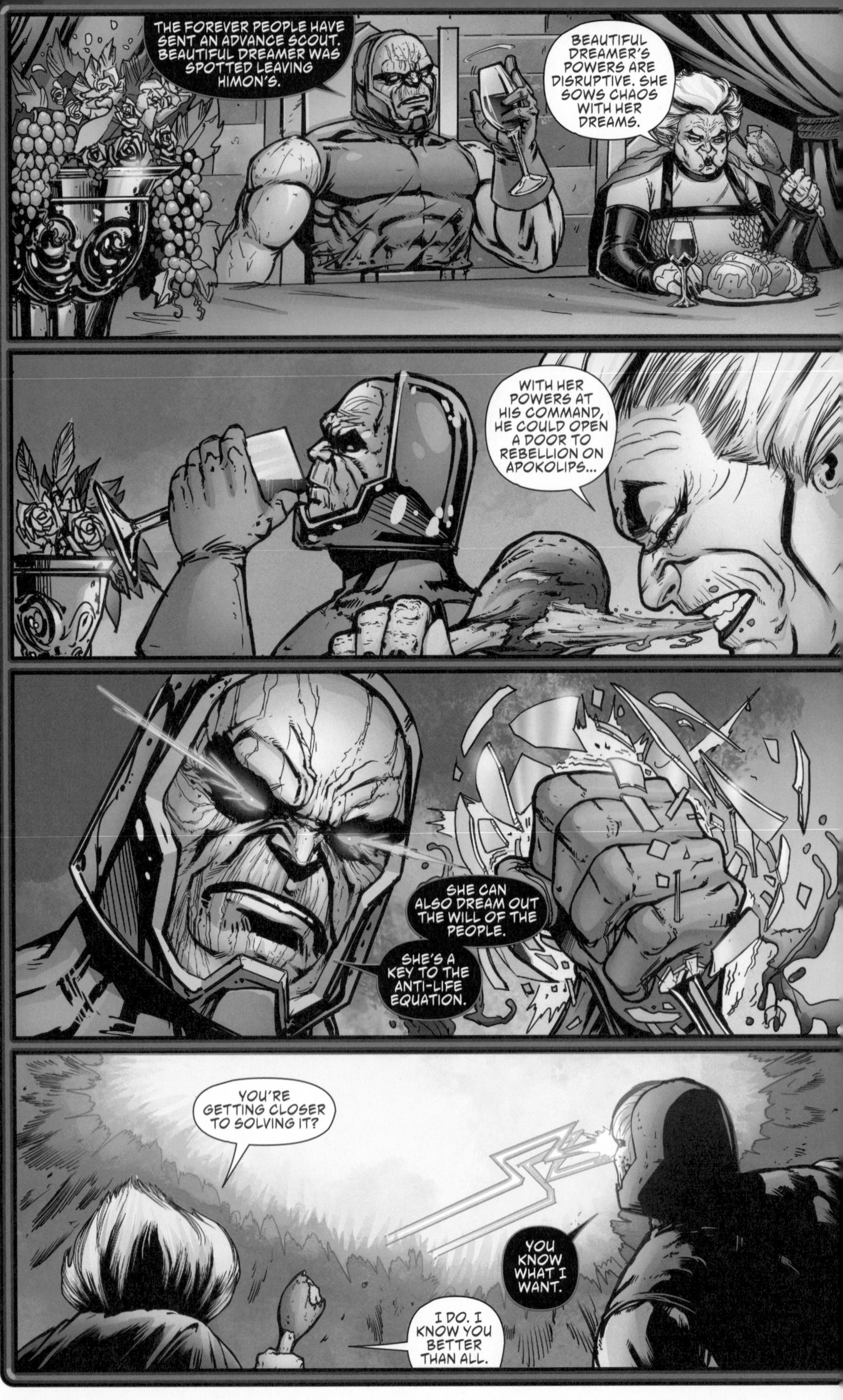
THE FOREVER PEOPLE HAVE SENT AN ADVANCE SCOUT. BEAUTIFUL DREAMER WAS SPOTTED LEAVING HIMON'S.
BEAUTIFUL DREAMER'S POWERS ARE DISRUPTIVE. SHE SOWS CHAOS WITH HER DREAMS.
WITH HER POWERS AT HIS COMMAND, HE COULD OPEN A DOOR TO REBELLION ON APOKOLIPS...
SHE CAN ALSO DREAM OUT THE WILL OF THE PEOPLE.
SHE'S A KEY TO THE ANTI-LIFE EQUATION.
YOU'RE GETTING CLOSER TO SOLVING IT?
YOU KNOW WHAT I WANT.
I DO. I KNOW YOU BETTER THAN ALL.

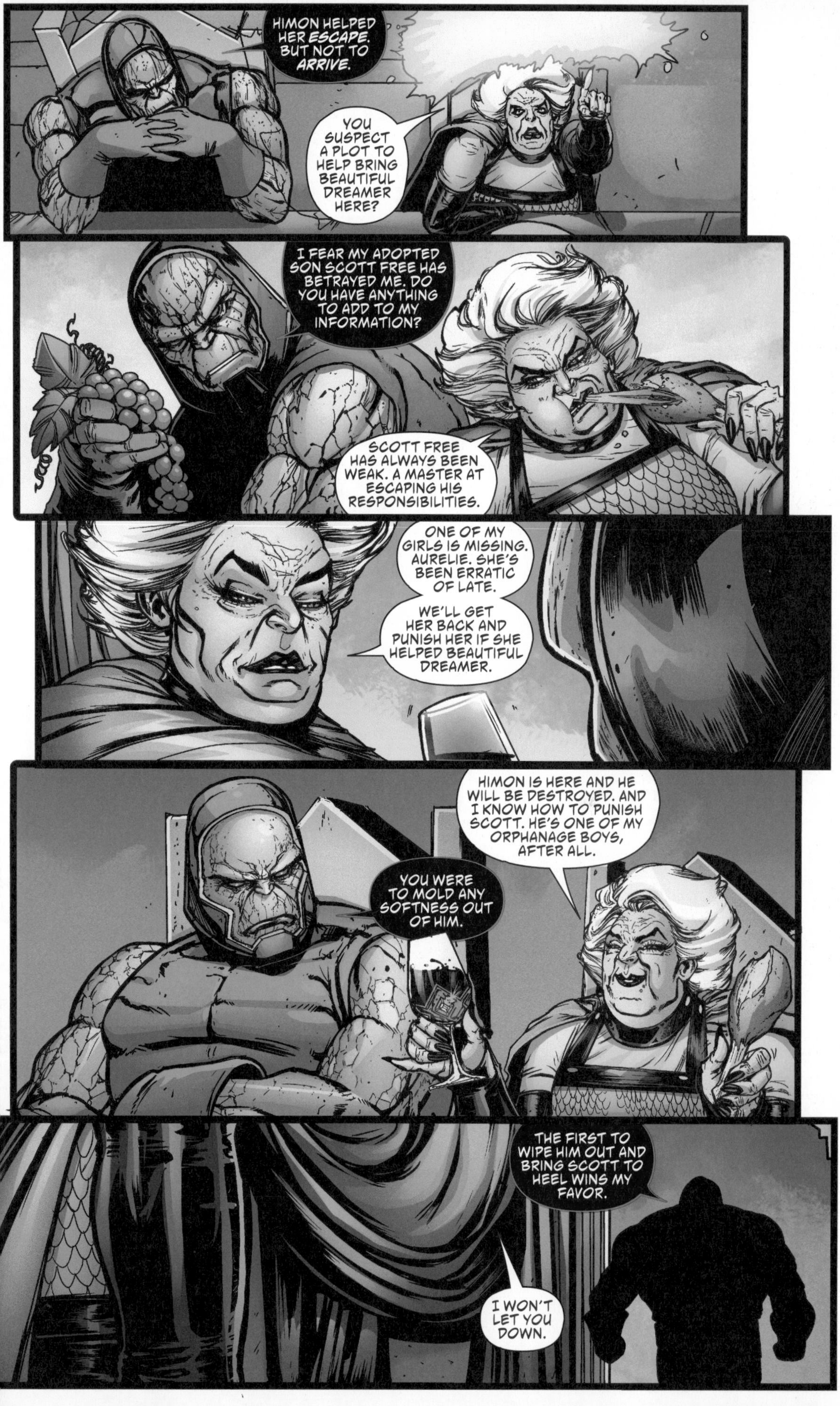
HIMON HELPED HER ESCAPE. BUT NOT TO ARRIVE.
YOU SUSPECT A PLOT TO HELP BRING BEAUTIFUL DREAMER HERE?
I FEAR MY ADOPTED SON SCOTT FREE HAS BETRAYED ME. DO YOU HAVE ANYTHING TO ADD TO MY INFORMATION?
SCOTT FREE HAS ALWAYS BEEN WEAK. A MASTER AT ESCAPING HIS RESPONSIBILITIES.
ONE OF MY GIRLS IS MISSING. AURELIE. SHE'S BEEN ERRATIC OF LATE.
WE'LL GET HER BACK AND PUNISH HER IF SHE HELPED BEAUTIFUL DREAMER.
HIMON IS HERE AND HE WILL BE DESTROYED. AND I KNOW HOW TO PUNISH SCOTT. HE'S ONE OF MY ORPHANAGE BOYS, AFTER ALL.
YOU WERE TO MOLD ANY SOFTNESS OUT OF HIM.
THE FIRST TO WIPE HIM OUT AND BRING SCOTT TO HEEL WINS MY FAVOR.
I WON'T LET YOU DOWN.

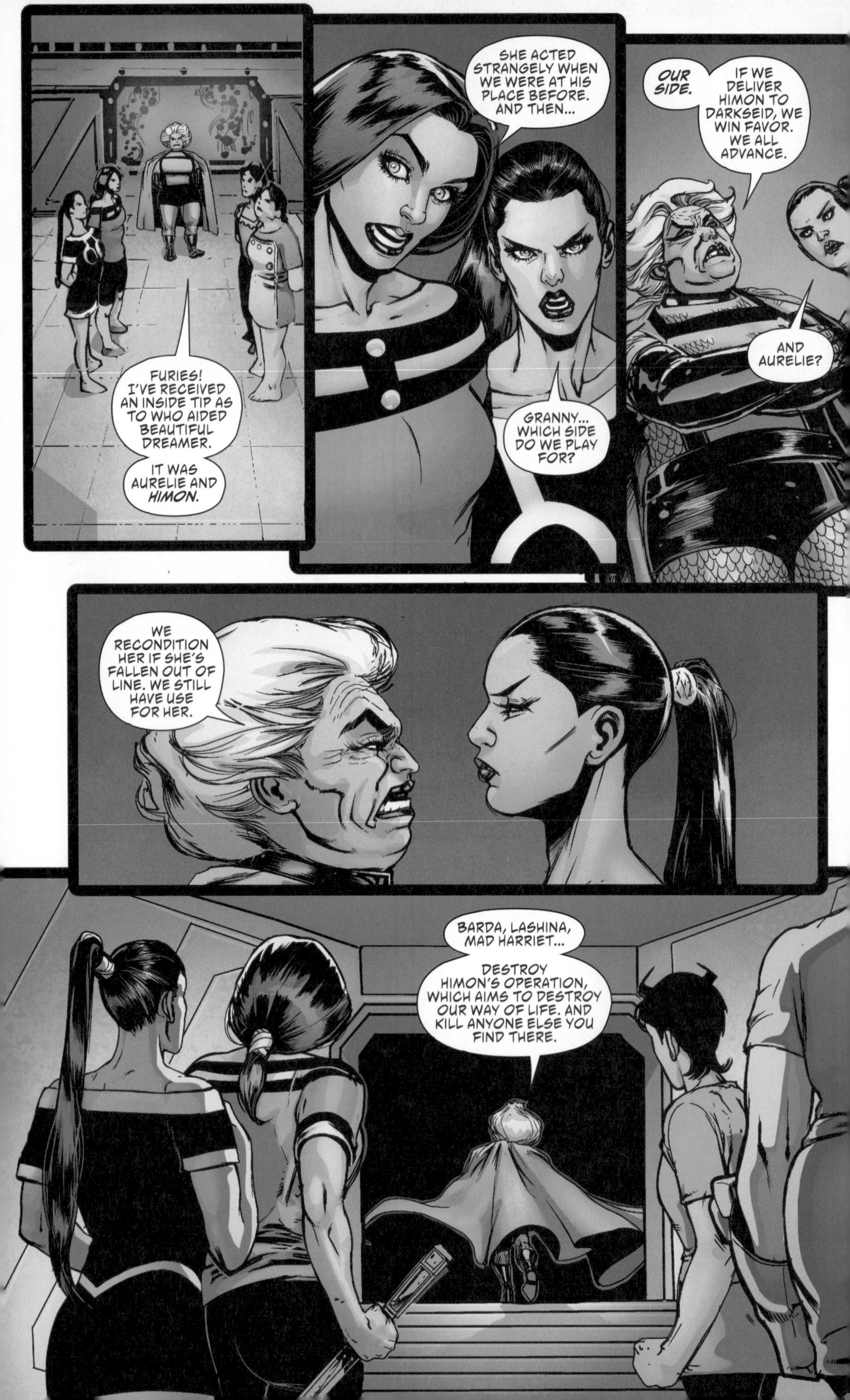
FURIES! I'VE RECEIVED AN INSIDE TIP AS TO WHO AIDED BEAUTIFUL DREAMER.
IT WAS AURELIE AND *HIMON*.
SHE ACTED STRANGELY WHEN WE WERE AT HIS PLACE BEFORE. AND THEN...
GRANNY... WHICH SIDE DO WE PLAY FOR?
OUR SIDE.
IF WE DELIVER HIMON TO DARKSEID, WE WIN FAVOR. WE ALL ADVANCE.
AND AURELIE?
WE RECONDITION HER IF SHE'S FALLEN OUT OF LINE. WE STILL HAVE USE FOR HER.
BARDA, LASHINA, MAD HARRIET...
DESTROY HIMON'S OPERATION, WHICH AIMS TO DESTROY OUR WAY OF LIFE. AND KILL ANYONE ELSE YOU FIND THERE.

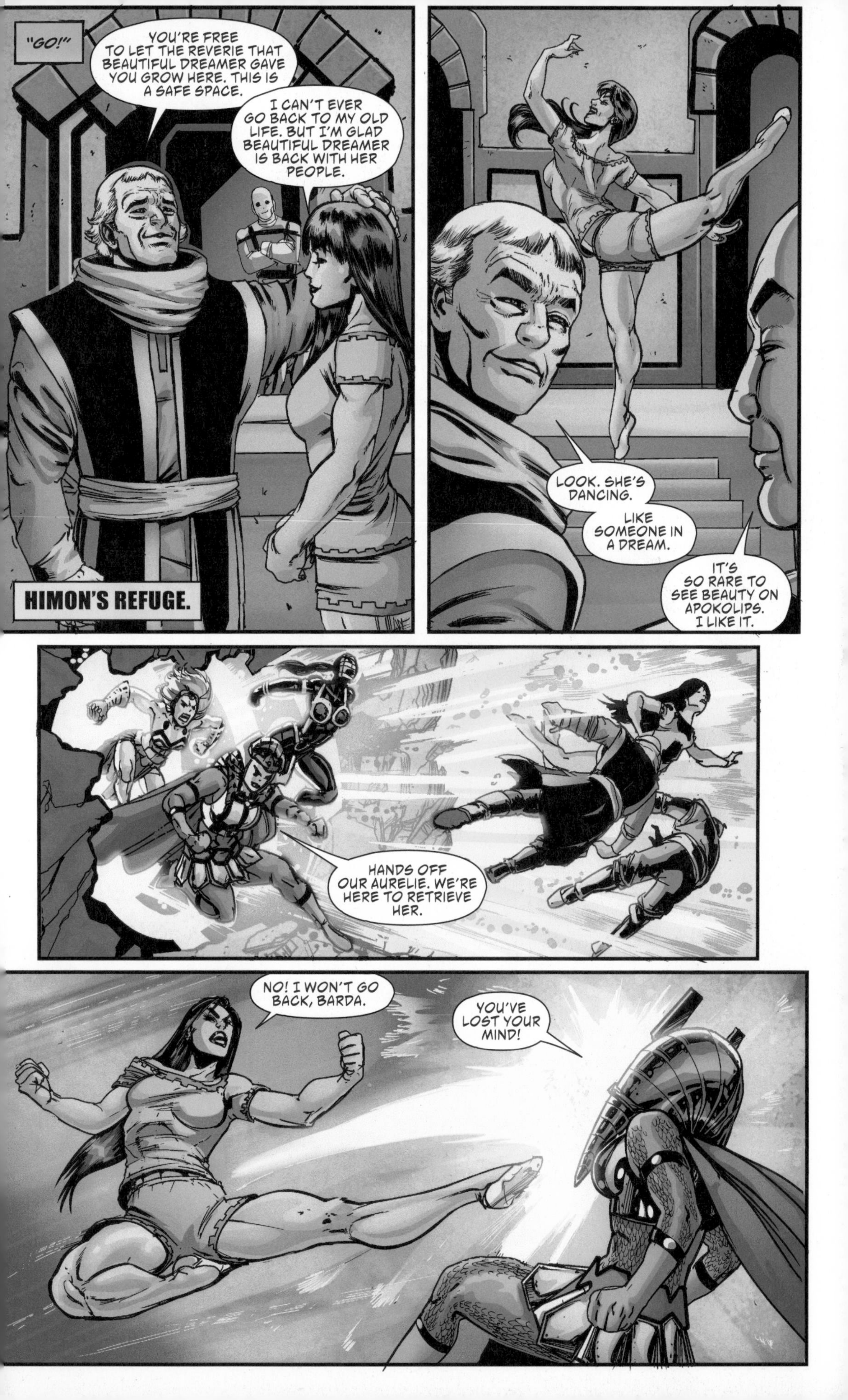
"GO!"
YOU'RE FREE TO LET THE REVERIE THAT BEAUTIFUL DREAMER GAVE YOU GROW HERE. THIS IS A SAFE SPACE.
I CAN'T EVER GO BACK TO MY OLD LIFE. BUT I'M GLAD BEAUTIFUL DREAMER IS BACK WITH HER PEOPLE.
HIMON'S REFUGE.
LOOK. SHE'S DANCING.
LIKE SOMEONE IN A DREAM.
IT'S SO RARE TO SEE BEAUTY ON APOKOLIPS. I LIKE IT.
HANDS OFF OUR AURELIE. WE'RE HERE TO RETRIEVE HER.
NO! I WON'T GO BACK, BARDA.
YOU'VE LOST YOUR MIND!

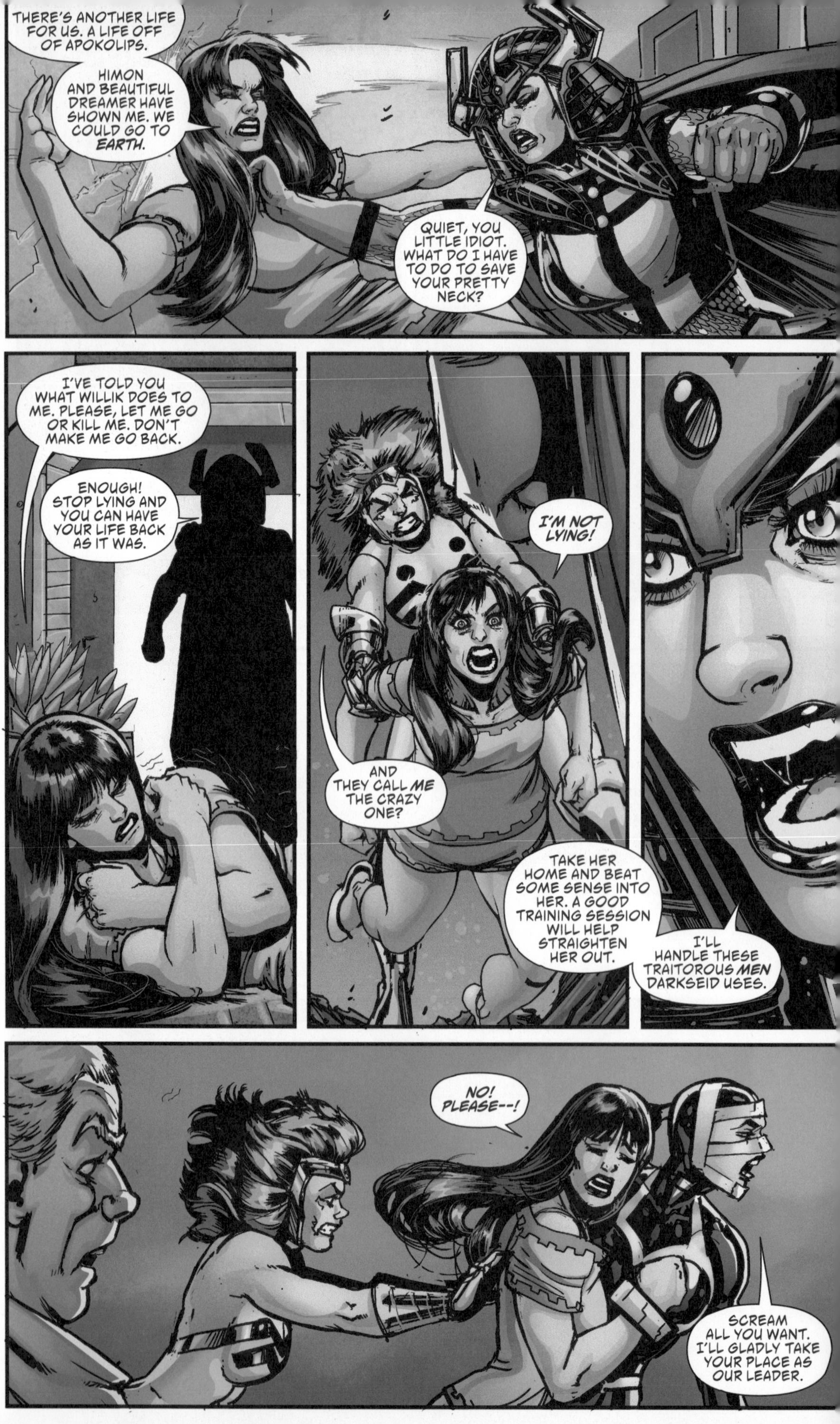
THERE'S ANOTHER LIFE FOR US. A LIFE OFF OF APOKOLIPS.
HIMON AND BEAUTIFUL DREAMER HAVE SHOWN ME. WE COULD GO TO *EARTH*.
QUIET, YOU LITTLE IDIOT. WHAT DO I HAVE TO DO TO SAVE YOUR PRETTY NECK?
I'VE TOLD YOU WHAT WILLIK DOES TO ME. PLEASE, LET ME GO OR KILL ME. DON'T MAKE ME GO BACK.
ENOUGH! STOP LYING AND YOU CAN HAVE YOUR LIFE BACK AS IT WAS.
I'M NOT LYING!
AND THEY CALL *ME* THE CRAZY ONE?
TAKE HER HOME AND BEAT SOME SENSE INTO HER. A GOOD TRAINING SESSION WILL HELP STRAIGHTEN HER OUT.
I'LL HANDLE THESE TRAITOROUS *MEN* DARKSEID USES.
NO! PLEASE--!
SCREAM ALL YOU WANT. I'LL GLADLY TAKE YOUR PLACE AS OUR LEADER.

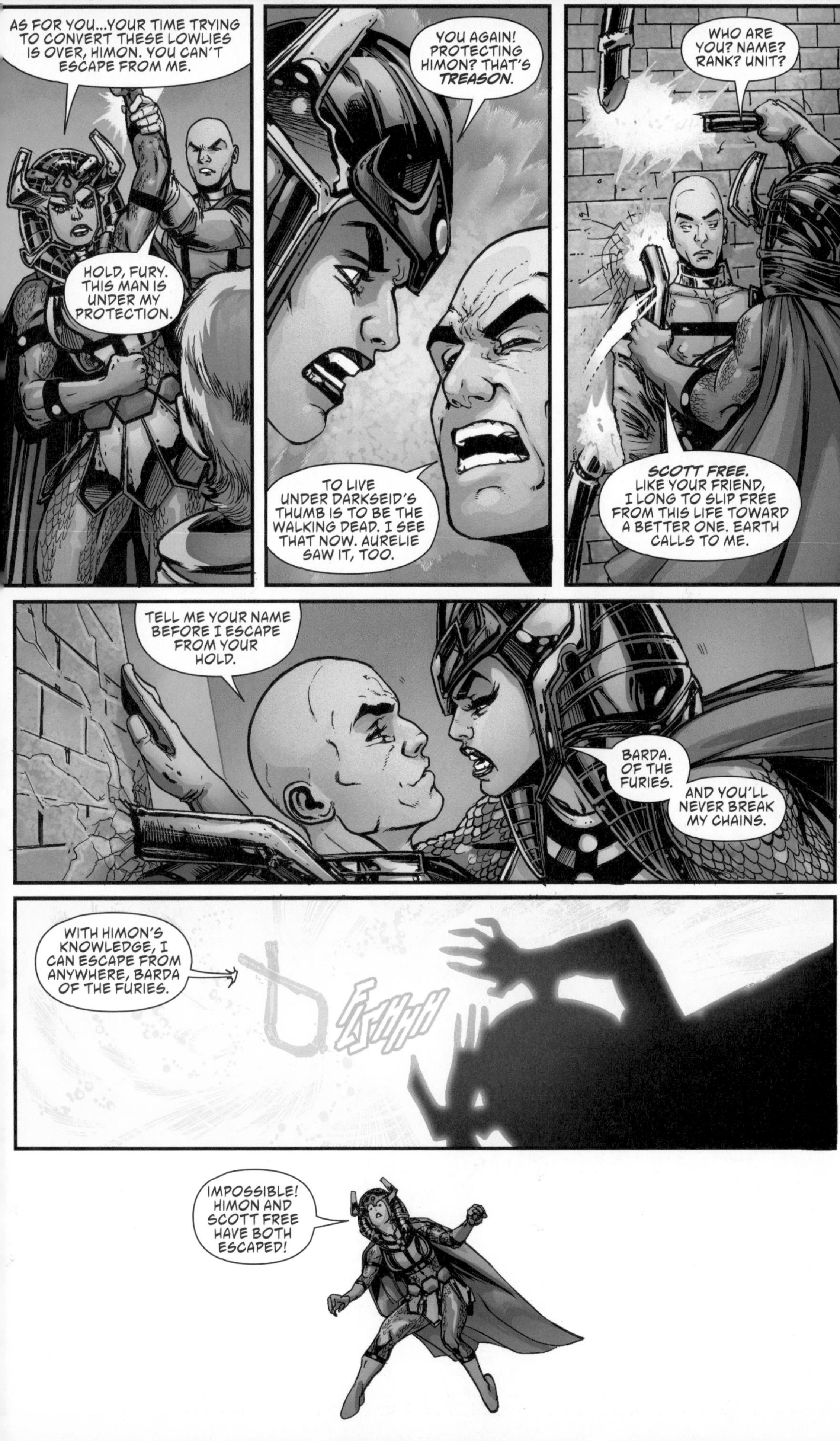
AS FOR YOU...YOUR TIME TRYING TO CONVERT THESE LOWLIES IS OVER, HIMON. YOU CAN'T ESCAPE FROM ME.
HOLD, FURY. THIS MAN IS UNDER MY PROTECTION.
YOU AGAIN! PROTECTING HIMON? THAT'S *TREASON*.
TO LIVE UNDER DARKSEID'S THUMB IS TO BE THE WALKING DEAD. I SEE THAT NOW. AURELIE SAW IT, TOO.
WHO ARE YOU? NAME? RANK? UNIT?
SCOTT FREE. LIKE YOUR FRIEND, I LONG TO SLIP FREE FROM THIS LIFE TOWARD A BETTER ONE. EARTH CALLS TO ME.
TELL ME YOUR NAME BEFORE I ESCAPE FROM YOUR HOLD.
BARDA. OF THE FURIES.
AND YOU'LL NEVER BREAK MY CHAINS.
WITH HIMON'S KNOWLEDGE, I CAN ESCAPE FROM ANYWHERE, BARDA OF THE FURIES.
IMPOSSIBLE! HIMON AND SCOTT FREE HAVE BOTH ESCAPED!

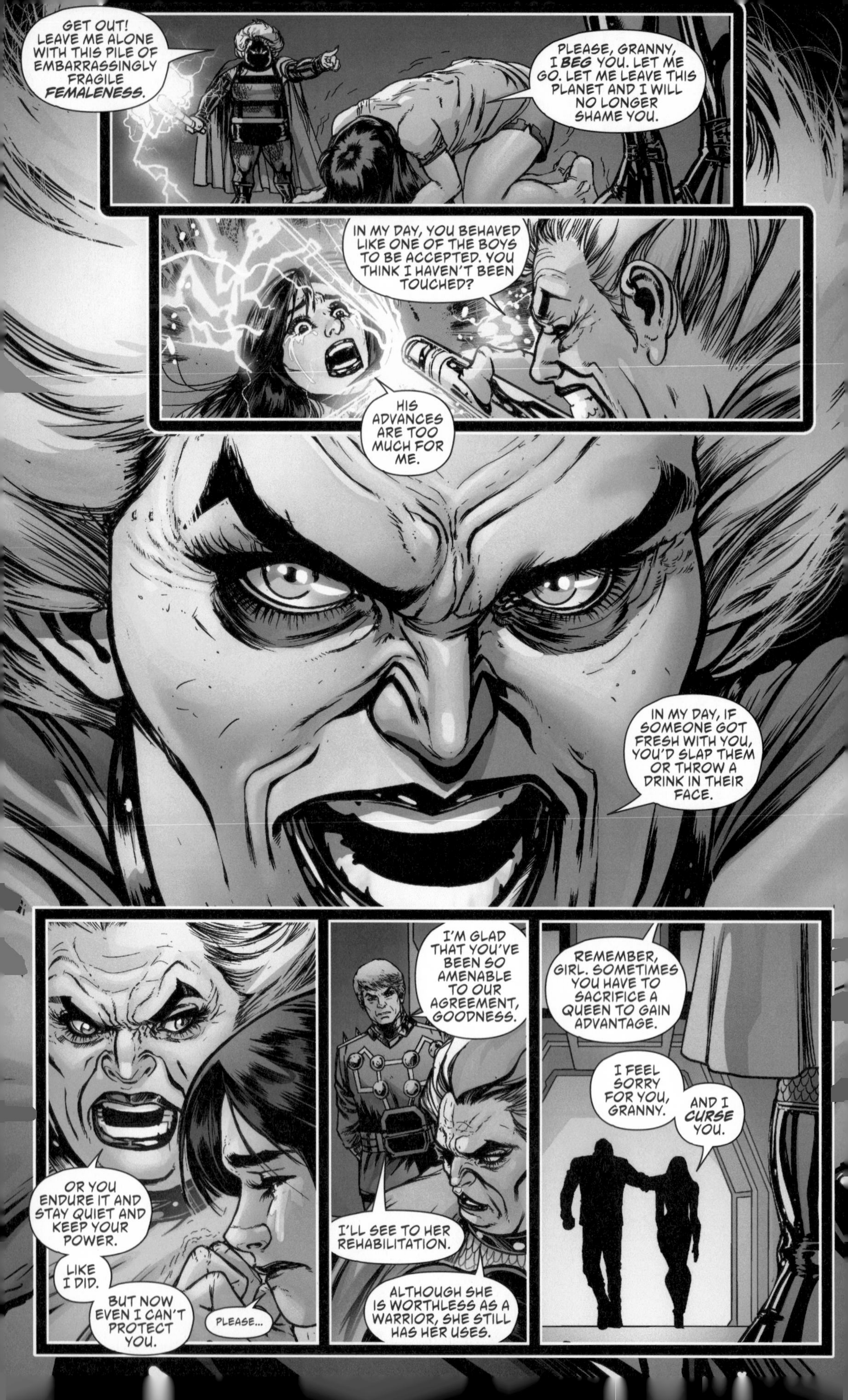
GET OUT! LEAVE ME ALONE WITH THIS PILE OF EMBARRASSINGLY FRAGILE *FEMALENESS*.
PLEASE, GRANNY, I *BEG* YOU. LET ME GO. LET ME LEAVE THIS PLANET AND I WILL NO LONGER SHAME YOU.
IN MY DAY, YOU BEHAVED LIKE ONE OF THE BOYS TO BE ACCEPTED. YOU THINK I HAVEN'T BEEN TOUCHED?
HIS ADVANCES ARE TOO MUCH FOR ME.
IN MY DAY, IF SOMEONE GOT FRESH WITH YOU, YOU'D SLAP THEM OR THROW A DRINK IN THEIR FACE.
OR YOU ENDURE IT AND STAY QUIET AND KEEP YOUR POWER.
LIKE I DID.
BUT NOW EVEN I CAN'T PROTECT YOU.
PLEASE...
I'M GLAD THAT YOU'VE BEEN SO AMENABLE TO OUR AGREEMENT, GOODNESS.
I'LL SEE TO HER REHABILITATION.
ALTHOUGH SHE IS WORTHLESS AS A WARRIOR, SHE STILL HAS HER USES.
REMEMBER, GIRL. SOMETIMES YOU HAVE TO SACRIFICE A QUEEN TO GAIN ADVANTAGE.
I FEEL SORRY FOR YOU, GRANNY.
AND I *CURSE* YOU.

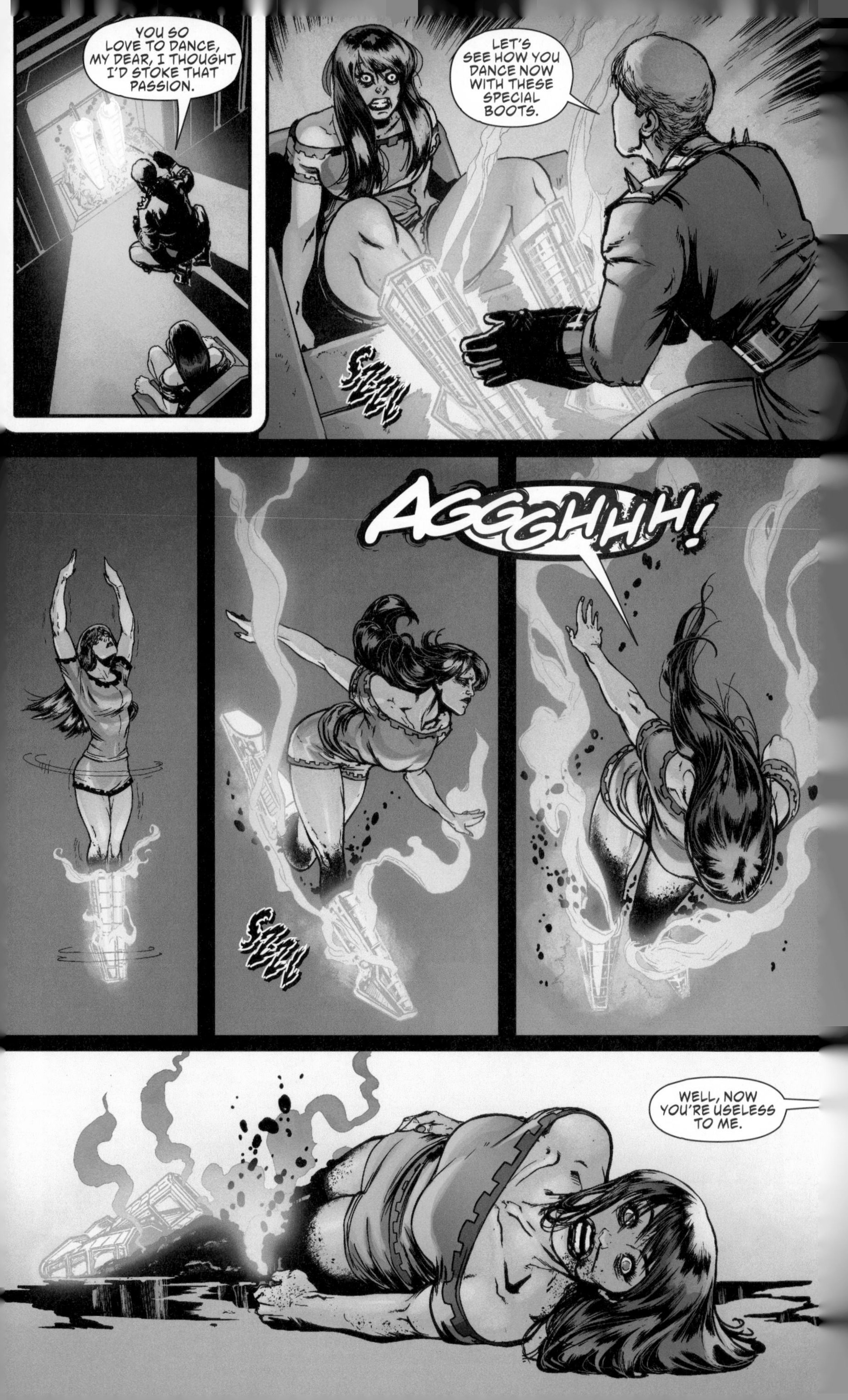
YOU SO LOVE TO DANCE, MY DEAR, I THOUGHT I'D STOKE THAT PASSION.
LET'S SEE HOW YOU DANCE NOW WITH THESE SPECIAL BOOTS.
SSSSS
AGGGHHHH!
SSSSS
WELL, NOW YOU'RE USELESS TO ME.

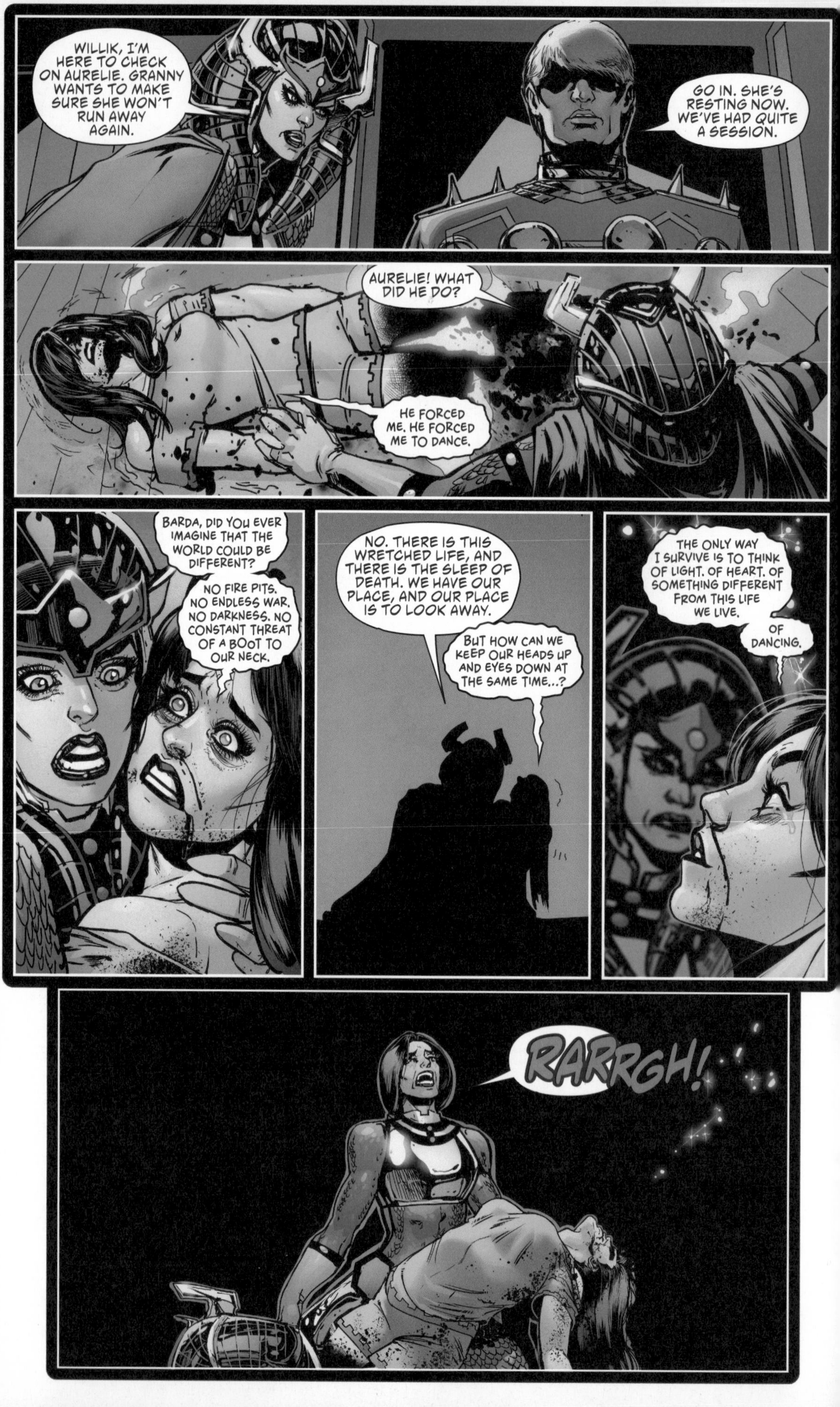
WILLIK, I'M HERE TO CHECK ON AURELIE. GRANNY WANTS TO MAKE SURE SHE WON'T RUN AWAY AGAIN.
GO IN. SHE'S RESTING NOW. WE'VE HAD QUITE A SESSION.
AURELIE! WHAT DID HE DO?
HE FORCED ME. HE FORCED ME TO DANCE.
BARDA, DID YOU EVER IMAGINE THAT THE WORLD COULD BE DIFFERENT?
NO FIRE PITS. NO ENDLESS WAR. NO DARKNESS. NO CONSTANT THREAT OF A BOOT TO OUR NECK.
NO. THERE IS THIS WRETCHED LIFE, AND THERE IS THE SLEEP OF DEATH. WE HAVE OUR PLACE, AND OUR PLACE IS TO LOOK AWAY.
BUT HOW CAN WE KEEP OUR HEADS UP AND EYES DOWN AT THE SAME TIME...?
THE ONLY WAY I SURVIVE IS TO THINK OF LIGHT. OF HEART. OF SOMETHING DIFFERENT FROM THIS LIFE WE LIVE.
OF DANCING.
RARRGH!

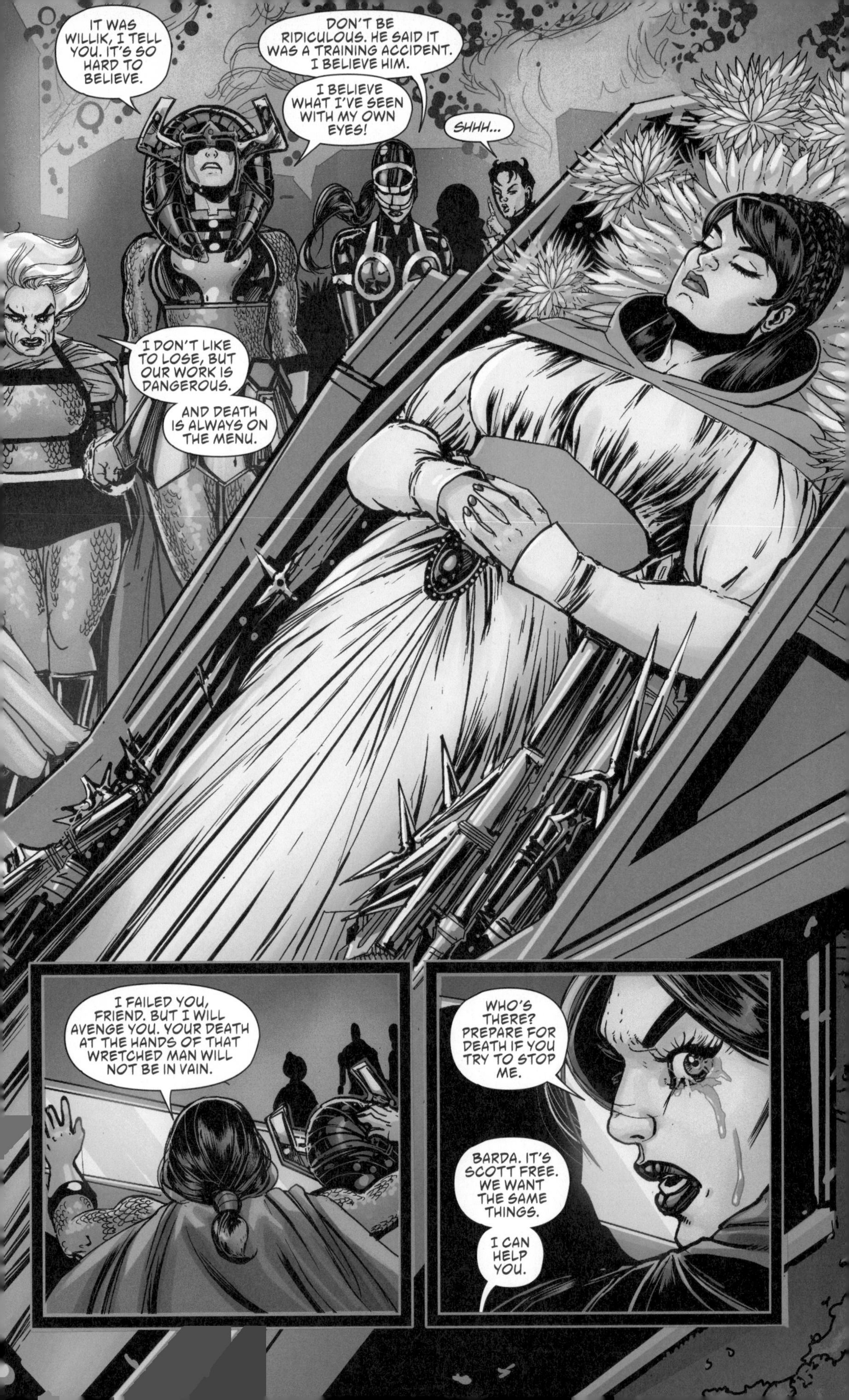
IT WAS WILLIK, I TELL YOU. IT'S SO HARD TO BELIEVE.
DON'T BE RIDICULOUS. HE SAID IT WAS A TRAINING ACCIDENT. I BELIEVE HIM.
I BELIEVE WHAT I'VE SEEN WITH MY OWN EYES!
SHHH...
I DON'T LIKE TO LOSE, BUT OUR WORK IS DANGEROUS.
AND DEATH IS ALWAYS ON THE MENU.
I FAILED YOU, FRIEND. BUT I WILL AVENGE YOU. YOUR DEATH AT THE HANDS OF THAT WRETCHED MAN WILL NOT BE IN VAIN.
WHO'S THERE? PREPARE FOR DEATH IF YOU TRY TO STOP ME.
BARDA. IT'S SCOTT FREE. WE WANT THE SAME THINGS.
I CAN HELP YOU.

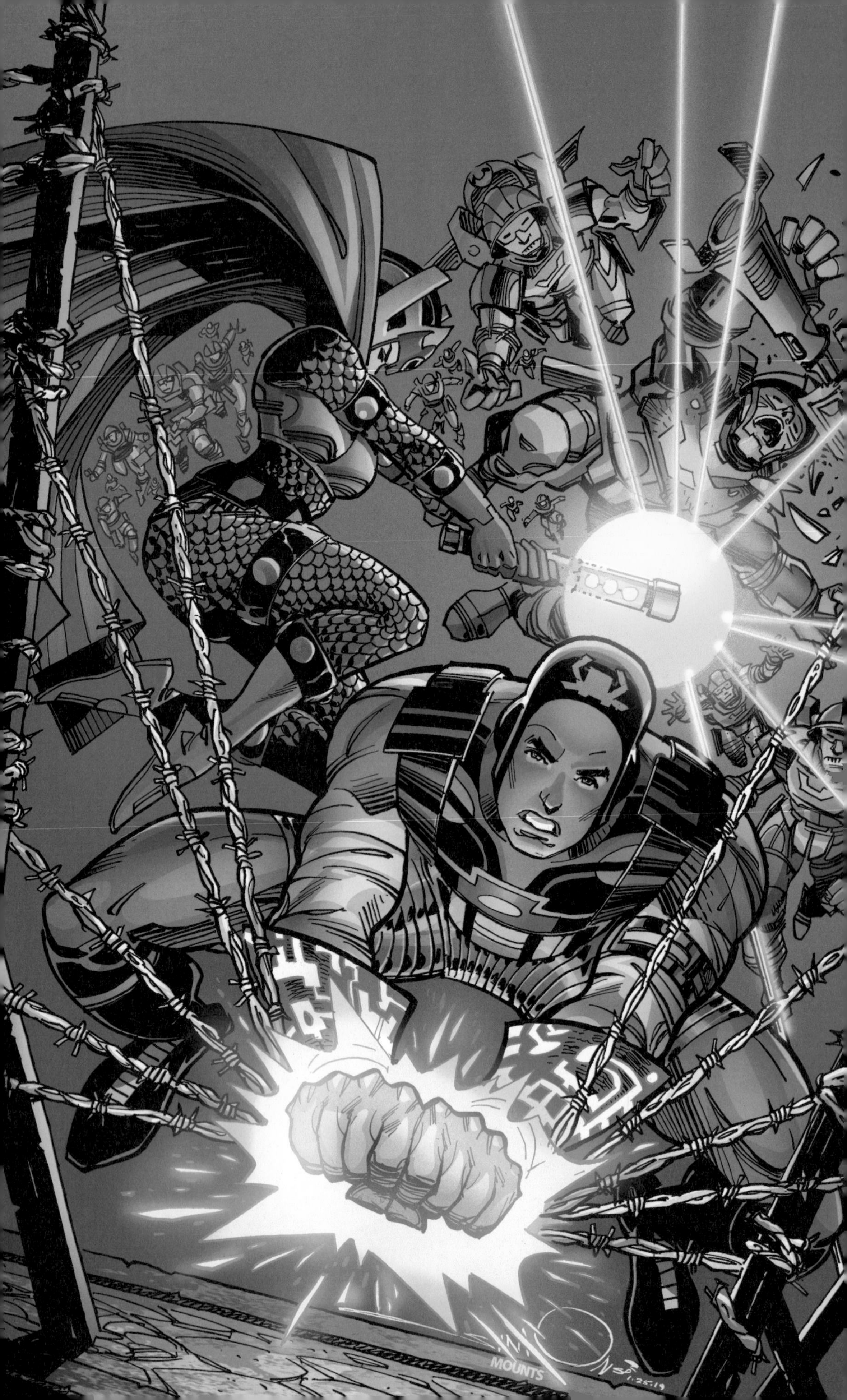
MOUNTS
1.25.19

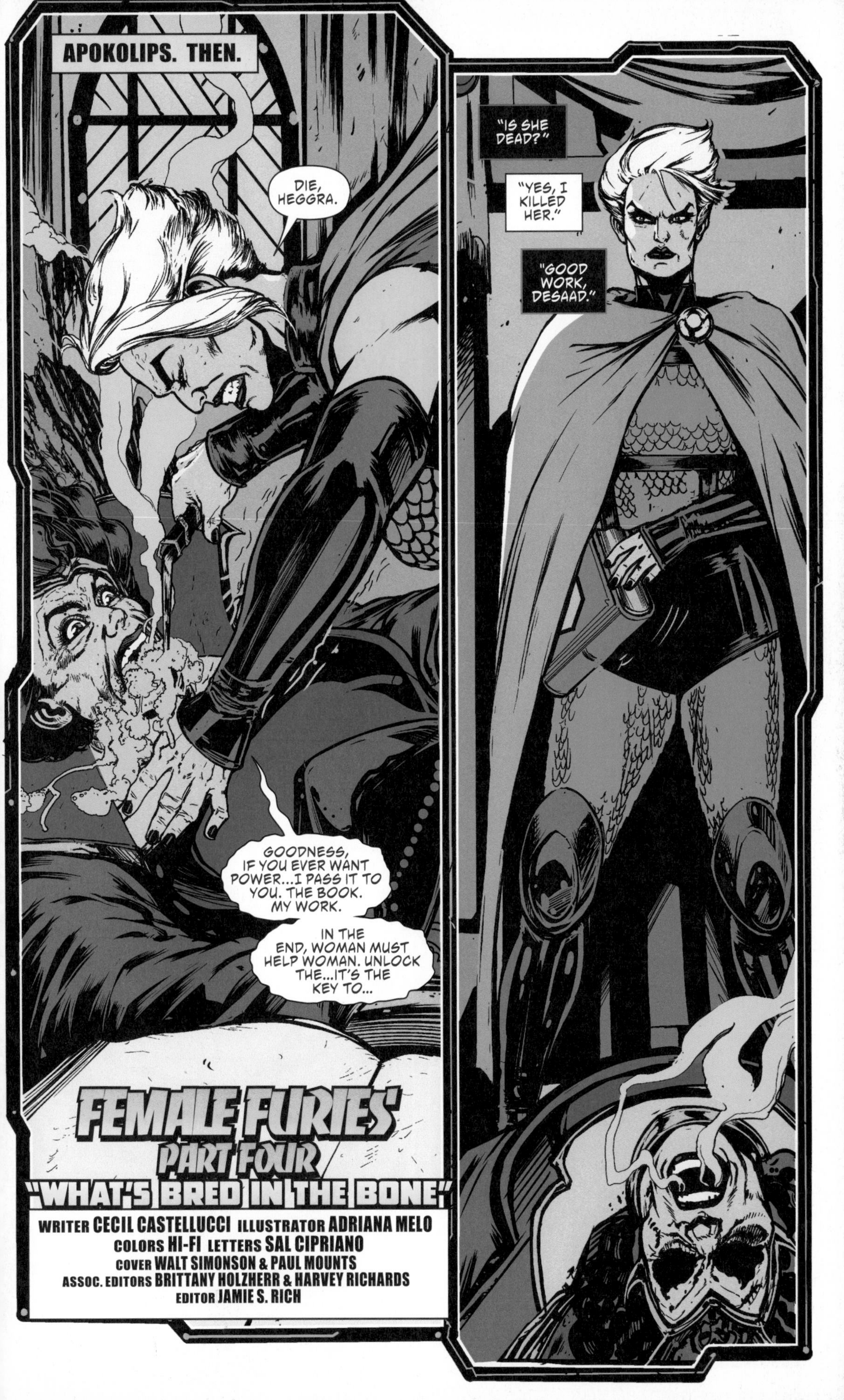

APOKOLIPS. THEN.
DIE, HEGGRA.
GOODNESS, IF YOU EVER WANT POWER...I PASS IT TO YOU. THE BOOK. MY WORK.
IN THE END, WOMAN MUST HELP WOMAN. UNLOCK THE...IT'S THE KEY TO...
FEMALE FURIES' PART FOUR
"WHAT'S BRED IN THE BONE"
WRITER CECIL CASTELLUCCI ILLUSTRATOR ADRIANA MELO
COLORS HI-FI LETTERS SAL CIPRIANO
COVER WALT SIMONSON & PAUL MOUNTS
ASSOC. EDITORS BRITTANY HOLZHERR & HARVEY RICHARDS
EDITOR JAMIE S. RICH
"IS SHE DEAD?"
"YES, I KILLED HER."
"GOOD WORK, DESAAD."

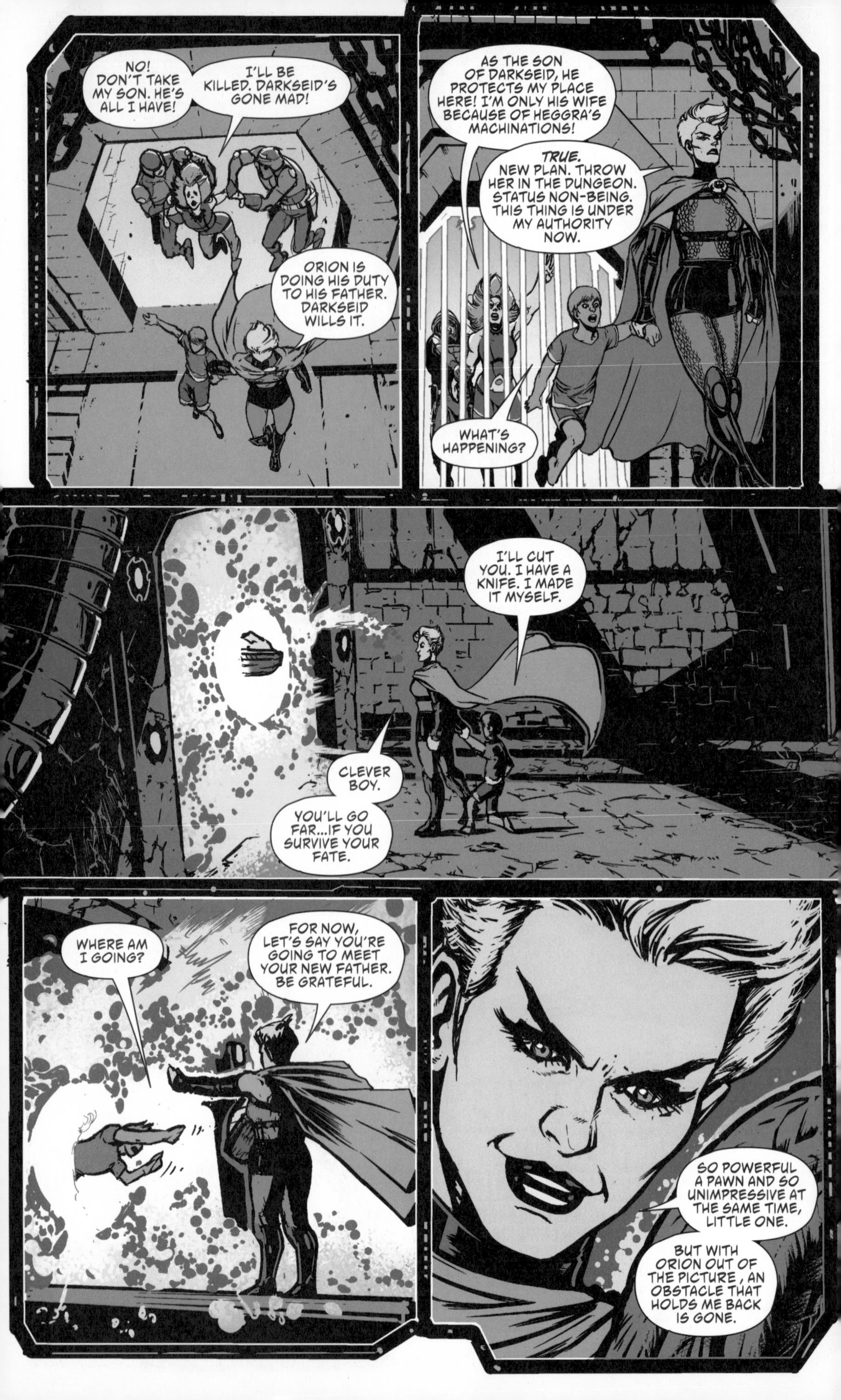
NO! DON'T TAKE MY SON. HE'S ALL I HAVE!
I'LL BE KILLED. DARKSEID'S GONE MAD!
ORION IS DOING HIS DUTY TO HIS FATHER. DARKSEID WILLS IT.
AS THE SON OF DARKSEID, HE PROTECTS MY PLACE HERE! I'M ONLY HIS WIFE BECAUSE OF HEGGRA'S MACHINATIONS!
TRUE. NEW PLAN. THROW HER IN THE DUNGEON. STATUS NON-BEING. THIS THING IS UNDER MY AUTHORITY NOW.
WHAT'S HAPPENING?
I'LL CUT YOU. I HAVE A KNIFE. I MADE IT MYSELF.
CLEVER BOY.
YOU'LL GO FAR...IF YOU SURVIVE YOUR FATE.
WHERE AM I GOING?
FOR NOW, LET'S SAY YOU'RE GOING TO MEET YOUR NEW FATHER. BE GRATEFUL.
SO POWERFUL A PAWN AND SO UNIMPRESSIVE AT THE SAME TIME, LITTLE ONE.
BUT WITH ORION OUT OF THE PICTURE, AN OBSTACLE THAT HOLDS ME BACK IS GONE.

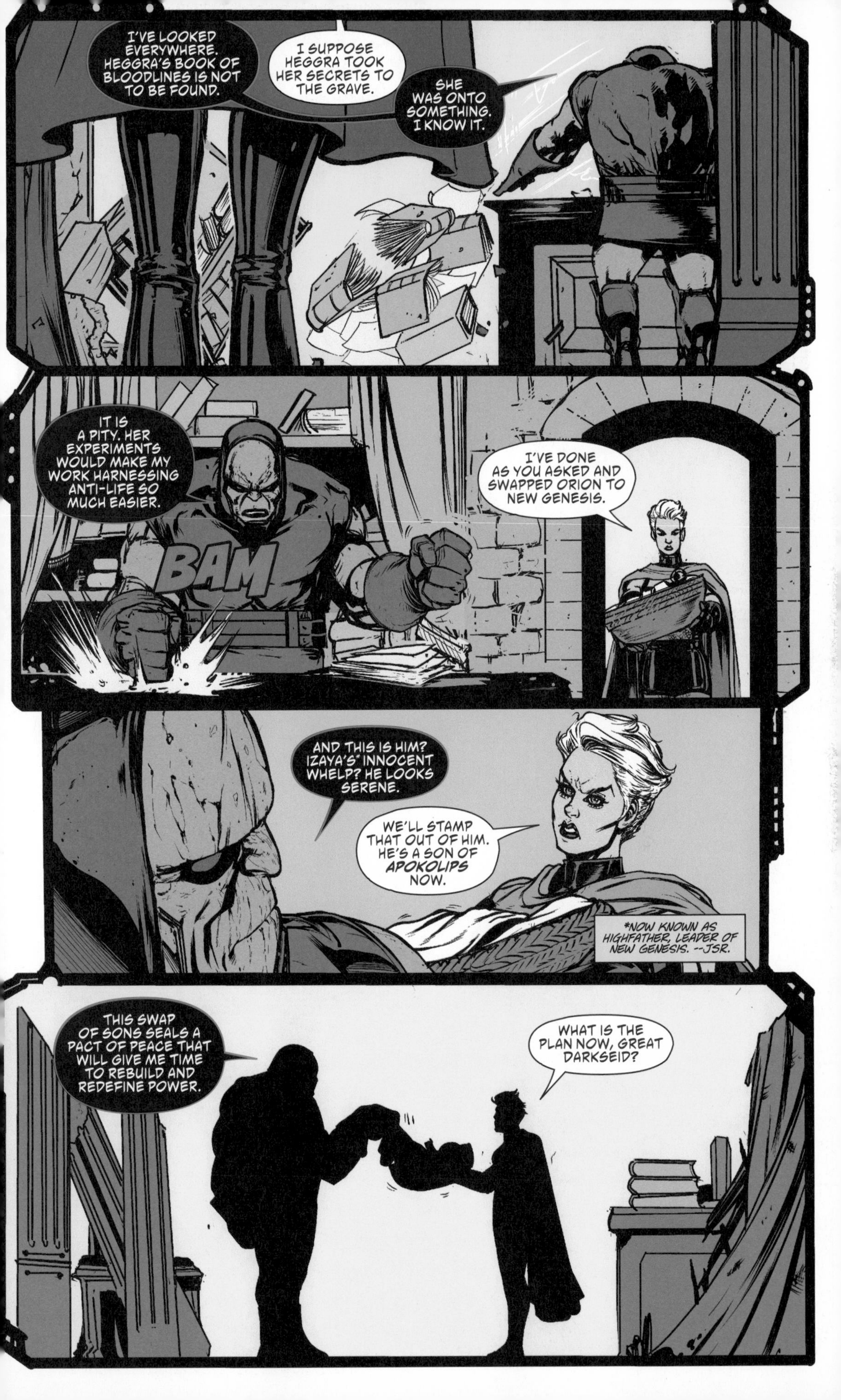
I'VE LOOKED EVERYWHERE. HEGGRA'S BOOK OF BLOODLINES IS NOT TO BE FOUND.
I SUPPOSE HEGGRA TOOK HER SECRETS TO THE GRAVE.
SHE WAS ONTO SOMETHING. I KNOW IT.
IT IS A PITY. HER EXPERIMENTS WOULD MAKE MY WORK HARNESSING ANTI-LIFE SO MUCH EASIER.
BAM
I'VE DONE AS YOU ASKED AND SWAPPED ORION TO NEW GENESIS.
AND THIS IS HIM? IZAYA'S* INNOCENT WHELP? HE LOOKS SERENE.
WE'LL STAMP THAT OUT OF HIM. HE'S A SON OF APOKOLIPS NOW.
*NOW KNOWN AS HIGHFATHER, LEADER OF NEW GENESIS. --JSR.
THIS SWAP OF SONS SEALS A PACT OF PEACE THAT WILL GIVE ME TIME TO REBUILD AND REDEFINE POWER.
WHAT IS THE PLAN NOW, GREAT DARKSEID?

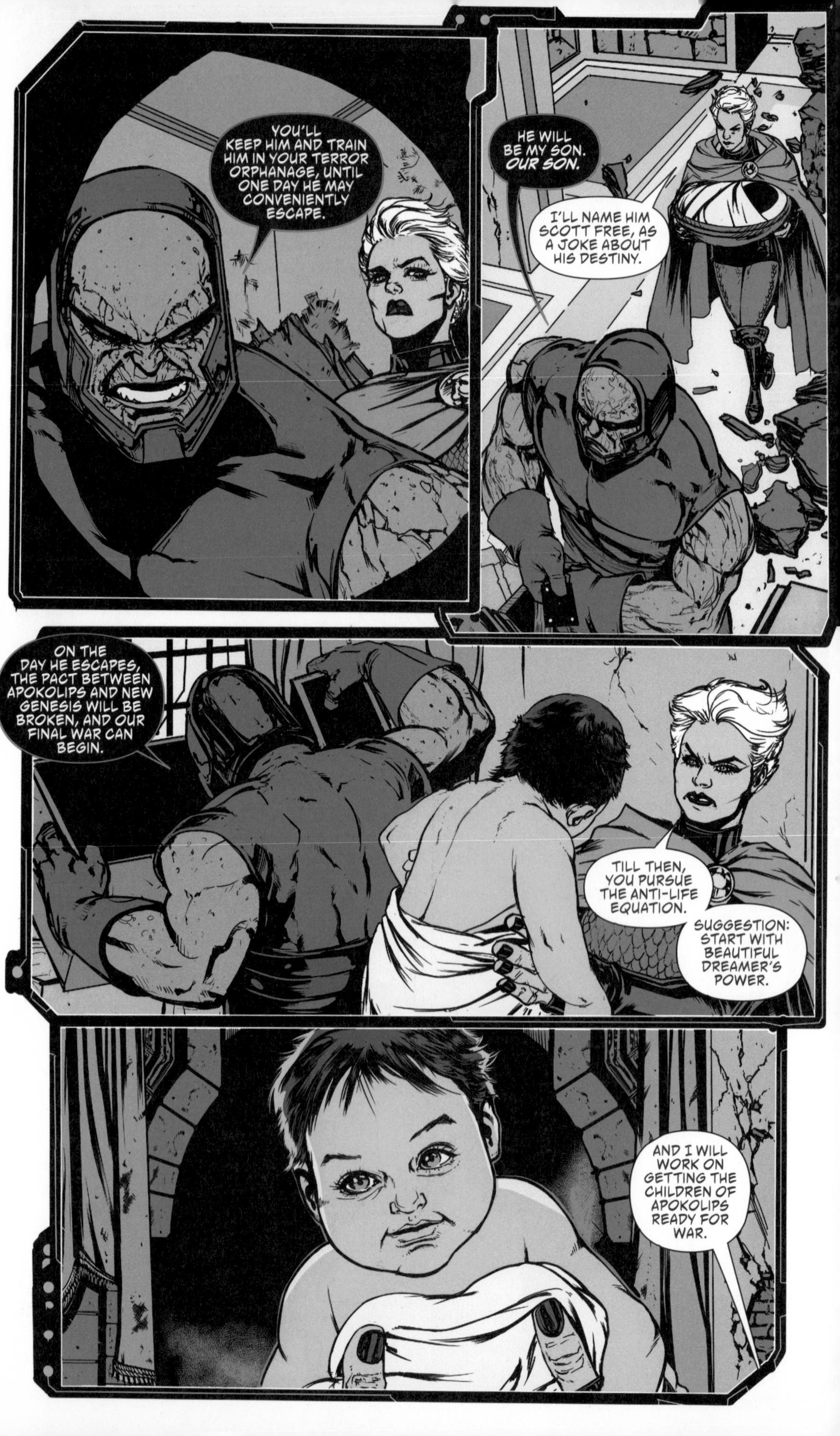
YOU'LL KEEP HIM AND TRAIN HIM IN YOUR TERROR ORPHANAGE, UNTIL ONE DAY HE MAY CONVENIENTLY ESCAPE.
HE WILL BE MY SON. *OUR SON.*
I'LL NAME HIM SCOTT FREE, AS A JOKE ABOUT HIS DESTINY.
ON THE DAY HE ESCAPES, THE PACT BETWEEN APOKOLIPS AND NEW GENESIS WILL BE BROKEN, AND OUR FINAL WAR CAN BEGIN.
TILL THEN, YOU PURSUE THE ANTI-LIFE EQUATION.
SUGGESTION: START WITH BEAUTIFUL DREAMER'S POWER.
AND I WILL WORK ON GETTING THE CHILDREN OF APOKOLIPS READY FOR WAR.

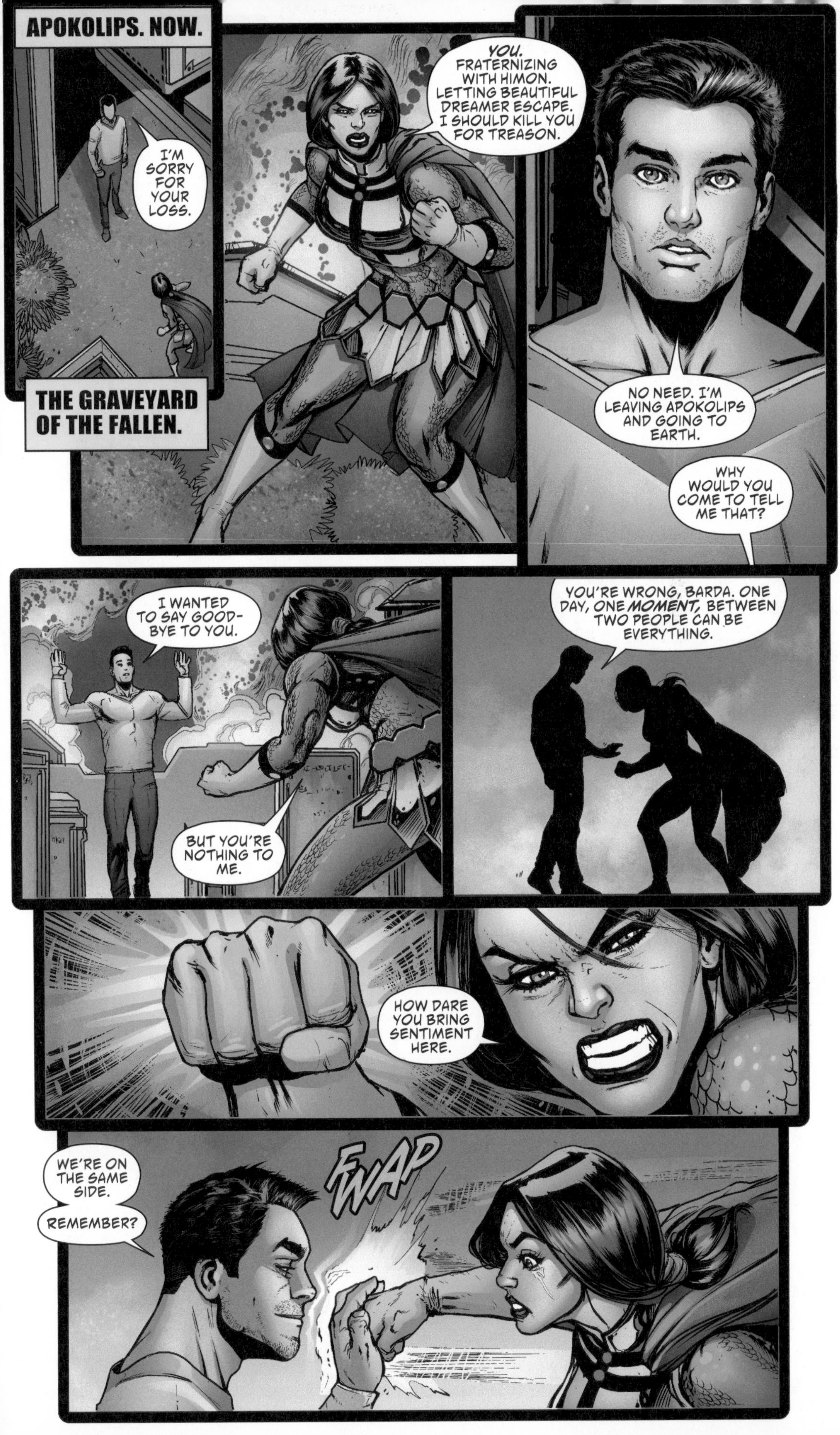
APOKOLIPS. NOW.
I'M SORRY FOR YOUR LOSS.
THE GRAVEYARD OF THE FALLEN.
YOU. FRATERNIZING WITH HIMON. LETTING BEAUTIFUL DREAMER ESCAPE. I SHOULD KILL YOU FOR TREASON.
NO NEED. I'M LEAVING APOKOLIPS AND GOING TO EARTH.
WHY WOULD YOU COME TO TELL ME THAT?
I WANTED TO SAY GOOD-BYE TO YOU.
BUT YOU'RE NOTHING TO ME.
YOU'RE WRONG, BARDA. ONE DAY, ONE MOMENT, BETWEEN TWO PEOPLE CAN BE EVERYTHING.
HOW DARE YOU BRING SENTIMENT HERE.
FWAP
WE'RE ON THE SAME SIDE.
REMEMBER?

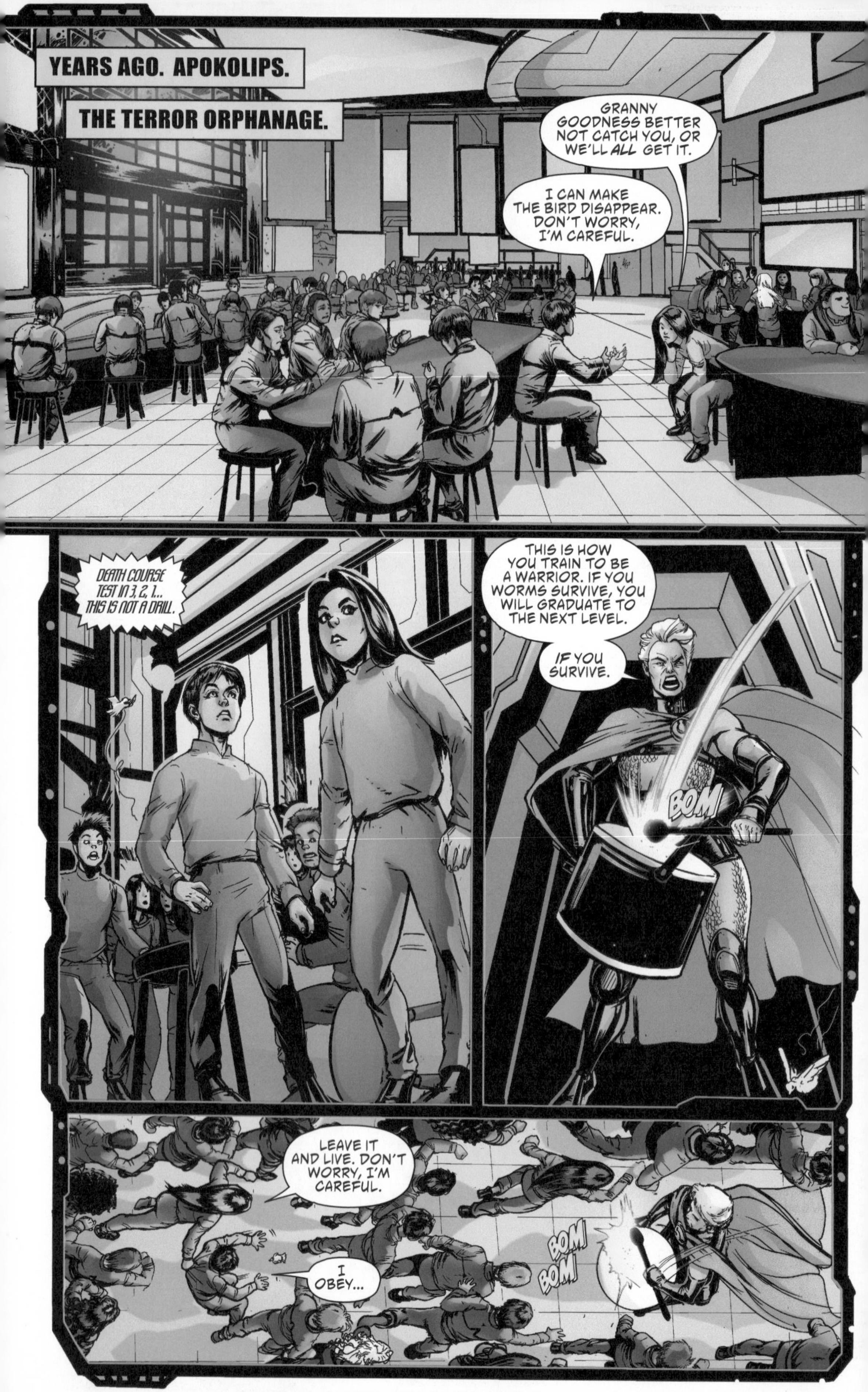

YEARS AGO. APOKOLIPS.
THE TERROR ORPHANAGE.
GRANNY GOODNESS BETTER NOT CATCH YOU, OR WE'LL ALL GET IT.
I CAN MAKE THE BIRD DISAPPEAR. DON'T WORRY, I'M CAREFUL.
DEATH COURSE TEST IN 3, 2, 1... THIS IS NOT A DRILL.
THIS IS HOW YOU TRAIN TO BE A WARRIOR. IF YOU WORMS SURVIVE, YOU WILL GRADUATE TO THE NEXT LEVEL.
IF YOU SURVIVE.
BOM
LEAVE IT AND LIVE. DON'T WORRY, I'M CAREFUL.
I OBEY...
BOM
BOM

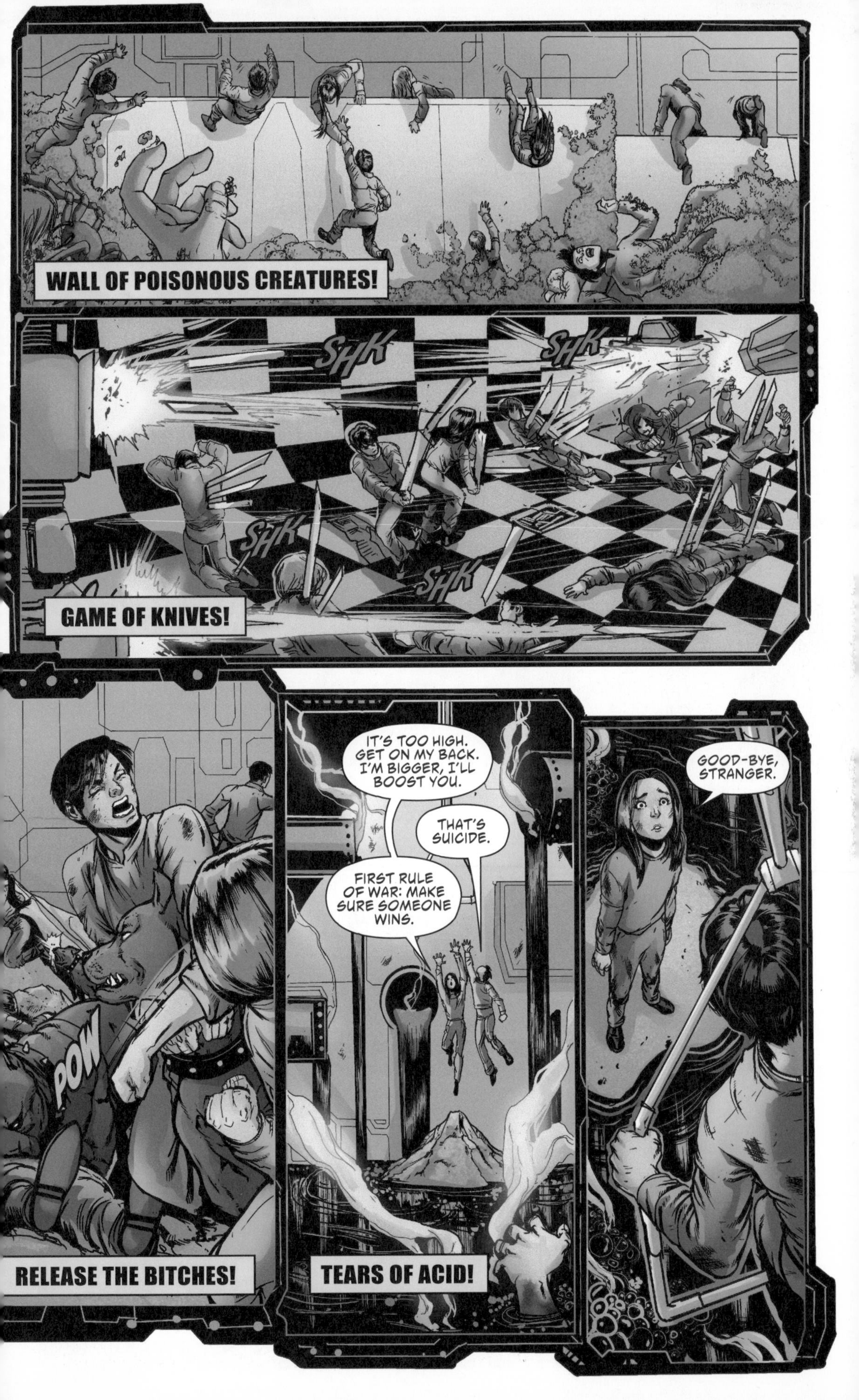
WALL OF POISONOUS CREATURES!
SHK
SHK
SHK
SHK
GAME OF KNIVES!
POW
RELEASE THE BITCHES!
IT'S TOO HIGH. GET ON MY BACK. I'M BIGGER, I'LL BOOST YOU.
THAT'S SUICIDE.
FIRST RULE OF WAR: MAKE SURE SOMEONE WINS.
TEARS OF ACID!
GOOD-BYE, STRANGER.

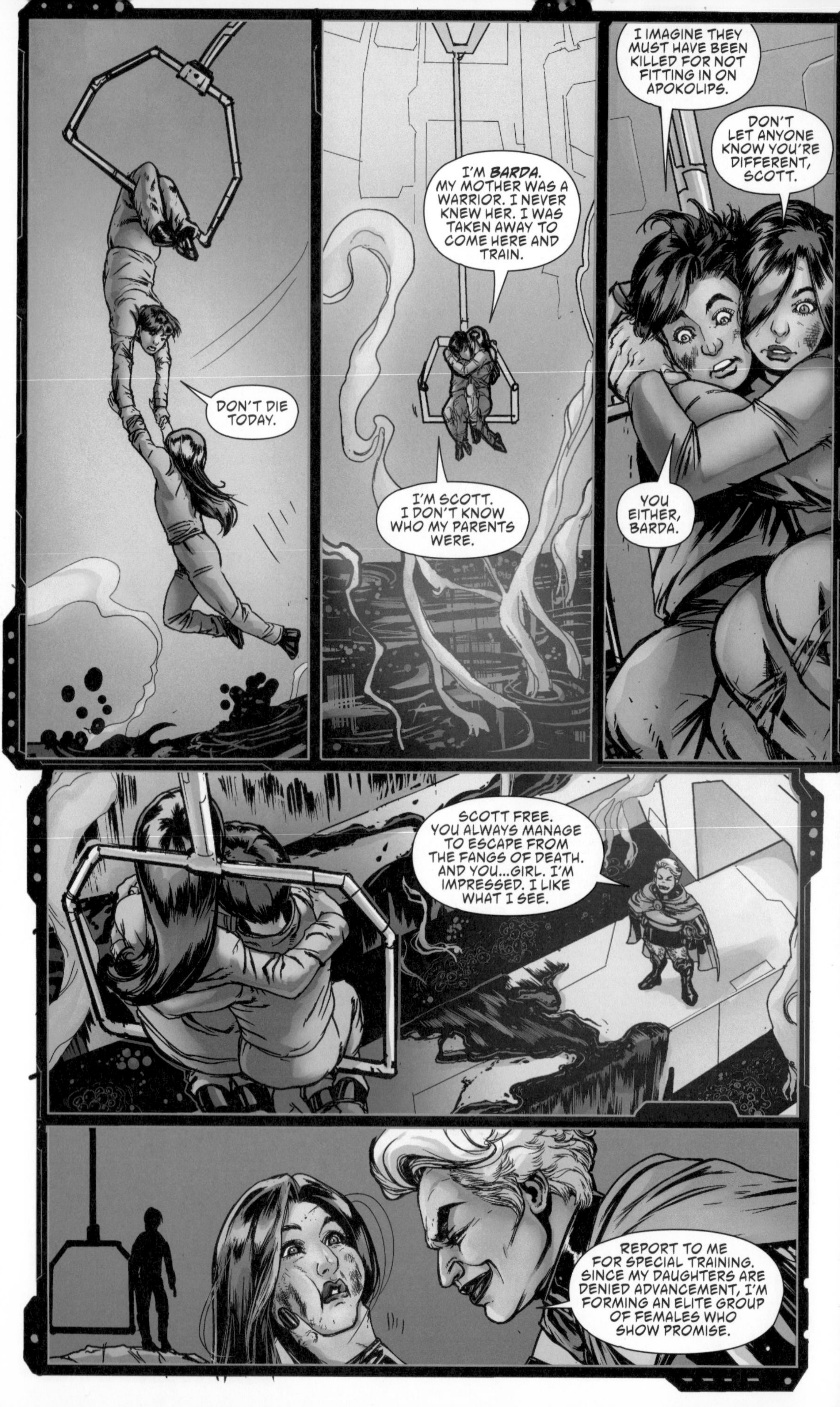
DON'T DIE TODAY.
I'M BARDA. MY MOTHER WAS A WARRIOR. I NEVER KNEW HER. I WAS TAKEN AWAY TO COME HERE AND TRAIN.
I'M SCOTT. I DON'T KNOW WHO MY PARENTS WERE.
I IMAGINE THEY MUST HAVE BEEN KILLED FOR NOT FITTING IN ON APOKOLIPS.
DON'T LET ANYONE KNOW YOU'RE DIFFERENT, SCOTT.
YOU EITHER, BARDA.
SCOTT FREE. YOU ALWAYS MANAGE TO ESCAPE FROM THE FANGS OF DEATH. AND YOU...GIRL. I'M IMPRESSED. I LIKE WHAT I SEE.
REPORT TO ME FOR SPECIAL TRAINING. SINCE MY DAUGHTERS ARE DENIED ADVANCEMENT, I'M FORMING AN ELITE GROUP OF FEMALES WHO SHOW PROMISE.

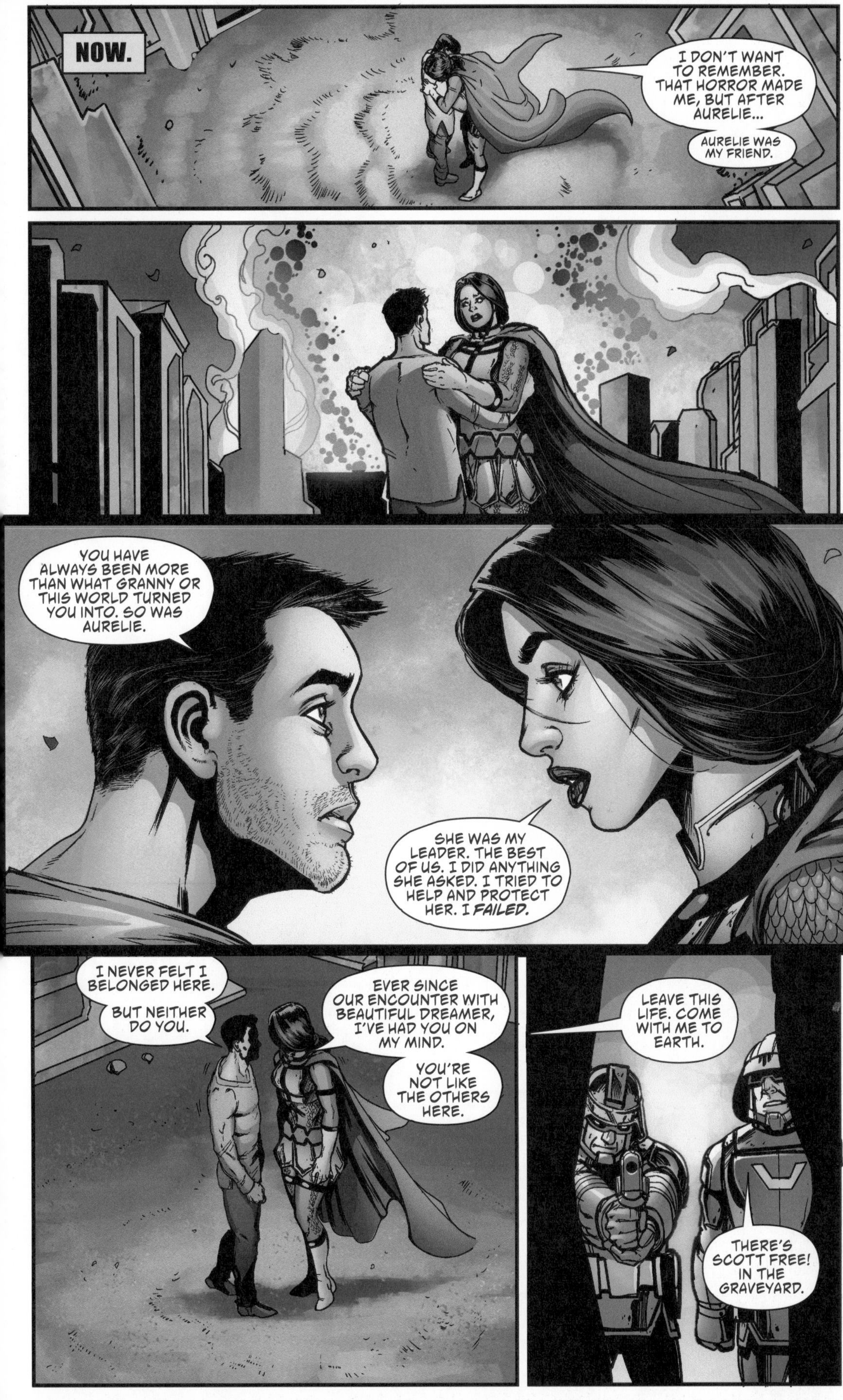
NOW.
I DON'T WANT TO REMEMBER. THAT HORROR MADE ME, BUT AFTER AURELIE...
AURELIE WAS MY FRIEND.
YOU HAVE ALWAYS BEEN MORE THAN WHAT GRANNY OR THIS WORLD TURNED YOU INTO. SO WAS AURELIE.
SHE WAS MY LEADER. THE BEST OF US. I DID ANYTHING SHE ASKED. I TRIED TO HELP AND PROTECT HER. I FAILED.
I NEVER FELT I BELONGED HERE.
BUT NEITHER DO YOU.
EVER SINCE OUR ENCOUNTER WITH BEAUTIFUL DREAMER, I'VE HAD YOU ON MY MIND.
YOU'RE NOT LIKE THE OTHERS HERE.
LEAVE THIS LIFE. COME WITH ME TO EARTH.
THERE'S SCOTT FREE! IN THE GRAVEYARD.

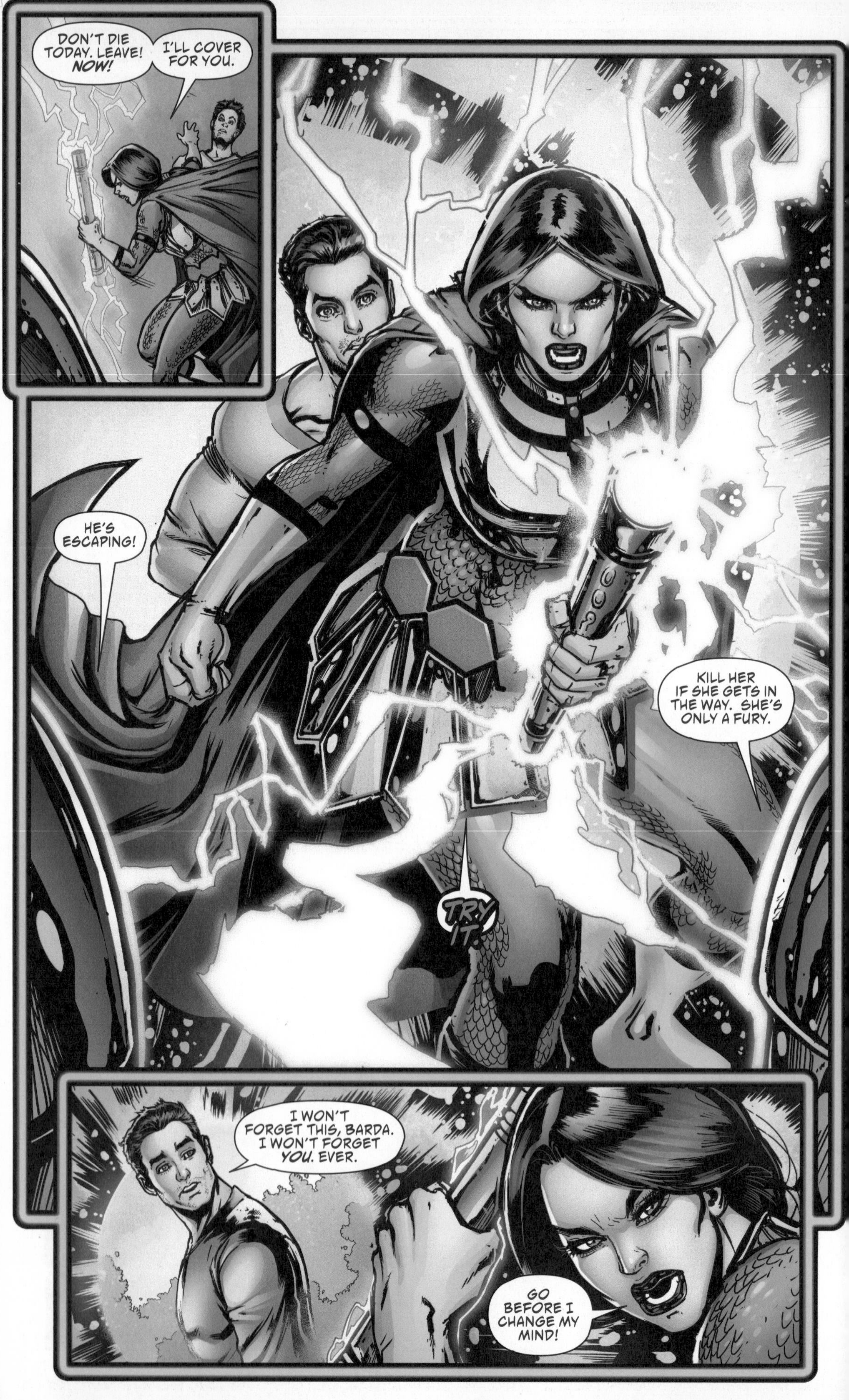
DON'T DIE TODAY. LEAVE! NOW!
I'LL COVER FOR YOU.
HE'S ESCAPING!
KILL HER IF SHE GETS IN THE WAY. SHE'S ONLY A FURY.
TRY IT.
I WON'T FORGET THIS, BARDA. I WON'T FORGET YOU. EVER.
GO BEFORE I CHANGE MY MIND!

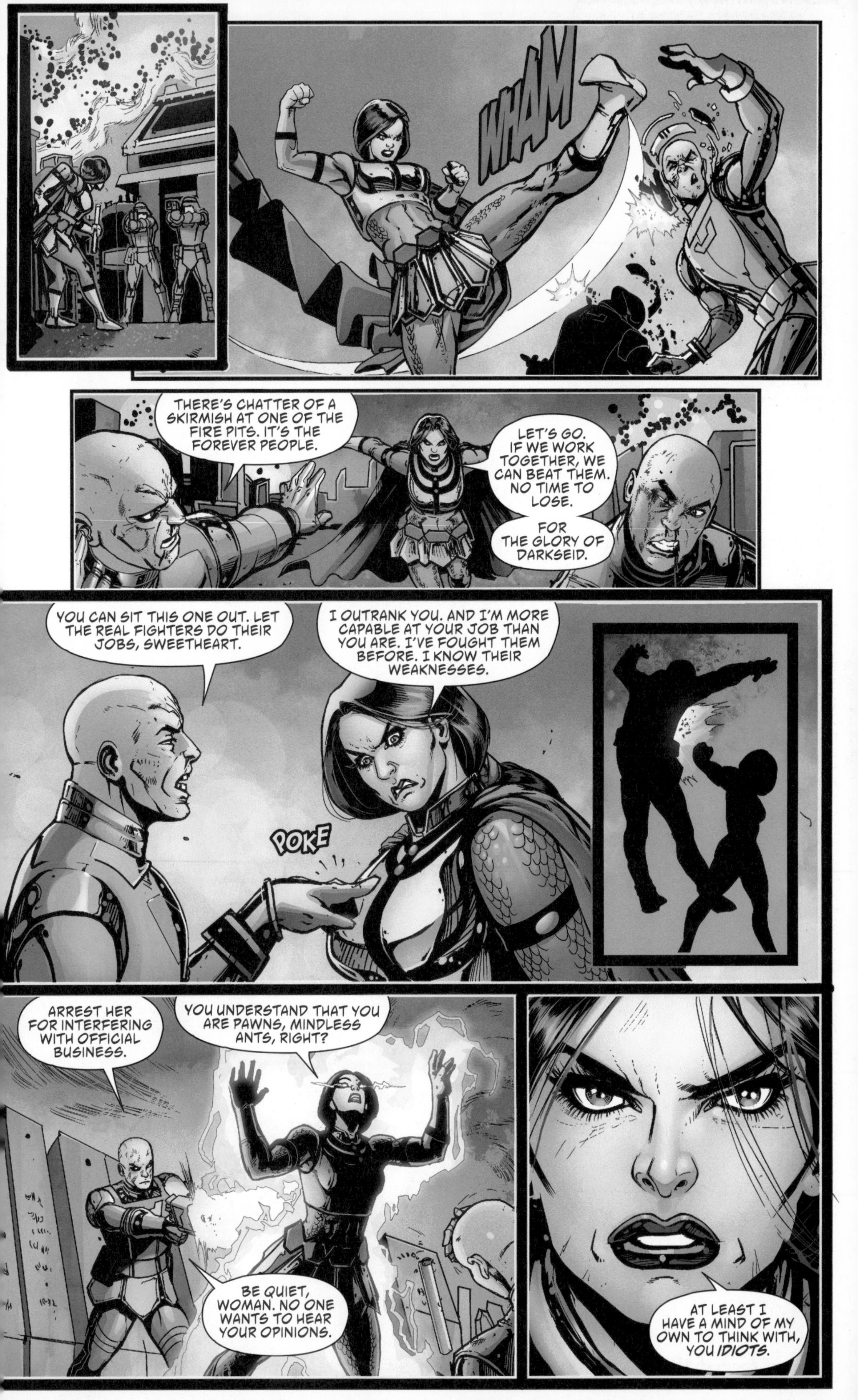
WHAM
THERE'S CHATTER OF A SKIRMISH AT ONE OF THE FIRE PITS. IT'S THE FOREVER PEOPLE.
LET'S GO. IF WE WORK TOGETHER, WE CAN BEAT THEM. NO TIME TO LOSE.
FOR THE GLORY OF DARKSEID.
YOU CAN SIT THIS ONE OUT. LET THE REAL FIGHTERS DO THEIR JOBS, SWEETHEART.
I OUTRANK YOU. AND I'M MORE CAPABLE AT YOUR JOB THAN YOU ARE. I'VE FOUGHT THEM BEFORE. I KNOW THEIR WEAKNESSES.
POKE
ARREST HER FOR INTERFERING WITH OFFICIAL BUSINESS.
YOU UNDERSTAND THAT YOU ARE PAWNS, MINDLESS ANTS, RIGHT?
BE QUIET, WOMAN. NO ONE WANTS TO HEAR YOUR OPINIONS.
AT LEAST I HAVE A MIND OF MY OWN TO THINK WITH, YOU *IDIOTS*.

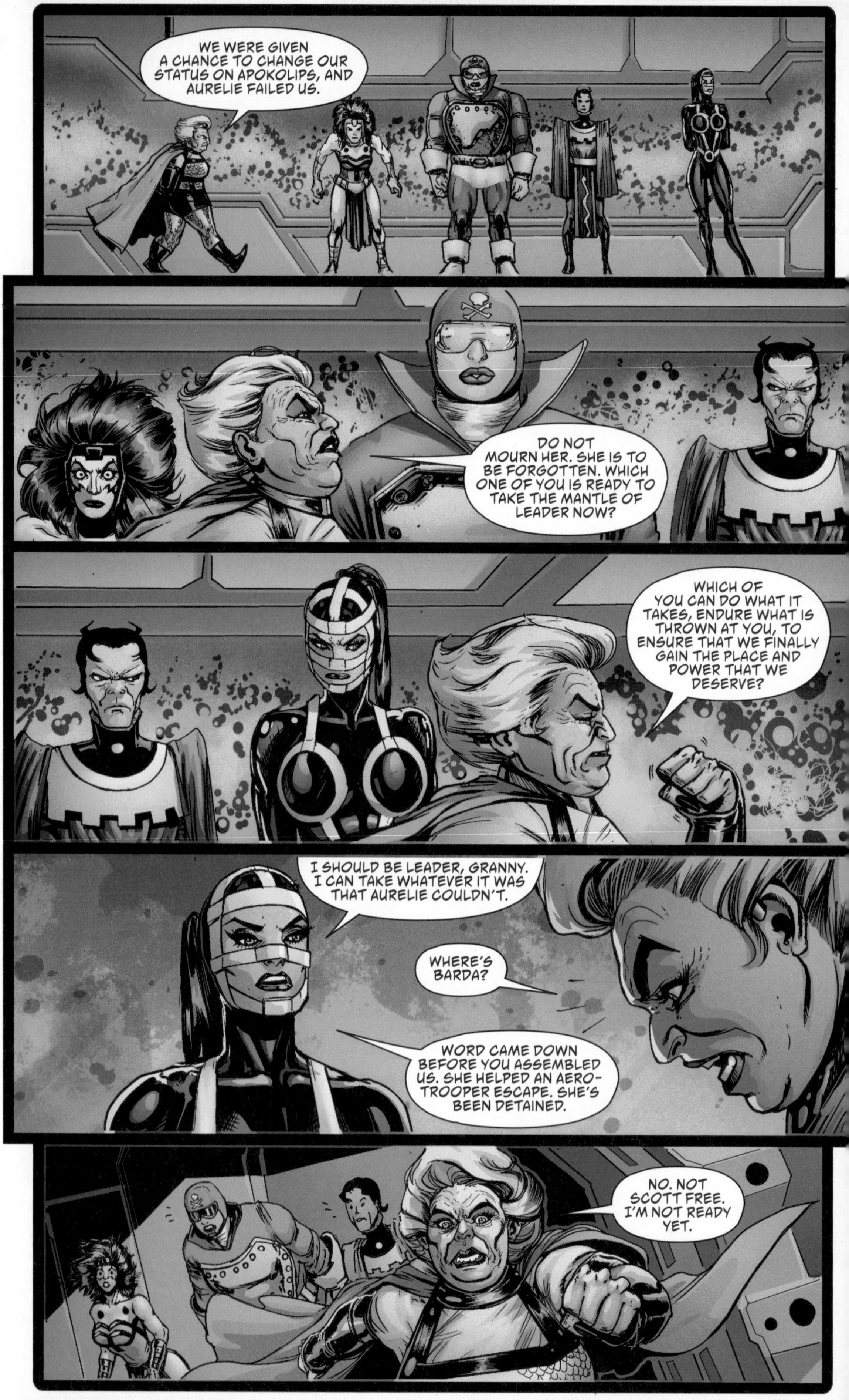
WE WERE GIVEN A CHANCE TO CHANGE OUR STATUS ON APOKOLIPS, AND AURELIE FAILED US.
DO NOT MOURN HER. SHE IS TO BE FORGOTTEN. WHICH ONE OF YOU IS READY TO TAKE THE MANTLE OF LEADER NOW?
WHICH OF YOU CAN DO WHAT IT TAKES, ENDURE WHAT IS THROWN AT YOU, TO ENSURE THAT WE FINALLY GAIN THE PLACE AND POWER THAT WE DESERVE?
I SHOULD BE LEADER, GRANNY. I CAN TAKE WHATEVER IT WAS THAT AURELIE COULDN'T.
WHERE'S BARDA?
WORD CAME DOWN BEFORE YOU ASSEMBLED US. SHE HELPED AN AERO-TROOPER ESCAPE. SHE'S BEEN DETAINED.
NO. NOT SCOTT FREE. I'M NOT READY YET.

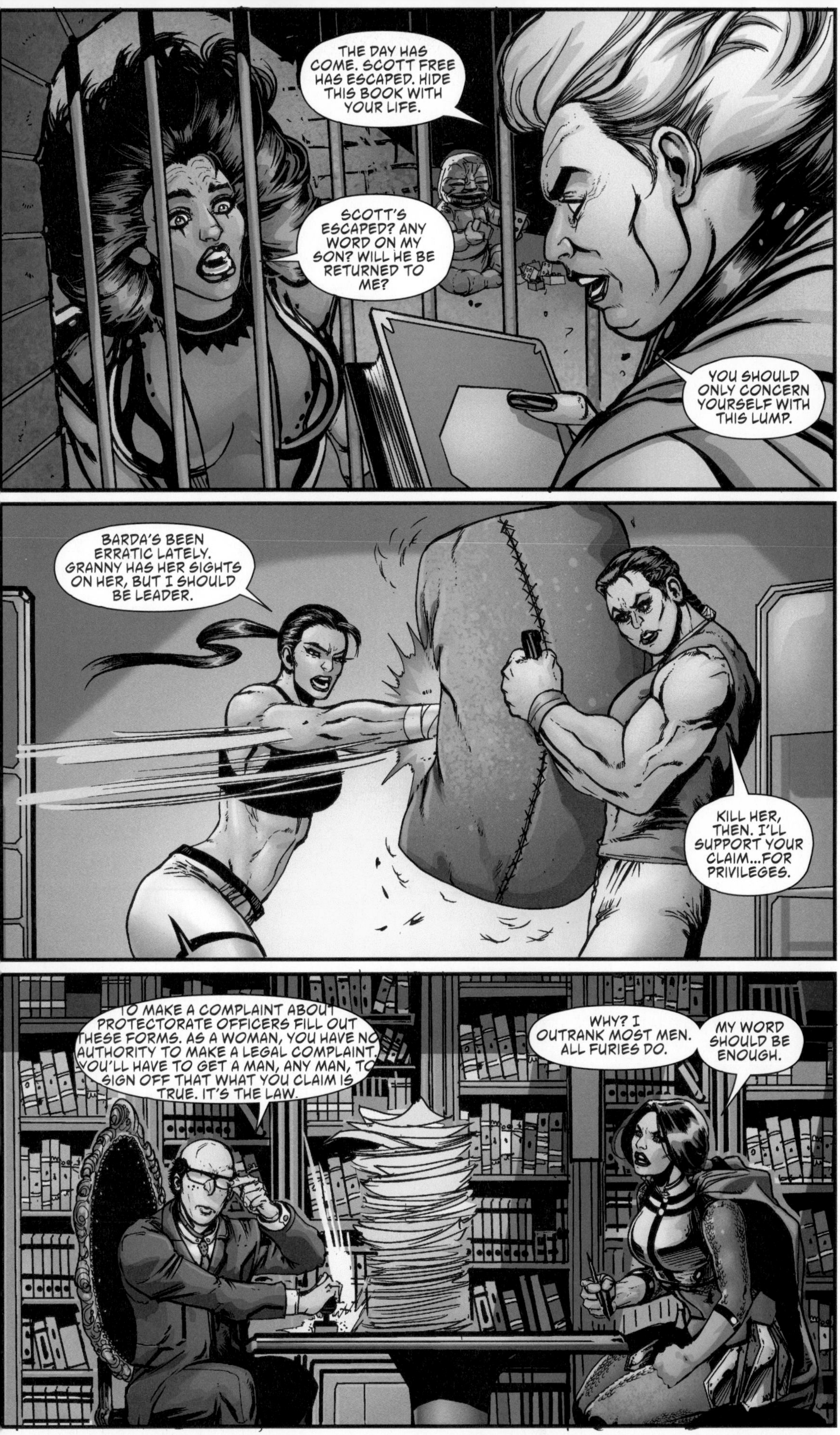
THE DAY HAS COME. SCOTT FREE HAS ESCAPED. HIDE THIS BOOK WITH YOUR LIFE.
SCOTT'S ESCAPED? ANY WORD ON MY SON? WILL HE BE RETURNED TO ME?
YOU SHOULD ONLY CONCERN YOURSELF WITH THIS LUMP.
BARDA'S BEEN ERRATIC LATELY. GRANNY HAS HER SIGHTS ON HER, BUT I SHOULD BE LEADER.
KILL HER, THEN. I'LL SUPPORT YOUR CLAIM...FOR PRIVILEGES.
TO MAKE A COMPLAINT ABOUT PROTECTORATE OFFICERS FILL OUT THESE FORMS. AS A WOMAN, YOU HAVE NO AUTHORITY TO MAKE A LEGAL COMPLAINT. YOU'LL HAVE TO GET A MAN, ANY MAN, TO SIGN OFF THAT WHAT YOU CLAIM IS TRUE. IT'S THE LAW.
WHY? I OUTRANK MOST MEN. ALL FURIES DO.
MY WORD SHOULD BE ENOUGH.

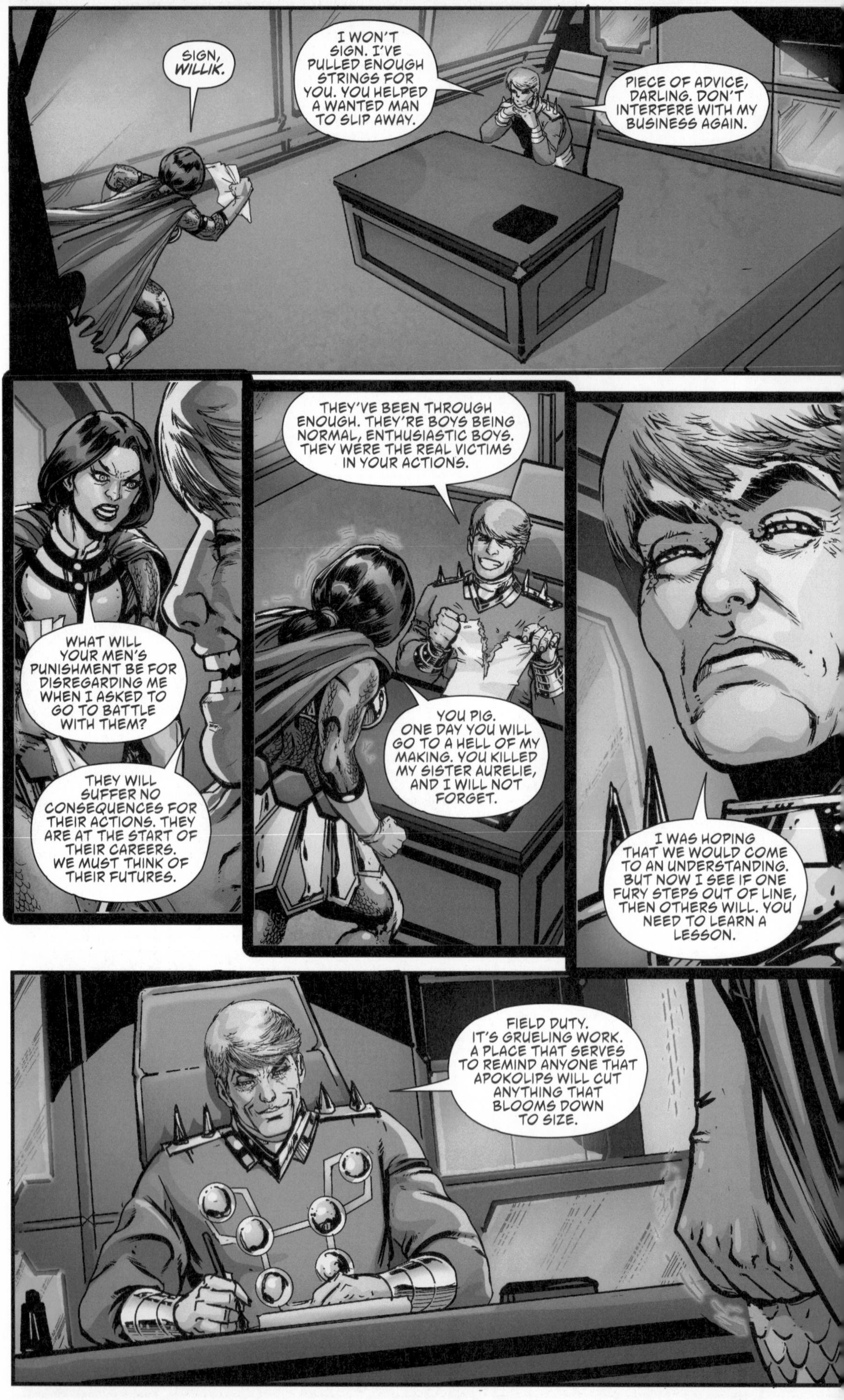
SIGN, WILLIK.
I WON'T SIGN. I'VE PULLED ENOUGH STRINGS FOR YOU. YOU HELPED A WANTED MAN TO SLIP AWAY.
PIECE OF ADVICE, DARLING. DON'T INTERFERE WITH MY BUSINESS AGAIN.
WHAT WILL YOUR MEN'S PUNISHMENT BE FOR DISREGARDING ME WHEN I ASKED TO GO TO BATTLE WITH THEM?
THEY WILL SUFFER NO CONSEQUENCES FOR THEIR ACTIONS. THEY ARE AT THE START OF THEIR CAREERS. WE MUST THINK OF THEIR FUTURES.
THEY'VE BEEN THROUGH ENOUGH. THEY'RE BOYS BEING NORMAL, ENTHUSIASTIC BOYS. THEY WERE THE REAL VICTIMS IN YOUR ACTIONS.
YOU PIG. ONE DAY YOU WILL GO TO A HELL OF MY MAKING. YOU KILLED MY SISTER AURELIE, AND I WILL NOT FORGET.
I WAS HOPING THAT WE WOULD COME TO AN UNDERSTANDING. BUT NOW I SEE IF ONE FURY STEPS OUT OF LINE, THEN OTHERS WILL. YOU NEED TO LEARN A LESSON.
FIELD DUTY. IT'S GRUELING WORK. A PLACE THAT SERVES TO REMIND ANYONE THAT APOKOLIPS WILL CUT ANYTHING THAT BLOOMS DOWN TO SIZE.

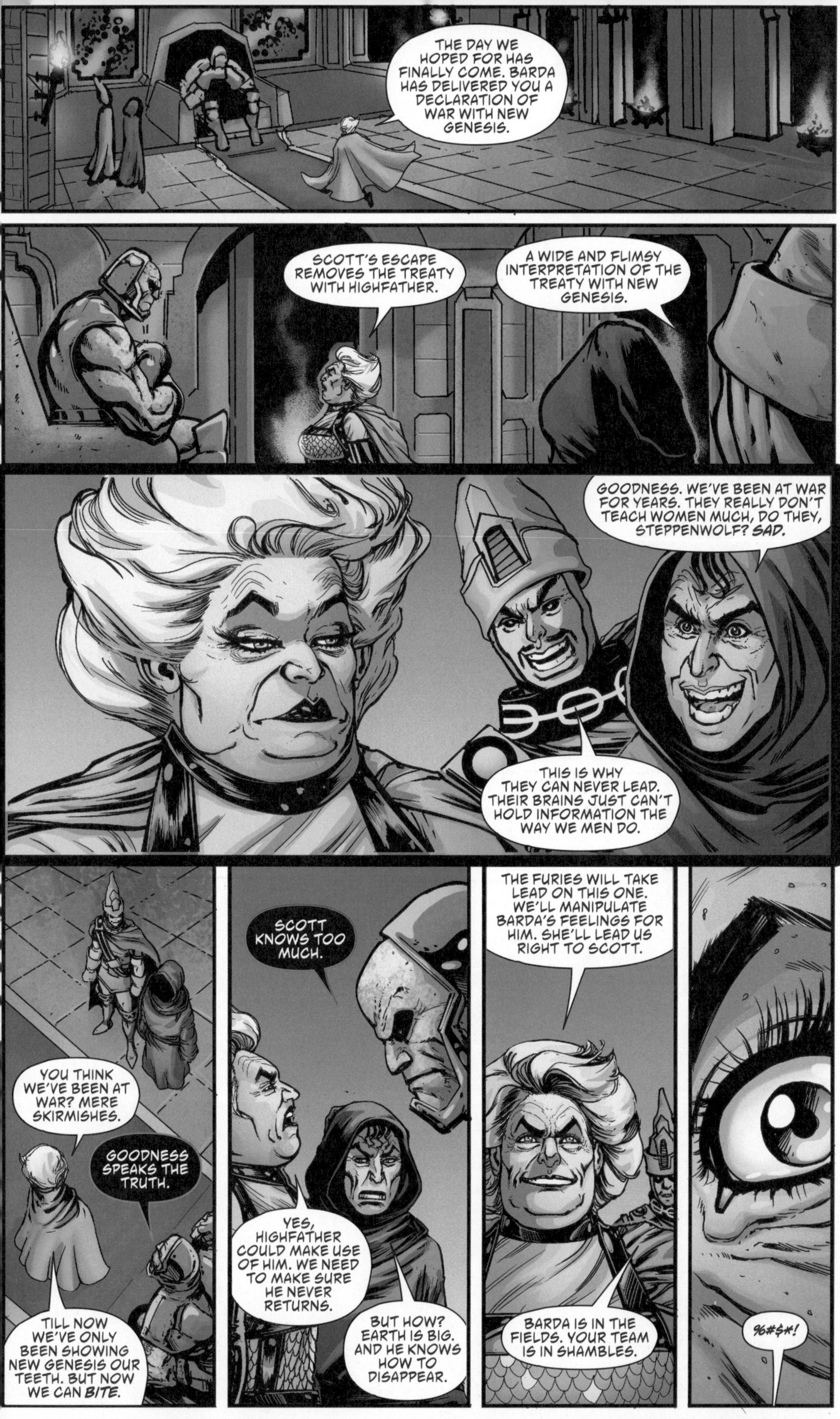
THE DAY WE HOPED FOR HAS FINALLY COME. BARDA HAS DELIVERED YOU A DECLARATION OF WAR WITH NEW GENESIS.
SCOTT'S ESCAPE REMOVES THE TREATY WITH HIGHFATHER.
A WIDE AND FLIMSY INTERPRETATION OF THE TREATY WITH NEW GENESIS.
GOODNESS. WE'VE BEEN AT WAR FOR YEARS. THEY REALLY DON'T TEACH WOMEN MUCH, DO THEY, STEPPENWOLF? SAD.
THIS IS WHY THEY CAN NEVER LEAD. THEIR BRAINS JUST CAN'T HOLD INFORMATION THE WAY WE MEN DO.
YOU THINK WE'VE BEEN AT WAR? MERE SKIRMISHES.
GOODNESS SPEAKS THE TRUTH.
TILL NOW WE'VE ONLY BEEN SHOWING NEW GENESIS OUR TEETH. BUT NOW WE CAN BITE.
SCOTT KNOWS TOO MUCH.
YES, HIGHFATHER COULD MAKE USE OF HIM. WE NEED TO MAKE SURE HE NEVER RETURNS.
BUT HOW? EARTH IS BIG. AND HE KNOWS HOW TO DISAPPEAR.
THE FURIES WILL TAKE LEAD ON THIS ONE. WE'LL MANIPULATE BARDA'S FEELINGS FOR HIM. SHE'LL LEAD US RIGHT TO SCOTT.
BARDA IS IN THE FIELDS. YOUR TEAM IS IN SHAMBLES.
%#$*!

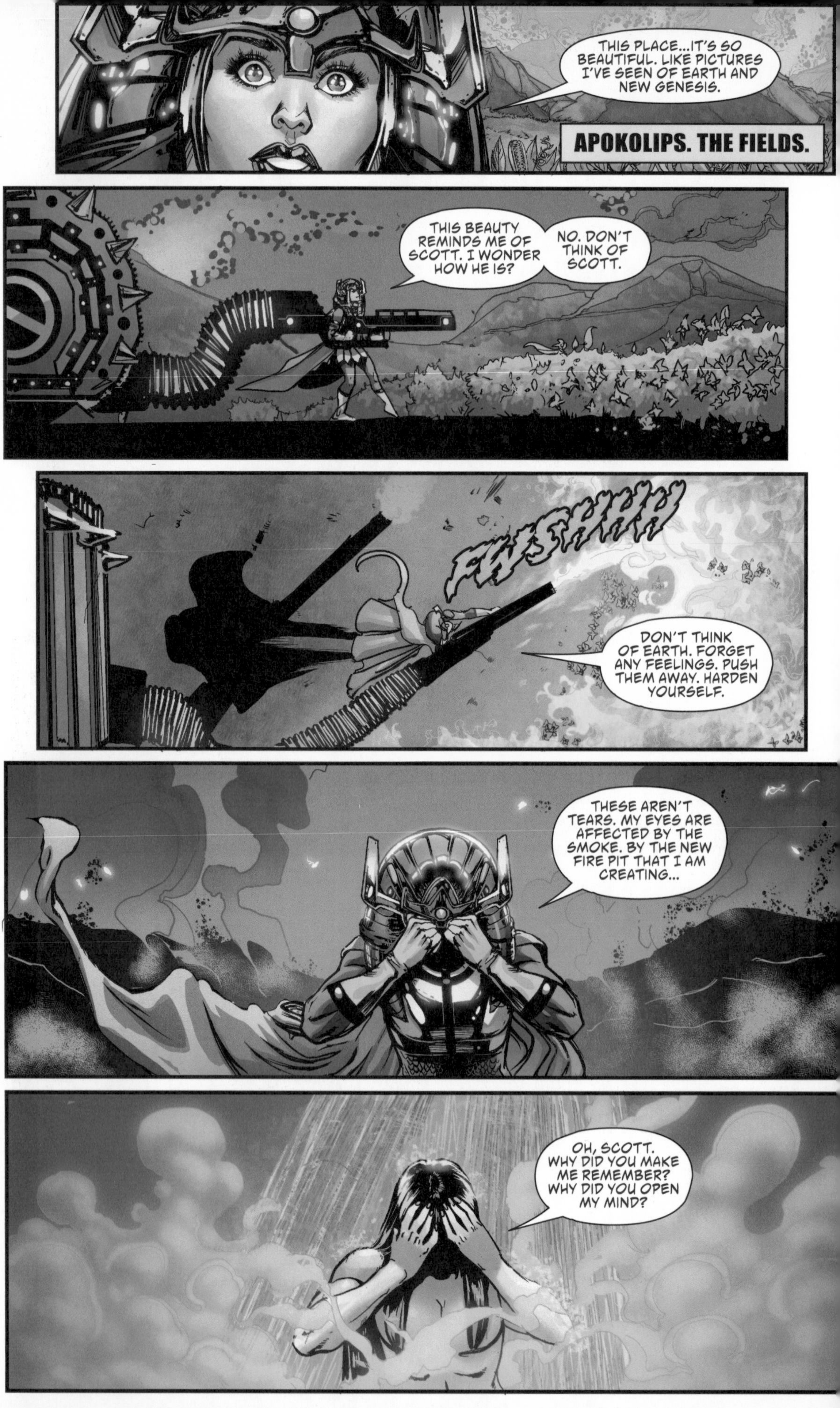
THIS PLACE...IT'S SO BEAUTIFUL. LIKE PICTURES I'VE SEEN OF EARTH AND NEW GENESIS.
APOKOLIPS. THE FIELDS.
THIS BEAUTY REMINDS ME OF SCOTT. I WONDER HOW HE IS?
NO. DON'T THINK OF SCOTT.
FWSHHH
DON'T THINK OF EARTH. FORGET ANY FEELINGS. PUSH THEM AWAY. HARDEN YOURSELF.
THESE AREN'T TEARS. MY EYES ARE AFFECTED BY THE SMOKE. BY THE NEW FIRE PIT THAT I AM CREATING...
OH, SCOTT. WHY DID YOU MAKE ME REMEMBER? WHY DID YOU OPEN MY MIND?

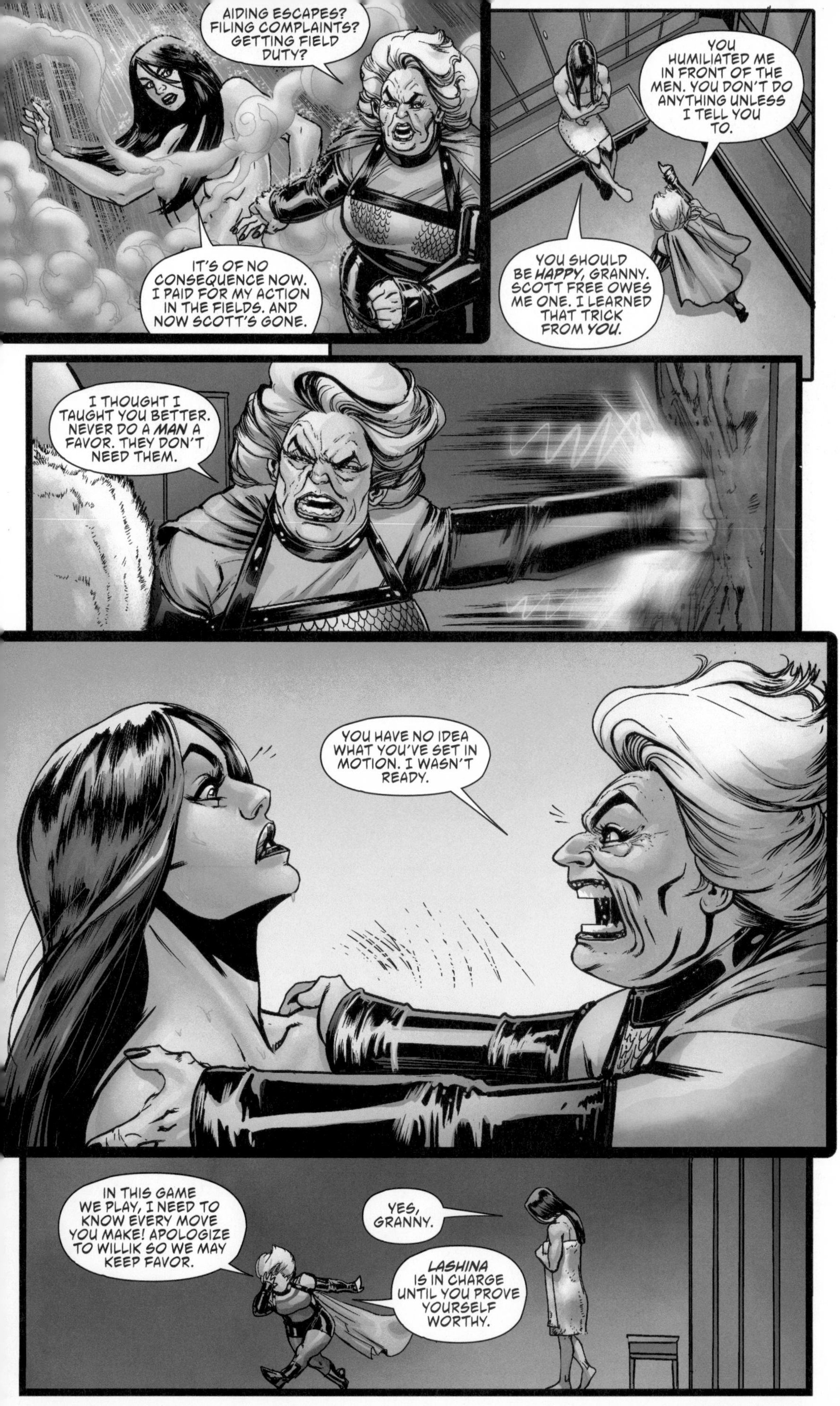
AIDING ESCAPES? FILING COMPLAINTS? GETTING FIELD DUTY?
IT'S OF NO CONSEQUENCE NOW. I PAID FOR MY ACTION IN THE FIELDS. AND NOW SCOTT'S GONE.
YOU HUMILIATED ME IN FRONT OF THE MEN. YOU DON'T DO ANYTHING UNLESS I TELL YOU TO.
YOU SHOULD BE *HAPPY*, GRANNY. SCOTT FREE OWES ME ONE. I LEARNED THAT TRICK FROM *YOU*.
I THOUGHT I TAUGHT YOU BETTER. NEVER DO A *MAN* A FAVOR. THEY DON'T NEED THEM.
YOU HAVE NO IDEA WHAT YOU'VE SET IN MOTION. I WASN'T READY.
IN THIS GAME WE PLAY, I NEED TO KNOW EVERY MOVE YOU MAKE! APOLOGIZE TO WILLIK SO WE MAY KEEP FAVOR.
YES, GRANNY.
LASHINA IS IN CHARGE UNTIL YOU PROVE YOURSELF WORTHY.

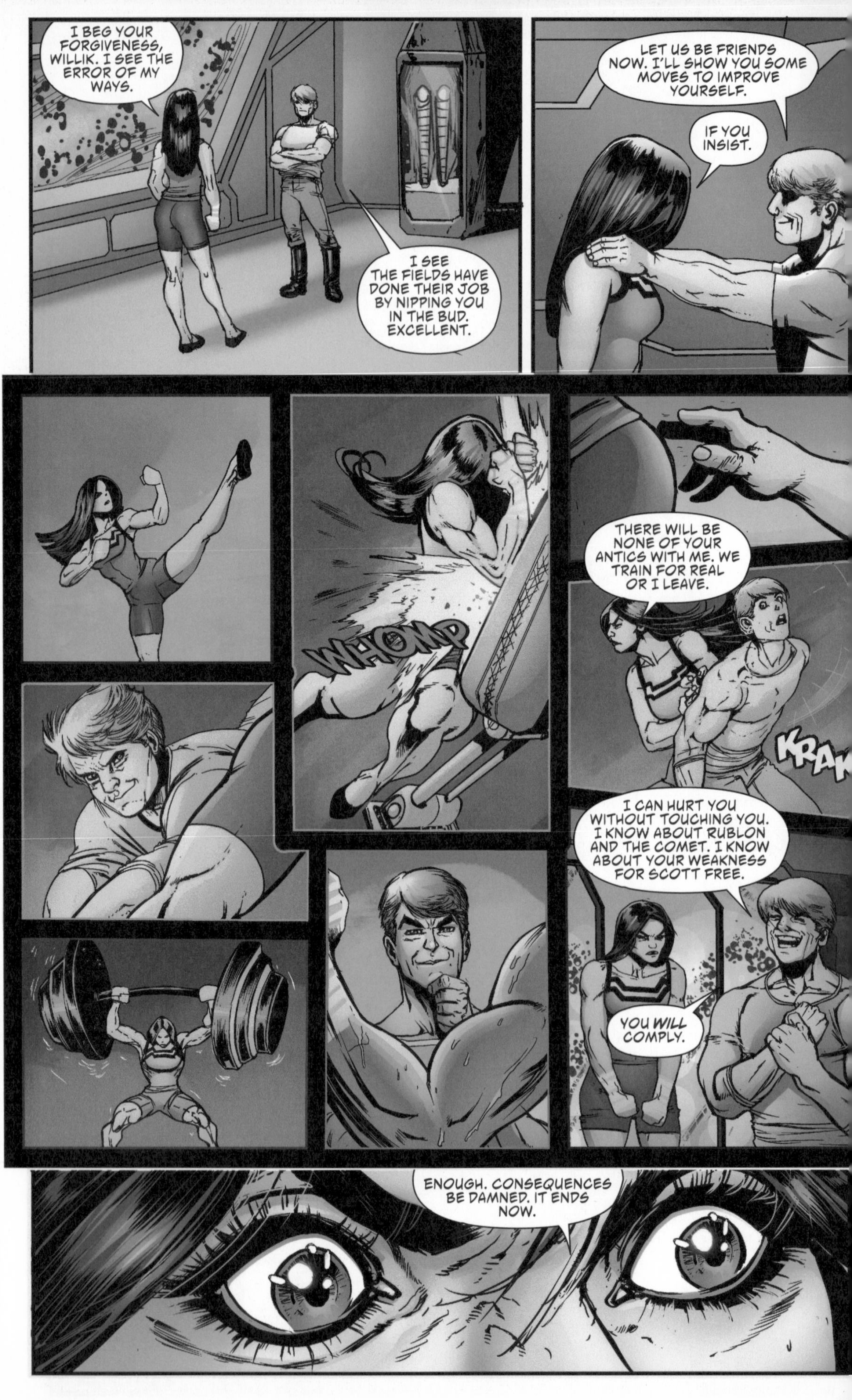
I BEG YOUR FORGIVENESS, WILLIK. I SEE THE ERROR OF MY WAYS.
I SEE THE FIELDS HAVE DONE THEIR JOB BY NIPPING YOU IN THE BUD. EXCELLENT.
LET US BE FRIENDS NOW. I'LL SHOW YOU SOME MOVES TO IMPROVE YOURSELF.
IF YOU INSIST.
WHOMP
THERE WILL BE NONE OF YOUR ANTICS WITH ME. WE TRAIN FOR REAL OR I LEAVE.
KRAK
I CAN HURT YOU WITHOUT TOUCHING YOU. I KNOW ABOUT RUBLON AND THE COMET. I KNOW ABOUT YOUR WEAKNESS FOR SCOTT FREE.
YOU WILL COMPLY.
ENOUGH. CONSEQUENCES BE DAMNED. IT ENDS NOW.

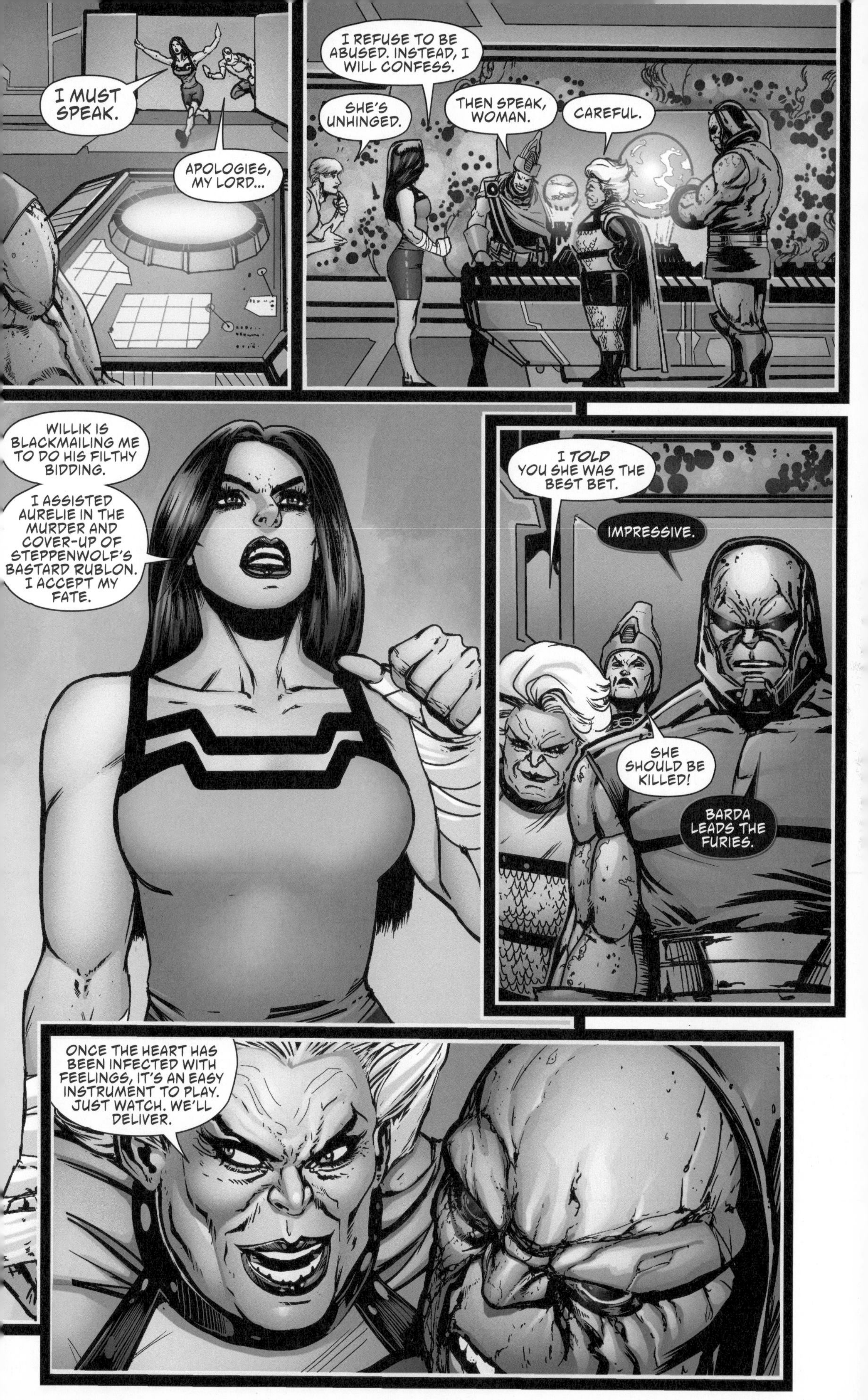
I MUST SPEAK.
APOLOGIES, MY LORD...
I REFUSE TO BE ABUSED. INSTEAD, I WILL CONFESS.
SHE'S UNHINGED.
THEN SPEAK, WOMAN.
CAREFUL.
WILLIK IS BLACKMAILING ME TO DO HIS FILTHY BIDDING.
I ASSISTED AURELIE IN THE MURDER AND COVER-UP OF STEPPENWOLF'S BASTARD RUBLON. I ACCEPT MY FATE.
I TOLD YOU SHE WAS THE BEST BET.
IMPRESSIVE.
SHE SHOULD BE KILLED!
BARDA LEADS THE FURIES.
ONCE THE HEART HAS BEEN INFECTED WITH FEELINGS, IT'S AN EASY INSTRUMENT TO PLAY. JUST WATCH. WE'LL DELIVER.

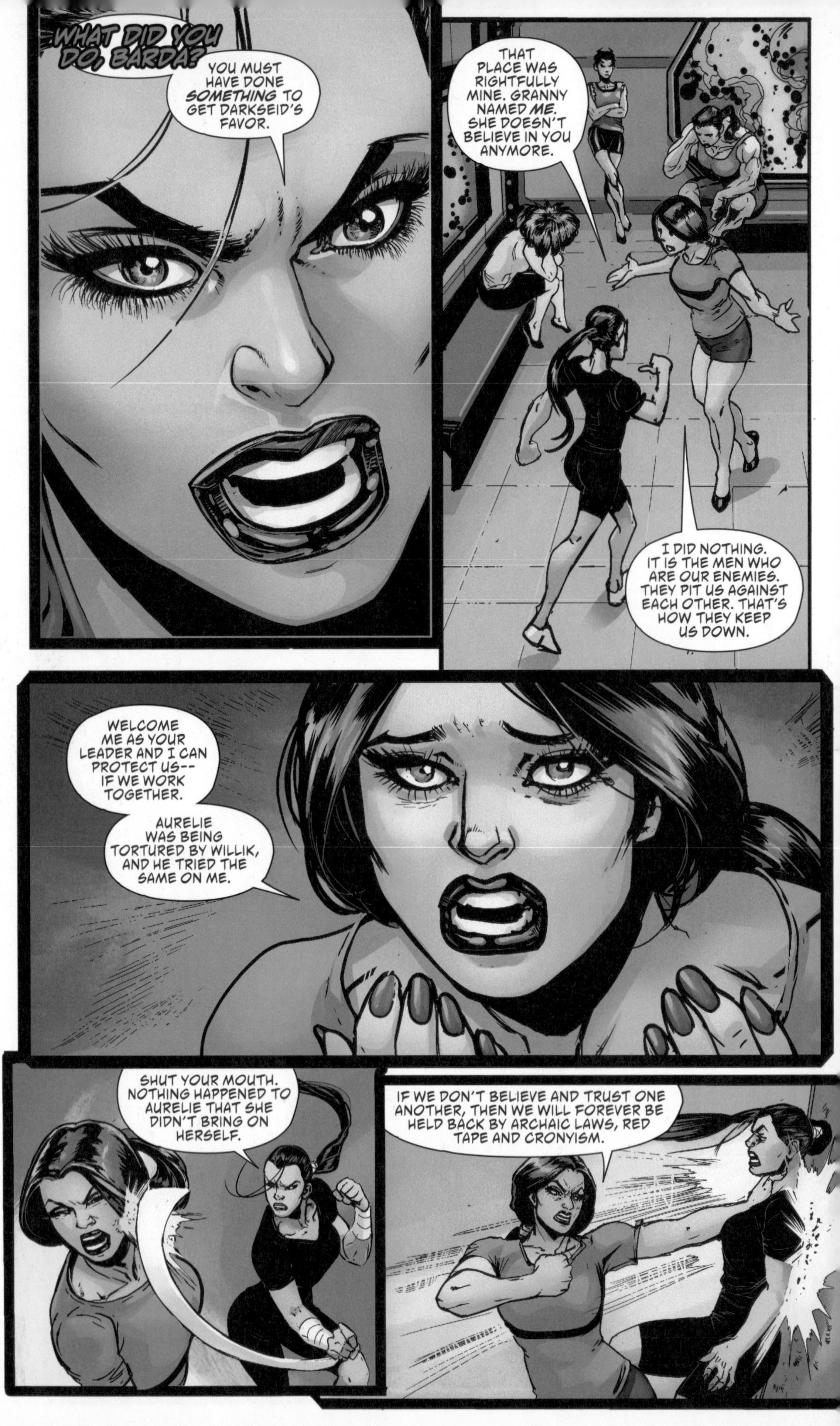
WHAT DID YOU DO, BARDA?
YOU MUST HAVE DONE SOMETHING TO GET DARKSEID'S FAVOR.
THAT PLACE WAS RIGHTFULLY MINE. GRANNY NAMED ME. SHE DOESN'T BELIEVE IN YOU ANYMORE.
I DID NOTHING. IT IS THE MEN WHO ARE OUR ENEMIES. THEY PIT US AGAINST EACH OTHER. THAT'S HOW THEY KEEP US DOWN.
WELCOME ME AS YOUR LEADER AND I CAN PROTECT US-- IF WE WORK TOGETHER.
AURELIE WAS BEING TORTURED BY WILLIK, AND HE TRIED THE SAME ON ME.
SHUT YOUR MOUTH. NOTHING HAPPENED TO AURELIE THAT SHE DIDN'T BRING ON HERSELF.
IF WE DON'T BELIEVE AND TRUST ONE ANOTHER, THEN WE WILL FOREVER BE HELD BACK BY ARCHAIC LAWS, RED TAPE AND CRONYISM.

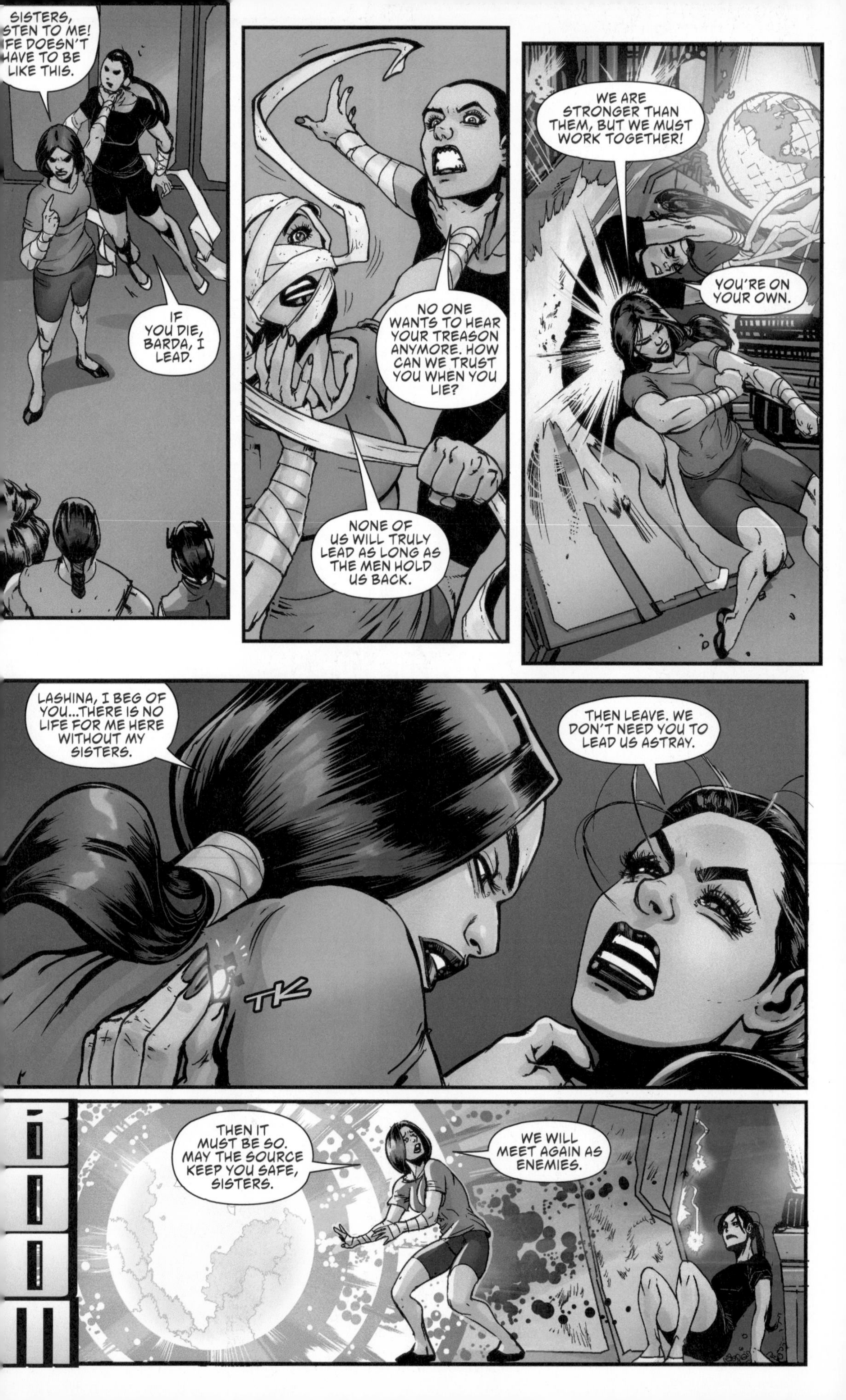
SISTERS, STEN TO ME! IFE DOESN'T HAVE TO BE LIKE THIS.
IF YOU DIE, BARDA, I LEAD.
NO ONE WANTS TO HEAR YOUR TREASON ANYMORE. HOW CAN WE TRUST YOU WHEN YOU LIE?
NONE OF US WILL TRULY LEAD AS LONG AS THE MEN HOLD US BACK.
WE ARE STRONGER THAN THEM, BUT WE MUST WORK TOGETHER!
YOU'RE ON YOUR OWN.
LASHINA, I BEG OF YOU...THERE IS NO LIFE FOR ME HERE WITHOUT MY SISTERS.
THEN LEAVE. WE DON'T NEED YOU TO LEAD US ASTRAY.
TK
BOOM
THEN IT MUST BE SO. MAY THE SOURCE KEEP YOU SAFE, SISTERS.
WE WILL MEET AGAIN AS ENEMIES.

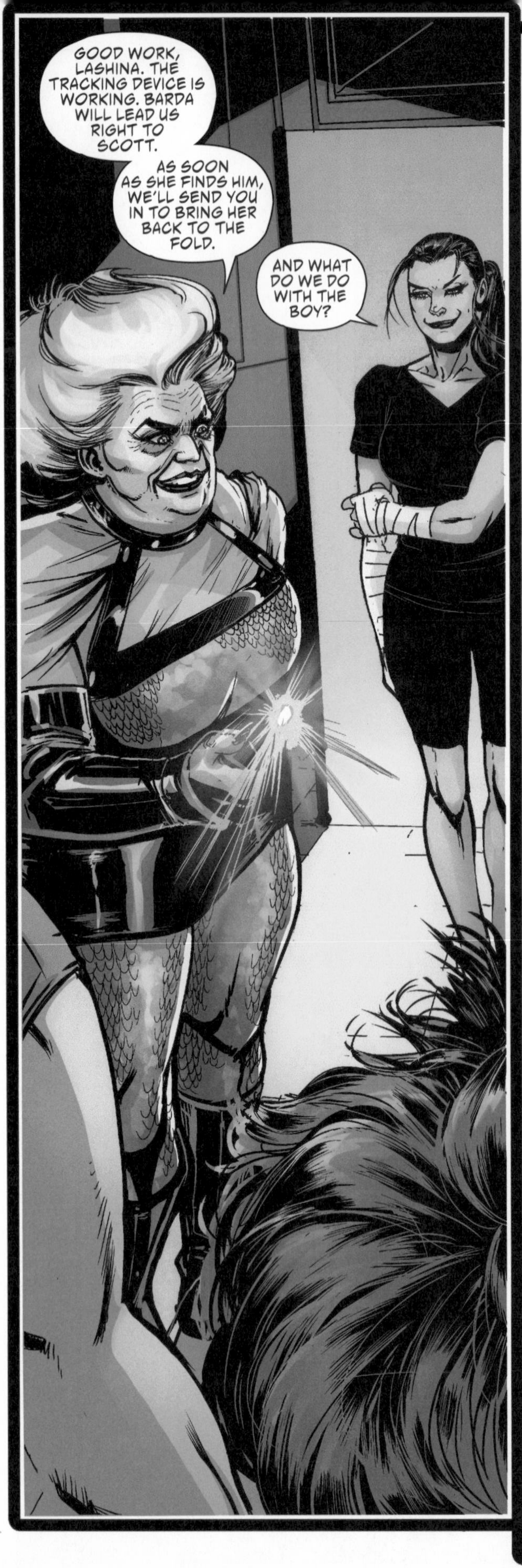
GOOD WORK, LASHINA. THE TRACKING DEVICE IS WORKING. BARDA WILL LEAD US RIGHT TO SCOTT.
AS SOON AS SHE FINDS HIM, WE'LL SEND YOU IN TO BRING HER BACK TO THE FOLD.
AND WHAT DO WE DO WITH THE BOY?
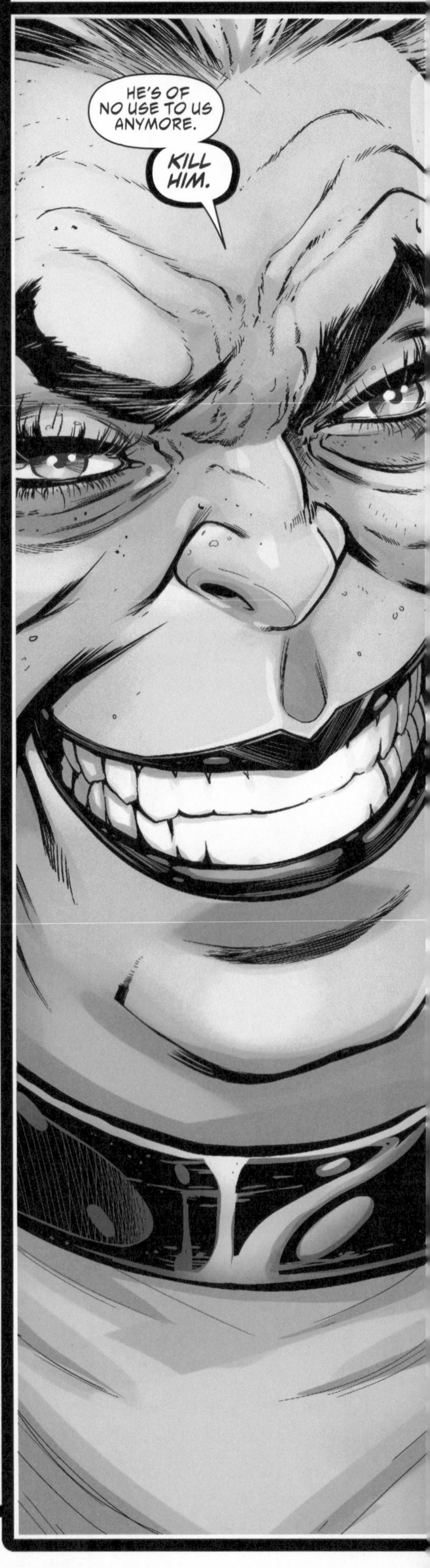
HE'S OF NO USE TO US ANYMORE.
KILL HIM.

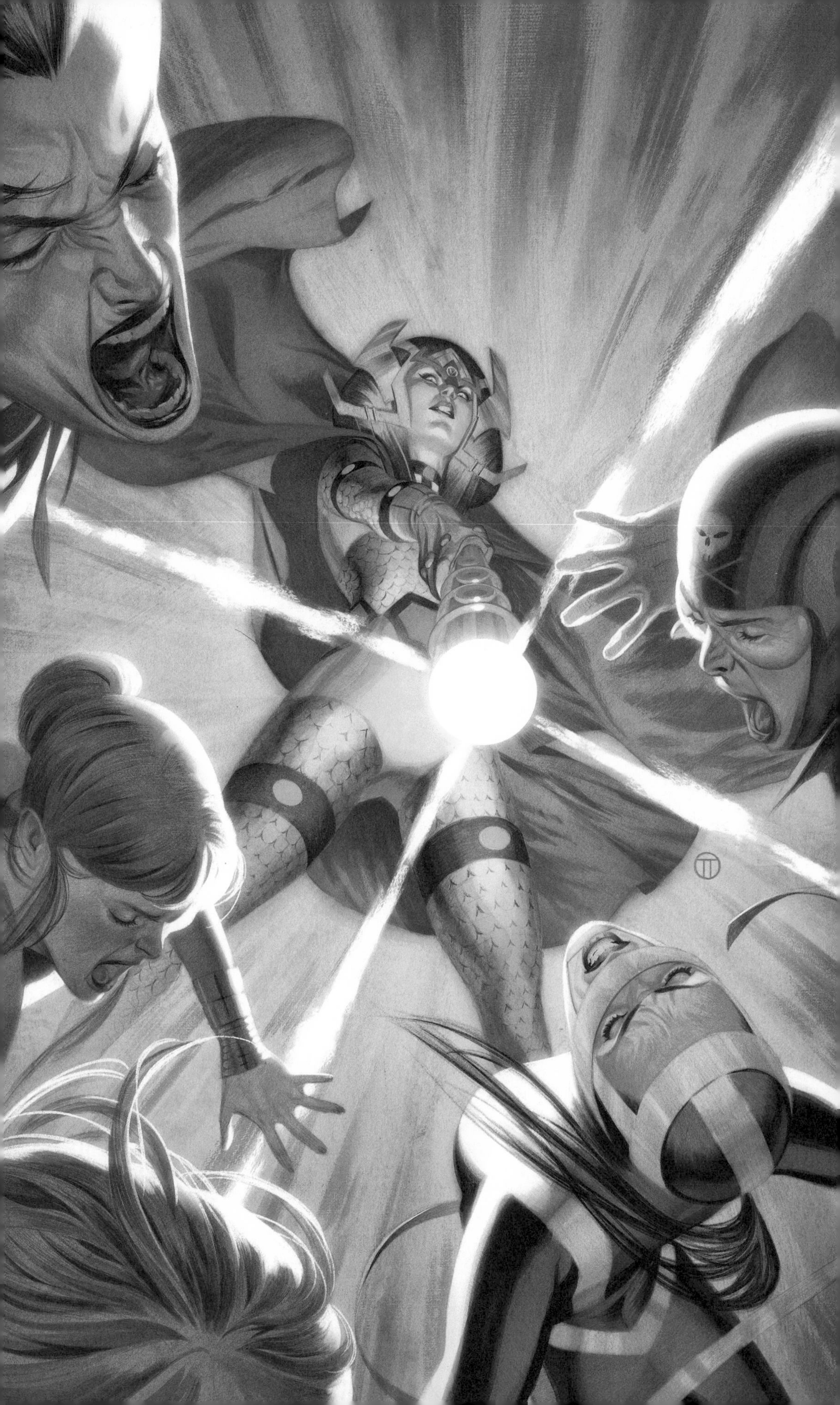

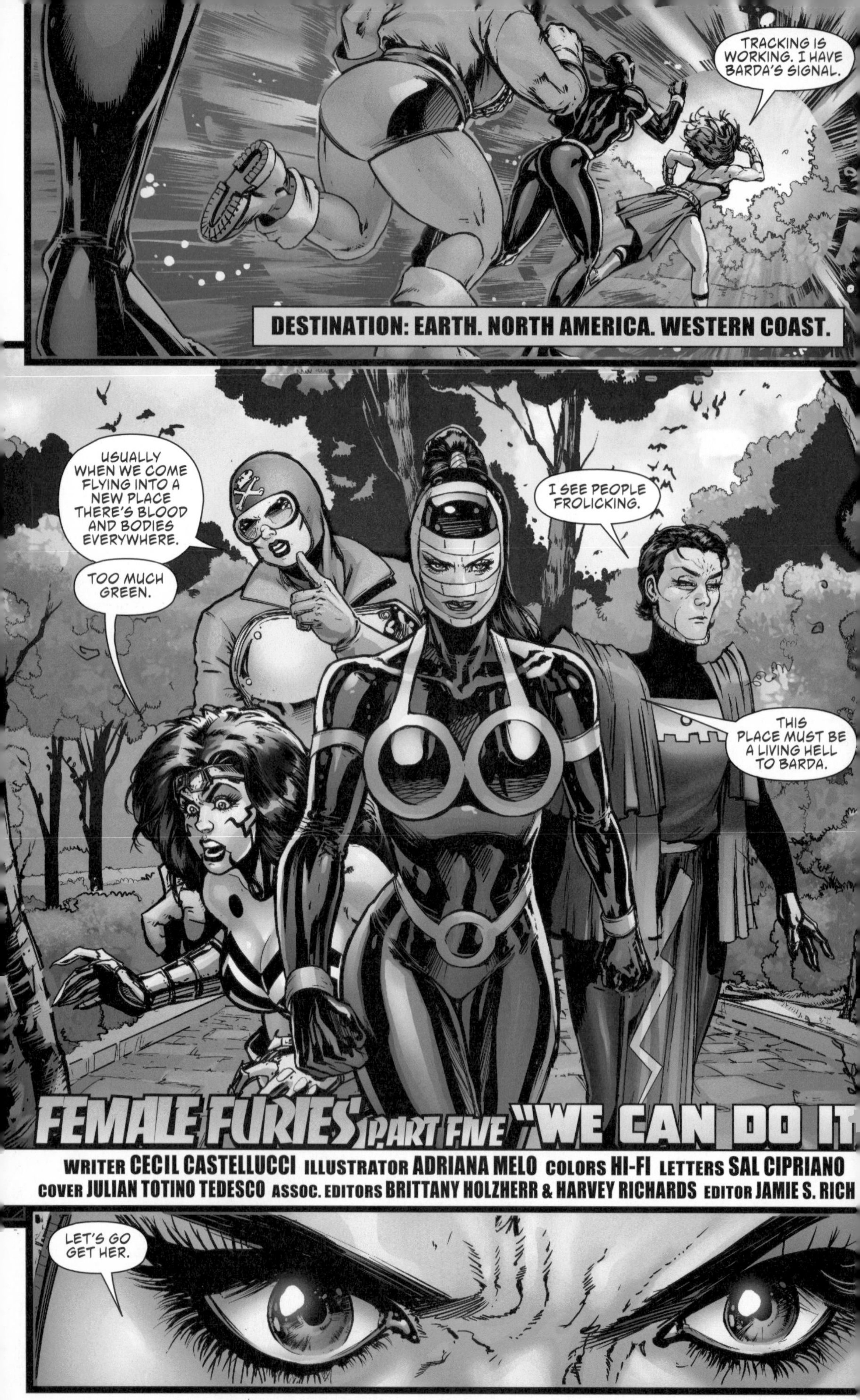
TRACKING IS WORKING. I HAVE BARDA'S SIGNAL.
DESTINATION: EARTH. NORTH AMERICA. WESTERN COAST.
USUALLY WHEN WE COME FLYING INTO A NEW PLACE THERE'S BLOOD AND BODIES EVERYWHERE.
TOO MUCH GREEN.
I SEE PEOPLE FROLICKING.
THIS PLACE MUST BE A LIVING HELL TO BARDA.
FEMALE FURIES PART FIVE "WE CAN DO IT
WRITER CECIL CASTELLUCCI ILLUSTRATOR ADRIANA MELO COLORS HI-FI LETTERS SAL CIPRIANO
COVER JULIAN TOTINO TEDESCO ASSOC. EDITORS BRITTANY HOLZHERR & HARVEY RICHARDS EDITOR JAMIE S. RICH
LET'S GO GET HER.

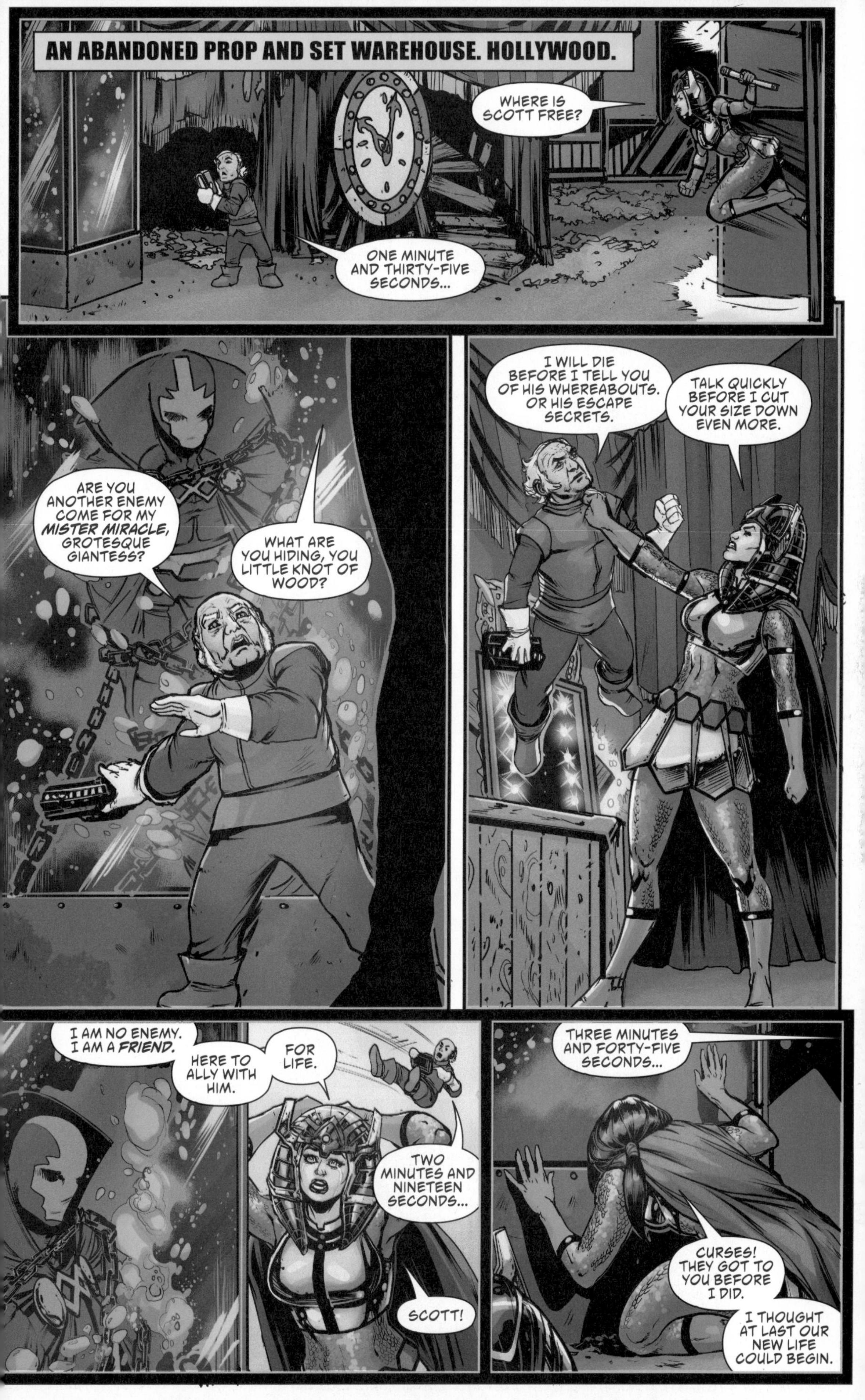
AN ABANDONED PROP AND SET WAREHOUSE. HOLLYWOOD.
WHERE IS SCOTT FREE?
ONE MINUTE AND THIRTY-FIVE SECONDS...
ARE YOU ANOTHER ENEMY COME FOR MY MISTER MIRACLE, GROTESQUE GIANTESS?
WHAT ARE YOU HIDING, YOU LITTLE KNOT OF WOOD?
I WILL DIE BEFORE I TELL YOU OF HIS WHEREABOUTS. OR HIS ESCAPE SECRETS.
TALK QUICKLY BEFORE I CUT YOUR SIZE DOWN EVEN MORE.
I AM NO ENEMY. I AM A FRIEND.
HERE TO ALLY WITH HIM.
FOR LIFE.
TWO MINUTES AND NINETEEN SECONDS...
SCOTT!
THREE MINUTES AND FORTY-FIVE SECONDS...
CURSES! THEY GOT TO YOU BEFORE I DID.
I THOUGHT AT LAST OUR NEW LIFE COULD BEGIN.

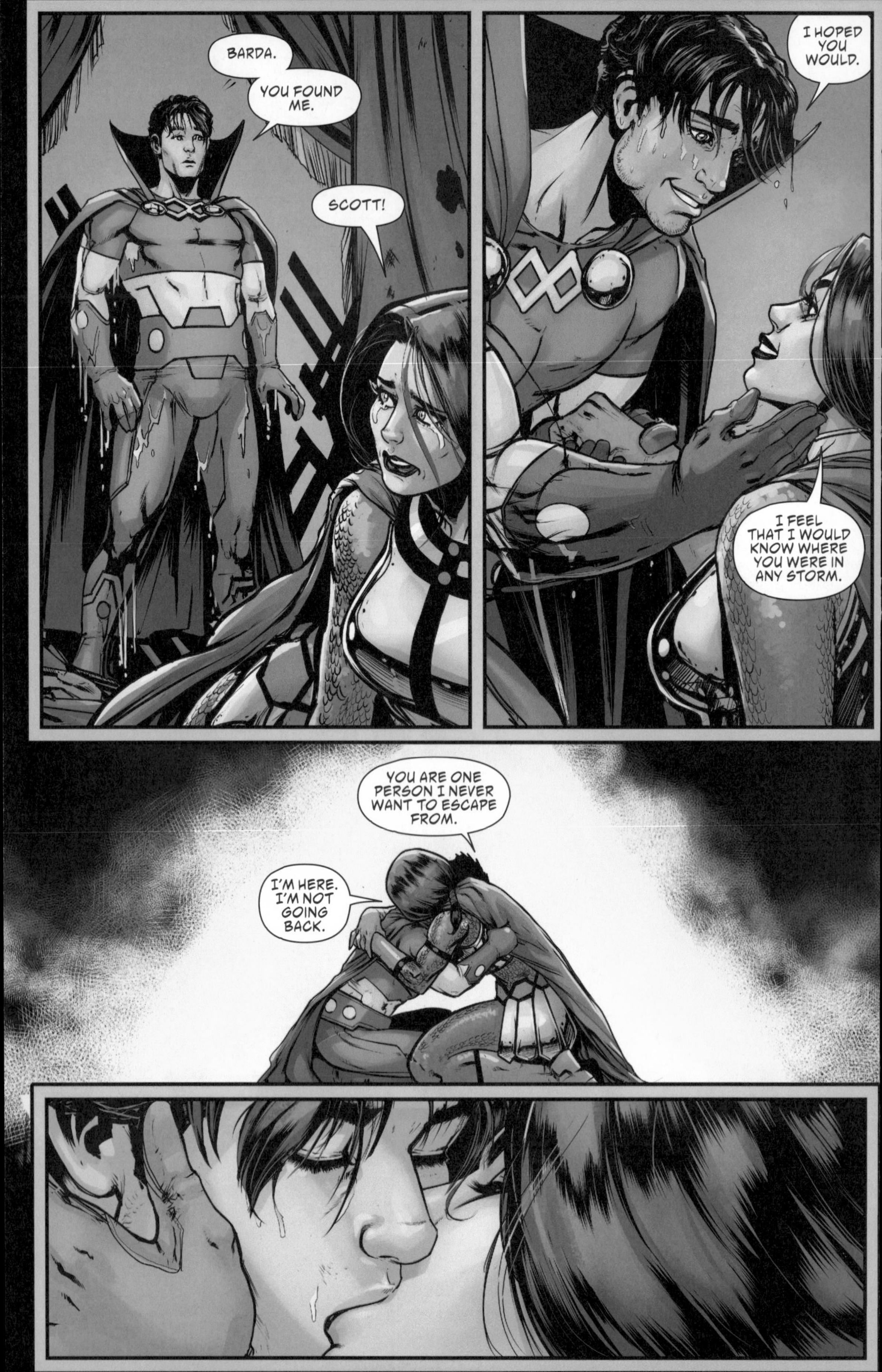
BARDA.
YOU FOUND ME.
SCOTT!
I HOPED YOU WOULD.
I FEEL THAT I WOULD KNOW WHERE YOU WERE IN ANY STORM.
YOU ARE ONE PERSON I NEVER WANT TO ESCAPE FROM.
I'M HERE. I'M NOT GOING BACK.

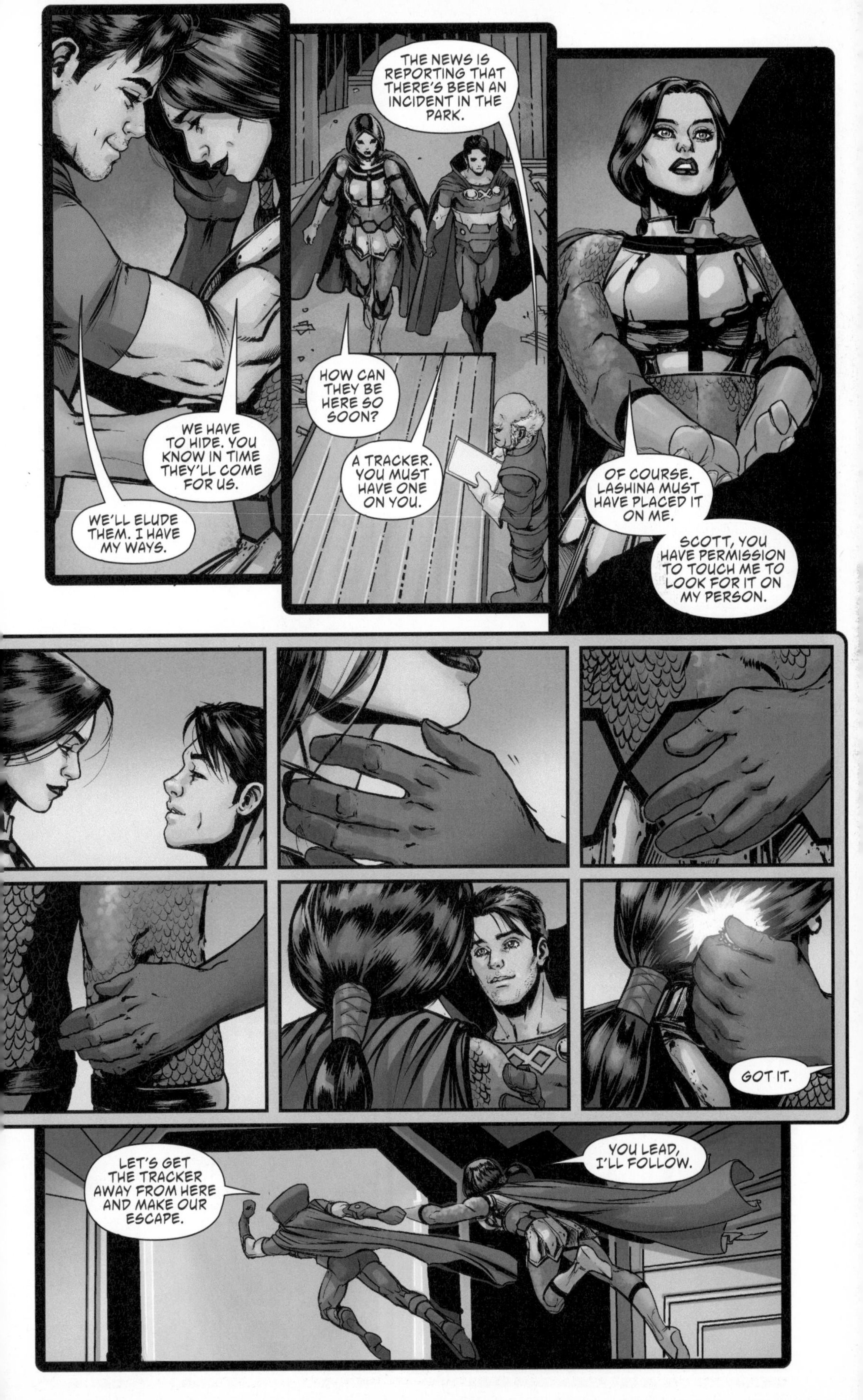

WE HAVE TO HIDE. YOU KNOW IN TIME THEY'LL COME FOR US.
WE'LL ELUDE THEM. I HAVE MY WAYS.
THE NEWS IS REPORTING THAT THERE'S BEEN AN INCIDENT IN THE PARK.
HOW CAN THEY BE HERE SO SOON?
A TRACKER. YOU MUST HAVE ONE ON YOU.
OF COURSE. LASHINA MUST HAVE PLACED IT ON ME.
SCOTT, YOU HAVE PERMISSION TO TOUCH ME TO LOOK FOR IT ON MY PERSON.
GOT IT.
LET'S GET THE TRACKER AWAY FROM HERE AND MAKE OUR ESCAPE.
YOU LEAD, I'LL FOLLOW.

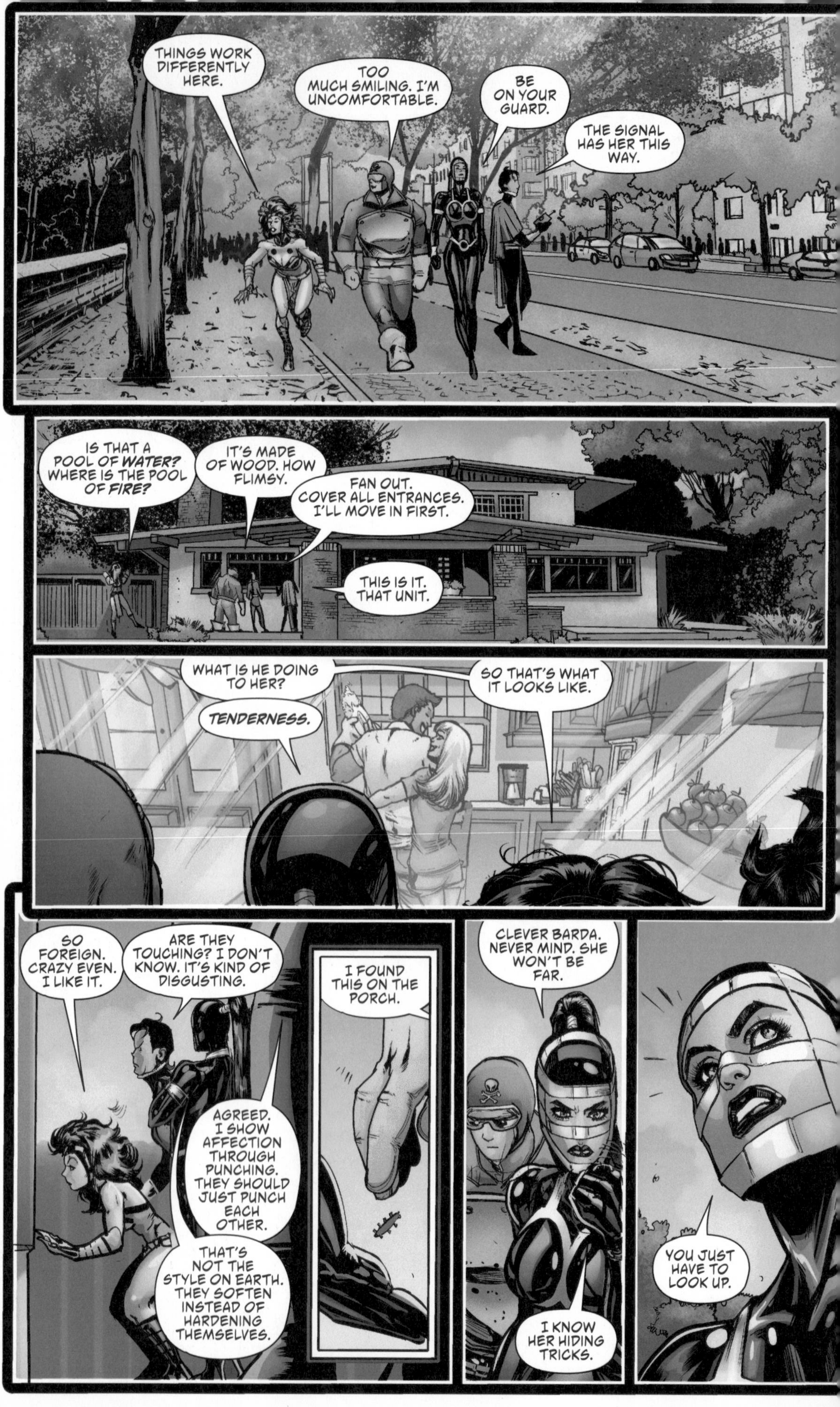
THINGS WORK DIFFERENTLY HERE.
TOO MUCH SMILING. I'M UNCOMFORTABLE.
BE ON YOUR GUARD.
THE SIGNAL HAS HER THIS WAY.
IS THAT A POOL OF WATER? WHERE IS THE POOL OF FIRE?
IT'S MADE OF WOOD. HOW FLIMSY.
FAN OUT. COVER ALL ENTRANCES. I'LL MOVE IN FIRST.
THIS IS IT. THAT UNIT.
WHAT IS HE DOING TO HER?
TENDERNESS.
SO THAT'S WHAT IT LOOKS LIKE.
SO FOREIGN. CRAZY EVEN. I LIKE IT.
ARE THEY TOUCHING? I DON'T KNOW. IT'S KIND OF DISGUSTING.
AGREED. I SHOW AFFECTION THROUGH PUNCHING. THEY SHOULD JUST PUNCH EACH OTHER.
THAT'S NOT THE STYLE ON EARTH. THEY SOFTEN INSTEAD OF HARDENING THEMSELVES.
I FOUND THIS ON THE PORCH.
CLEVER BARDA. NEVER MIND. SHE WON'T BE FAR.
I KNOW HER HIDING TRICKS.
YOU JUST HAVE TO LOOK UP.

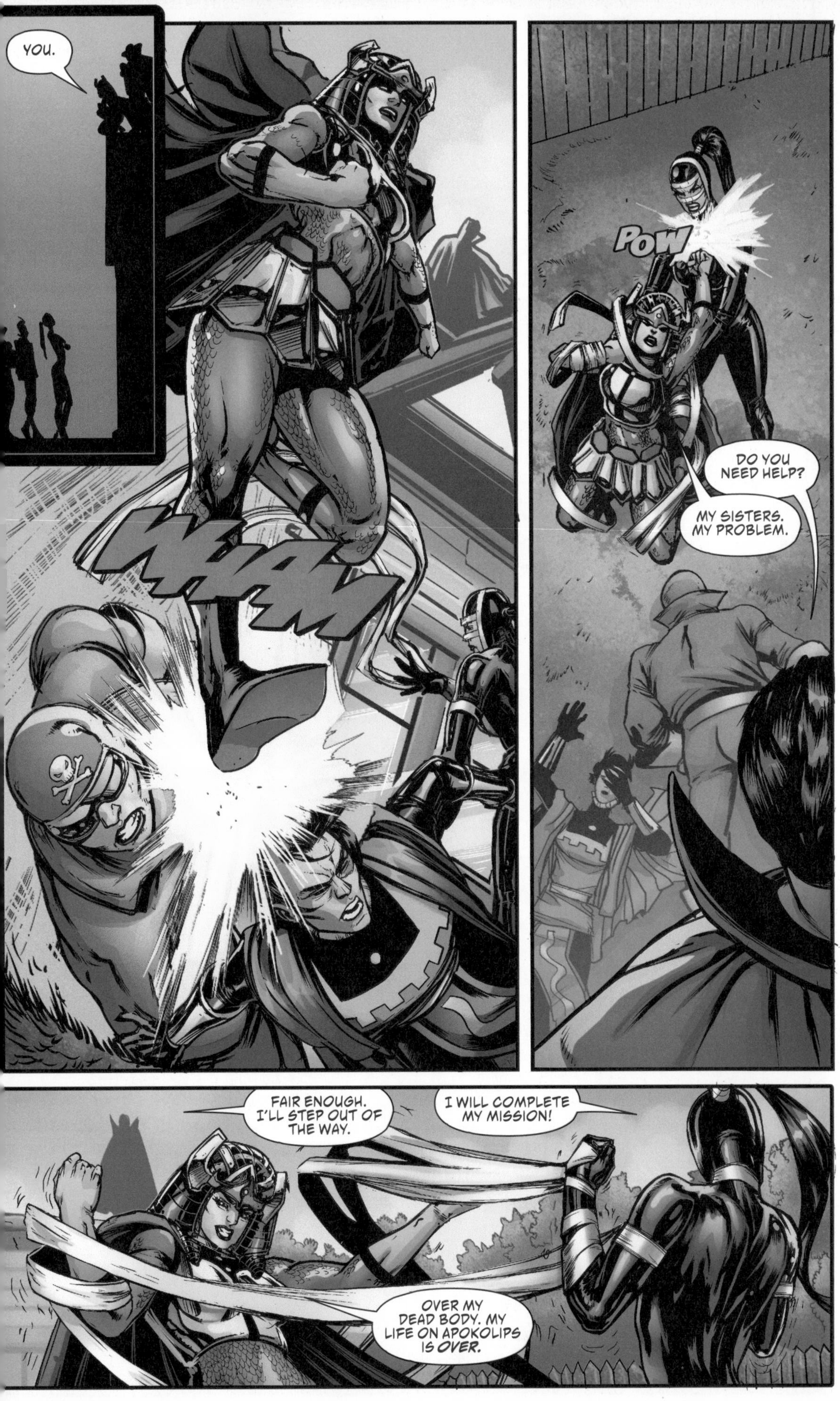

YOU.
WHAM
POW
DO YOU NEED HELP?
MY SISTERS. MY PROBLEM.
FAIR ENOUGH. I'LL STEP OUT OF THE WAY.
I WILL COMPLETE MY MISSION!
OVER MY DEAD BODY. MY LIFE ON APOKOLIPS IS *OVER*.

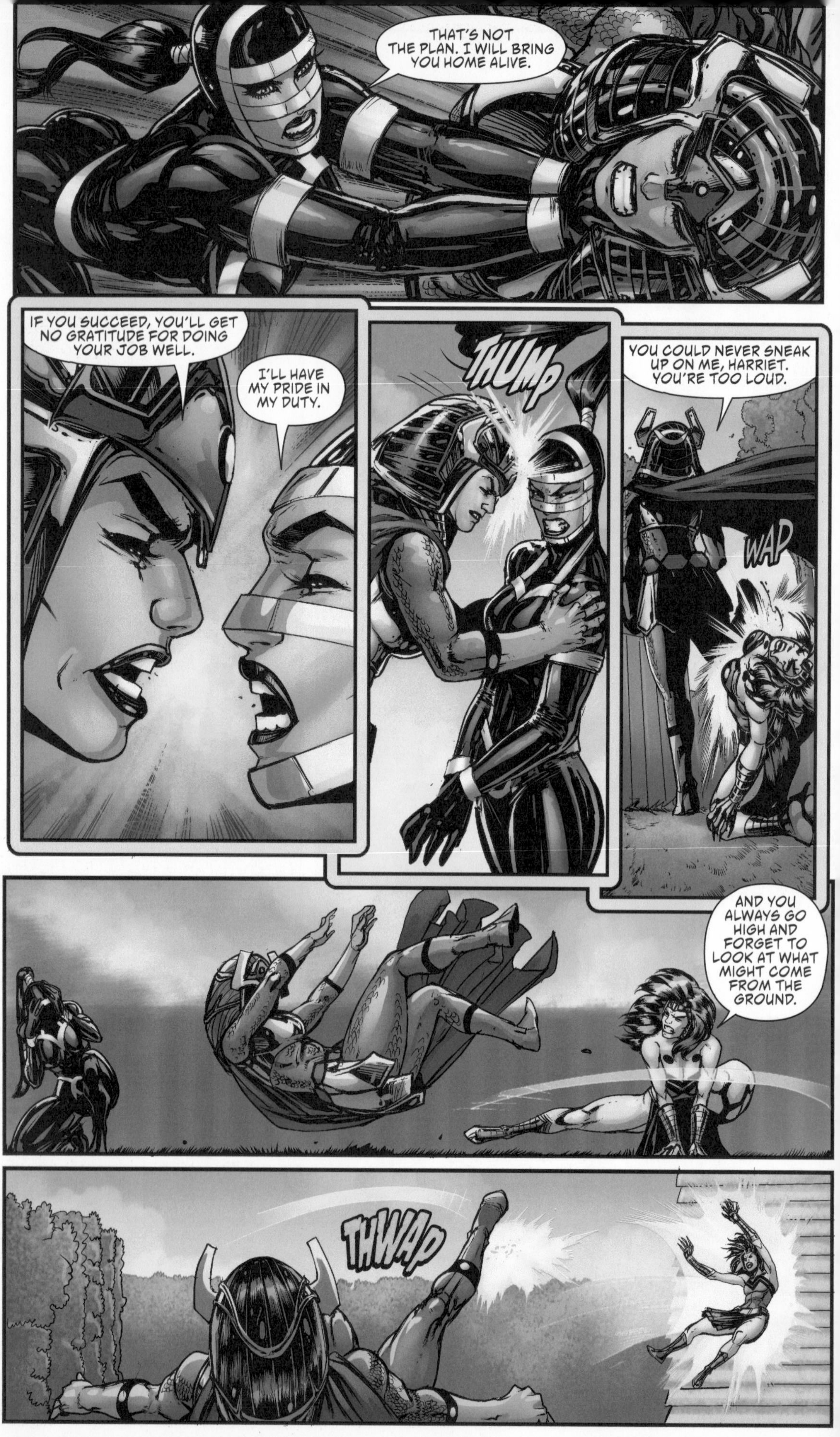
THAT'S NOT THE PLAN. I WILL BRING YOU HOME ALIVE.
IF YOU SUCCEED, YOU'LL GET NO GRATITUDE FOR DOING YOUR JOB WELL.
I'LL HAVE MY PRIDE IN MY DUTY.
THUMP
YOU COULD NEVER SNEAK UP ON ME, HARRIET. YOU'RE TOO LOUD.
WAP
AND YOU ALWAYS GO HIGH AND FORGET TO LOOK AT WHAT MIGHT COME FROM THE GROUND.
THWAP

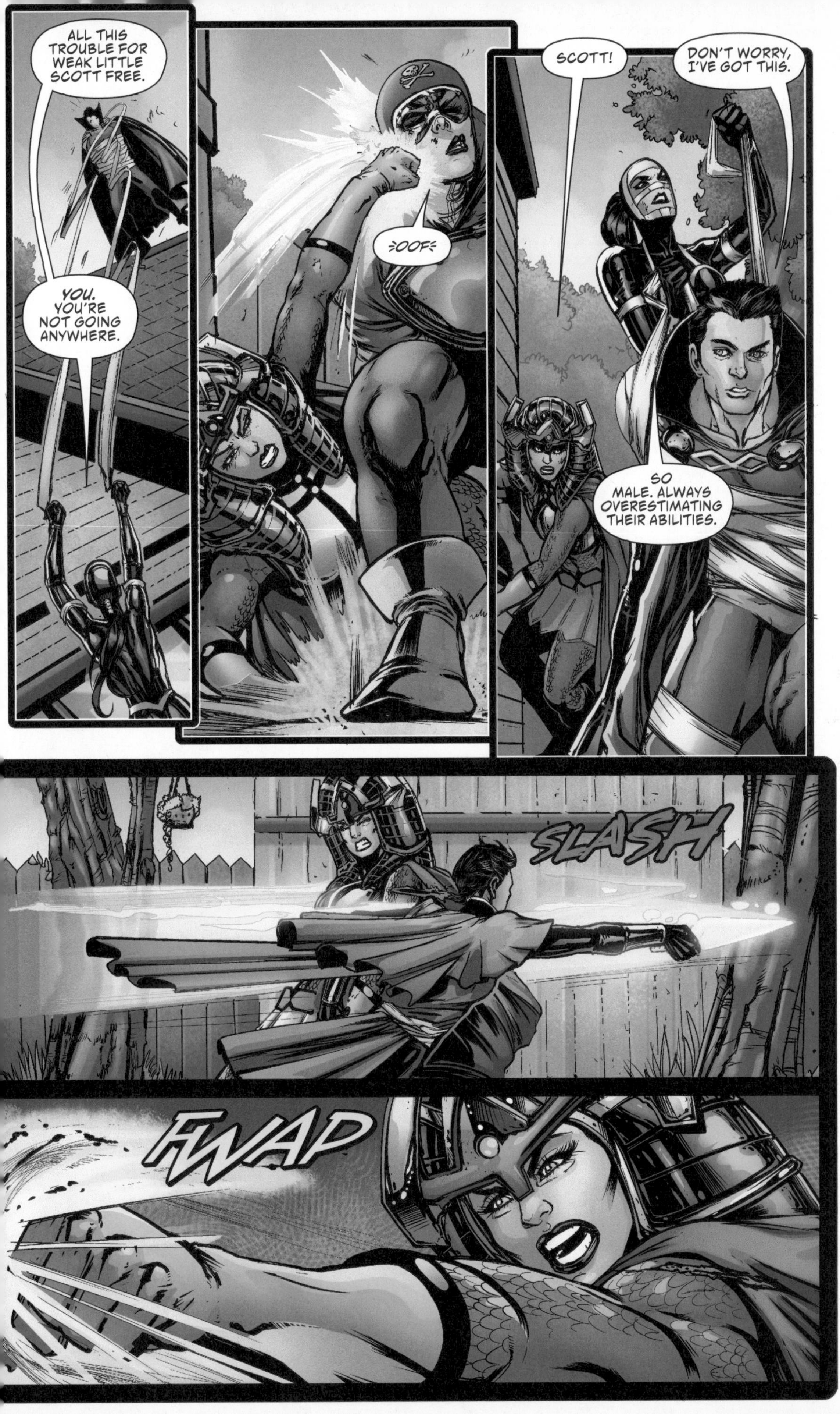
ALL THIS TROUBLE FOR WEAK LITTLE SCOTT FREE.
YOU. YOU'RE NOT GOING ANYWHERE.
OOF
SCOTT!
DON'T WORRY, I'VE GOT THIS.
SO MALE. ALWAYS OVERESTIMATING THEIR ABILITIES.
SLASH
FWAP

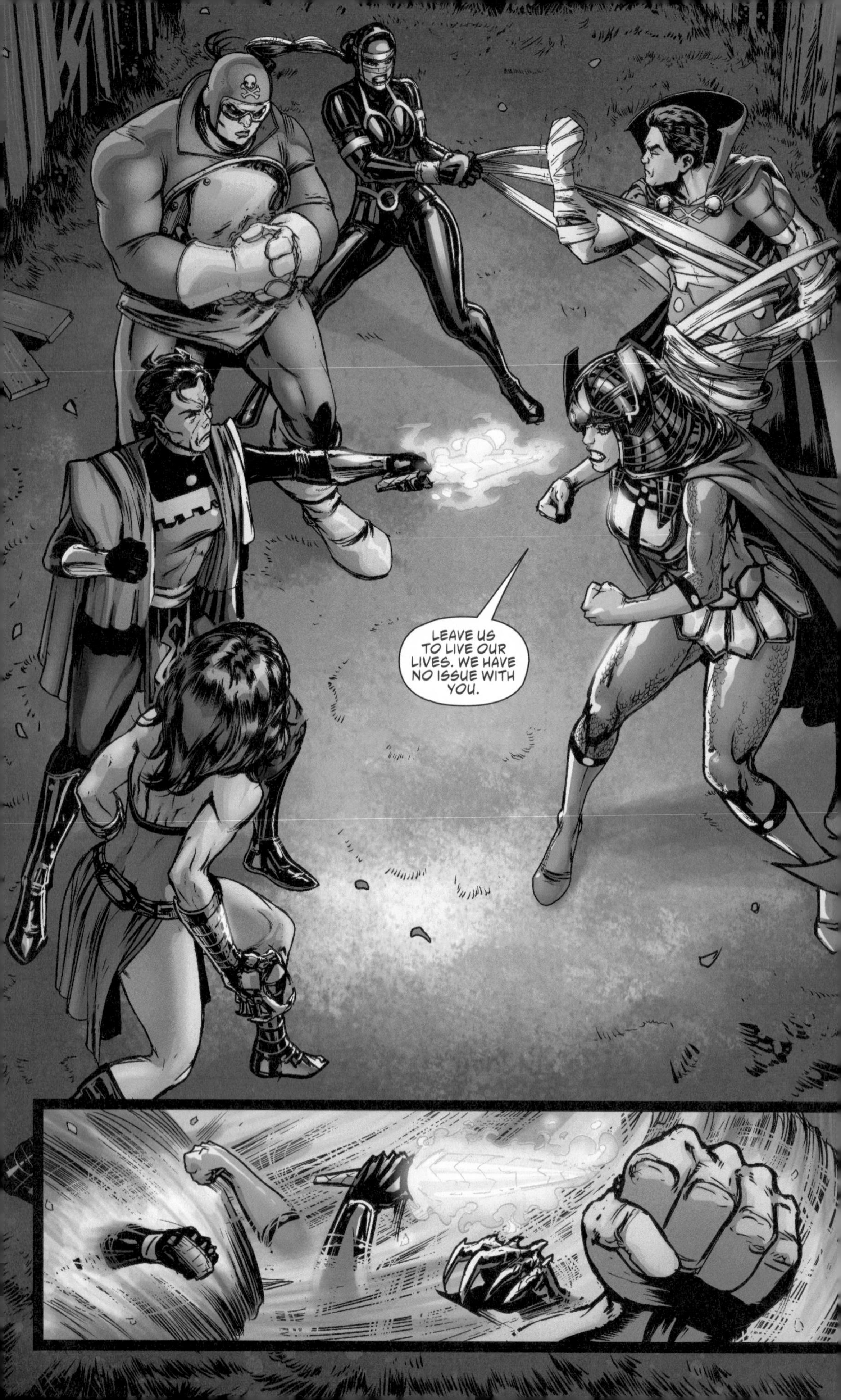
LEAVE US TO LIVE OUR LIVES. WE HAVE NO ISSUE WITH YOU.

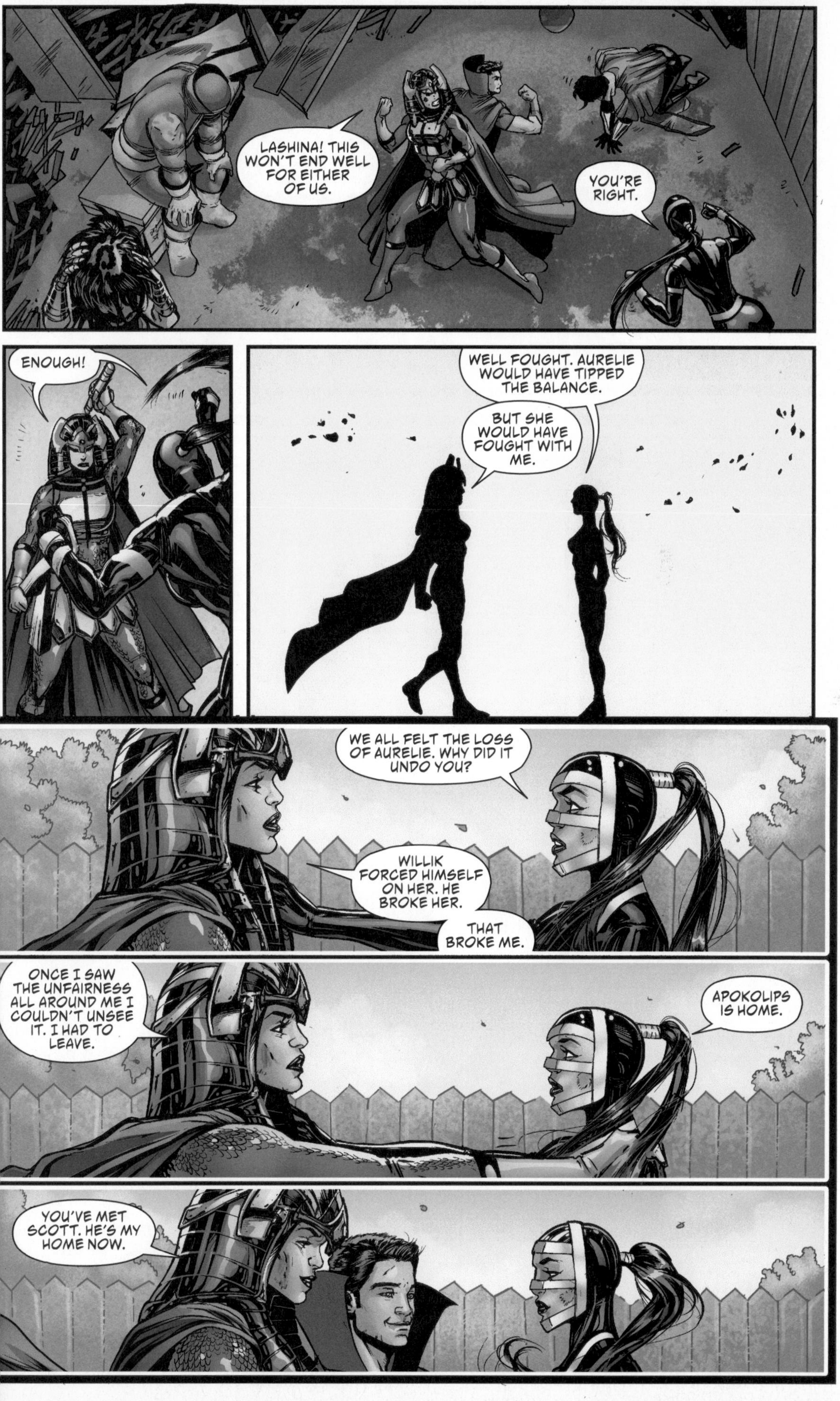
LASHINA! THIS WON'T END WELL FOR EITHER OF US.
YOU'RE RIGHT.
ENOUGH!
WELL FOUGHT. AURELIE WOULD HAVE TIPPED THE BALANCE.
BUT SHE WOULD HAVE FOUGHT WITH ME.
WE ALL FELT THE LOSS OF AURELIE. WHY DID IT UNDO YOU?
WILLIK FORCED HIMSELF ON HER. HE BROKE HER.
THAT BROKE ME.
ONCE I SAW THE UNFAIRNESS ALL AROUND ME I COULDN'T UNSEE IT. I HAD TO LEAVE.
APOKOLIPS IS HOME.
YOU'VE MET SCOTT. HE'S MY HOME NOW.

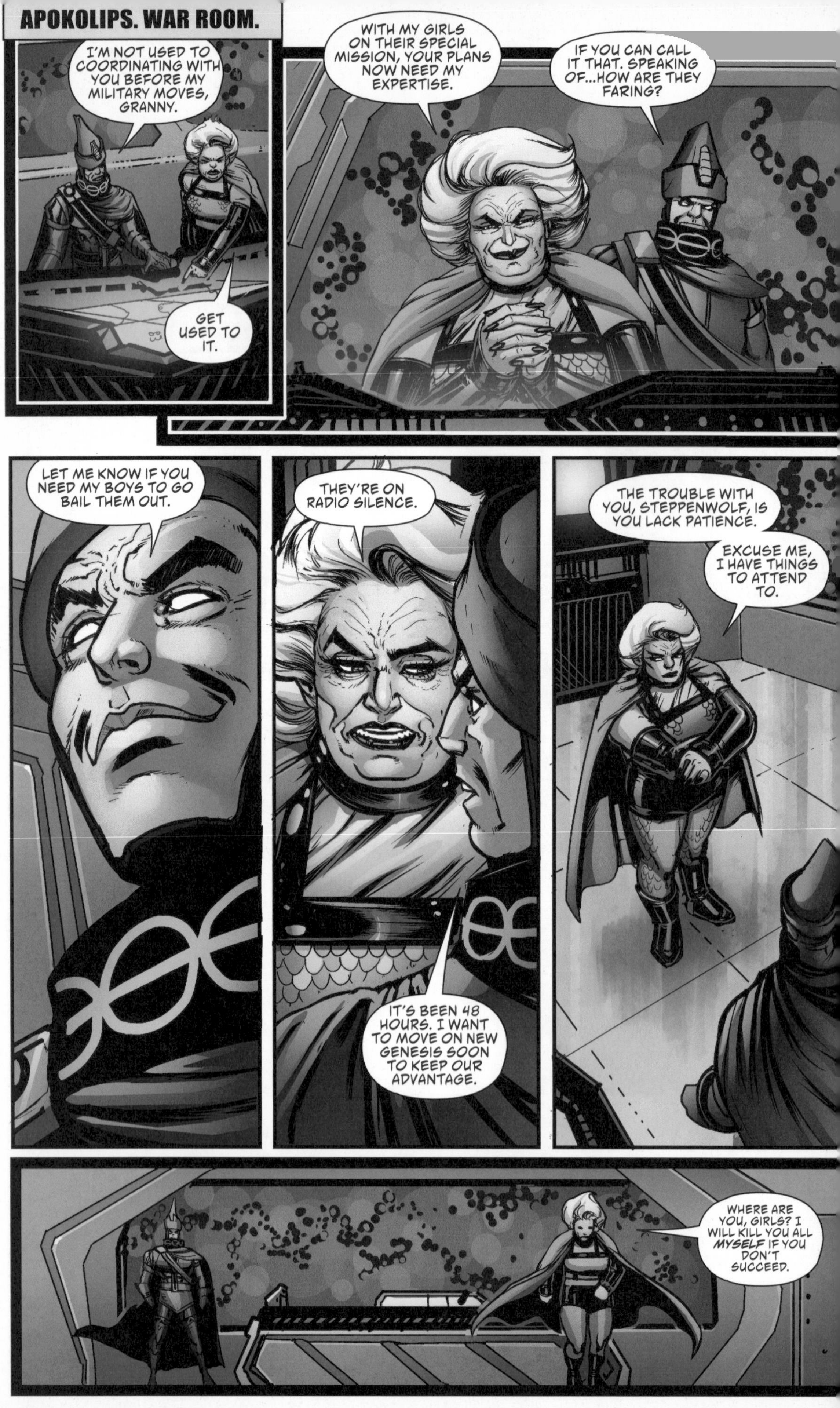

APOKOLIPS. WAR ROOM.
I'M NOT USED TO COORDINATING WITH YOU BEFORE MY MILITARY MOVES, GRANNY.
GET USED TO IT.
WITH MY GIRLS ON THEIR SPECIAL MISSION, YOUR PLANS NOW NEED MY EXPERTISE.
IF YOU CAN CALL IT THAT. SPEAKING OF...HOW ARE THEY FARING?
LET ME KNOW IF YOU NEED MY BOYS TO GO BAIL THEM OUT.
THEY'RE ON RADIO SILENCE.
IT'S BEEN 48 HOURS. I WANT TO MOVE ON NEW GENESIS SOON TO KEEP OUR ADVANTAGE.
THE TROUBLE WITH YOU, STEPPENWOLF, IS YOU LACK PATIENCE.
EXCUSE ME, I HAVE THINGS TO ATTEND TO.
WHERE ARE YOU, GIRLS? I WILL KILL YOU ALL *MYSELF* IF YOU DON'T SUCCEED.

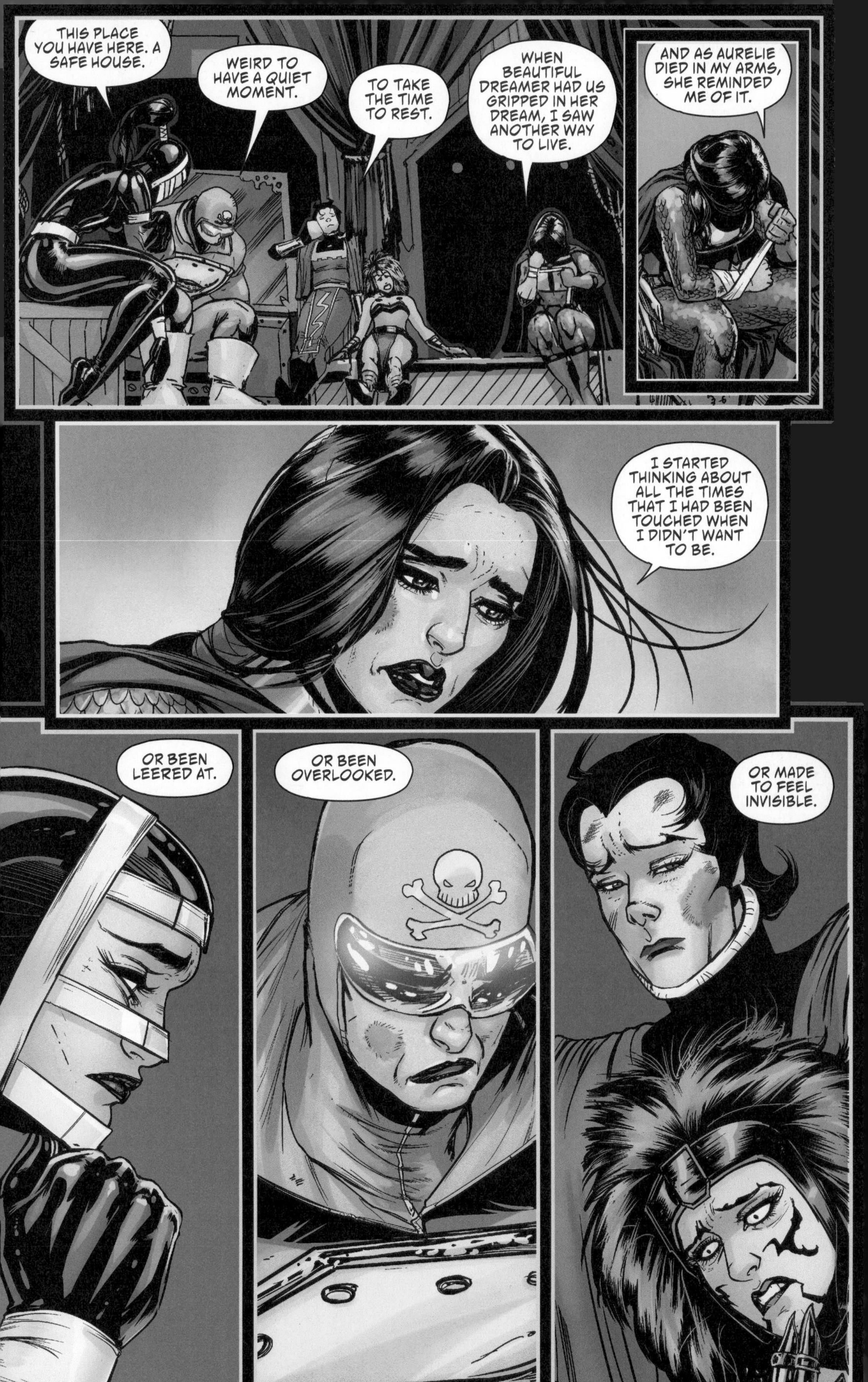
THIS PLACE YOU HAVE HERE. A SAFE HOUSE.
WEIRD TO HAVE A QUIET MOMENT.
TO TAKE THE TIME TO REST.
WHEN BEAUTIFUL DREAMER HAD US GRIPPED IN HER DREAM, I SAW ANOTHER WAY TO LIVE.
AND AS AURELIE DIED IN MY ARMS, SHE REMINDED ME OF IT.
I STARTED THINKING ABOUT ALL THE TIMES THAT I HAD BEEN TOUCHED WHEN I DIDN'T WANT TO BE.
OR BEEN LEERED AT.
OR BEEN OVERLOOKED.
OR MADE TO FEEL INVISIBLE.

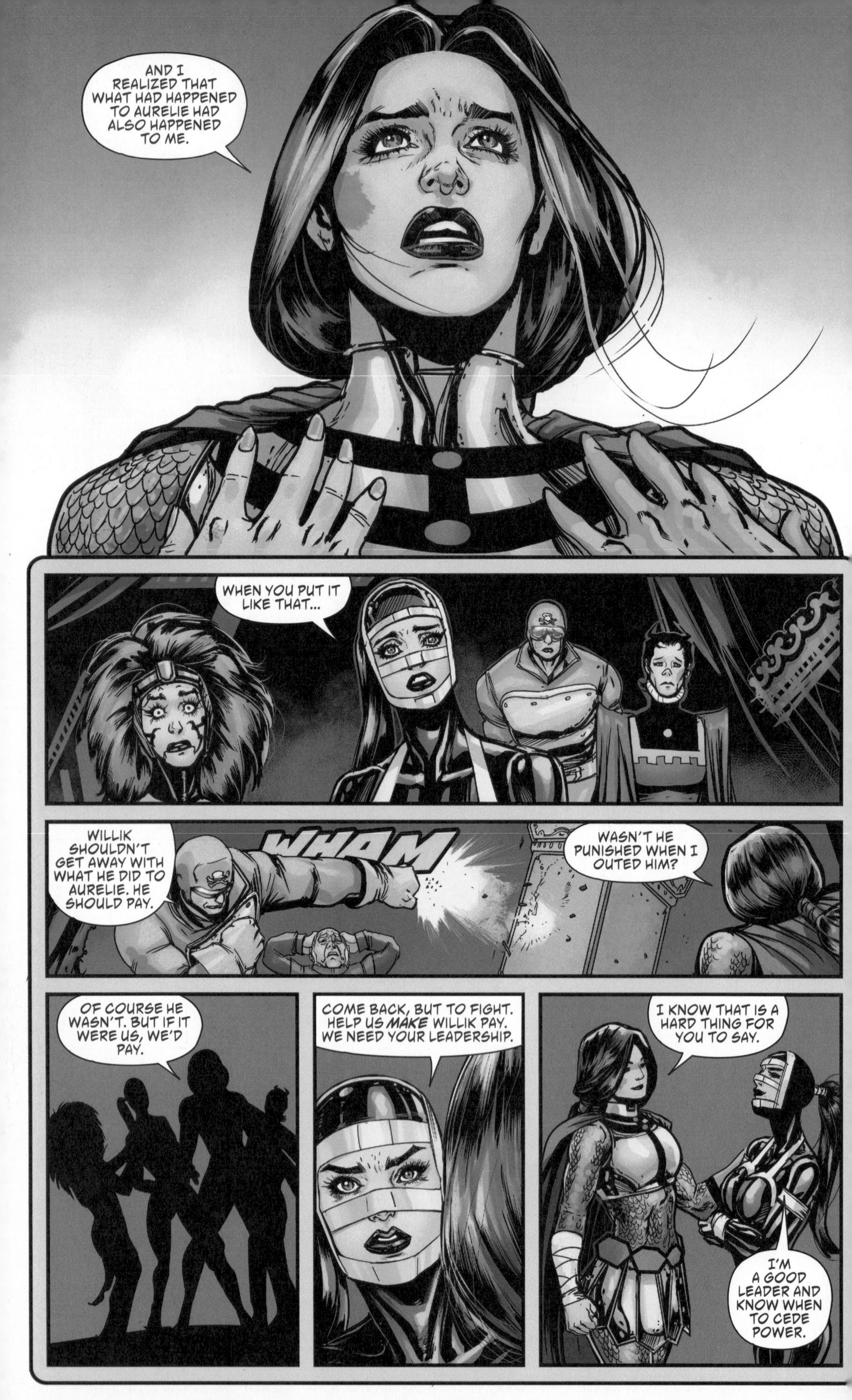
AND I REALIZED THAT WHAT HAD HAPPENED TO AURELIE HAD ALSO HAPPENED TO ME.
WHEN YOU PUT IT LIKE THAT...
WILLIK SHOULDN'T GET AWAY WITH WHAT HE DID TO AURELIE. HE SHOULD PAY.
WHAM
WASN'T HE PUNISHED WHEN I OUTED HIM?
OF COURSE HE WASN'T. BUT IF IT WERE US, WE'D PAY.
COME BACK, BUT TO FIGHT. HELP US *MAKE* WILLIK PAY. WE NEED YOUR LEADERSHIP.
I KNOW THAT IS A HARD THING FOR YOU TO SAY.
I'M A GOOD LEADER AND KNOW WHEN TO CEDE POWER.

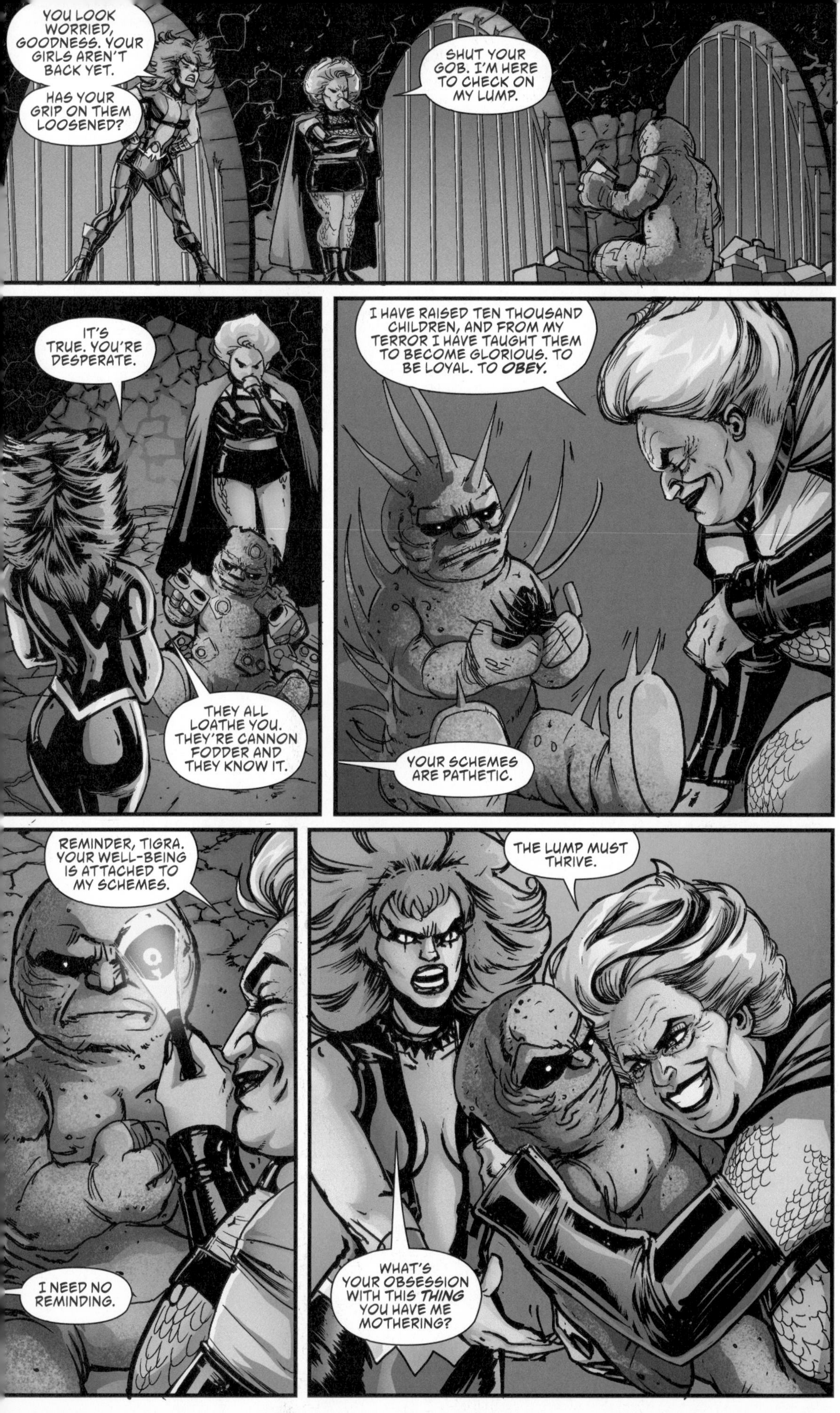
YOU LOOK WORRIED, GOODNESS. YOUR GIRLS AREN'T BACK YET.
HAS YOUR GRIP ON THEM LOOSENED?
SHUT YOUR GOB. I'M HERE TO CHECK ON MY LUMP.
IT'S TRUE. YOU'RE DESPERATE.
THEY ALL LOATHE YOU. THEY'RE CANNON FODDER AND THEY KNOW IT.
I HAVE RAISED TEN THOUSAND CHILDREN, AND FROM MY TERROR I HAVE TAUGHT THEM TO BECOME GLORIOUS. TO BE LOYAL. TO *OBEY.*
YOUR SCHEMES ARE PATHETIC.
REMINDER, TIGRA. YOUR WELL-BEING IS ATTACHED TO MY SCHEMES.
I NEED NO REMINDING.
THE LUMP MUST THRIVE.
WHAT'S YOUR OBSESSION WITH THIS *THING* YOU HAVE ME MOTHERING?

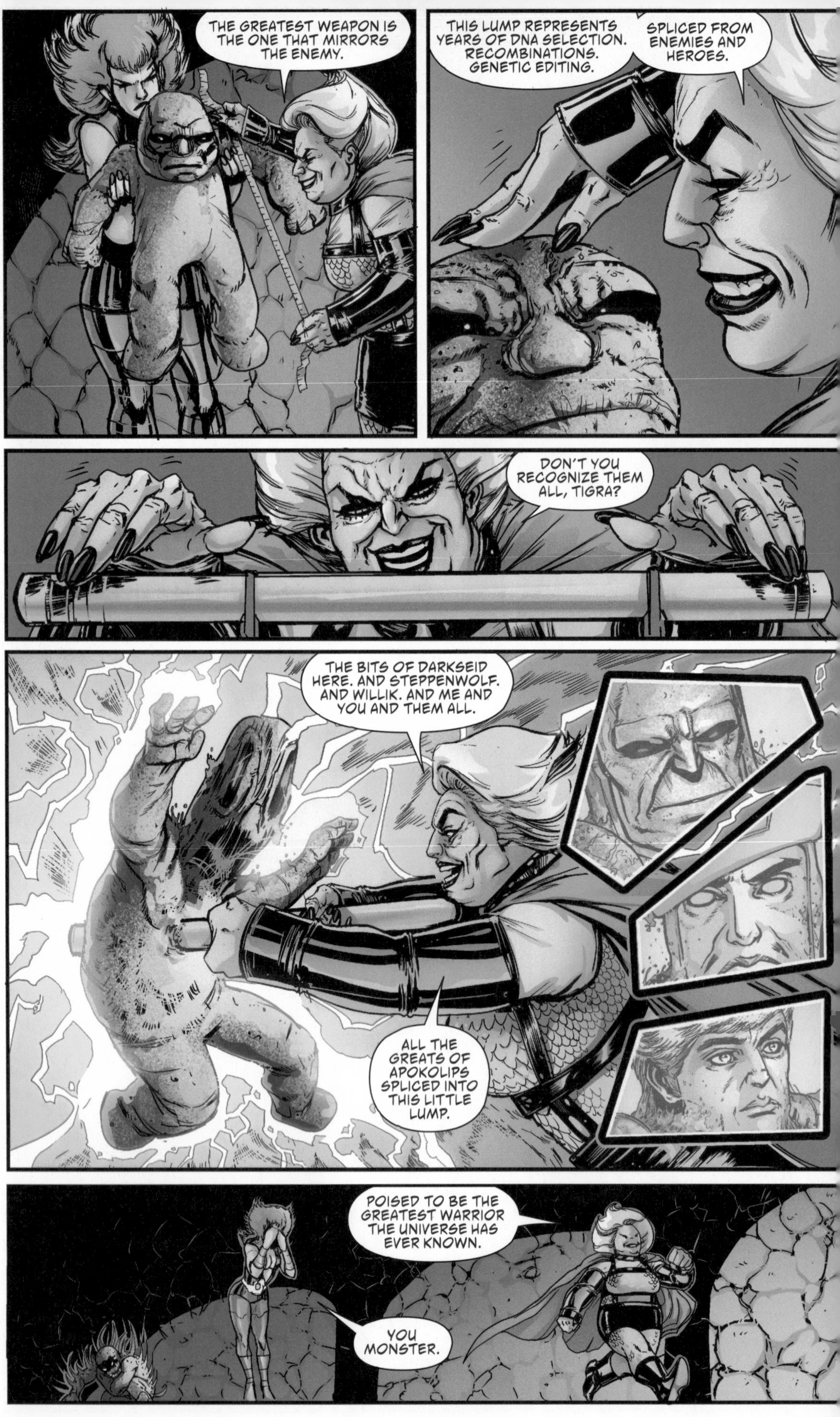
THE GREATEST WEAPON IS THE ONE THAT MIRRORS THE ENEMY.
THIS LUMP REPRESENTS YEARS OF DNA SELECTION. RECOMBINATIONS. GENETIC EDITING.
SPLICED FROM ENEMIES AND HEROES.
DON'T YOU RECOGNIZE THEM ALL, TIGRA?
THE BITS OF DARKSEID HERE. AND STEPPENWOLF. AND WILLIK. AND ME AND YOU AND THEM ALL.
ALL THE GREATS OF APOKOLIPS SPLICED INTO THIS LITTLE LUMP.
POISED TO BE THE GREATEST WARRIOR THE UNIVERSE HAS EVER KNOWN.
YOU MONSTER.

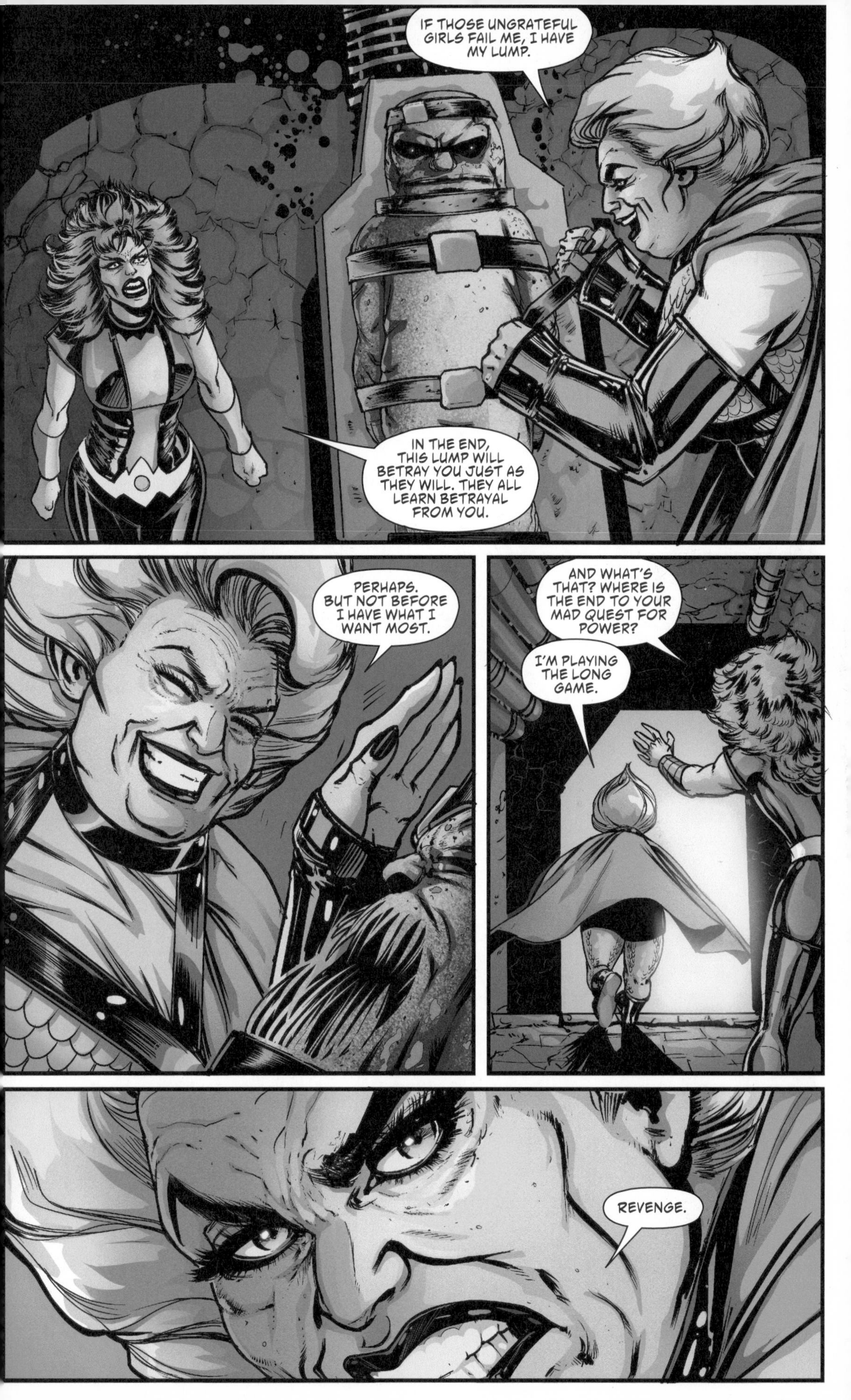
IF THOSE UNGRATEFUL GIRLS FAIL ME, I HAVE MY LUMP.
IN THE END, THIS LUMP WILL BETRAY YOU JUST AS THEY WILL. THEY ALL LEARN BETRAYAL FROM YOU.
PERHAPS. BUT NOT BEFORE I HAVE WHAT I WANT MOST.
AND WHAT'S THAT? WHERE IS THE END TO YOUR MAD QUEST FOR POWER?
I'M PLAYING THE LONG GAME.
REVENGE.

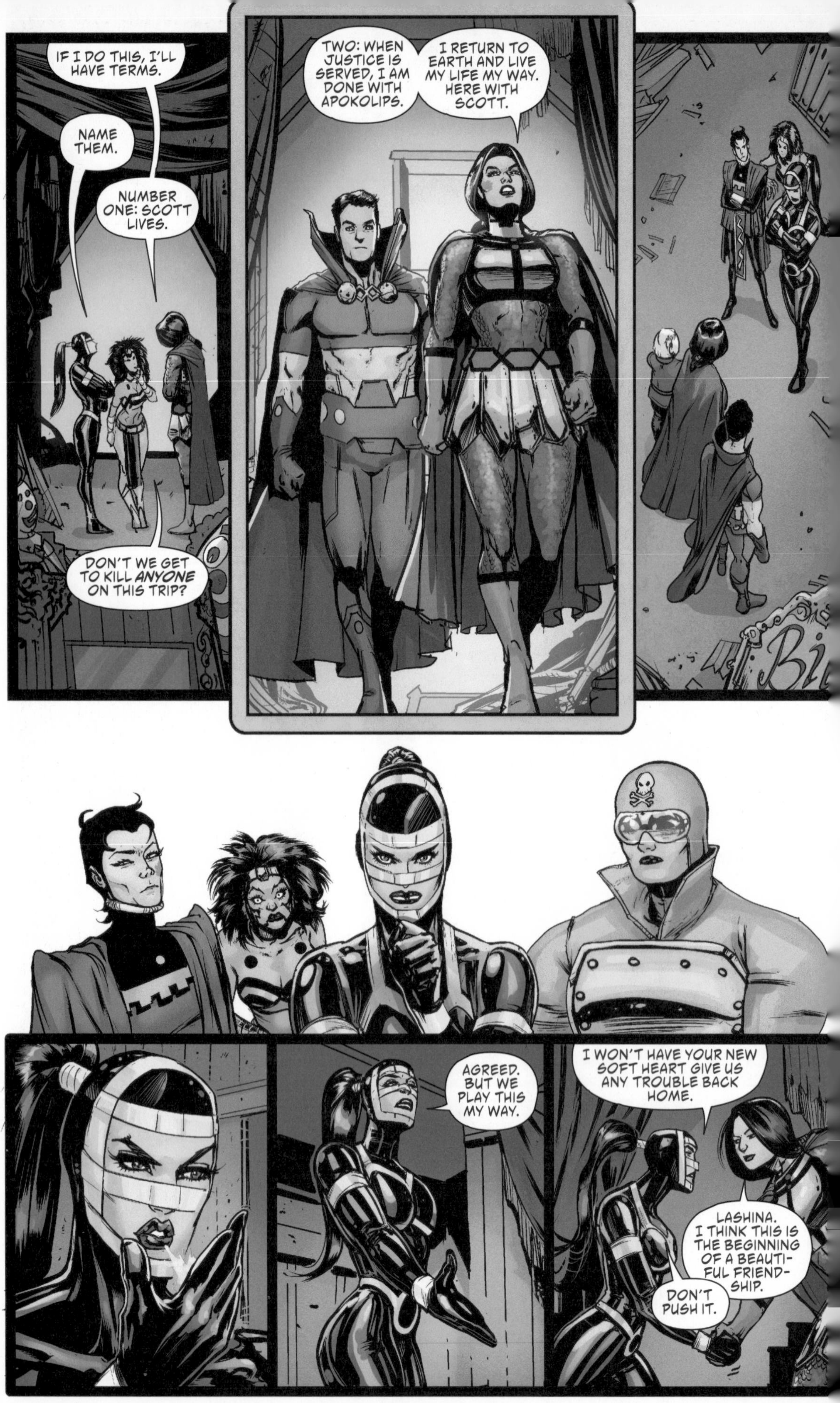

IF I DO THIS, I'LL HAVE TERMS.
NAME THEM.
NUMBER ONE: SCOTT LIVES.
DON'T WE GET TO KILL *ANYONE* ON THIS TRIP?
TWO: WHEN JUSTICE IS SERVED, I AM DONE WITH APOKOLIPS.
I RETURN TO EARTH AND LIVE MY LIFE MY WAY. HERE WITH SCOTT.
AGREED. BUT WE PLAY THIS MY WAY.
I WON'T HAVE YOUR NEW SOFT HEART GIVE US ANY TROUBLE BACK HOME.
LASHINA. I THINK THIS IS THE BEGINNING OF A BEAUTI-FUL FRIEND-SHIP.
DON'T PUSH IT.

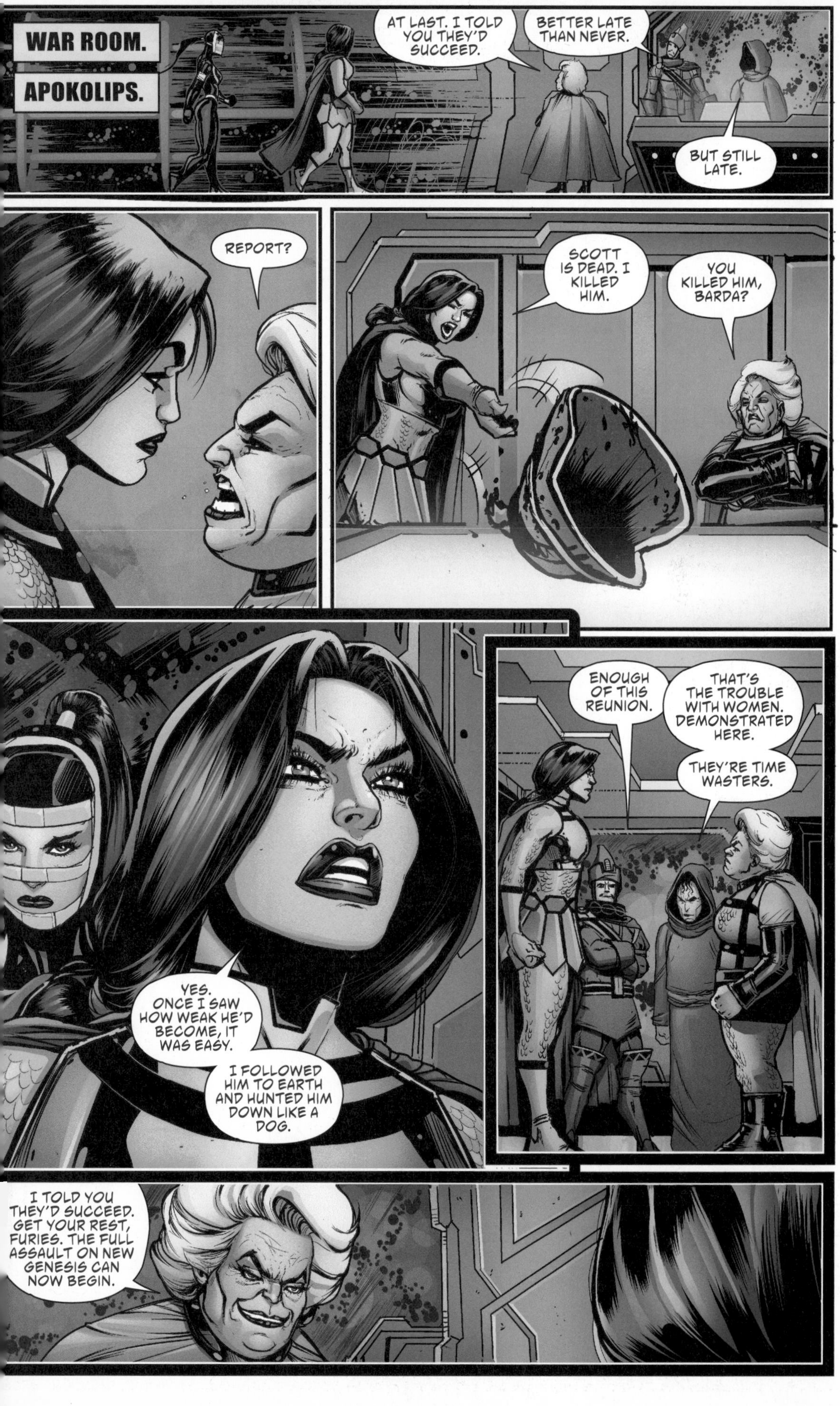
WAR ROOM.
APOKOLIPS.
AT LAST. I TOLD YOU THEY'D SUCCEED.
BETTER LATE THAN NEVER.
BUT STILL LATE.
REPORT?
SCOTT IS DEAD. I KILLED HIM.
YOU KILLED HIM, BARDA?
YES. ONCE I SAW HOW WEAK HE'D BECOME, IT WAS EASY.
I FOLLOWED HIM TO EARTH AND HUNTED HIM DOWN LIKE A DOG.
ENOUGH OF THIS REUNION.
THAT'S THE TROUBLE WITH WOMEN. DEMONSTRATED HERE.
THEY'RE TIME WASTERS.
I TOLD YOU THEY'D SUCCEED. GET YOUR REST, FURIES. THE FULL ASSAULT ON NEW GENESIS CAN NOW BEGIN.

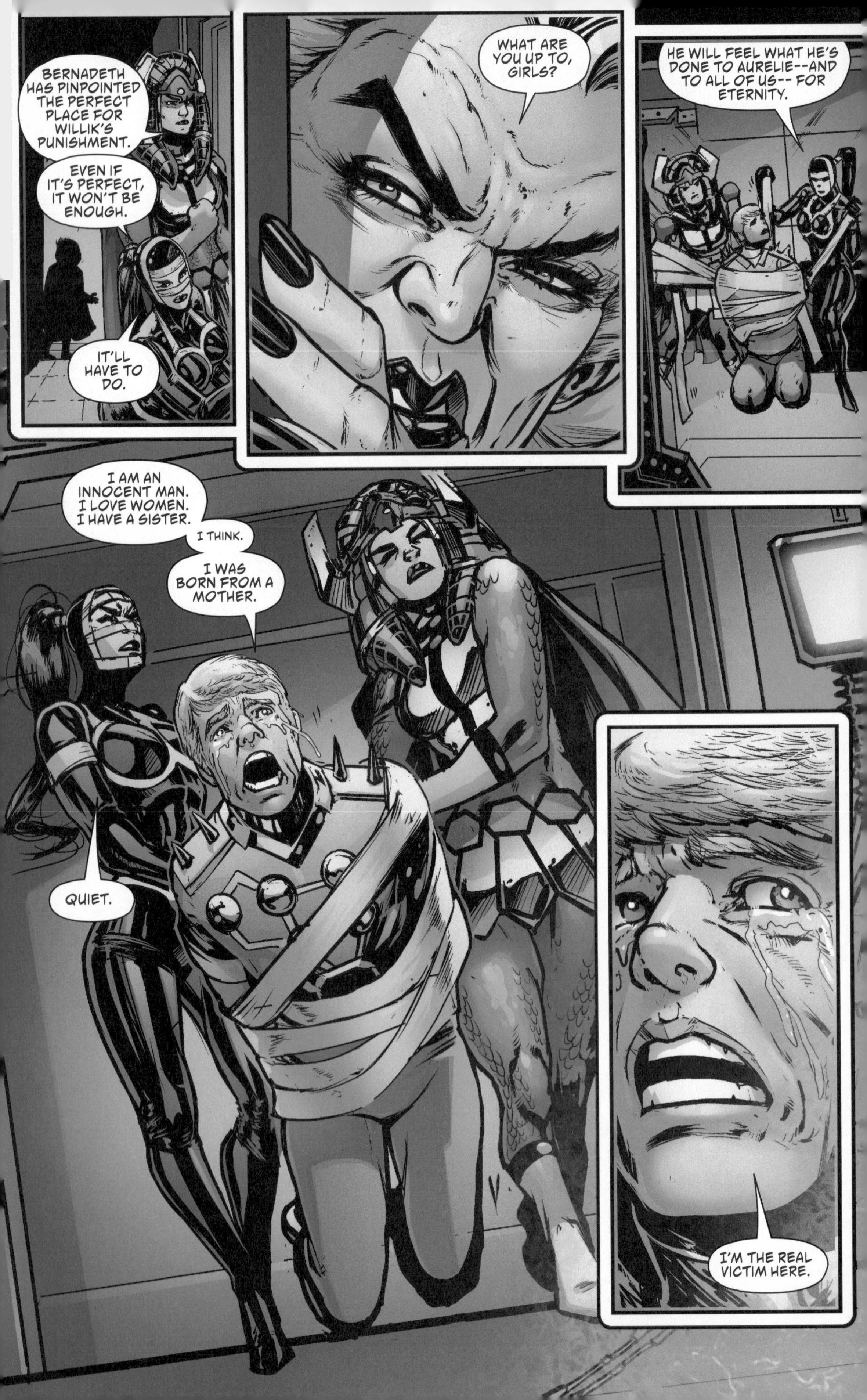
BERNADETH HAS PINPOINTED THE PERFECT PLACE FOR WILLIK'S PUNISHMENT.
EVEN IF IT'S PERFECT, IT WON'T BE ENOUGH.
IT'LL HAVE TO DO.
WHAT ARE YOU UP TO, GIRLS?
HE WILL FEEL WHAT HE'S DONE TO AURELIE--AND TO ALL OF US-- FOR ETERNITY.
I AM AN INNOCENT MAN. I LOVE WOMEN. I HAVE A SISTER.
I THINK.
I WAS BORN FROM A MOTHER.
QUIET.
I'M THE REAL VICTIM HERE.

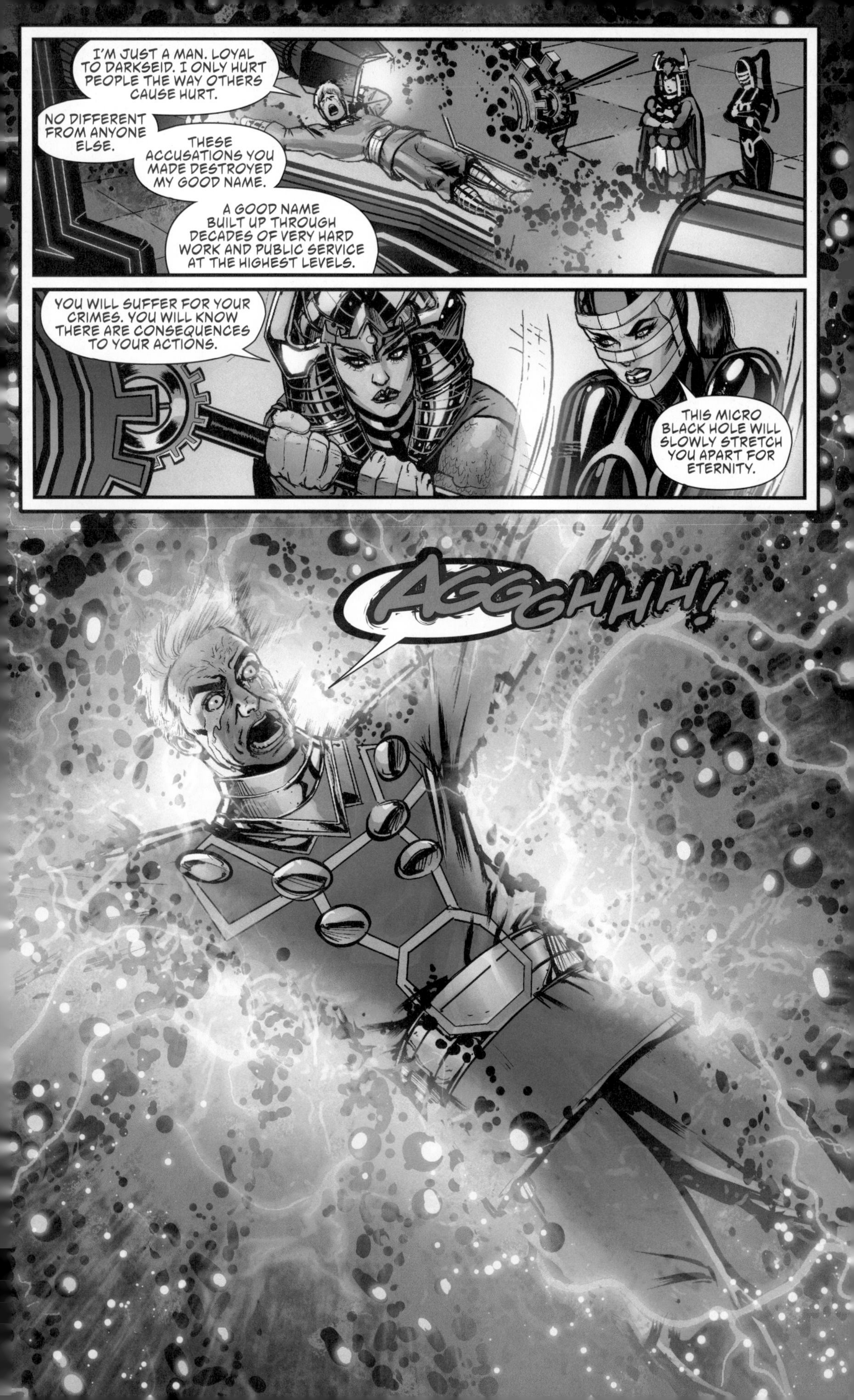
I'M JUST A MAN. LOYAL TO DARKSEID. I ONLY HURT PEOPLE THE WAY OTHERS CAUSE HURT.
NO DIFFERENT FROM ANYONE ELSE.
THESE ACCUSATIONS YOU MADE DESTROYED MY GOOD NAME.
A GOOD NAME BUILT UP THROUGH DECADES OF VERY HARD WORK AND PUBLIC SERVICE AT THE HIGHEST LEVELS.
YOU WILL SUFFER FOR YOUR CRIMES. YOU WILL KNOW THERE ARE CONSEQUENCES TO YOUR ACTIONS.
THIS MICRO BLACK HOLE WILL SLOWLY STRETCH YOU APART FOR ETERNITY.
AGGGHHHH!

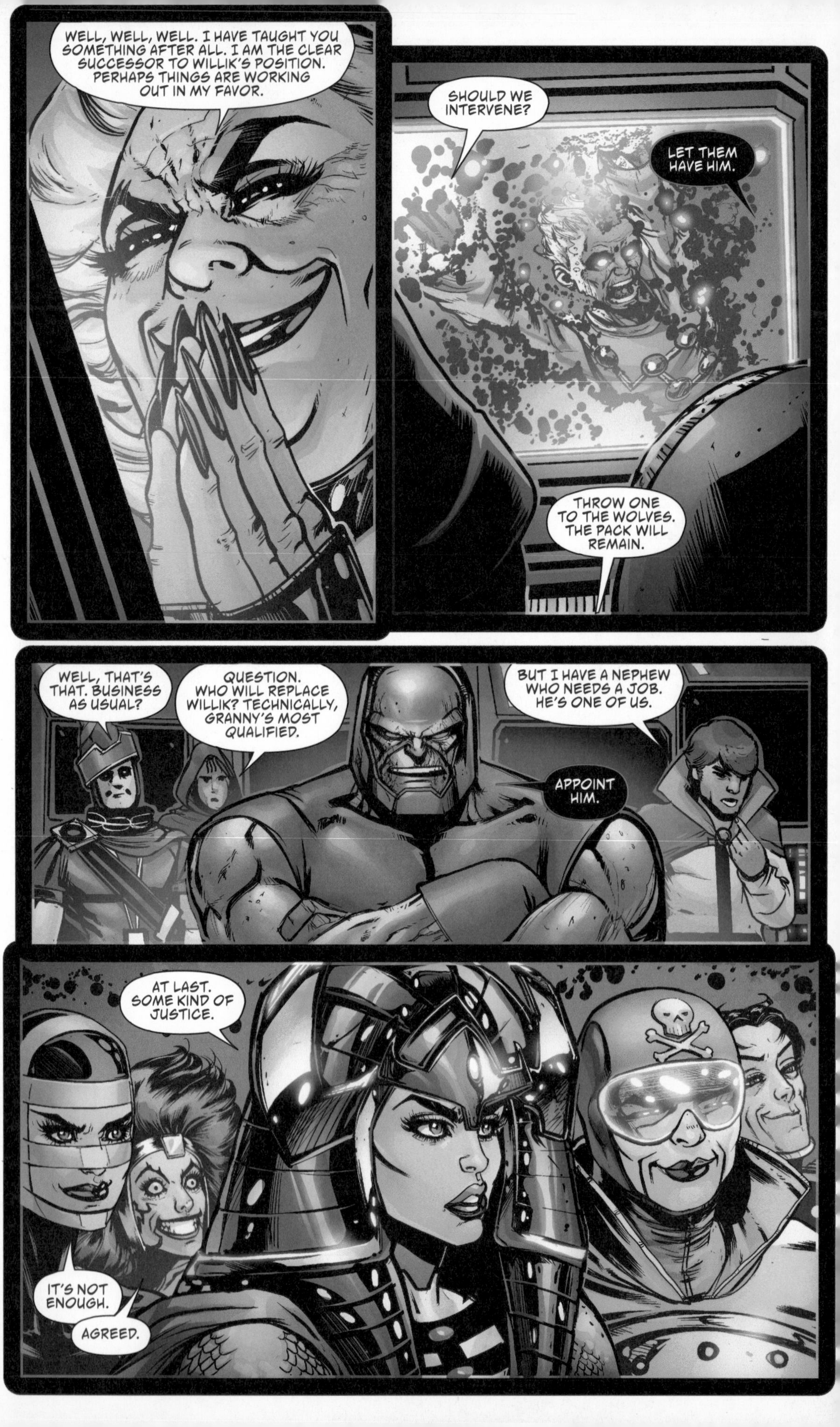
WELL, WELL, WELL. I HAVE TAUGHT YOU SOMETHING AFTER ALL. I AM THE CLEAR SUCCESSOR TO WILLIK'S POSITION. PERHAPS THINGS ARE WORKING OUT IN MY FAVOR.
SHOULD WE INTERVENE?
LET THEM HAVE HIM.
THROW ONE TO THE WOLVES. THE PACK WILL REMAIN.
WELL, THAT'S THAT. BUSINESS AS USUAL?
QUESTION. WHO WILL REPLACE WILLIK? TECHNICALLY, GRANNY'S MOST QUALIFIED.
BUT I HAVE A NEPHEW WHO NEEDS A JOB. HE'S ONE OF US.
APPOINT HIM.
AT LAST. SOME KIND OF JUSTICE.
IT'S NOT ENOUGH.
AGREED.

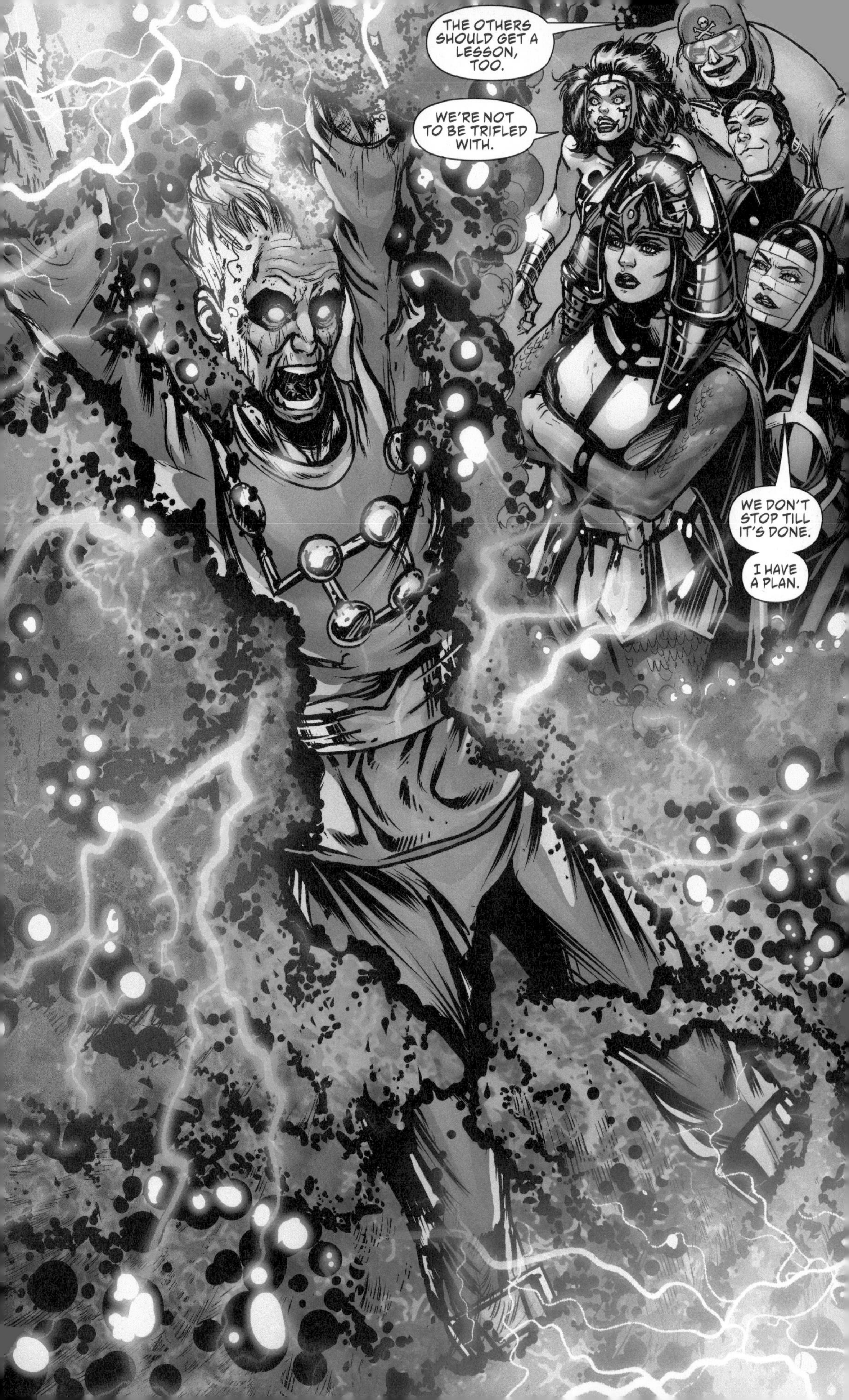
THE OTHERS SHOULD GET A LESSON, TOO.
WE'RE NOT TO BE TRIFLED WITH.
WE DON'T STOP TILL IT'S DONE.
I HAVE A PLAN.

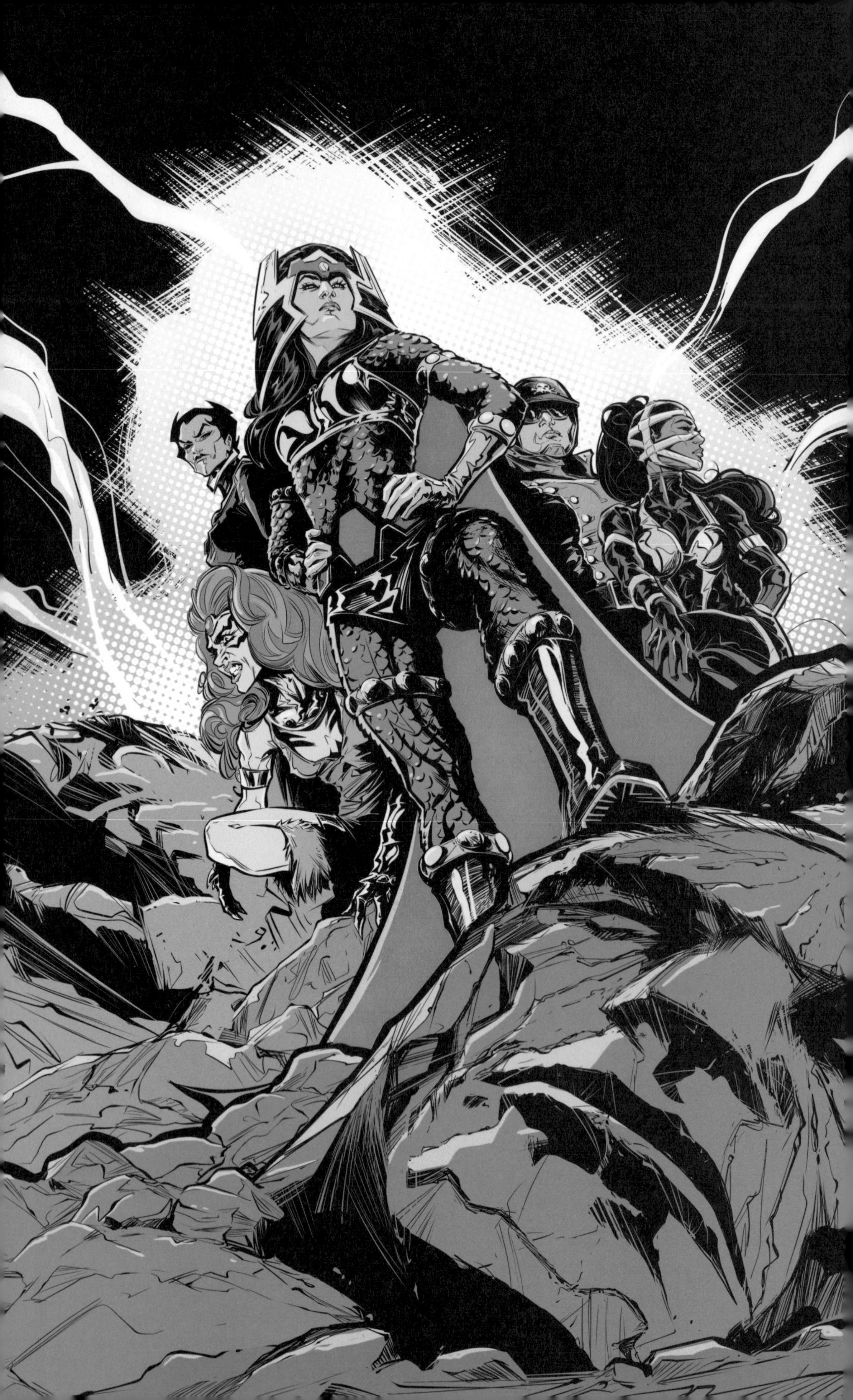

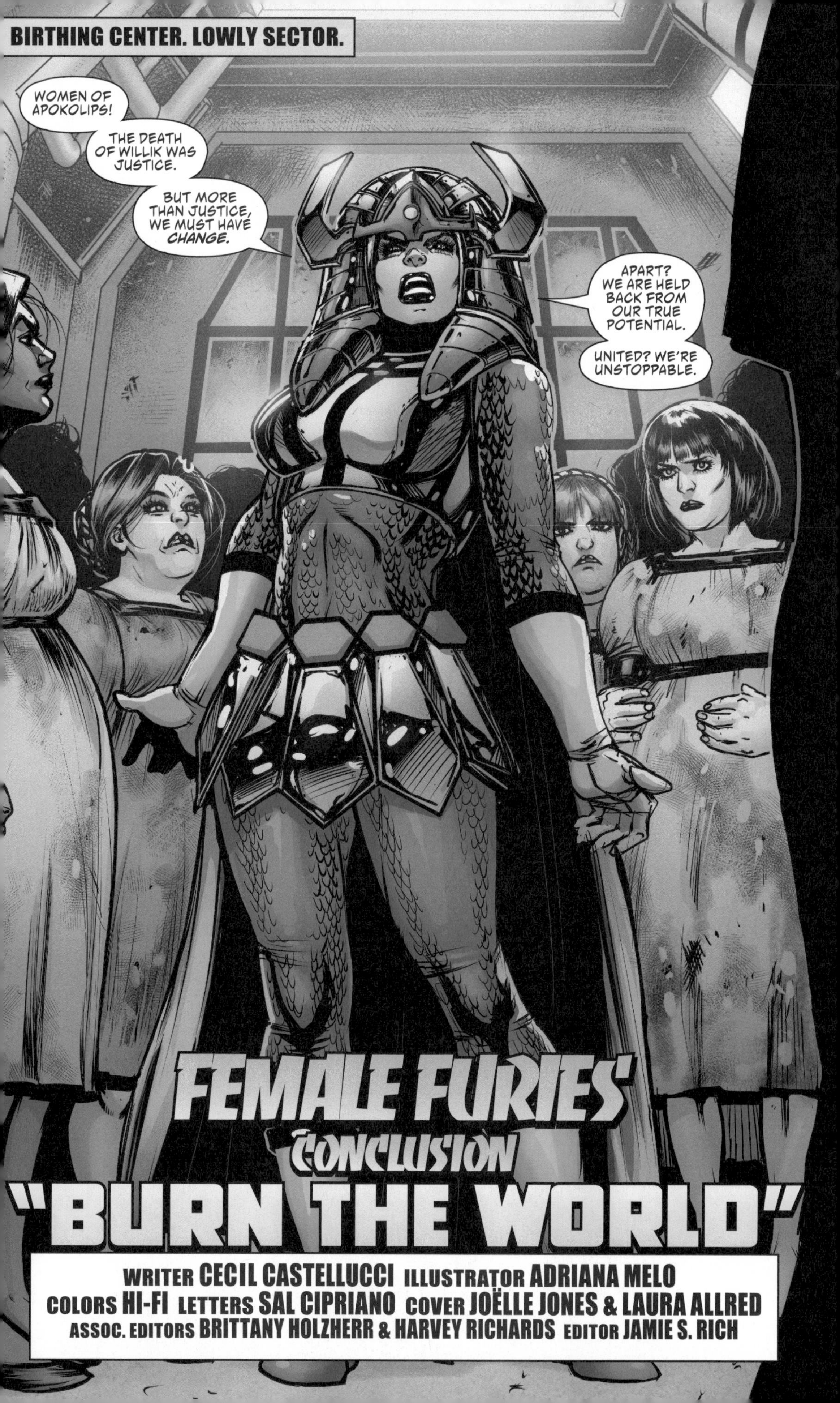
BIRTHING CENTER. LOWLY SECTOR.
WOMEN OF APOKOLIPS!
THE DEATH OF WILLIK WAS JUSTICE.
BUT MORE THAN JUSTICE, WE MUST HAVE CHANGE.
APART? WE ARE HELD BACK FROM OUR TRUE POTENTIAL.
UNITED? WE'RE UNSTOPPABLE.
FEMALE FURIES' CONCLUSION
"BURN THE WORLD"
WRITER CECIL CASTELLUCCI ILLUSTRATOR ADRIANA MELO
COLORS HI-FI LETTERS SAL CIPRIANO COVER JOËLLE JONES & LAURA ALLRED
ASSOC. EDITORS BRITTANY HOLZHERR & HARVEY RICHARDS EDITOR JAMIE S. RICH

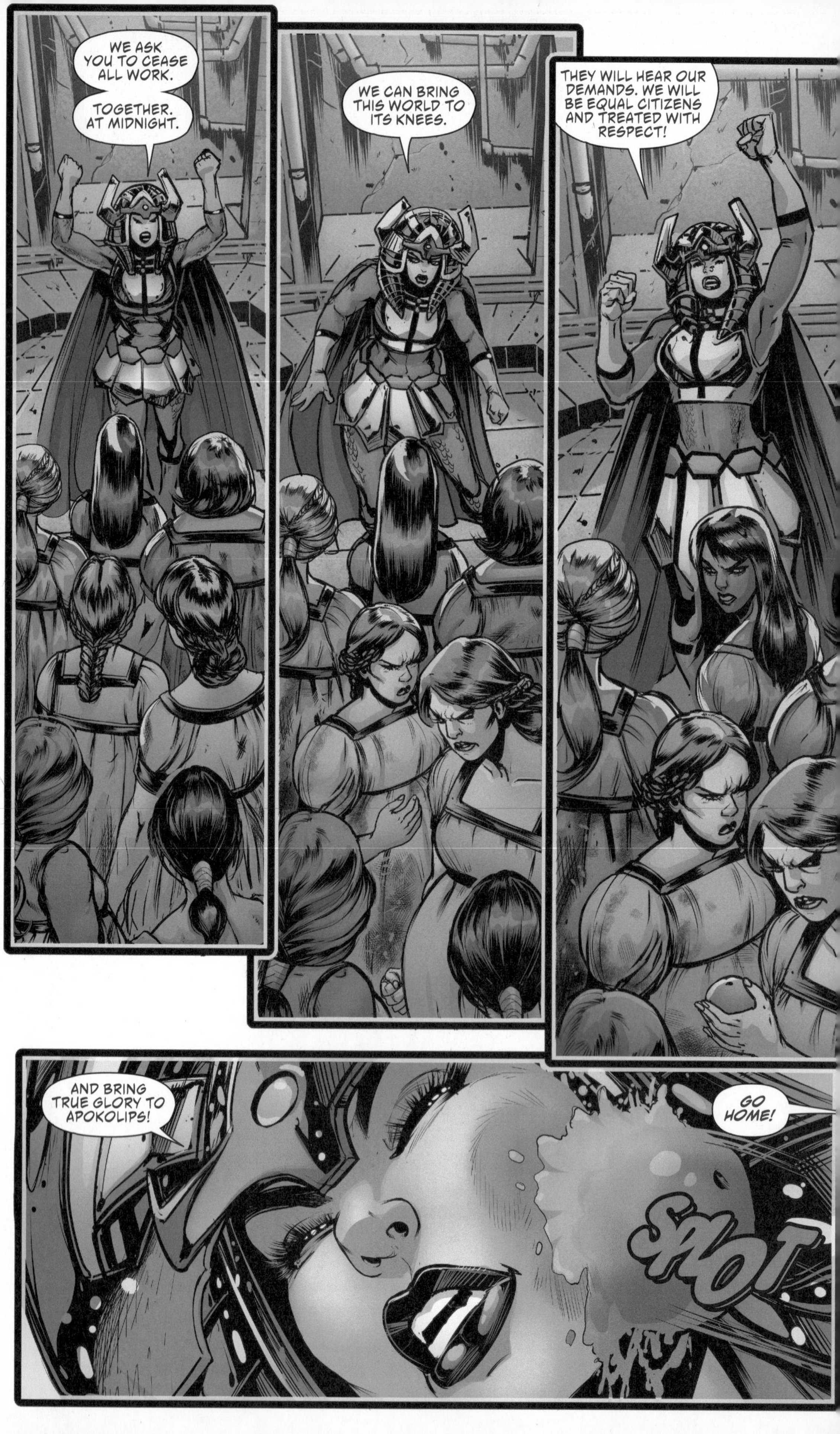

WE ASK YOU TO CEASE ALL WORK.
TOGETHER. AT MIDNIGHT.
WE CAN BRING THIS WORLD TO ITS KNEES.
THEY WILL HEAR OUR DEMANDS. WE WILL BE EQUAL CITIZENS AND TREATED WITH RESPECT!
AND BRING TRUE GLORY TO APOKOLIPS!
GO HOME!
SPLOT

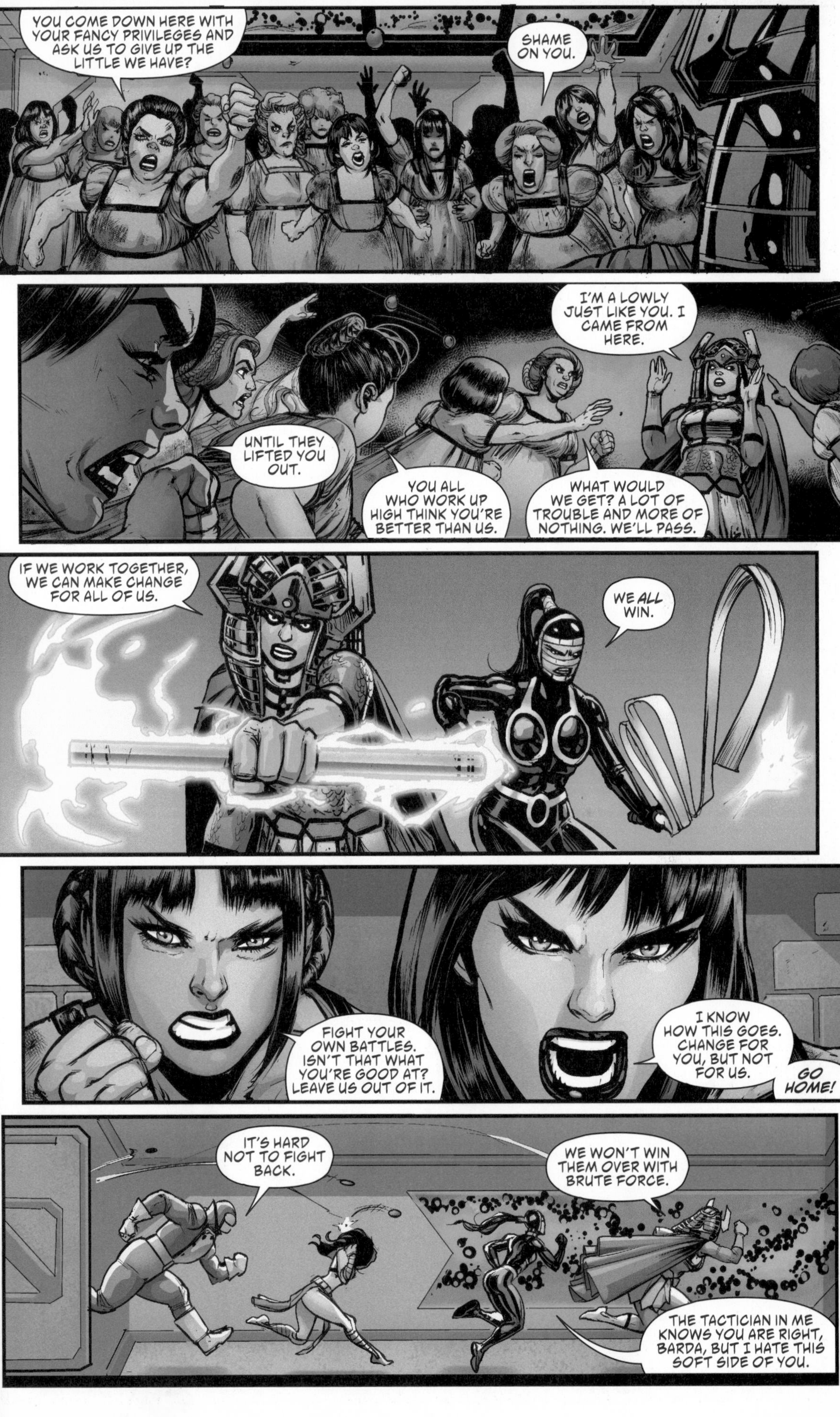

YOU COME DOWN HERE WITH YOUR FANCY PRIVILEGES AND ASK US TO GIVE UP THE LITTLE WE HAVE?
SHAME ON YOU.
I'M A LOWLY JUST LIKE YOU. I CAME FROM HERE.
UNTIL THEY LIFTED YOU OUT.
YOU ALL WHO WORK UP HIGH THINK YOU'RE BETTER THAN US.
WHAT WOULD WE GET? A LOT OF TROUBLE AND MORE OF NOTHING. WE'LL PASS.
IF WE WORK TOGETHER, WE CAN MAKE CHANGE FOR ALL OF US.
WE ALL WIN.
FIGHT YOUR OWN BATTLES. ISN'T THAT WHAT YOU'RE GOOD AT? LEAVE US OUT OF IT.
I KNOW HOW THIS GOES. CHANGE FOR YOU, BUT NOT FOR US.
GO HOME!
IT'S HARD NOT TO FIGHT BACK.
WE WON'T WIN THEM OVER WITH BRUTE FORCE.
THE TACTICIAN IN ME KNOWS YOU ARE RIGHT, BARDA, BUT I HATE THIS SOFT SIDE OF YOU.

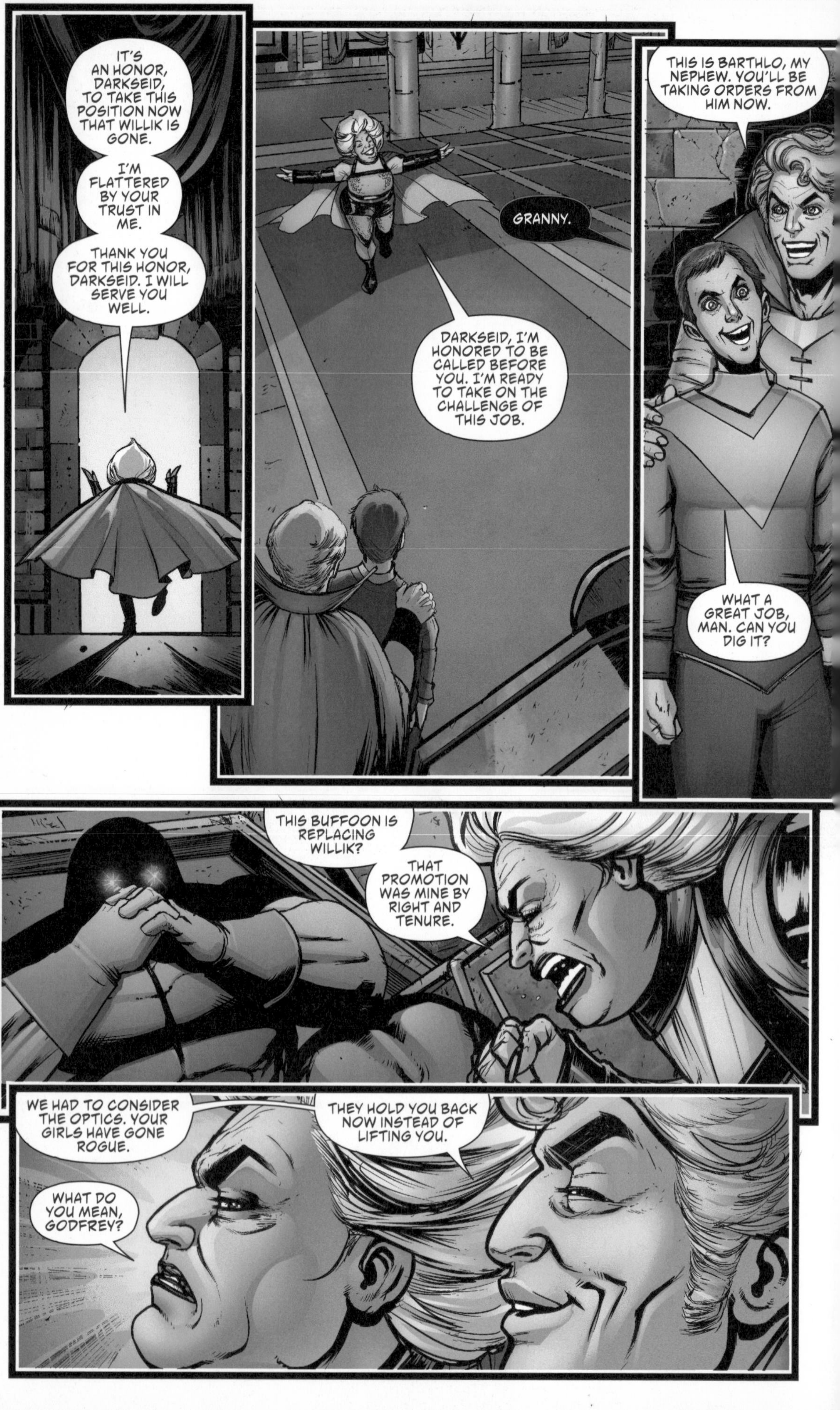
IT'S AN HONOR, DARKSEID, TO TAKE THIS POSITION NOW THAT WILLIK IS GONE.
I'M FLATTERED BY YOUR TRUST IN ME.
THANK YOU FOR THIS HONOR, DARKSEID. I WILL SERVE YOU WELL.
GRANNY.
DARKSEID, I'M HONORED TO BE CALLED BEFORE YOU. I'M READY TO TAKE ON THE CHALLENGE OF THIS JOB.
THIS IS BARTHLO, MY NEPHEW. YOU'LL BE TAKING ORDERS FROM HIM NOW.
WHAT A GREAT JOB, MAN. CAN YOU DIG IT?
THIS BUFFOON IS REPLACING WILLIK?
THAT PROMOTION WAS MINE BY RIGHT AND TENURE.
WE HAD TO CONSIDER THE OPTICS. YOUR GIRLS HAVE GONE ROGUE.
WHAT DO YOU MEAN, GODFREY?
THEY HOLD YOU BACK NOW INSTEAD OF LIFTING YOU.

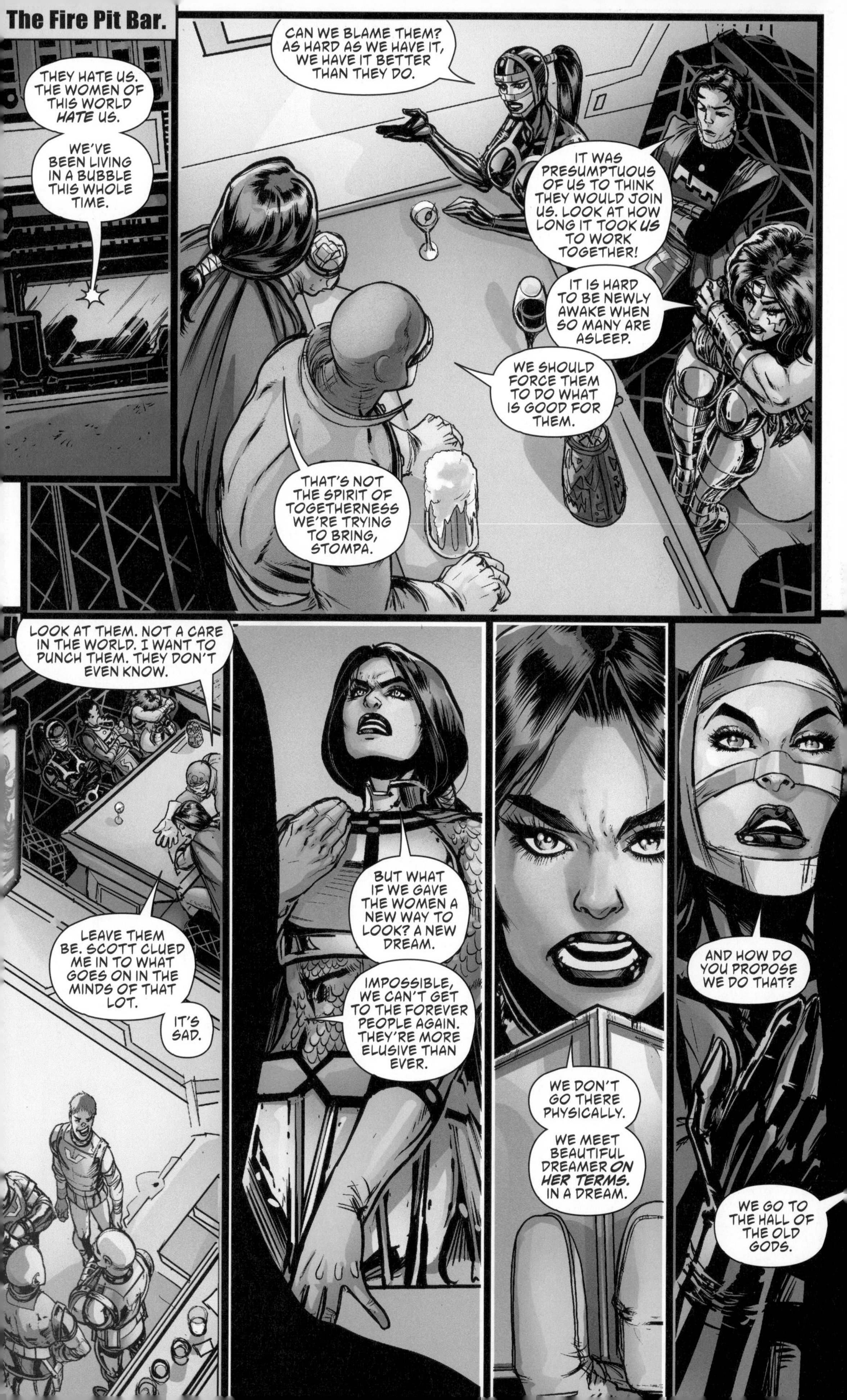

The Fire Pit Bar.
THEY HATE US. THE WOMEN OF THIS WORLD HATE US.
WE'VE BEEN LIVING IN A BUBBLE THIS WHOLE TIME.
CAN WE BLAME THEM? AS HARD AS WE HAVE IT, WE HAVE IT BETTER THAN THEY DO.
IT WAS PRESUMPTUOUS OF US TO THINK THEY WOULD JOIN US. LOOK AT HOW LONG IT TOOK US TO WORK TOGETHER!
IT IS HARD TO BE NEWLY AWAKE WHEN SO MANY ARE ASLEEP.
WE SHOULD FORCE THEM TO DO WHAT IS GOOD FOR THEM.
THAT'S NOT THE SPIRIT OF TOGETHERNESS WE'RE TRYING TO BRING, STOMPA.
LOOK AT THEM. NOT A CARE IN THE WORLD. I WANT TO PUNCH THEM. THEY DON'T EVEN KNOW.
LEAVE THEM BE. SCOTT CLUED ME IN TO WHAT GOES ON IN THE MINDS OF THAT LOT.
IT'S SAD.
BUT WHAT IF WE GAVE THE WOMEN A NEW WAY TO LOOK? A NEW DREAM.
IMPOSSIBLE, WE CAN'T GET TO THE FOREVER PEOPLE AGAIN. THEY'RE MORE ELUSIVE THAN EVER.
WE DON'T GO THERE PHYSICALLY.
WE MEET BEAUTIFUL DREAMER ON HER TERMS. IN A DREAM.
AND HOW DO YOU PROPOSE WE DO THAT?
WE GO TO THE HALL OF THE OLD GODS.

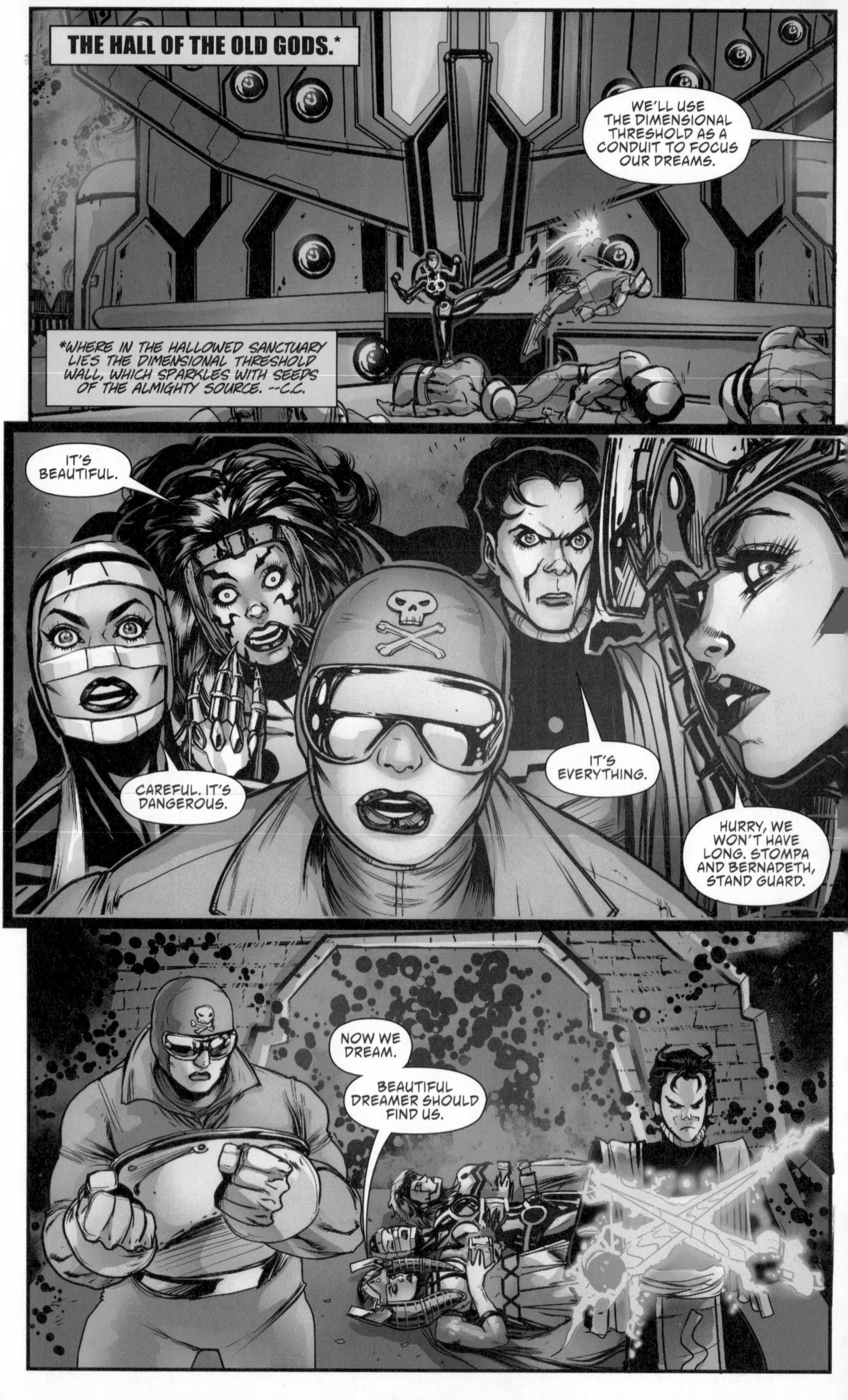
THE HALL OF THE OLD GODS.*
WE'LL USE THE DIMENSIONAL THRESHOLD AS A CONDUIT TO FOCUS OUR DREAMS.
*WHERE IN THE HALLOWED SANCTUARY LIES THE DIMENSIONAL THRESHOLD WALL, WHICH SPARKLES WITH SEEDS OF THE ALMIGHTY SOURCE. --C.C.
IT'S BEAUTIFUL.
CAREFUL. IT'S DANGEROUS.
IT'S EVERYTHING.
HURRY, WE WON'T HAVE LONG. STOMPA AND BERNADETH, STAND GUARD.
NOW WE DREAM.
BEAUTIFUL DREAMER SHOULD FIND US.

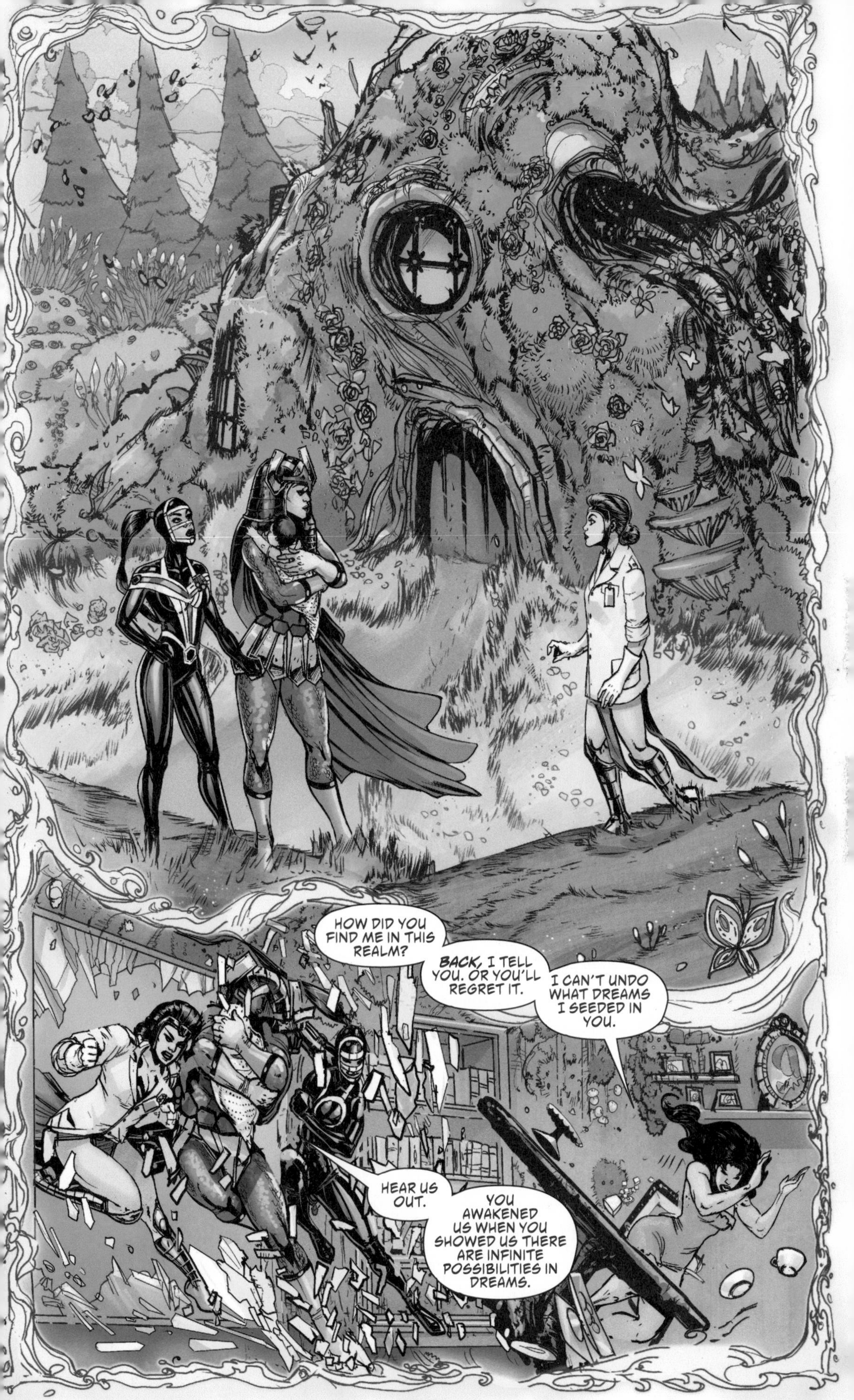
HOW DID YOU FIND ME IN THIS REALM?
BACK, I TELL YOU. OR YOU'LL REGRET IT.
I CAN'T UNDO WHAT DREAMS I SEEDED IN YOU.
HEAR US OUT.
YOU AWAKENED US WHEN YOU SHOWED US THERE ARE INFINITE POSSIBILITIES IN DREAMS.

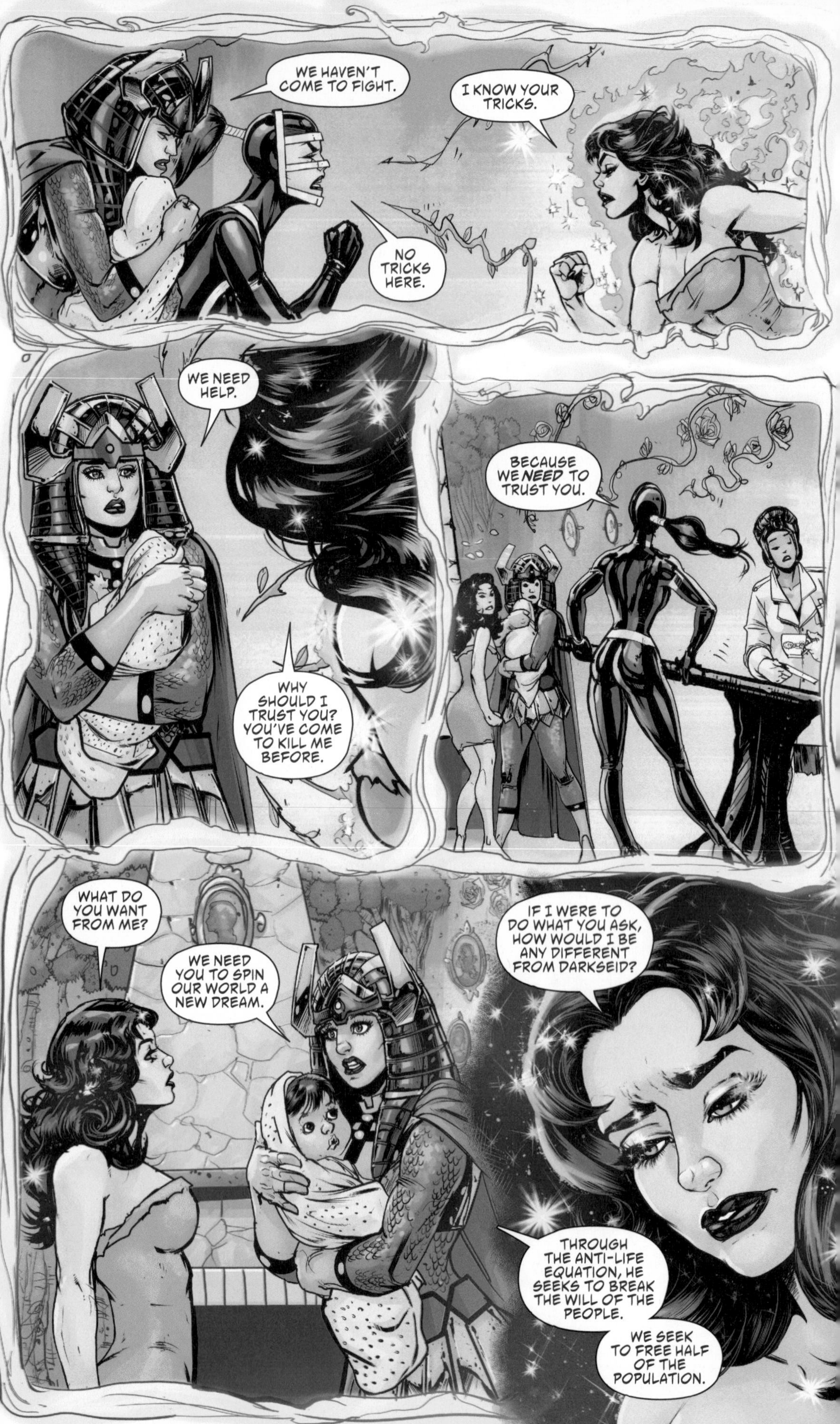
WE HAVEN'T COME TO FIGHT.
NO TRICKS HERE.
I KNOW YOUR TRICKS.
WE NEED HELP.
WHY SHOULD I TRUST YOU? YOU'VE COME TO KILL ME BEFORE.
BECAUSE WE *NEED* TO TRUST YOU.
WHAT DO YOU WANT FROM ME?
WE NEED YOU TO SPIN OUR WORLD A NEW DREAM.
IF I WERE TO DO WHAT YOU ASK, HOW WOULD I BE ANY DIFFERENT FROM DARKSEID?
THROUGH THE ANTI-LIFE EQUATION, HE SEEKS TO BREAK THE WILL OF THE PEOPLE.
WE SEEK TO FREE HALF OF THE POPULATION.

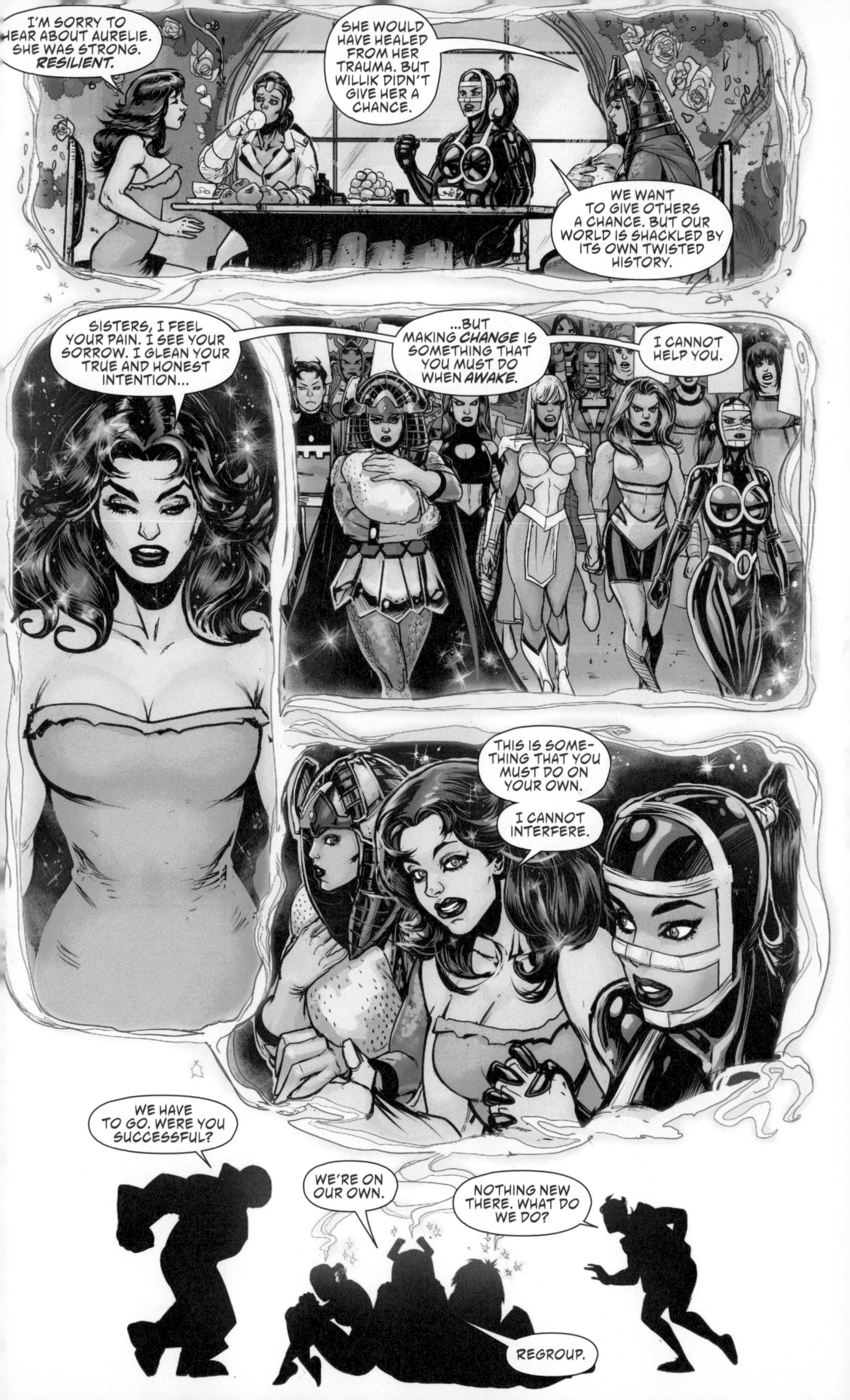
I'M SORRY TO HEAR ABOUT AURELIE. SHE WAS STRONG. *RESILIENT.*
SHE WOULD HAVE HEALED FROM HER TRAUMA. BUT WILLIK DIDN'T GIVE HER A CHANCE.
WE WANT TO GIVE OTHERS A CHANCE. BUT OUR WORLD IS SHACKLED BY ITS OWN TWISTED HISTORY.
SISTERS, I FEEL YOUR PAIN. I SEE YOUR SORROW. I GLEAN YOUR TRUE AND HONEST INTENTION...
...BUT MAKING *CHANGE* IS SOMETHING THAT YOU MUST DO WHEN *AWAKE.*
I CANNOT HELP YOU.
THIS IS SOME-THING THAT YOU MUST DO ON YOUR OWN.
I CANNOT INTERFERE.
WE HAVE TO GO. WERE YOU SUCCESSFUL?
WE'RE ON OUR OWN.
NOTHING NEW THERE. WHAT DO WE DO?
REGROUP.

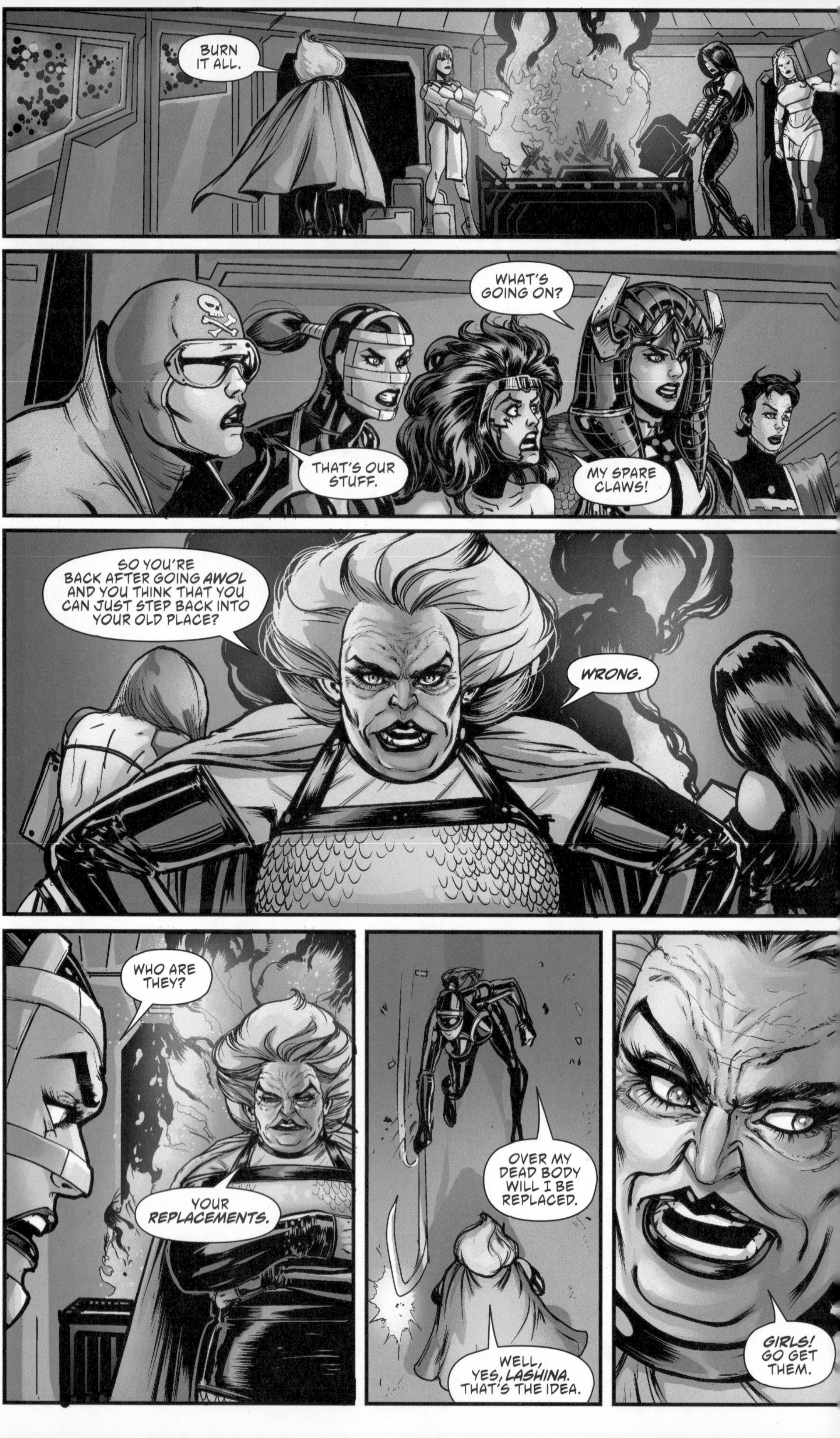
BURN IT ALL.
WHAT'S GOING ON?
THAT'S OUR STUFF.
MY SPARE CLAWS!
SO YOU'RE BACK AFTER GOING AWOL AND YOU THINK THAT YOU CAN JUST STEP BACK INTO YOUR OLD PLACE?
WRONG.
WHO ARE THEY?
YOUR REPLACEMENTS.
OVER MY DEAD BODY WILL I BE REPLACED.
WELL, YES, LASHINA. THAT'S THE IDEA.
GIRLS! GO GET THEM.

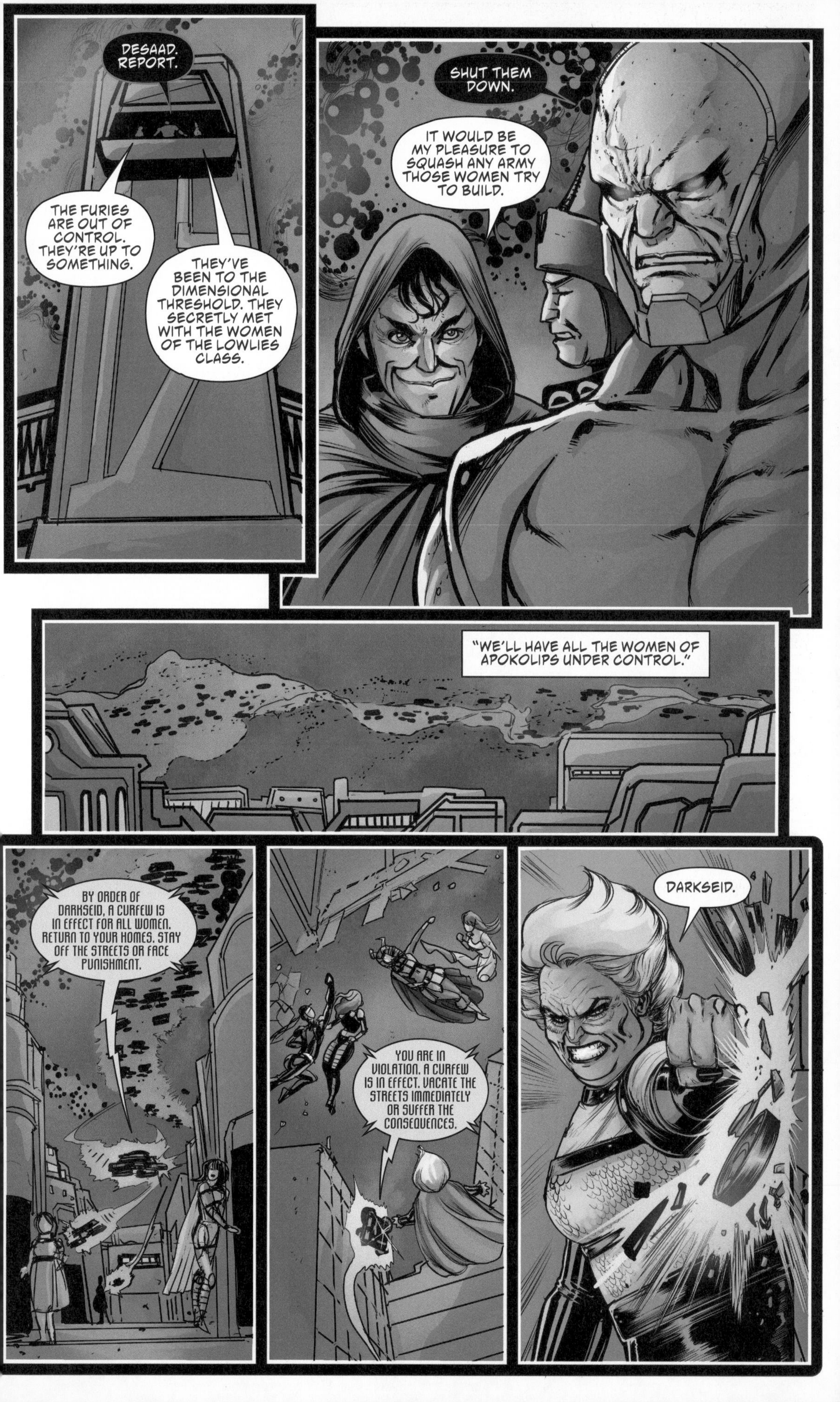
DESAAD. REPORT.
THE FURIES ARE OUT OF CONTROL. THEY'RE UP TO SOMETHING.
THEY'VE BEEN TO THE DIMENSIONAL THRESHOLD. THEY SECRETLY MET WITH THE WOMEN OF THE LOWLIES CLASS.
SHUT THEM DOWN.
IT WOULD BE MY PLEASURE TO SQUASH ANY ARMY THOSE WOMEN TRY TO BUILD.
"WE'LL HAVE ALL THE WOMEN OF APOKOLIPS UNDER CONTROL."
BY ORDER OF DARKSEID, A CURFEW IS IN EFFECT FOR ALL WOMEN. RETURN TO YOUR HOMES. STAY OFF THE STREETS OR FACE PUNISHMENT.
YOU ARE IN VIOLATION. A CURFEW IS IN EFFECT. VACATE THE STREETS IMMEDIATELY OR SUFFER THE CONSEQUENCES.
DARKSEID.

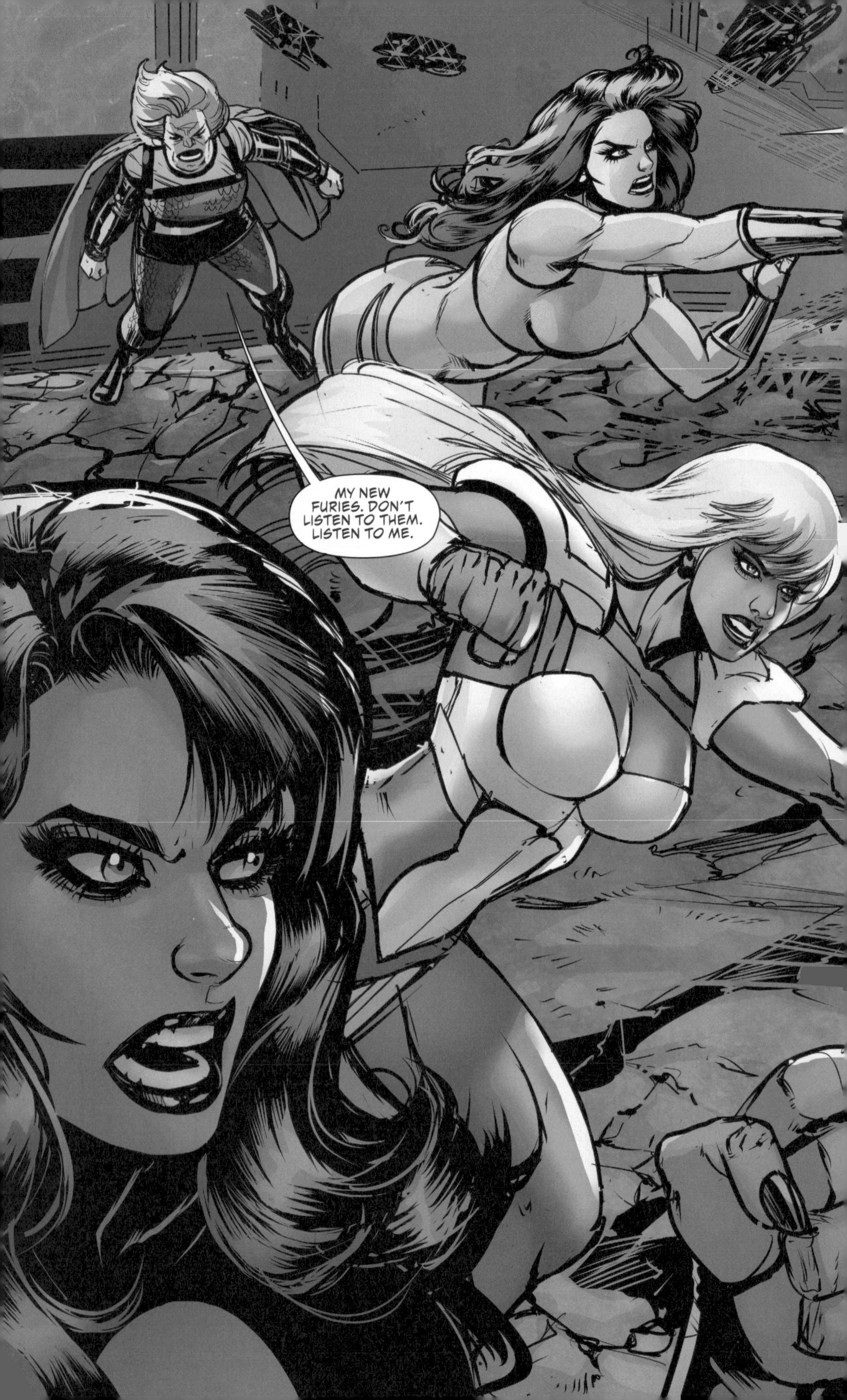
MY NEW FURIES. DON'T LISTEN TO THEM. LISTEN TO ME.

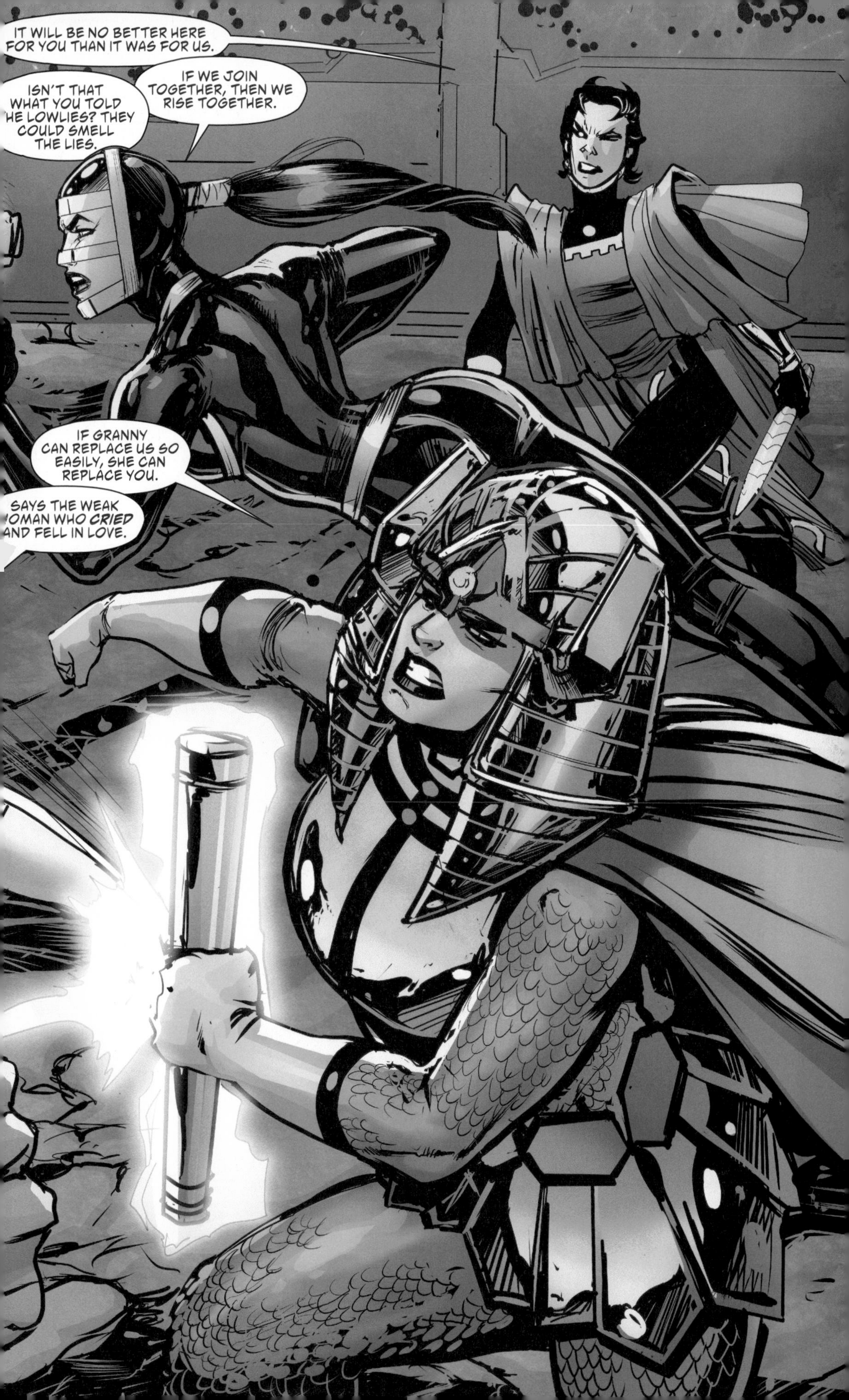
IT WILL BE NO BETTER HERE FOR YOU THAN IT WAS FOR US.
ISN'T THAT WHAT YOU TOLD HE LOWLIES? THEY COULD SMELL THE LIES.
IF WE JOIN TOGETHER, THEN WE RISE TOGETHER.
IF GRANNY CAN REPLACE US SO EASILY, SHE CAN REPLACE YOU.
SAYS THE WEAK OMAN WHO *CRIED* AND FELL IN LOVE.

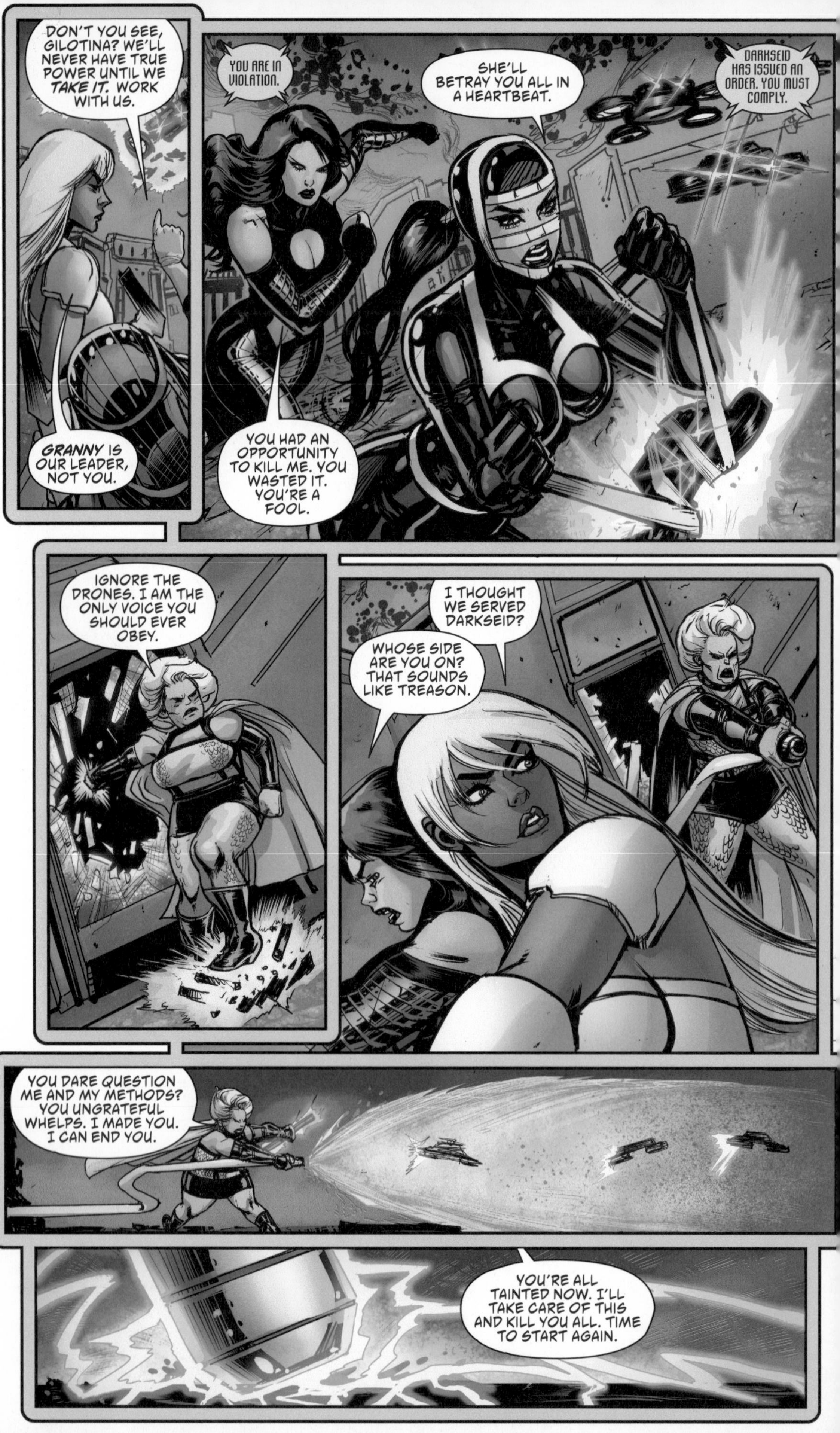
DON'T YOU SEE, GILOTINA? WE'LL NEVER HAVE TRUE POWER UNTIL WE TAKE IT. WORK WITH US.
GRANNY IS OUR LEADER, NOT YOU.
YOU ARE IN VIOLATION.
YOU HAD AN OPPORTUNITY TO KILL ME. YOU WASTED IT. YOU'RE A FOOL.
SHE'LL BETRAY YOU ALL IN A HEARTBEAT.
DARKSEID HAS ISSUED AN ORDER. YOU MUST COMPLY.
IGNORE THE DRONES. I AM THE ONLY VOICE YOU SHOULD EVER OBEY.
I THOUGHT WE SERVED DARKSEID?
WHOSE SIDE ARE YOU ON? THAT SOUNDS LIKE TREASON.
YOU DARE QUESTION ME AND MY METHODS? YOU UNGRATEFUL WHELPS. I MADE YOU. I CAN END YOU.
YOU'RE ALL TAINTED NOW. I'LL TAKE CARE OF THIS AND KILL YOU ALL. TIME TO START AGAIN.

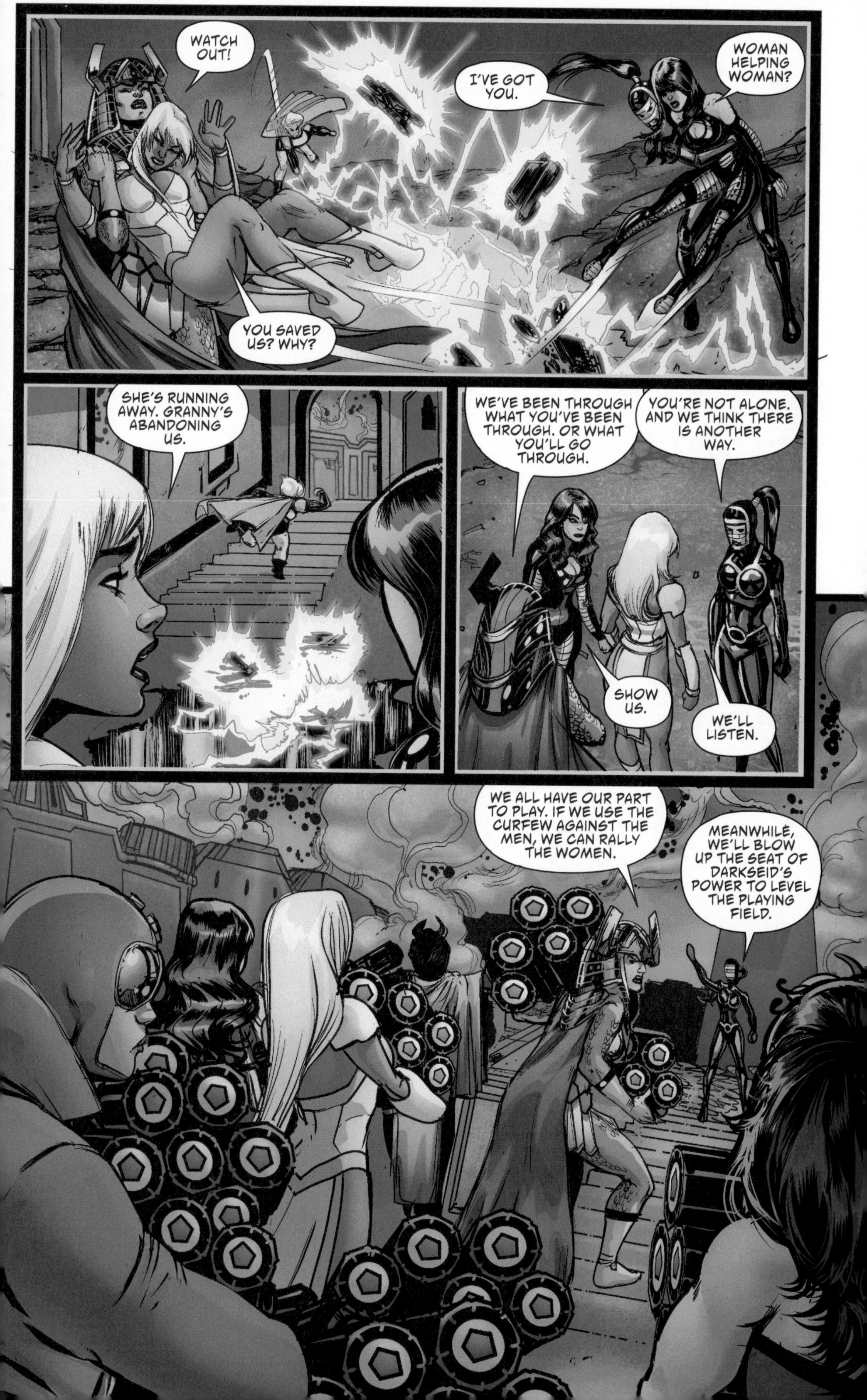
WATCH OUT!
I'VE GOT YOU.
WOMAN HELPING WOMAN?
YOU SAVED US? WHY?
SHE'S RUNNING AWAY. GRANNY'S ABANDONING US.
WE'VE BEEN THROUGH WHAT YOU'VE BEEN THROUGH. OR WHAT YOU'LL GO THROUGH.
YOU'RE NOT ALONE. AND WE THINK THERE IS ANOTHER WAY.
SHOW US.
WE'LL LISTEN.
WE ALL HAVE OUR PART TO PLAY. IF WE USE THE CURFEW AGAINST THE MEN, WE CAN RALLY THE WOMEN.
MEANWHILE, WE'LL BLOW UP THE SEAT OF DARKSEID'S POWER TO LEVEL THE PLAYING FIELD.

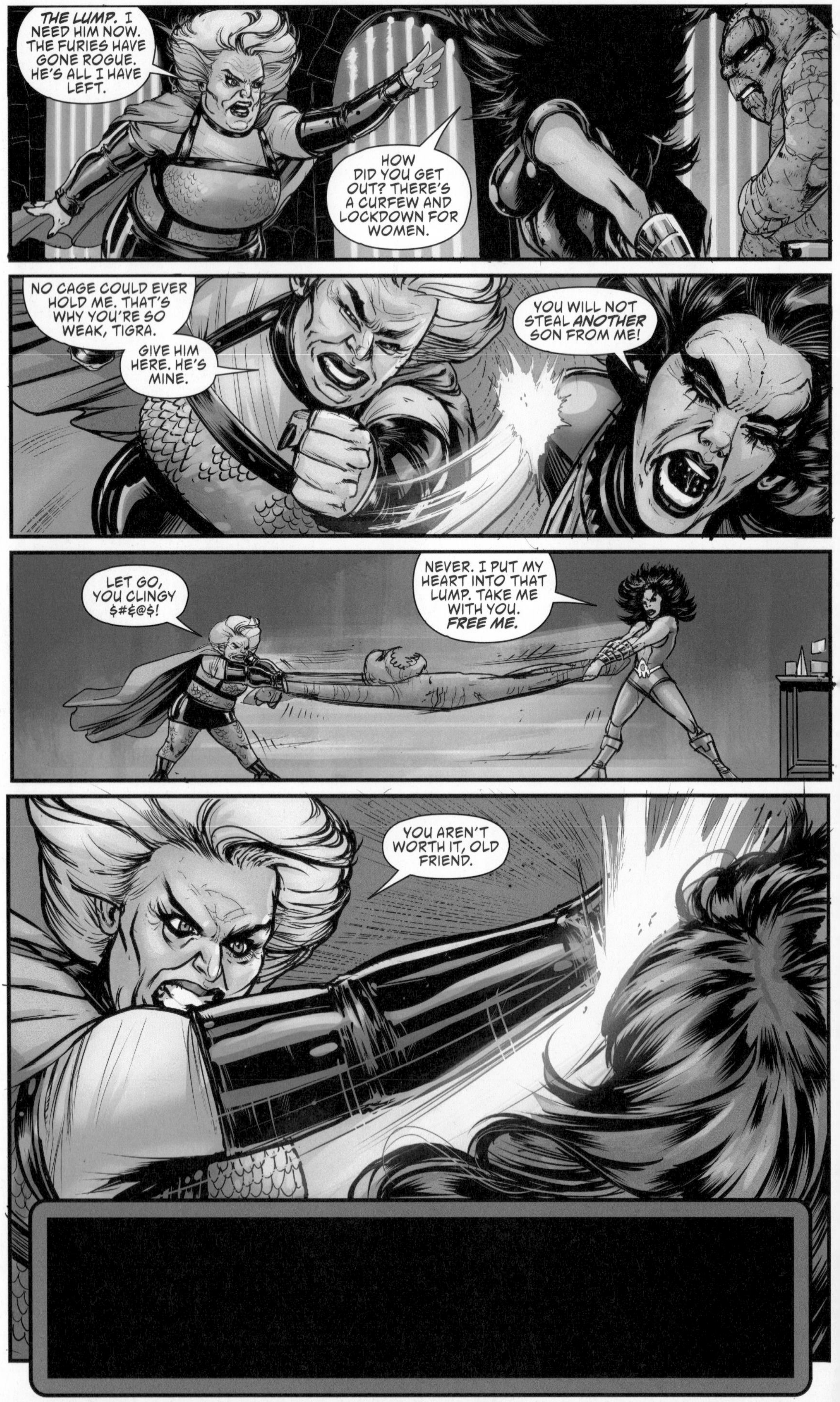

THE LUMP. I NEED HIM NOW. THE FURIES HAVE GONE ROGUE. HE'S ALL I HAVE LEFT.
HOW DID YOU GET OUT? THERE'S A CURFEW AND LOCKDOWN FOR WOMEN.
NO CAGE COULD EVER HOLD ME. THAT'S WHY YOU'RE SO WEAK, TIGRA.
GIVE HIM HERE. HE'S MINE.
YOU WILL NOT STEAL ANOTHER SON FROM ME!
LET GO, YOU CLINGY $#&@$!
NEVER. I PUT MY HEART INTO THAT LUMP. TAKE ME WITH YOU. FREE ME.
YOU AREN'T WORTH IT, OLD FRIEND.

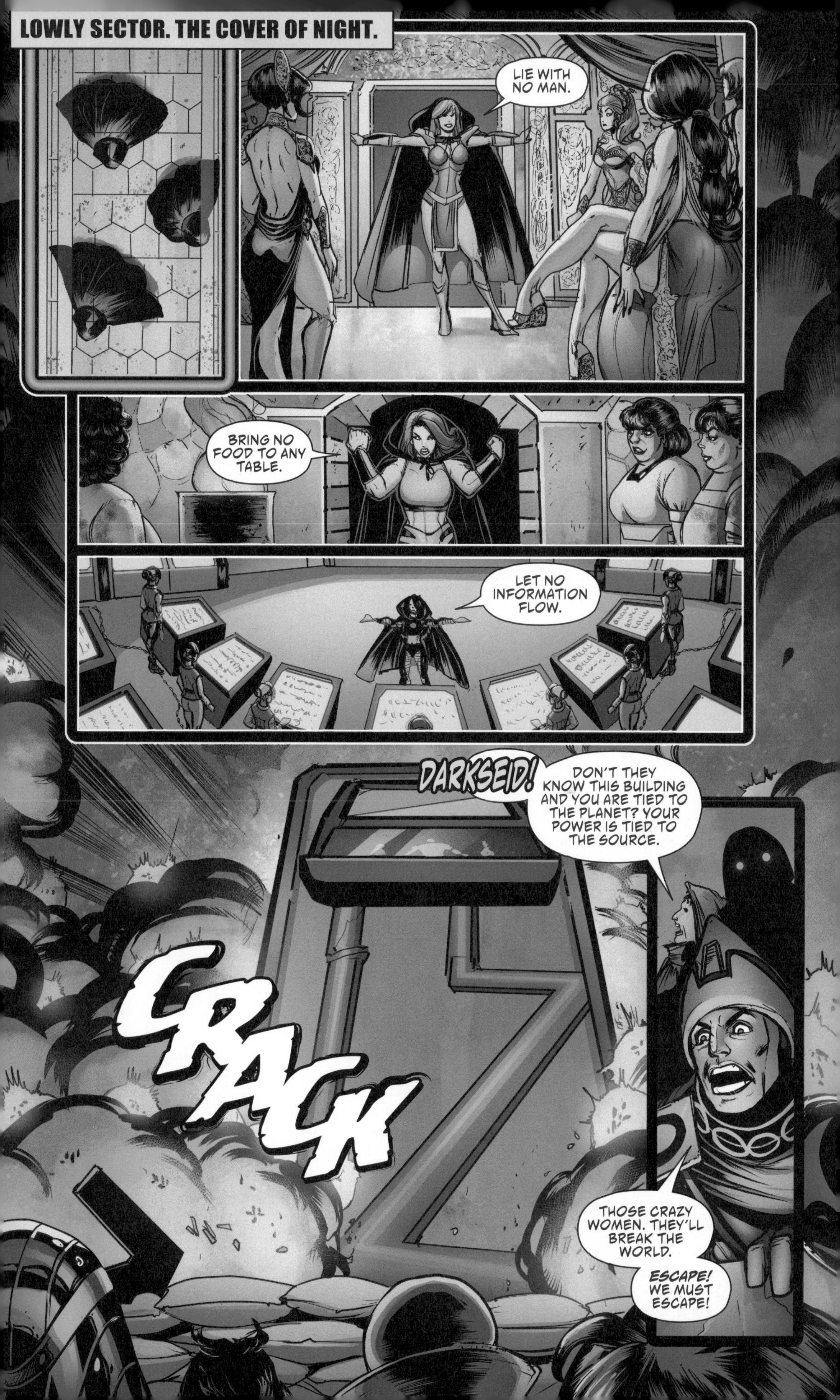
LOWLY SECTOR. THE COVER OF NIGHT.
LIE WITH NO MAN.
BRING NO FOOD TO ANY TABLE.
LET NO INFORMATION FLOW.
DARKSEID!
DON'T THEY KNOW THIS BUILDING AND YOU ARE TIED TO THE PLANET? YOUR POWER IS TIED TO THE SOURCE.
CRACK
THOSE CRAZY WOMEN. THEY'LL BREAK THE WORLD.
ESCAPE! WE MUST ESCAPE!

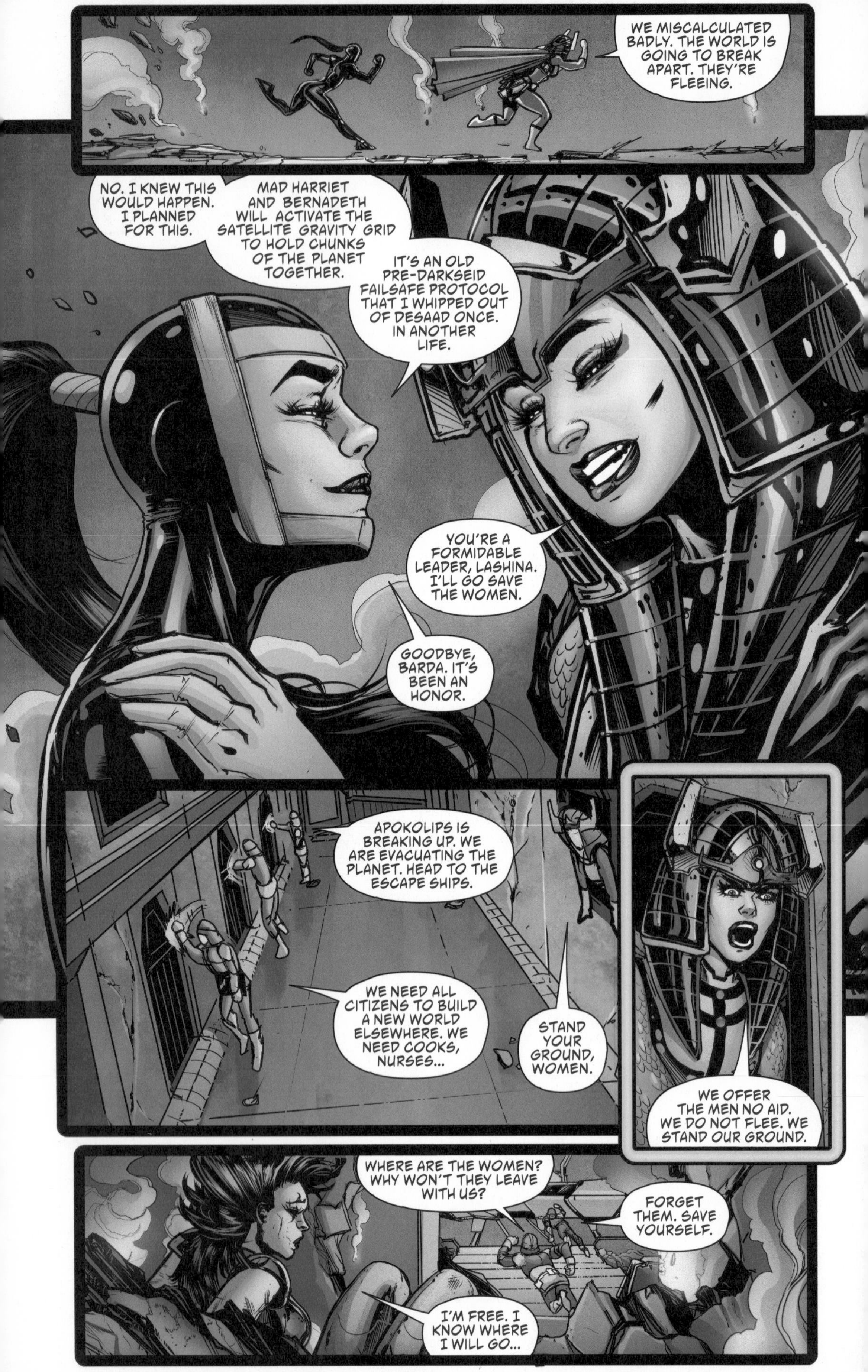
WE MISCALCULATED BADLY. THE WORLD IS GOING TO BREAK APART. THEY'RE FLEEING.
NO. I KNEW THIS WOULD HAPPEN. I PLANNED FOR THIS.
MAD HARRIET AND BERNADETH WILL ACTIVATE THE SATELLITE GRAVITY GRID TO HOLD CHUNKS OF THE PLANET TOGETHER.
IT'S AN OLD PRE-DARKSEID FAILSAFE PROTOCOL THAT I WHIPPED OUT OF DESAAD ONCE. IN ANOTHER LIFE.
YOU'RE A FORMIDABLE LEADER, LASHINA. I'LL GO SAVE THE WOMEN.
GOODBYE, BARDA. IT'S BEEN AN HONOR.
APOKOLIPS IS BREAKING UP. WE ARE EVACUATING THE PLANET. HEAD TO THE ESCAPE SHIPS.
WE NEED ALL CITIZENS TO BUILD A NEW WORLD ELSEWHERE. WE NEED COOKS, NURSES...
STAND YOUR GROUND, WOMEN.
WE OFFER THE MEN NO AID. WE DO NOT FLEE. WE STAND OUR GROUND.
WHERE ARE THE WOMEN? WHY WON'T THEY LEAVE WITH US?
FORGET THEM. SAVE YOURSELF.
I'M FREE. I KNOW WHERE I WILL GO...

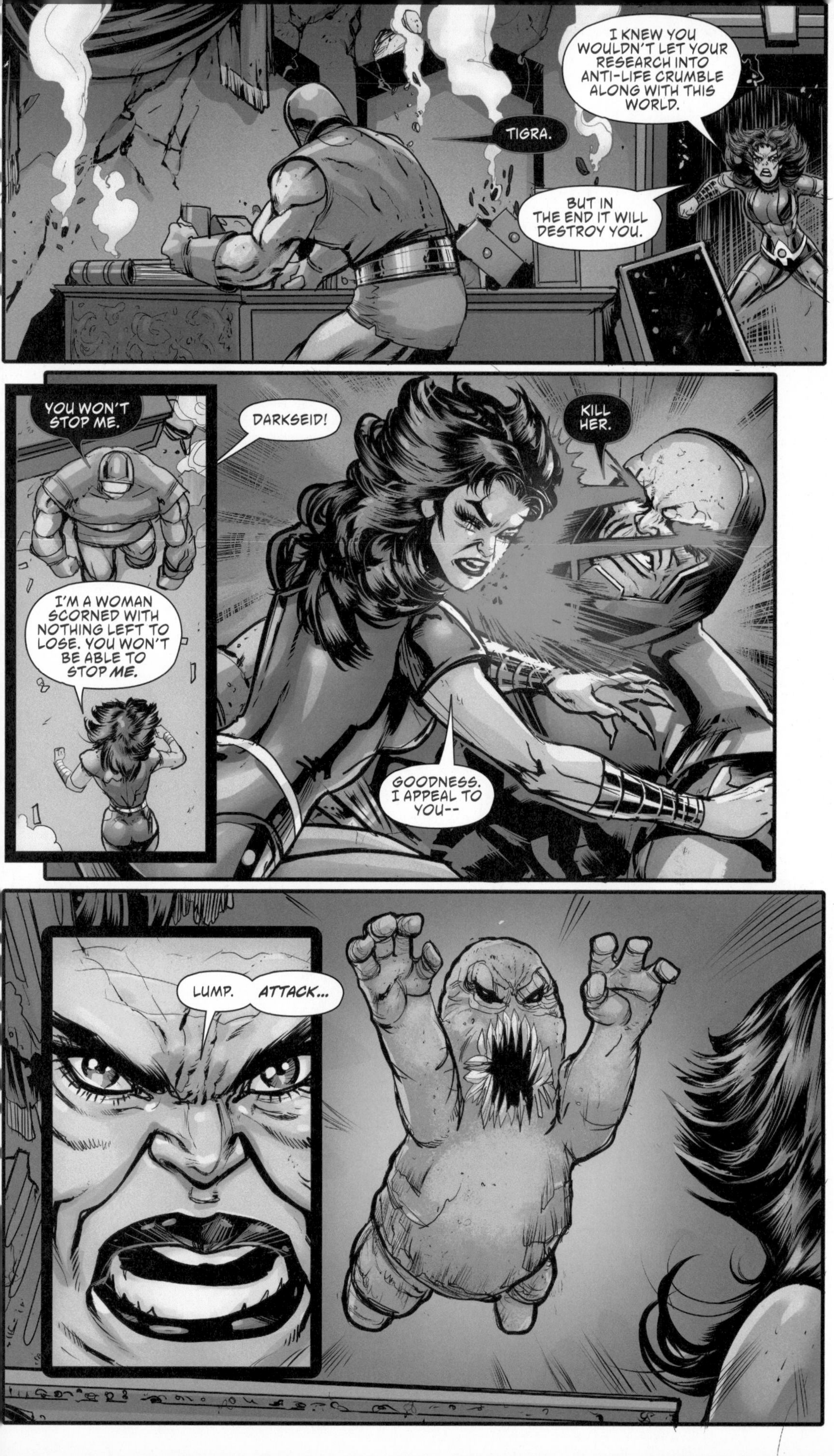
I KNEW YOU WOULDN'T LET YOUR RESEARCH INTO ANTI-LIFE CRUMBLE ALONG WITH THIS WORLD.
TIGRA.
BUT IN THE END IT WILL DESTROY YOU.
YOU WON'T STOP ME.
I'M A WOMAN SCORNED WITH NOTHING LEFT TO LOSE. YOU WON'T BE ABLE TO STOP ME.
DARKSEID!
KILL HER.
GOODNESS. I APPEAL TO YOU--
LUMP.
ATTACK...

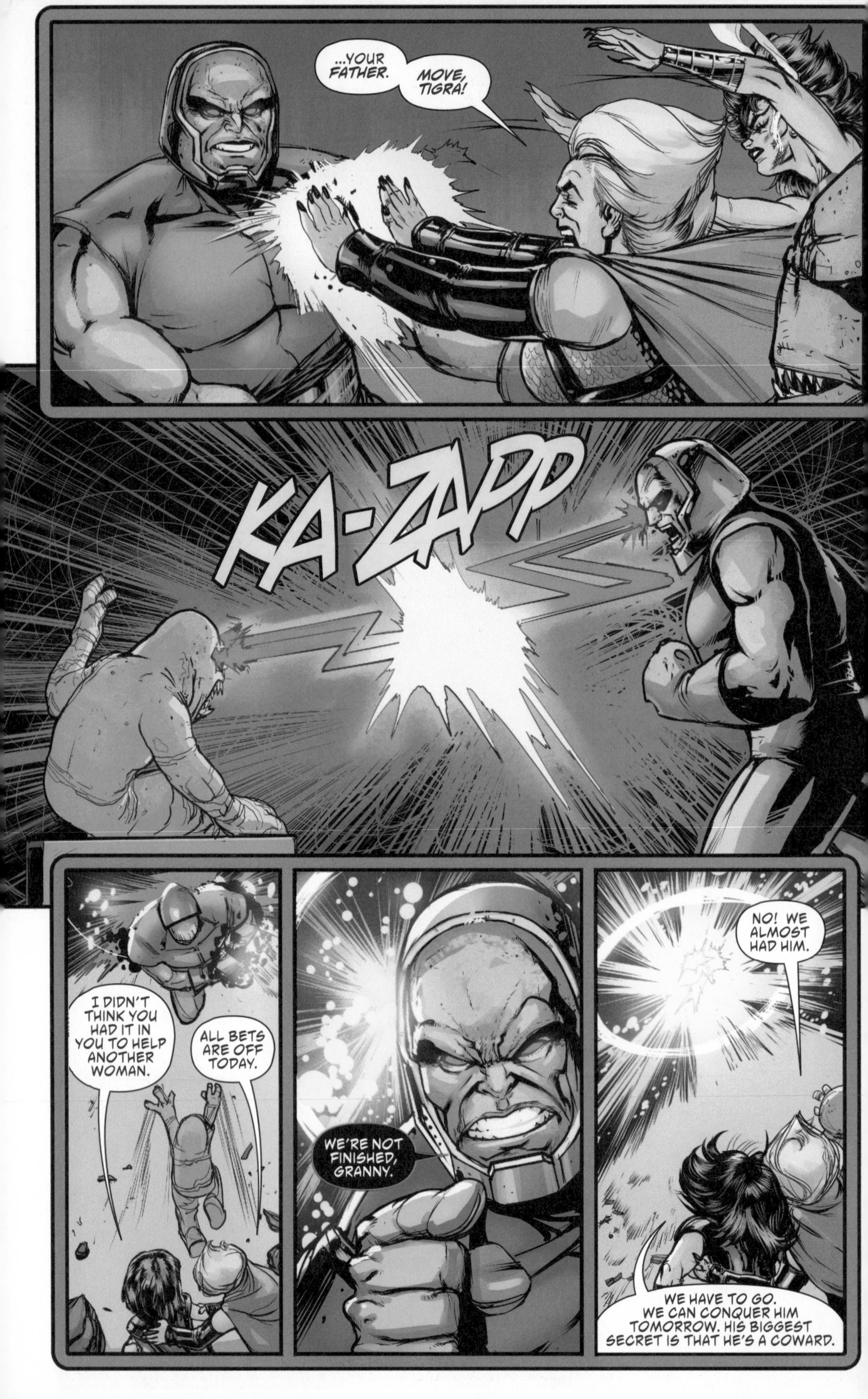

...YOUR FATHER.
MOVE, TIGRA!
KA-ZAPP
I DIDN'T THINK YOU HAD IT IN YOU TO HELP ANOTHER WOMAN.
ALL BETS ARE OFF TODAY.
WE'RE NOT FINISHED, GRANNY.
NO! WE ALMOST HAD HIM.
WE HAVE TO GO. WE CAN CONQUER HIM TOMORROW. HIS BIGGEST SECRET IS THAT HE'S A COWARD.

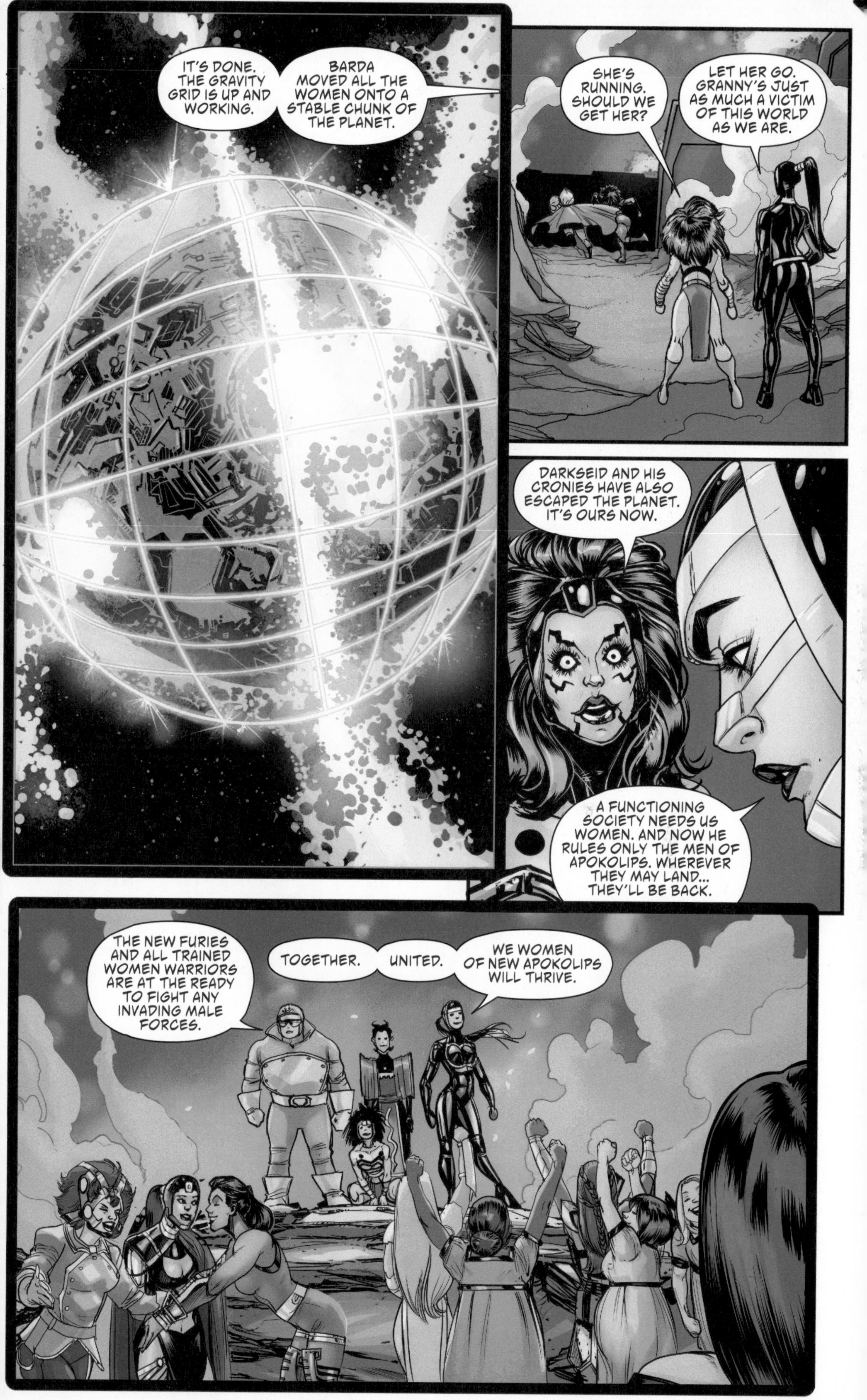
IT'S DONE. THE GRAVITY GRID IS UP AND WORKING.
BARDA MOVED ALL THE WOMEN ONTO A STABLE CHUNK OF THE PLANET.
SHE'S RUNNING. SHOULD WE GET HER?
LET HER GO. GRANNY'S JUST AS MUCH A VICTIM OF THIS WORLD AS WE ARE.
DARKSEID AND HIS CRONIES HAVE ALSO ESCAPED THE PLANET. IT'S OURS NOW.
A FUNCTIONING SOCIETY NEEDS US WOMEN. AND NOW HE RULES ONLY THE MEN OF APOKOLIPS. WHEREVER THEY MAY LAND... THEY'LL BE BACK.
THE NEW FURIES AND ALL TRAINED WOMEN WARRIORS ARE AT THE READY TO FIGHT ANY INVADING MALE FORCES.
TOGETHER.
UNITED.
WE WOMEN OF NEW APOKOLIPS WILL THRIVE.

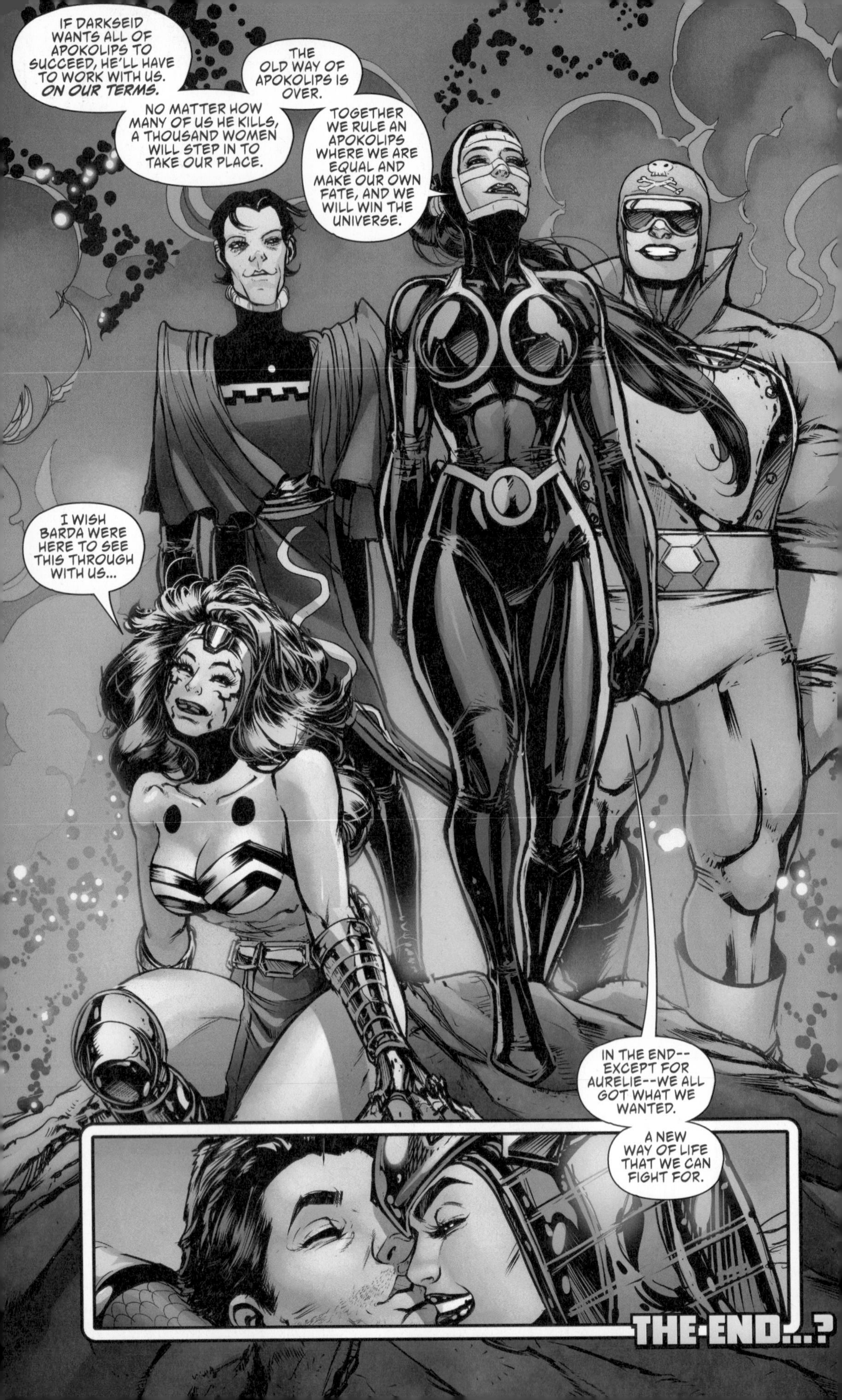
IF DARKSEID WANTS ALL OF APOKOLIPS TO SUCCEED, HE'LL HAVE TO WORK WITH US. *ON OUR TERMS.*
NO MATTER HOW MANY OF US HE KILLS, A THOUSAND WOMEN WILL STEP IN TO TAKE OUR PLACE.
THE OLD WAY OF APOKOLIPS IS OVER.
TOGETHER WE RULE AN APOKOLIPS WHERE WE ARE EQUAL AND MAKE OUR OWN FATE, AND WE WILL WIN THE UNIVERSE.
I WISH BARDA WERE HERE TO SEE THIS THROUGH WITH US...
IN THE END-- EXCEPT FOR AURELIE--WE ALL GOT WHAT WE WANTED.
A NEW WAY OF LIFE THAT WE CAN FIGHT FOR.
THE END...?

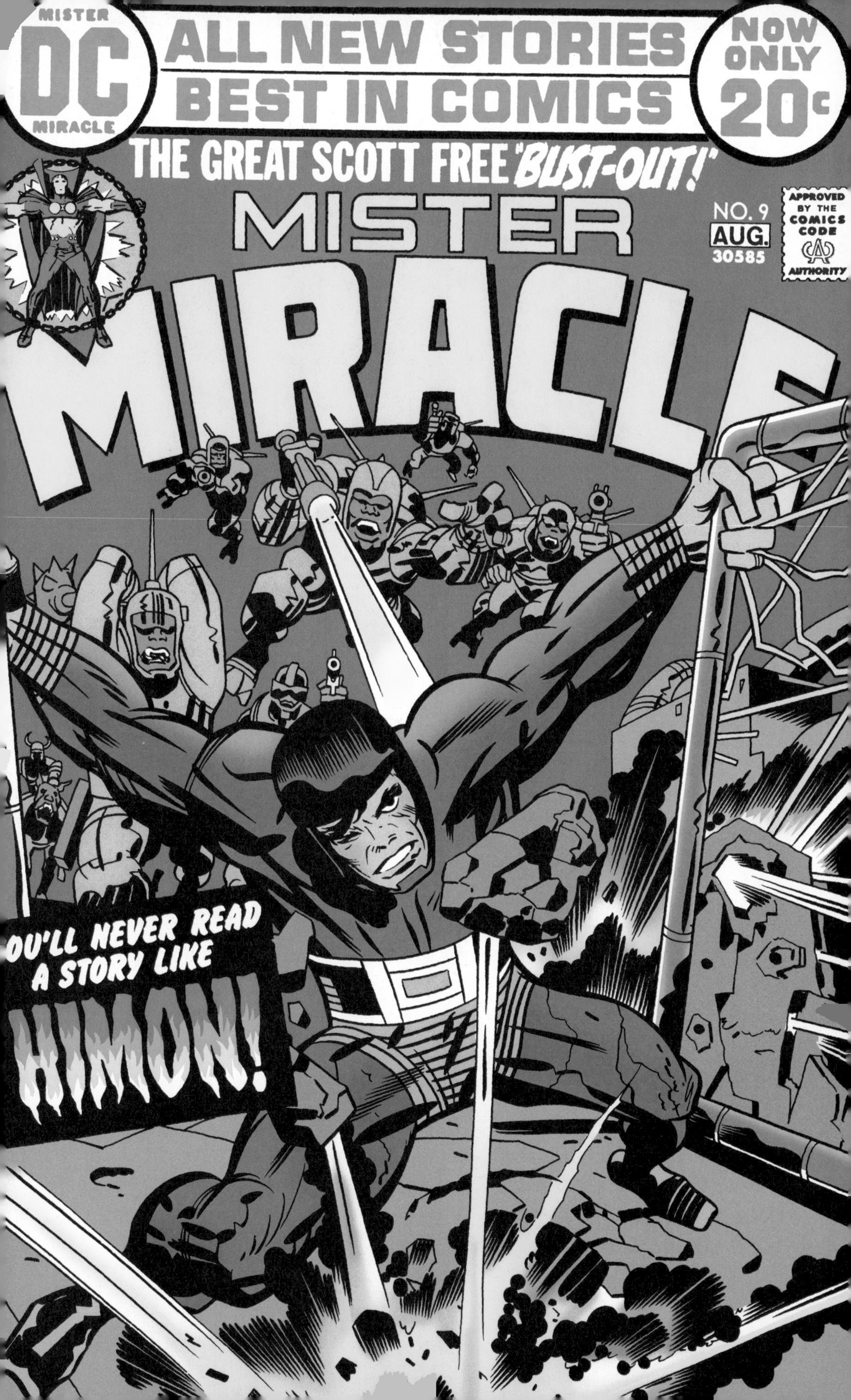
MISTER DC MIRACLE
ALL NEW STORIES
BEST IN COMICS
NOW ONLY 20¢
THE GREAT SCOTT FREE "BUST-OUT!"
MISTER MIRACLE
NO. 9
AUG.
30585
APPROVED BY THE COMICS CODE AUTHORITY
OU'LL NEVER READ A STORY LIKE
HIMON!

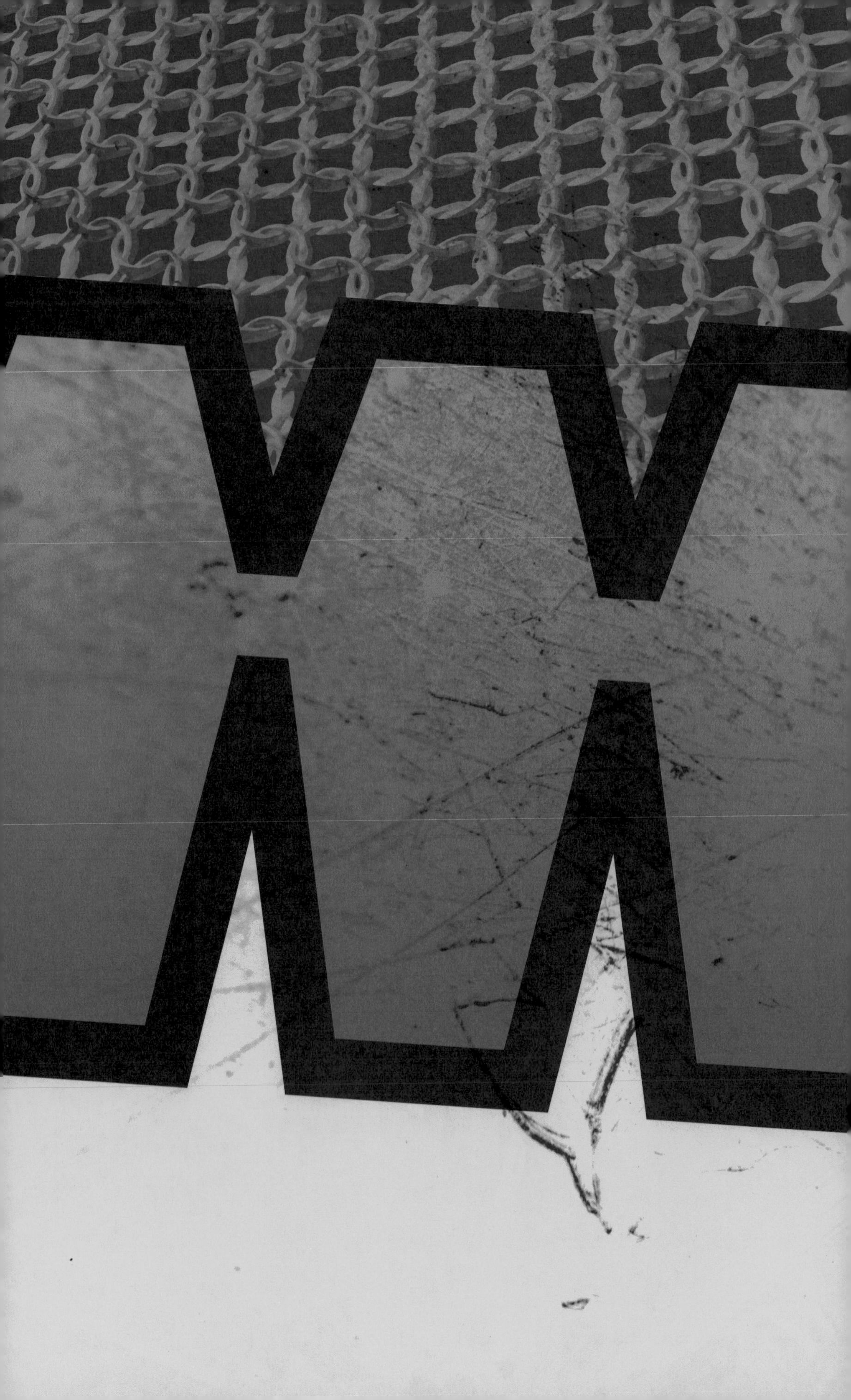
XX

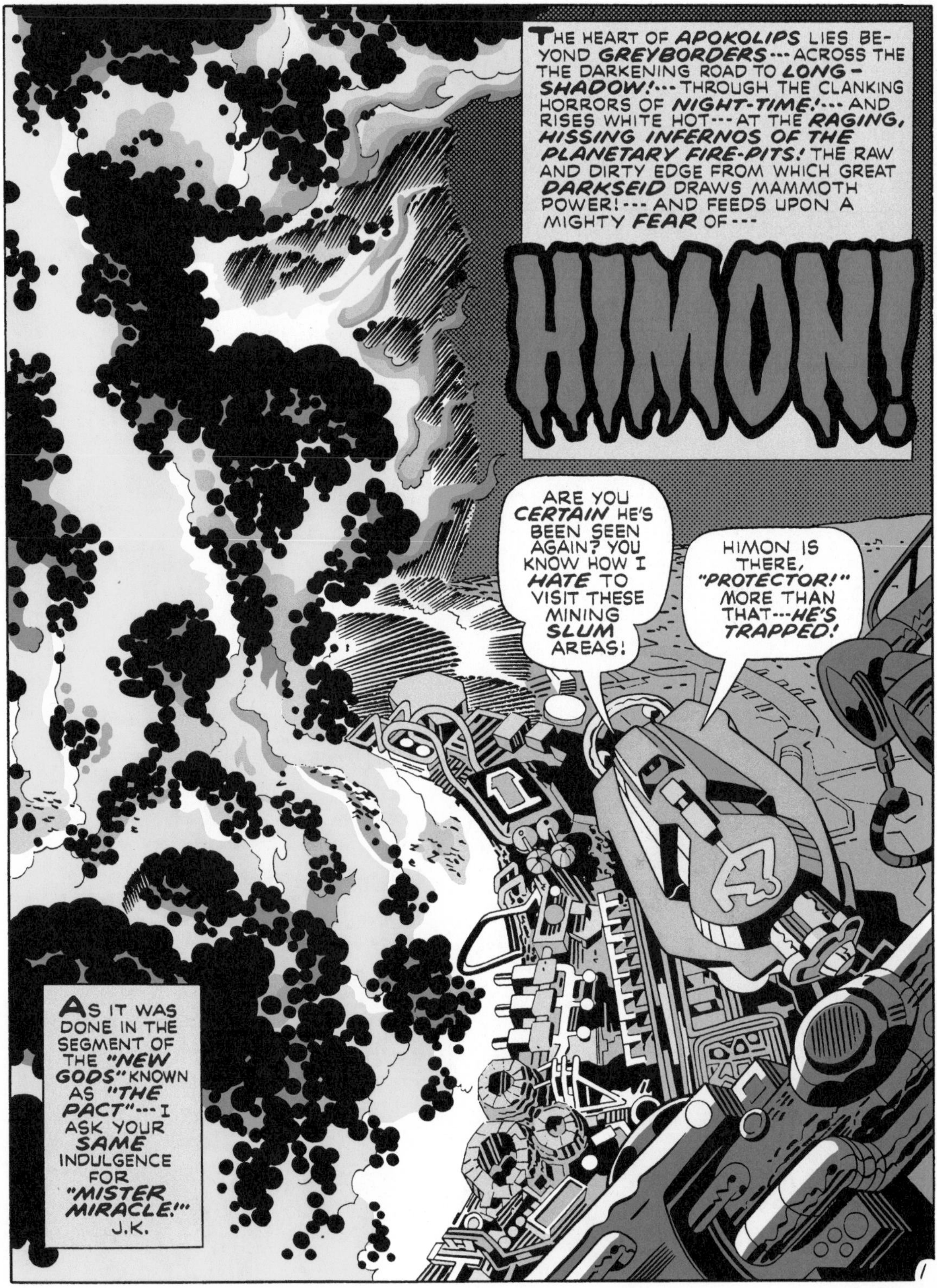
THE HEART OF APOKOLIPS LIES BEYOND GREYBORDERS--- ACROSS THE THE DARKENING ROAD TO LONG-SHADOW!--- THROUGH THE CLANKING HORRORS OF NIGHT-TIME!--- AND RISES WHITE HOT--- AT THE RAGING, HISSING INFERNOS OF THE PLANETARY FIRE-PITS! THE RAW AND DIRTY EDGE FROM WHICH GREAT DARKSEID DRAWS MAMMOTH POWER!--- AND FEEDS UPON A MIGHTY FEAR OF---
HIMON!
ARE YOU CERTAIN HE'S BEEN SEEN AGAIN? YOU KNOW HOW I HATE TO VISIT THESE MINING SLUM AREAS!
HIMON IS THERE, "PROTECTOR!" MORE THAN THAT---HE'S TRAPPED!
AS IT WAS DONE IN THE SEGMENT OF THE "NEW GODS" KNOWN AS "THE PACT"--- I ASK YOUR SAME INDULGENCE FOR "MISTER MIRACLE!" J.K.

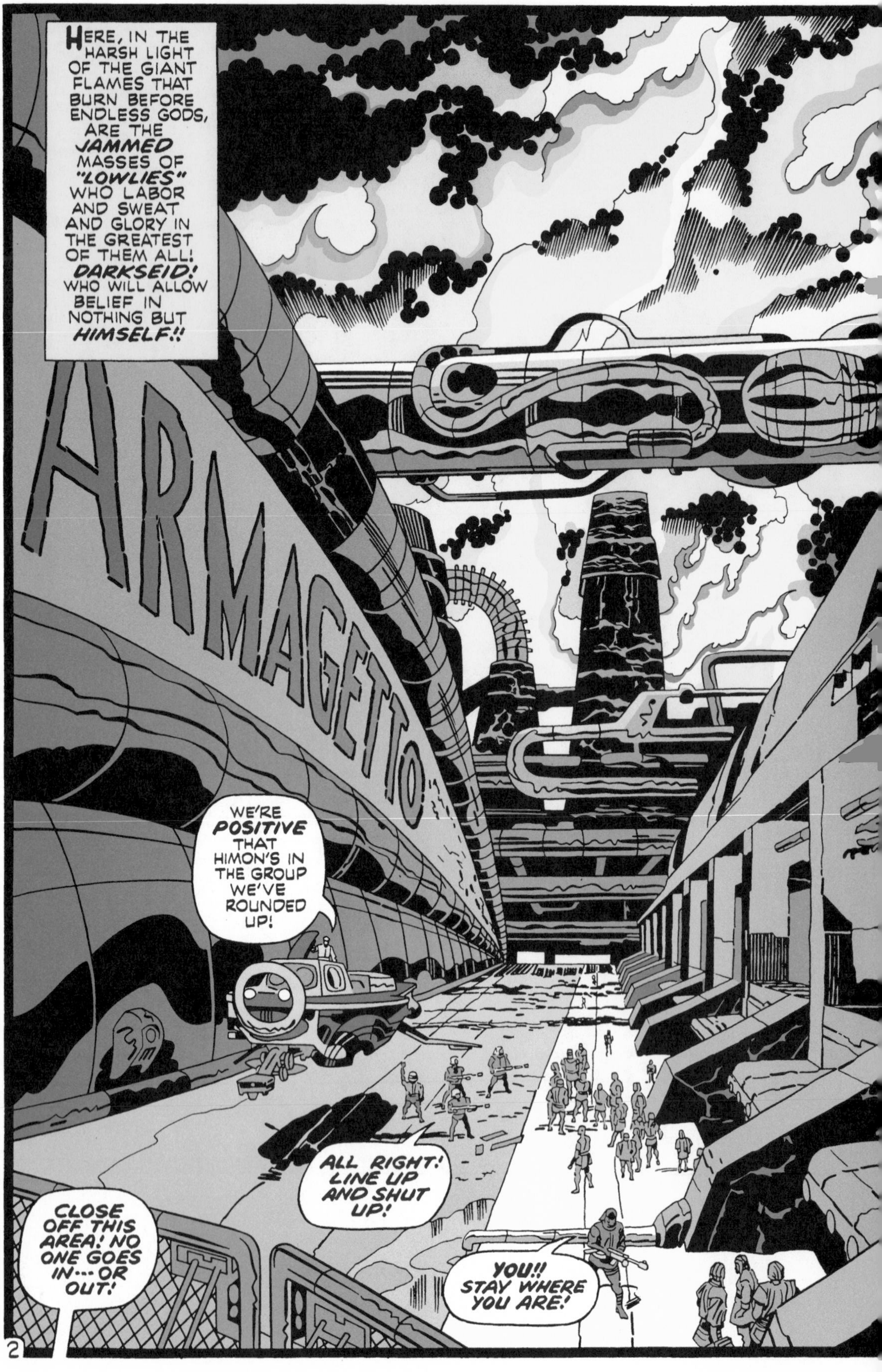
HERE, IN THE HARSH LIGHT OF THE GIANT FLAMES THAT BURN BEFORE ENDLESS GODS, ARE THE JAMMED MASSES OF "LOWLIES" WHO LABOR AND SWEAT AND GLORY IN THE GREATEST OF THEM ALL! DARKSEID! WHO WILL ALLOW BELIEF IN NOTHING BUT HIMSELF!!
ARMAGETTO
WE'RE POSITIVE THAT HIMON'S IN THE GROUP WE'VE ROUNDED UP!
ALL RIGHT! LINE UP AND SHUT UP!
CLOSE OFF THIS AREA! NO ONE GOES IN... OR OUT!
YOU!! STAY WHERE YOU ARE!

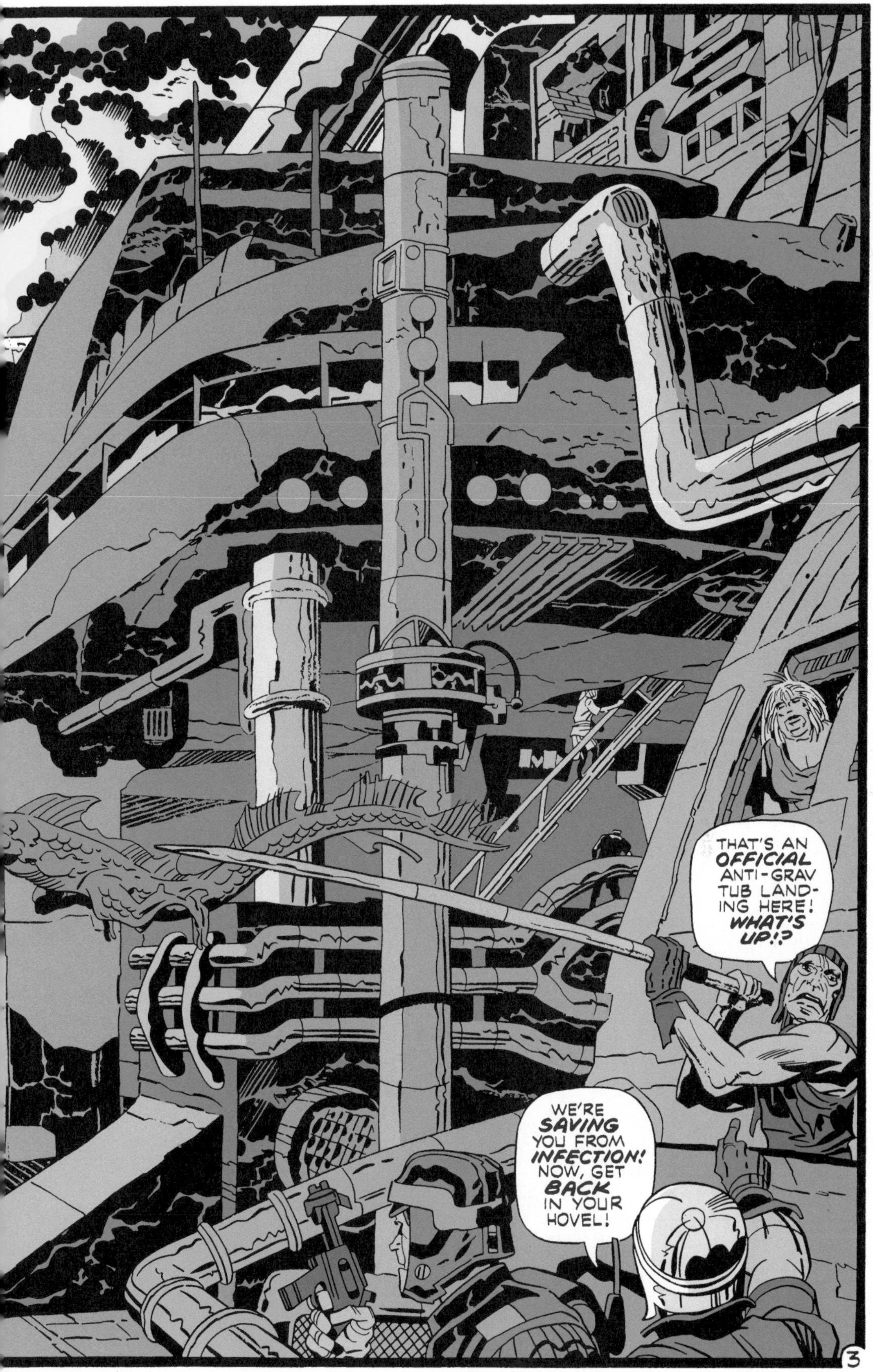
THAT'S AN OFFICIAL ANTI-GRAV TUB LANDING HERE! WHAT'S UP!?
WE'RE SAVING YOU FROM INFECTION! NOW, GET BACK IN YOUR HOVEL!
3

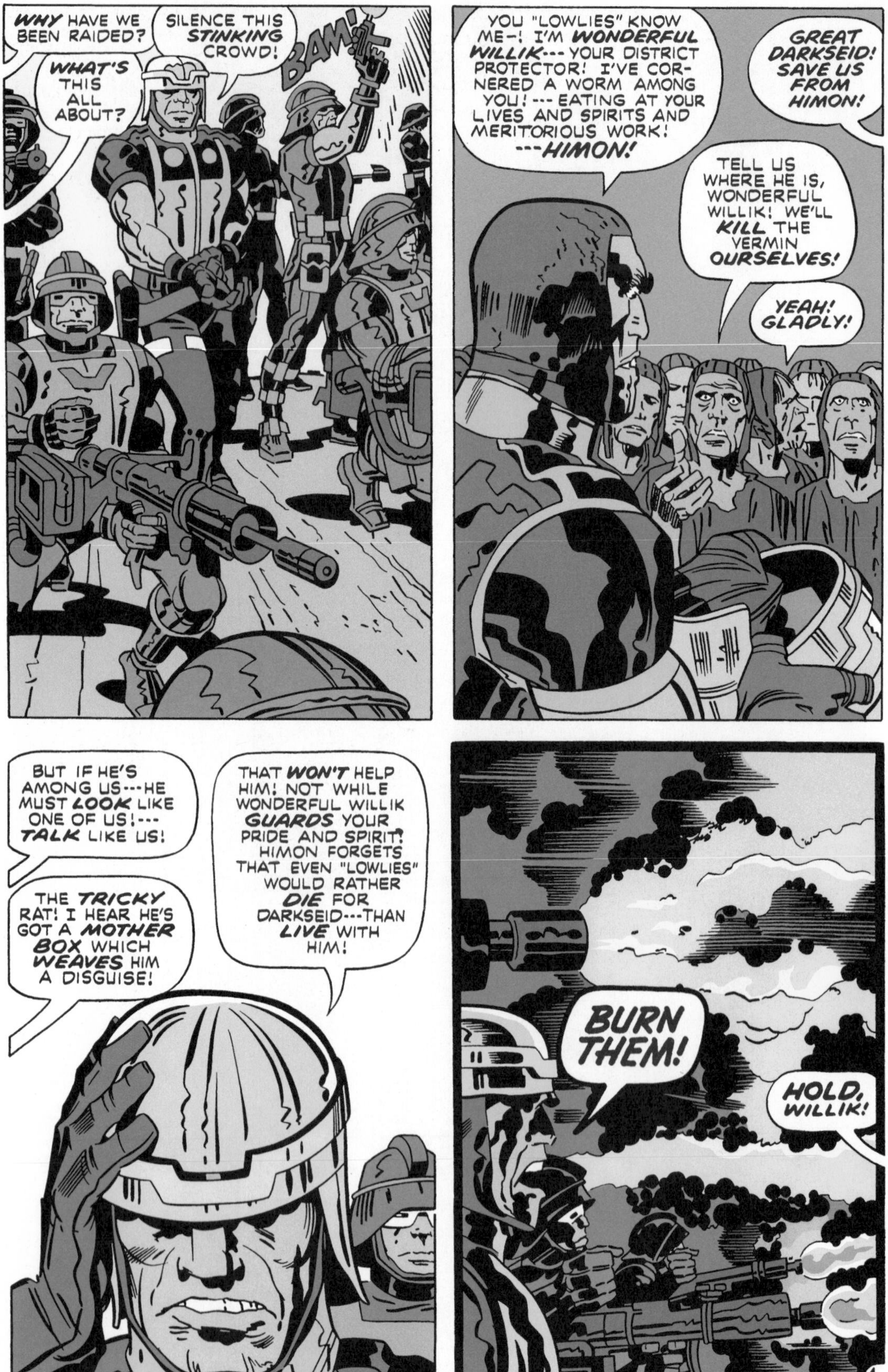
WHY HAVE WE BEEN RAIDED?
WHAT'S THIS ALL ABOUT?
SILENCE THIS STINKING CROWD!
BAM!
YOU "LOWLIES" KNOW ME--! I'M WONDERFUL WILLIK--- YOUR DISTRICT PROTECTOR! I'VE CORNERED A WORM AMONG YOU! --- EATING AT YOUR LIVES AND SPIRITS AND MERITORIOUS WORK! ---HIMON!
GREAT DARKSEID! SAVE US FROM HIMON!
TELL US WHERE HE IS, WONDERFUL WILLIK! WE'LL KILL THE VERMIN OURSELVES!
YEAH! GLADLY!
BUT IF HE'S AMONG US---HE MUST LOOK LIKE ONE OF US!--- TALK LIKE US!
THE TRICKY RAT! I HEAR HE'S GOT A MOTHER BOX WHICH WEAVES HIM A DISGUISE!
THAT WON'T HELP HIM! NOT WHILE WONDERFUL WILLIK GUARDS YOUR PRIDE AND SPIRIT! HIMON FORGETS THAT EVEN "LOWLIES" WOULD RATHER DIE FOR DARKSEID---THAN LIVE WITH HIM!
BURN THEM!
HOLD, WILLIK!
4

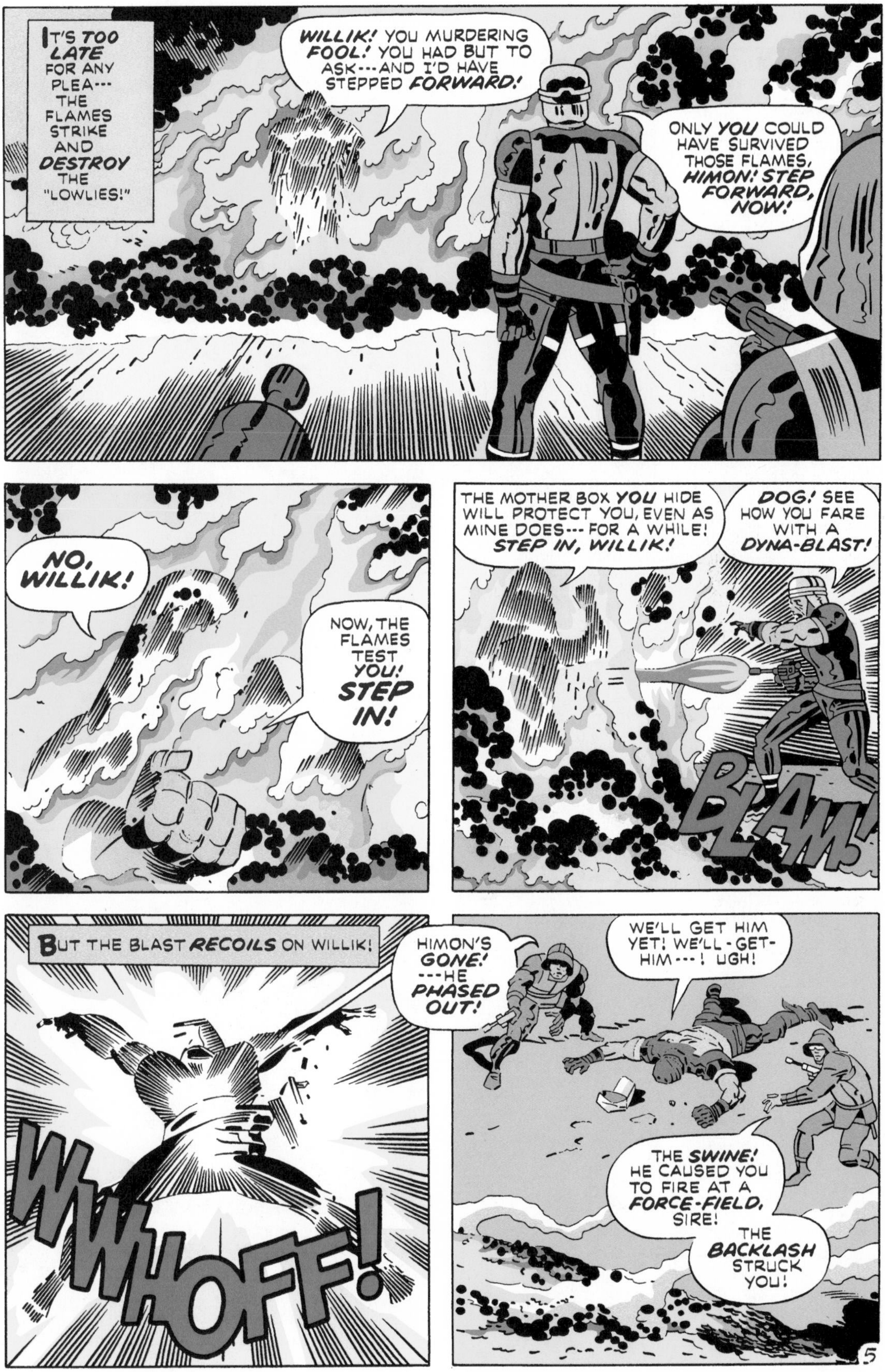
IT'S TOO LATE FOR ANY PLEA--- THE FLAMES STRIKE AND DESTROY THE "LOWLIES!"
WILLIK! YOU MURDERING FOOL! YOU HAD BUT TO ASK---AND I'D HAVE STEPPED FORWARD!
ONLY YOU COULD HAVE SURVIVED THOSE FLAMES, HIMON! STEP FORWARD, NOW!
NO, WILLIK!
NOW, THE FLAMES TEST YOU! STEP IN!
THE MOTHER BOX YOU HIDE WILL PROTECT YOU, EVEN AS MINE DOES--- FOR A WHILE! STEP IN, WILLIK!
DOG! SEE HOW YOU FARE WITH A DYNA-BLAST!
BLAM!
BUT THE BLAST RECOILS ON WILLIK!
WWHOFF!
HIMON'S GONE! ---HE PHASED OUT!
WE'LL GET HIM YET! WE'LL-GET-HIM---! UGH!
THE SWINE! HE CAUSED YOU TO FIRE AT A FORCE-FIELD, SIRE!
THE BACKLASH STRUCK YOU!

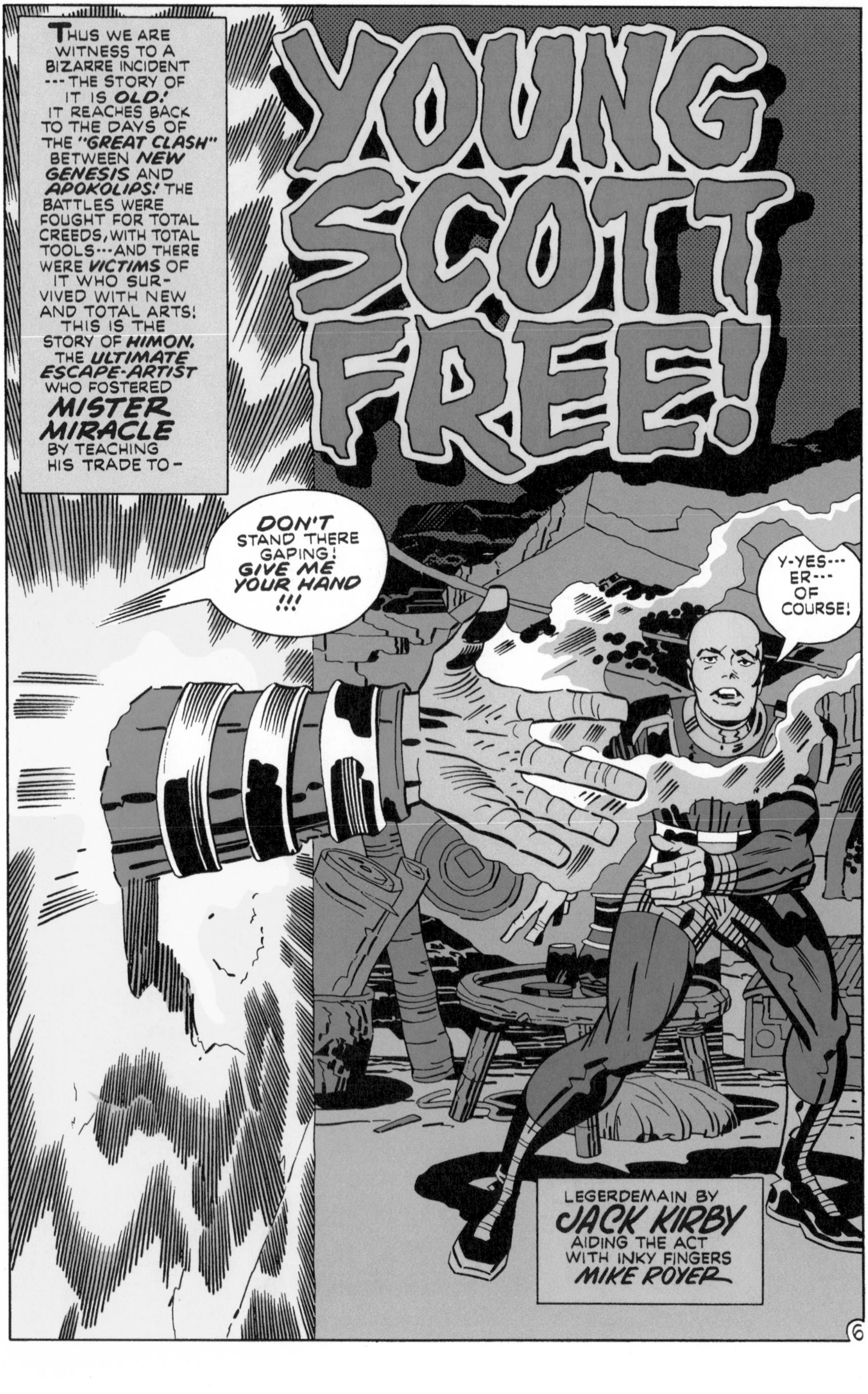
THUS WE ARE WITNESS TO A BIZARRE INCIDENT --- THE STORY OF IT IS OLD! IT REACHES BACK TO THE DAYS OF THE "GREAT CLASH" BETWEEN NEW GENESIS AND APOKOLIPS! THE BATTLES WERE FOUGHT FOR TOTAL CREEDS, WITH TOTAL TOOLS---AND THERE WERE VICTIMS OF IT WHO SURVIVED WITH NEW AND TOTAL ARTS! THIS IS THE STORY OF HIMON, THE ULTIMATE ESCAPE-ARTIST WHO FOSTERED MISTER MIRACLE BY TEACHING HIS TRADE TO -
YOUNG SCOTT FREE!
DON'T STAND THERE GAPING! GIVE ME YOUR HAND !!!
Y-YES--- ER--- OF COURSE!
LEGERDEMAIN BY JACK KIRBY AIDING THE ACT WITH INKY FINGERS MIKE ROYER
6

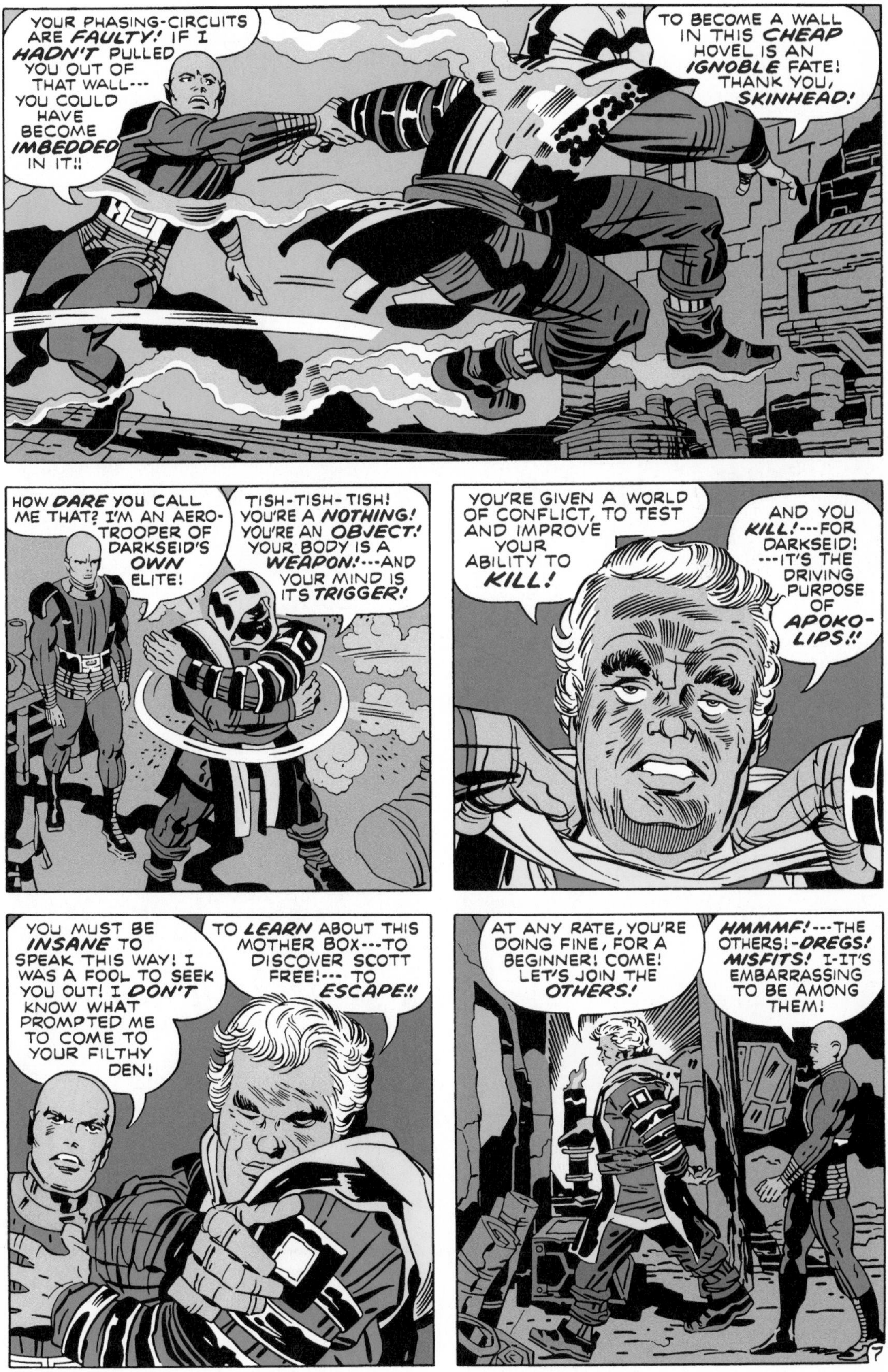
YOUR PHASING-CIRCUITS ARE FAULTY! IF I HADN'T PULLED YOU OUT OF THAT WALL--- YOU COULD HAVE BECOME IMBEDDED IN IT!!
TO BECOME A WALL IN THIS CHEAP HOVEL IS AN IGNOBLE FATE! THANK YOU, SKINHEAD!
HOW DARE YOU CALL ME THAT? I'M AN AERO-TROOPER OF DARKSEID'S OWN ELITE!
TISH-TISH-TISH! YOU'RE A NOTHING! YOU'RE AN OBJECT! YOUR BODY IS A WEAPON!---AND YOUR MIND IS ITS TRIGGER!
YOU'RE GIVEN A WORLD OF CONFLICT, TO TEST AND IMPROVE YOUR ABILITY TO KILL!
AND YOU KILL!---FOR DARKSEID! ---IT'S THE DRIVING PURPOSE OF APOKO-LIPS!!
YOU MUST BE INSANE TO SPEAK THIS WAY! I WAS A FOOL TO SEEK YOU OUT! I DON'T KNOW WHAT PROMPTED ME TO COME TO YOUR FILTHY DEN!
TO LEARN ABOUT THIS MOTHER BOX---TO DISCOVER SCOTT FREE!--- TO ESCAPE!!
AT ANY RATE, YOU'RE DOING FINE, FOR A BEGINNER! COME! LET'S JOIN THE OTHERS!
HMMMF!---THE OTHERS!-DREGS! MISFITS! I-IT'S EMBARRASSING TO BE AMONG THEM!
7

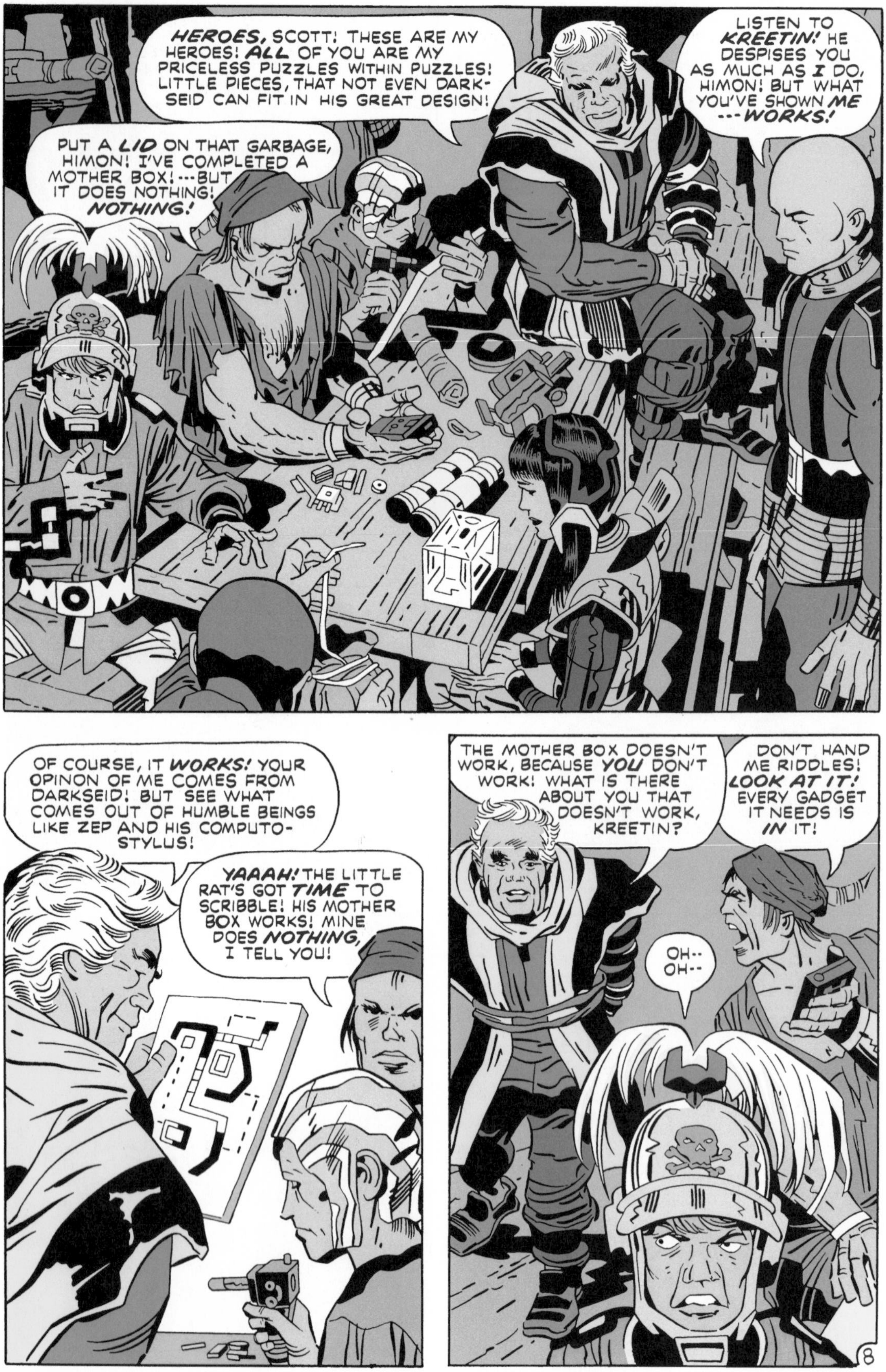
HEROES, SCOTT! THESE ARE MY HEROES! ALL OF YOU ARE MY PRICELESS PUZZLES WITHIN PUZZLES! LITTLE PIECES, THAT NOT EVEN DARK-SEID CAN FIT IN HIS GREAT DESIGN!
LISTEN TO KREETIN! HE DESPISES YOU AS MUCH AS I DO, HIMON! BUT WHAT YOU'VE SHOWN ME ---WORKS!
PUT A LID ON THAT GARBAGE, HIMON! I'VE COMPLETED A MOTHER BOX! ---BUT IT DOES NOTHING! NOTHING!
OF COURSE, IT WORKS! YOUR OPINON OF ME COMES FROM DARKSEID! BUT SEE WHAT COMES OUT OF HUMBLE BEINGS LIKE ZEP AND HIS COMPUTO-STYLUS!
YAAAH! THE LITTLE RAT'S GOT TIME TO SCRIBBLE! HIS MOTHER BOX WORKS! MINE DOES NOTHING, I TELL YOU!
THE MOTHER BOX DOESN'T WORK, BECAUSE YOU DON'T WORK! WHAT IS THERE ABOUT YOU THAT DOESN'T WORK, KREETIN?
DON'T HAND ME RIDDLES! LOOK AT IT! EVERY GADGET IT NEEDS IS IN IT!
OH-- OH--
8

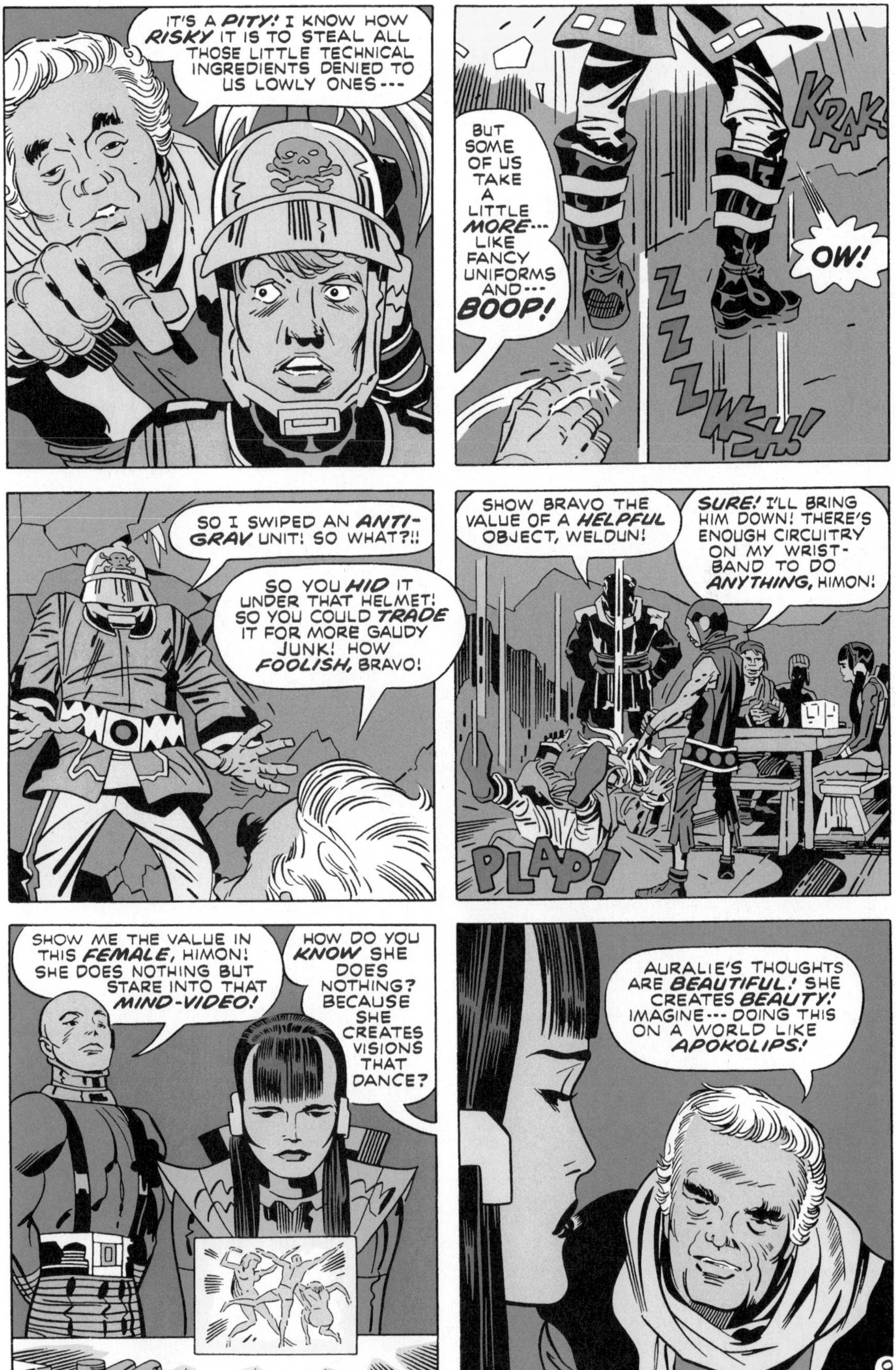
IT'S A PITY! I KNOW HOW RISKY IT IS TO STEAL ALL THOSE LITTLE TECHNICAL INGREDIENTS DENIED TO US LOWLY ONES---
BUT SOME OF US TAKE A LITTLE MORE--- LIKE FANCY UNIFORMS AND--- BOOP!
KRAK!
OW!
ZZZWSH!
SO I SWIPED AN ANTI-GRAV UNIT! SO WHAT?!!
SO YOU HID IT UNDER THAT HELMET! SO YOU COULD TRADE IT FOR MORE GAUDY JUNK! HOW FOOLISH, BRAVO!
SHOW BRAVO THE VALUE OF A HELPFUL OBJECT, WELDUN!
SURE! I'LL BRING HIM DOWN! THERE'S ENOUGH CIRCUITRY ON MY WRIST-BAND TO DO ANYTHING, HIMON!
PLAP!
SHOW ME THE VALUE IN THIS FEMALE, HIMON! SHE DOES NOTHING BUT STARE INTO THAT MIND-VIDEO!
HOW DO YOU KNOW SHE DOES NOTHING? BECAUSE SHE CREATES VISIONS THAT DANCE?
AURALIE'S THOUGHTS ARE BEAUTIFUL! SHE CREATES BEAUTY! IMAGINE--- DOING THIS ON A WORLD LIKE APOKOLIPS!
9

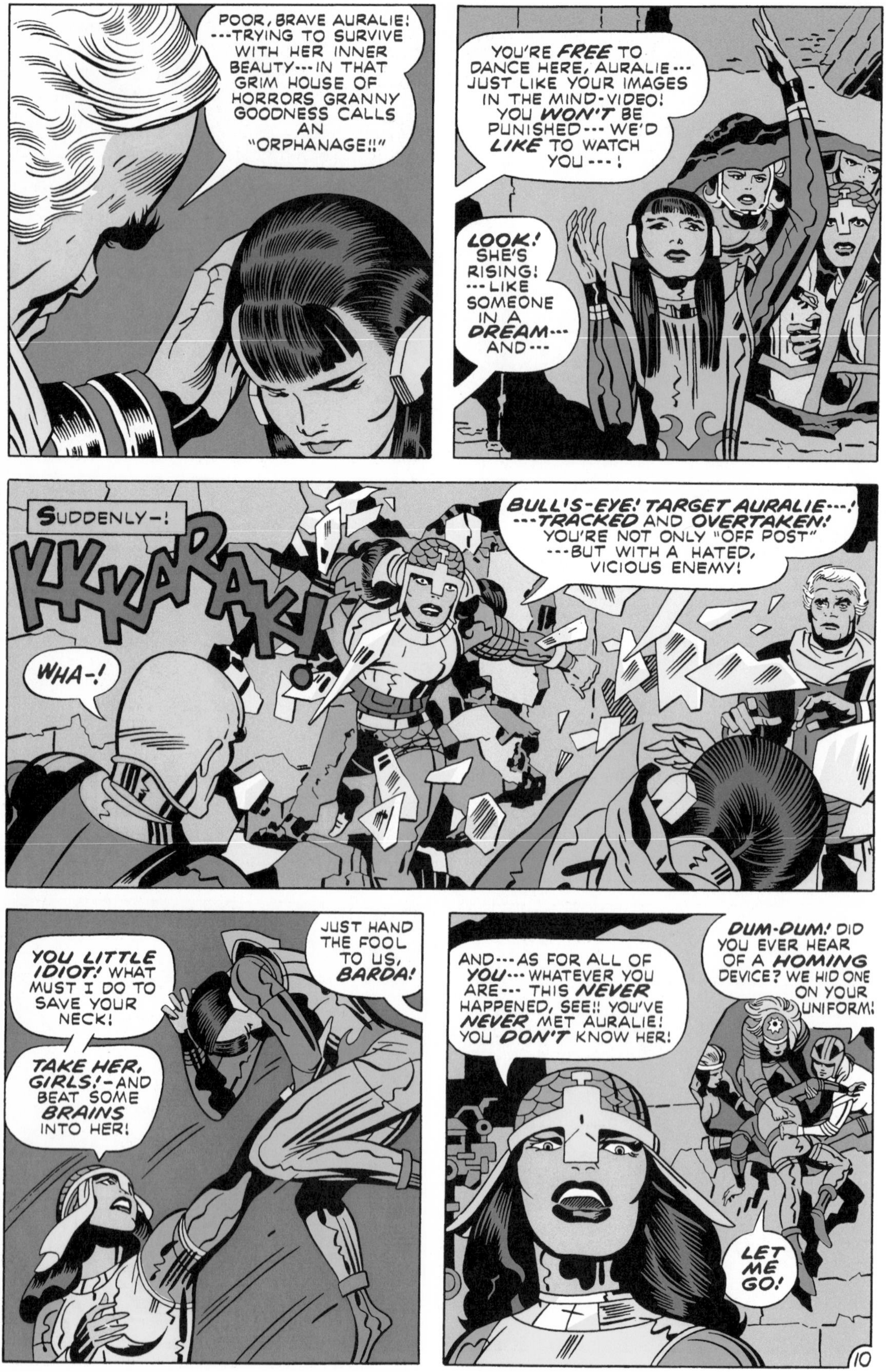
POOR, BRAVE AURALIE! ---TRYING TO SURVIVE WITH HER INNER BEAUTY---IN THAT GRIM HOUSE OF HORRORS GRANNY GOODNESS CALLS AN "ORPHANAGE!!"
YOU'RE FREE TO DANCE HERE, AURALIE--- JUST LIKE YOUR IMAGES IN THE MIND-VIDEO! YOU WON'T BE PUNISHED--- WE'D LIKE TO WATCH YOU---!
LOOK! SHE'S RISING! ---LIKE SOMEONE IN A DREAM--- AND---
SUDDENLY-!
KKKARAKK!
BULL'S-EYE! TARGET AURALIE---! ---TRACKED AND OVERTAKEN! YOU'RE NOT ONLY "OFF POST" ---BUT WITH A HATED, VICIOUS ENEMY!
WHA-!
YOU LITTLE IDIOT! WHAT MUST I DO TO SAVE YOUR NECK!
TAKE HER, GIRLS!-AND BEAT SOME BRAINS INTO HER!
JUST HAND THE FOOL TO US, BARDA!
AND---AS FOR ALL OF YOU---WHATEVER YOU ARE--- THIS NEVER HAPPENED, SEE!! YOU'VE NEVER MET AURALIE! YOU DON'T KNOW HER!
DUM-DUM! DID YOU EVER HEAR OF A HOMING DEVICE? WE HID ONE ON YOUR UNIFORM!
LET ME GO!

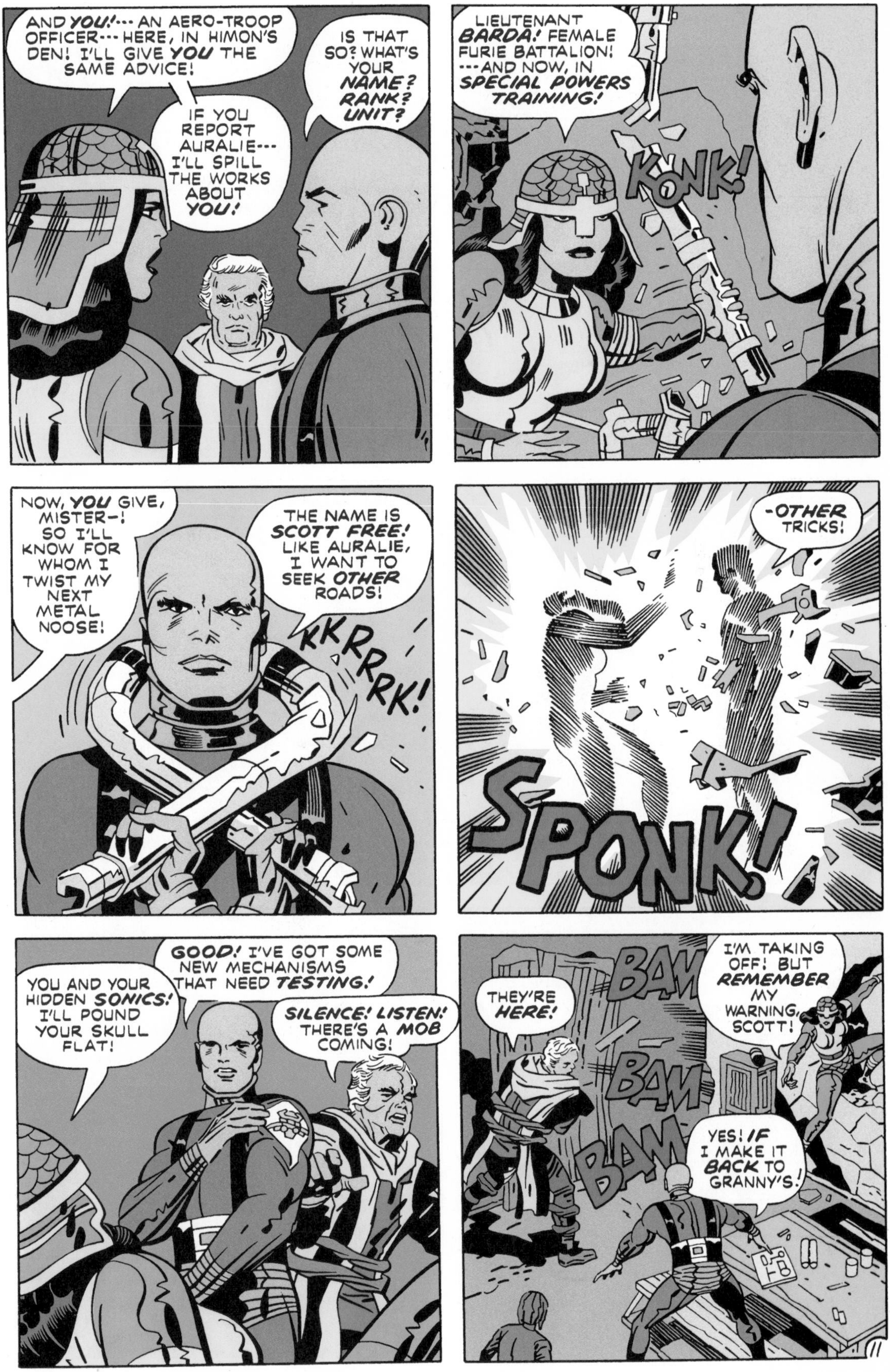
AND YOU!--- AN AERO-TROOP OFFICER--- HERE, IN HIMON'S DEN! I'LL GIVE YOU THE SAME ADVICE!
IF YOU REPORT AURALIE--- I'LL SPILL THE WORKS ABOUT YOU!
IS THAT SO? WHAT'S YOUR NAME? RANK? UNIT?
LIEUTENANT BARDA! FEMALE FURIE BATTALION! ---AND NOW, IN SPECIAL POWERS TRAINING!
KONK!
NOW, YOU GIVE, MISTER-! SO I'LL KNOW FOR WHOM I TWIST MY NEXT METAL NOOSE!
THE NAME IS SCOTT FREE! LIKE AURALIE, I WANT TO SEEK OTHER ROADS!
KKRRRRK!
-OTHER TRICKS!
SPONK!
YOU AND YOUR HIDDEN SONICS! I'LL POUND YOUR SKULL FLAT!
GOOD! I'VE GOT SOME NEW MECHANISMS THAT NEED TESTING!
SILENCE! LISTEN! THERE'S A MOB COMING!
BAM
BAM
BAM
THEY'RE HERE!
I'M TAKING OFF! BUT REMEMBER MY WARNING, SCOTT!
YES! IF I MAKE IT BACK TO GRANNY'S!

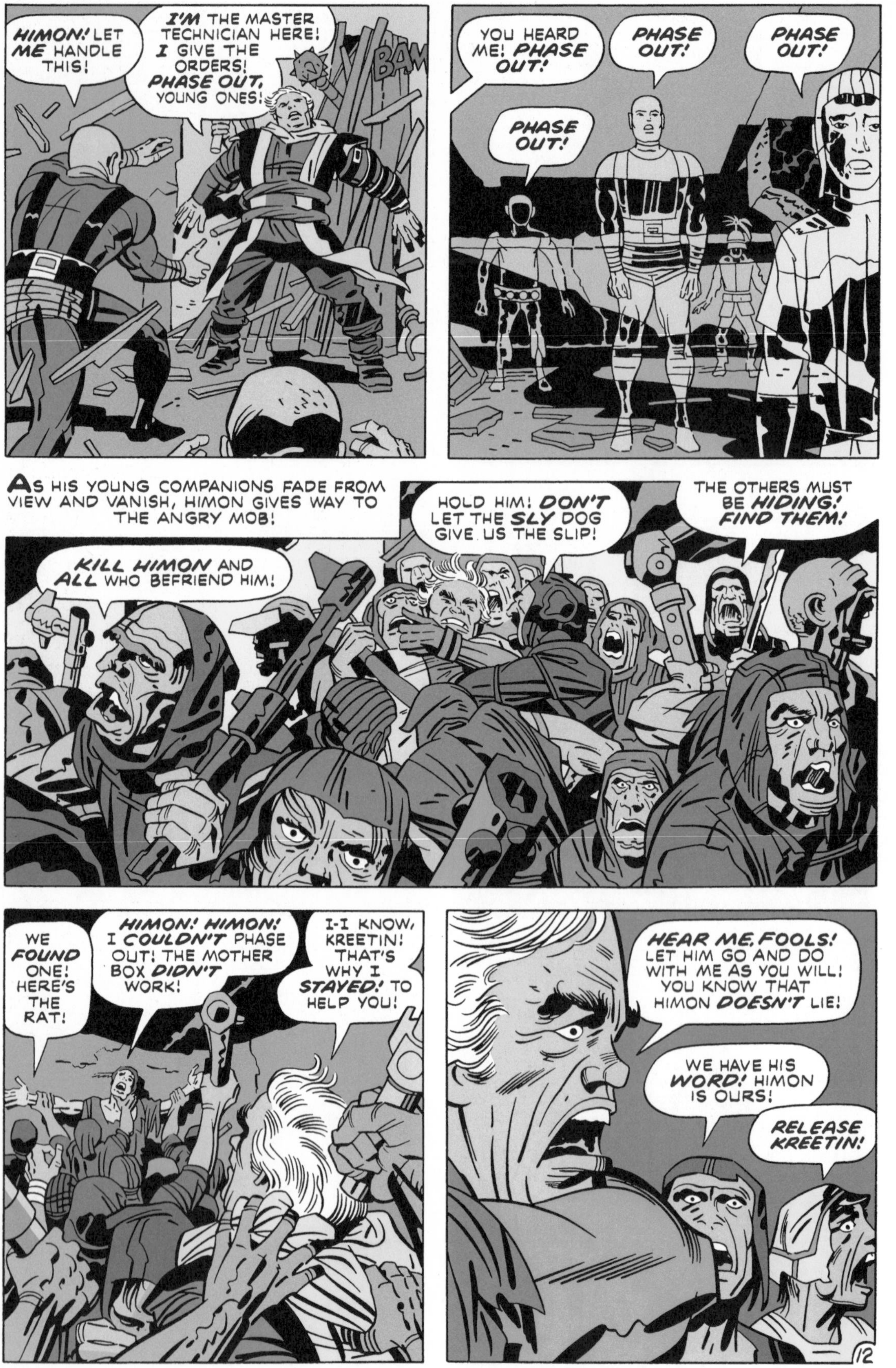
HIMON! LET ME HANDLE THIS!
I'M THE MASTER TECHNICIAN HERE! I GIVE THE ORDERS! PHASE OUT, YOUNG ONES!
BAM
YOU HEARD ME! PHASE OUT!
PHASE OUT!
PHASE OUT!
PHASE OUT!
AS HIS YOUNG COMPANIONS FADE FROM VIEW AND VANISH, HIMON GIVES WAY TO THE ANGRY MOB!
HOLD HIM! DON'T LET THE SLY DOG GIVE US THE SLIP!
THE OTHERS MUST BE HIDING! FIND THEM!
KILL HIMON AND ALL WHO BEFRIEND HIM!
WE FOUND ONE! HERE'S THE RAT!
HIMON! HIMON! I COULDN'T PHASE OUT! THE MOTHER BOX DIDN'T WORK!
I-I KNOW, KREETIN! THAT'S WHY I STAYED! TO HELP YOU!
HEAR ME, FOOLS! LET HIM GO AND DO WITH ME AS YOU WILL! YOU KNOW THAT HIMON DOESN'T LIE!
WE HAVE HIS WORD! HIMON IS OURS!
RELEASE KREETIN!
12

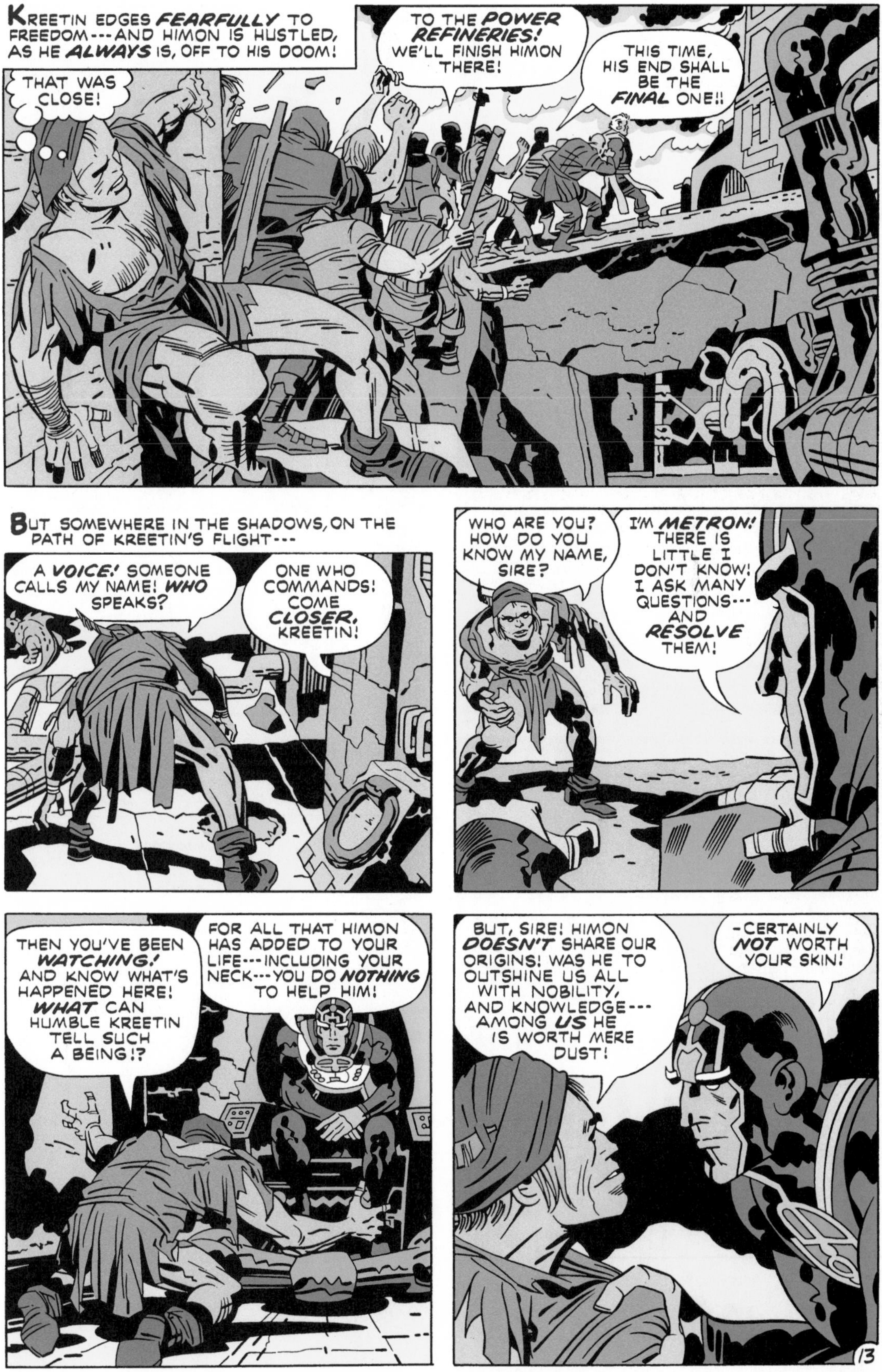
KREETIN EDGES FEARFULLY TO FREEDOM---AND HIMON IS HUSTLED, AS HE ALWAYS IS, OFF TO HIS DOOM!
THAT WAS CLOSE!
TO THE POWER REFINERIES! WE'LL FINISH HIMON THERE!
THIS TIME, HIS END SHALL BE THE FINAL ONE!!
BUT SOMEWHERE IN THE SHADOWS, ON THE PATH OF KREETIN'S FLIGHT---
A VOICE! SOMEONE CALLS MY NAME! WHO SPEAKS?
ONE WHO COMMANDS! COME CLOSER, KREETIN!
WHO ARE YOU? HOW DO YOU KNOW MY NAME, SIRE?
I'M METRON! THERE IS LITTLE I DON'T KNOW! I ASK MANY QUESTIONS--- AND RESOLVE THEM!
THEN YOU'VE BEEN WATCHING! AND KNOW WHAT'S HAPPENED HERE! WHAT CAN HUMBLE KREETIN TELL SUCH A BEING!?
FOR ALL THAT HIMON HAS ADDED TO YOUR LIFE---INCLUDING YOUR NECK---YOU DO NOTHING TO HELP HIM!
BUT, SIRE! HIMON DOESN'T SHARE OUR ORIGINS! WAS HE TO OUTSHINE US ALL WITH NOBILITY, AND KNOWLEDGE--- AMONG US HE IS WORTH MERE DUST!
-CERTAINLY NOT WORTH YOUR SKIN!

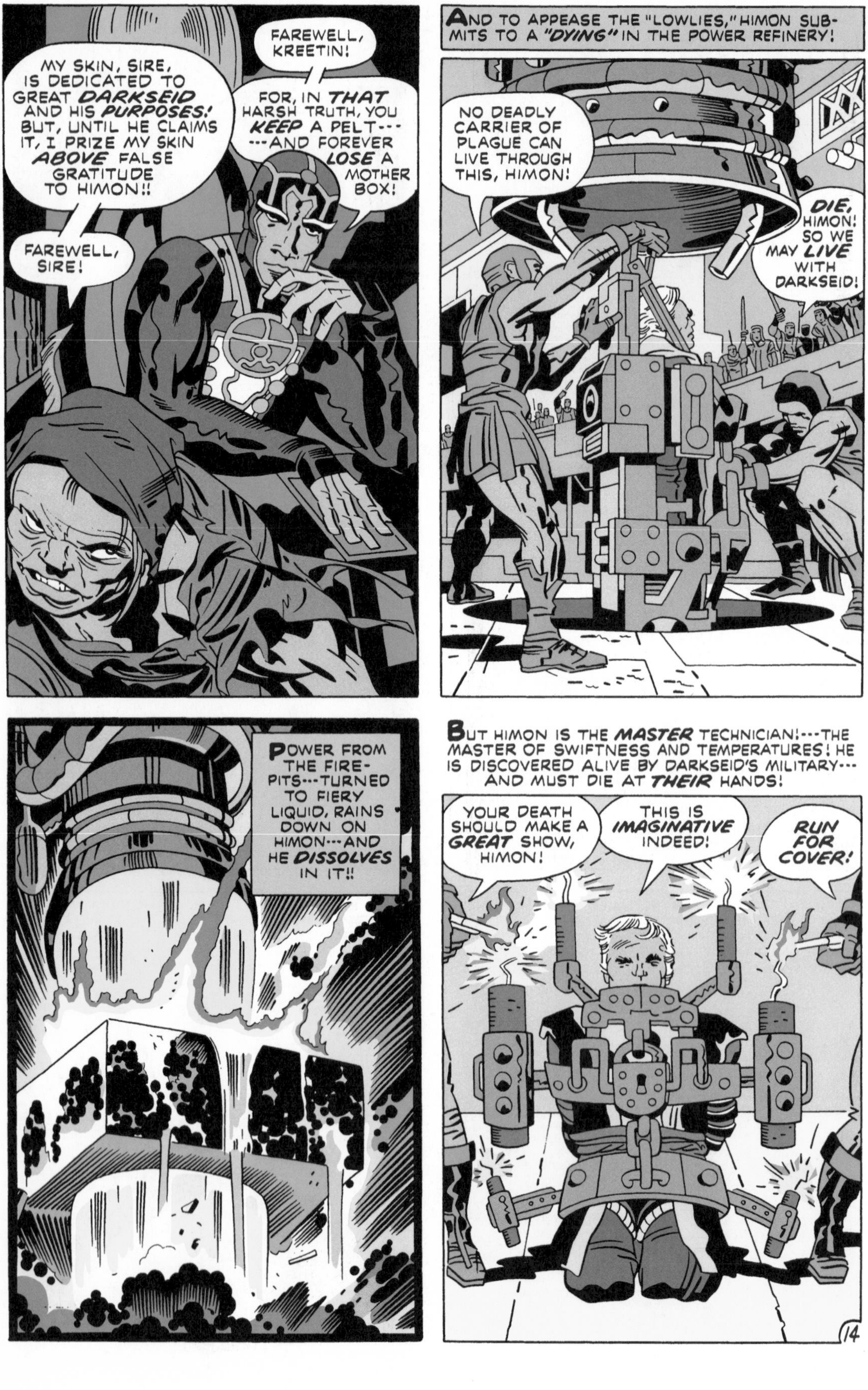

MY SKIN, SIRE, IS DEDICATED TO GREAT DARKSEID AND HIS PURPOSES! BUT, UNTIL HE CLAIMS IT, I PRIZE MY SKIN ABOVE FALSE GRATITUDE TO HIMON!!
FAREWELL, KREETIN!
FOR, IN THAT HARSH TRUTH, YOU KEEP A PELT--- ---AND FOREVER LOSE A MOTHER BOX!
FAREWELL, SIRE!
AND TO APPEASE THE "LOWLIES," HIMON SUBMITS TO A "DYING" IN THE POWER REFINERY!
NO DEADLY CARRIER OF PLAGUE CAN LIVE THROUGH THIS, HIMON!
DIE, HIMON! SO WE MAY LIVE WITH DARKSEID!
POWER FROM THE FIRE-PITS---TURNED TO FIERY LIQUID, RAINS DOWN ON HIMON---AND HE DISSOLVES IN IT!!
BUT HIMON IS THE MASTER TECHNICIAN!---THE MASTER OF SWIFTNESS AND TEMPERATURES! HE IS DISCOVERED ALIVE BY DARKSEID'S MILITARY--- AND MUST DIE AT THEIR HANDS!
YOUR DEATH SHOULD MAKE A GREAT SHOW, HIMON!
THIS IS IMAGINATIVE INDEED!
RUN FOR COVER!
14

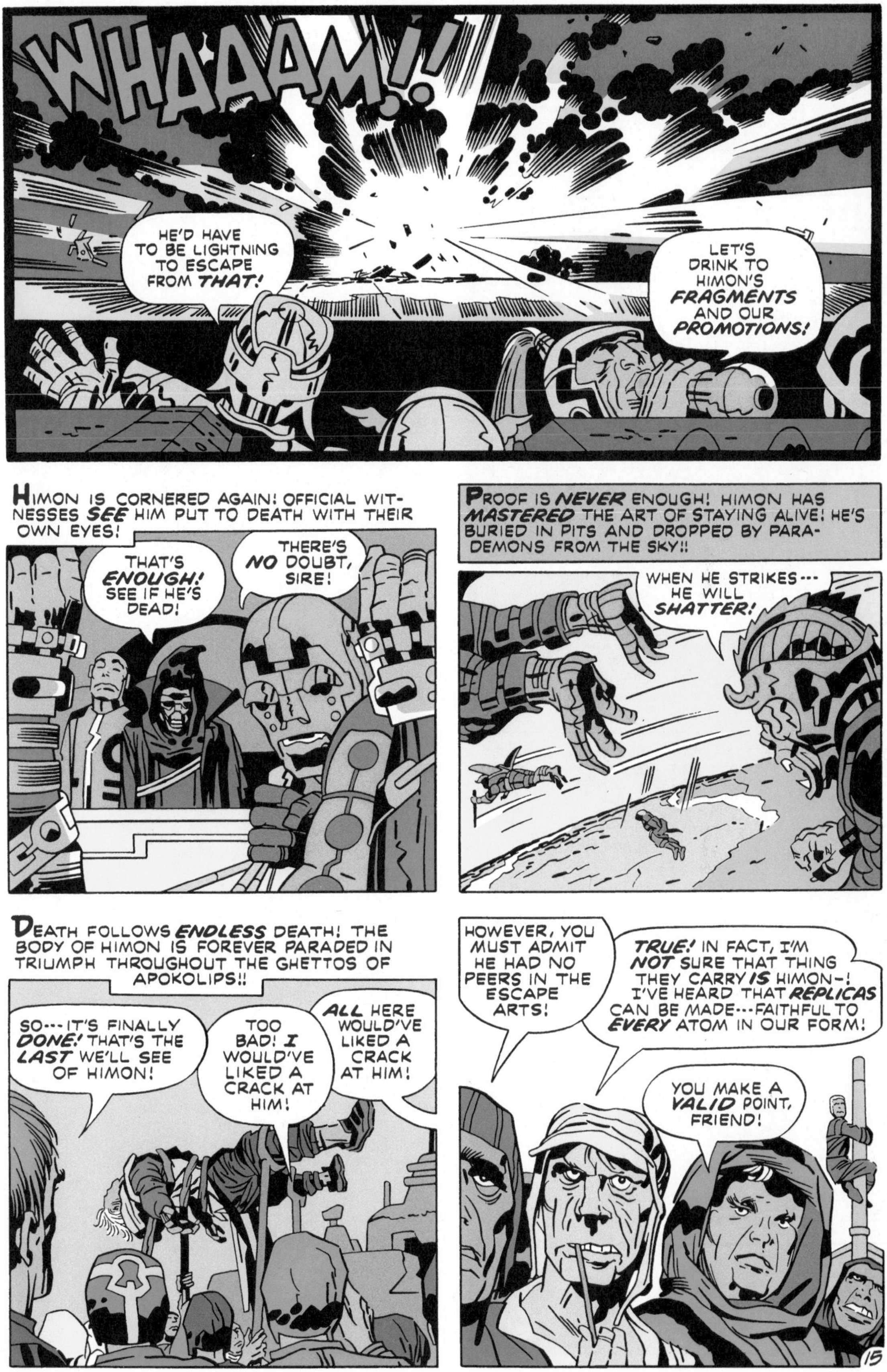
WHAAAM!!
HE'D HAVE TO BE LIGHTNING TO ESCAPE FROM THAT!
LET'S DRINK TO HIMON'S FRAGMENTS AND OUR PROMOTIONS!
HIMON IS CORNERED AGAIN! OFFICIAL WITNESSES SEE HIM PUT TO DEATH WITH THEIR OWN EYES!
THAT'S ENOUGH! SEE IF HE'S DEAD!
THERE'S NO DOUBT, SIRE!
PROOF IS NEVER ENOUGH! HIMON HAS MASTERED THE ART OF STAYING ALIVE! HE'S BURIED IN PITS AND DROPPED BY PARA-DEMONS FROM THE SKY!!
WHEN HE STRIKES--- HE WILL SHATTER!
DEATH FOLLOWS ENDLESS DEATH! THE BODY OF HIMON IS FOREVER PARADED IN TRIUMPH THROUGHOUT THE GHETTOS OF APOKOLIPS!!
SO---IT'S FINALLY DONE! THAT'S THE LAST WE'LL SEE OF HIMON!
TOO BAD! I WOULD'VE LIKED A CRACK AT HIM!
ALL HERE WOULD'VE LIKED A CRACK AT HIM!
HOWEVER, YOU MUST ADMIT HE HAD NO PEERS IN THE ESCAPE ARTS!
TRUE! IN FACT, I'M NOT SURE THAT THING THEY CARRY IS HIMON-! I'VE HEARD THAT REPLICAS CAN BE MADE---FAITHFUL TO EVERY ATOM IN OUR FORM!
YOU MAKE A VALID POINT, FRIEND!

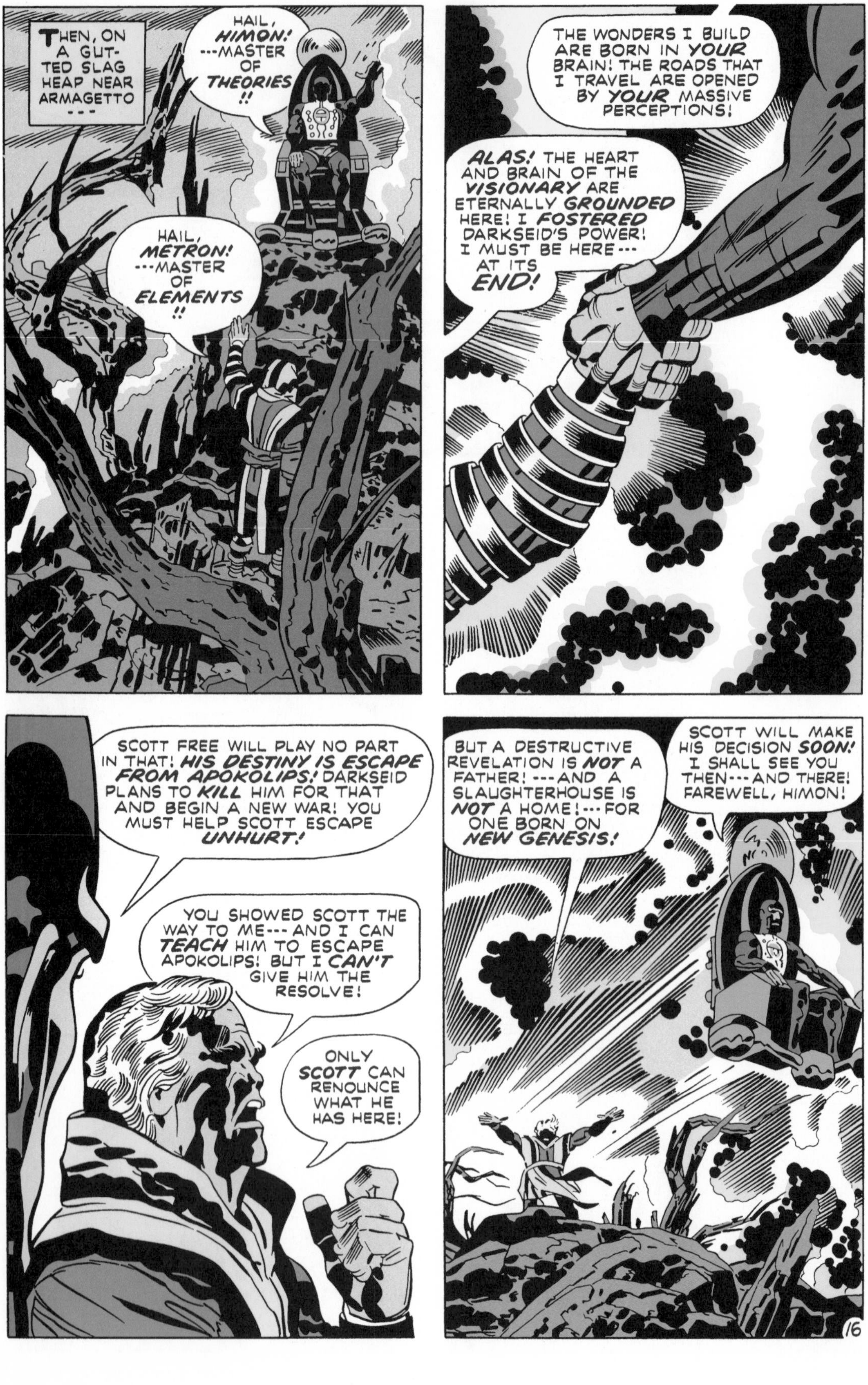
THEN, ON A GUTTED SLAG HEAP NEAR ARMAGETTO ---
HAIL, HIMON! ---MASTER OF THEORIES !!
HAIL, METRON! ---MASTER OF ELEMENTS !!
THE WONDERS I BUILD ARE BORN IN YOUR BRAIN! THE ROADS THAT I TRAVEL ARE OPENED BY YOUR MASSIVE PERCEPTIONS!
ALAS! THE HEART AND BRAIN OF THE VISIONARY ARE ETERNALLY GROUNDED HERE! I FOSTERED DARKSEID'S POWER! I MUST BE HERE--- AT ITS END!
SCOTT FREE WILL PLAY NO PART IN THAT! HIS DESTINY IS ESCAPE FROM APOKOLIPS! DARKSEID PLANS TO KILL HIM FOR THAT AND BEGIN A NEW WAR! YOU MUST HELP SCOTT ESCAPE UNHURT!
YOU SHOWED SCOTT THE WAY TO ME--- AND I CAN TEACH HIM TO ESCAPE APOKOLIPS! BUT I CAN'T GIVE HIM THE RESOLVE!
ONLY SCOTT CAN RENOUNCE WHAT HE HAS HERE!
BUT A DESTRUCTIVE REVELATION IS NOT A FATHER! ---AND A SLAUGHTERHOUSE IS NOT A HOME! --- FOR ONE BORN ON NEW GENESIS!
SCOTT WILL MAKE HIS DECISION SOON! I SHALL SEE YOU THEN--- AND THERE! FAREWELL, HIMON!

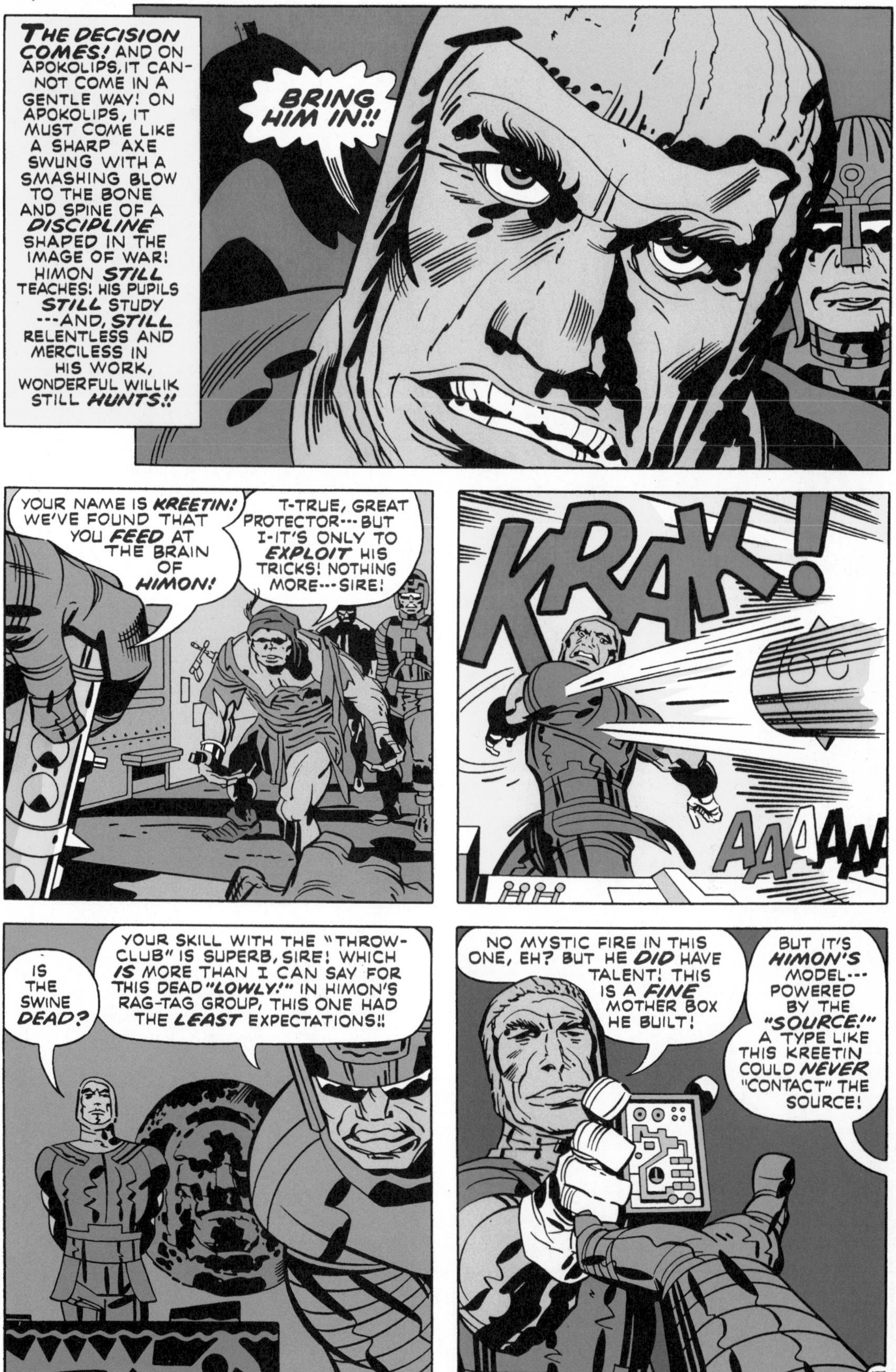
THE DECISION COMES! AND ON APOKOLIPS, IT CANNOT COME IN A GENTLE WAY! ON APOKOLIPS, IT MUST COME LIKE A SHARP AXE SWUNG WITH A SMASHING BLOW TO THE BONE AND SPINE OF A DISCIPLINE SHAPED IN THE IMAGE OF WAR! HIMON STILL TEACHES! HIS PUPILS STILL STUDY ---AND, STILL RELENTLESS AND MERCILESS IN HIS WORK, WONDERFUL WILLIK STILL HUNTS!!
BRING HIM IN!!
YOUR NAME IS KREETIN! WE'VE FOUND THAT YOU FEED AT THE BRAIN OF HIMON!
T-TRUE, GREAT PROTECTOR---BUT I-IT'S ONLY TO EXPLOIT HIS TRICKS! NOTHING MORE---SIRE!
KRAK!
AAAAAAA
IS THE SWINE DEAD?
YOUR SKILL WITH THE "THROW-CLUB" IS SUPERB, SIRE! WHICH IS MORE THAN I CAN SAY FOR THIS DEAD "LOWLY!" IN HIMON'S RAG-TAG GROUP, THIS ONE HAD THE LEAST EXPECTATIONS!!
NO MYSTIC FIRE IN THIS ONE, EH? BUT HE DID HAVE TALENT! THIS IS A FINE MOTHER BOX HE BUILT!
BUT IT'S HIMON'S MODEL---POWERED BY THE "SOURCE!" A TYPE LIKE THIS KREETIN COULD NEVER "CONTACT" THE SOURCE!
17

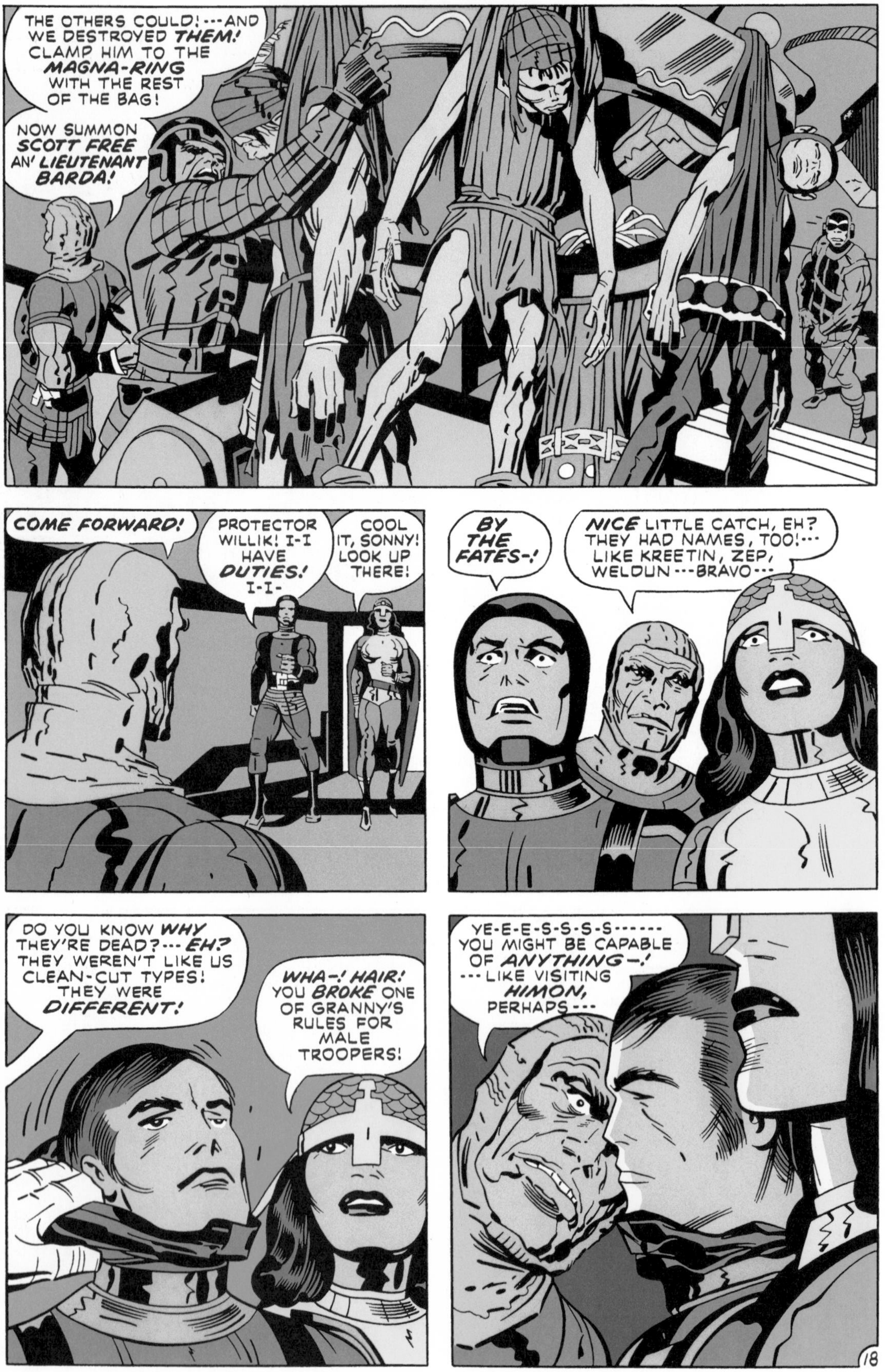
THE OTHERS COULD! ---AND WE DESTROYED THEM! CLAMP HIM TO THE MAGNA-RING WITH THE REST OF THE BAG!
NOW SUMMON SCOTT FREE AN' LIEUTENANT BARDA!
COME FORWARD!
PROTECTOR WILLIK! I-I HAVE DUTIES! I-I-
COOL IT, SONNY! LOOK UP THERE!
BY THE FATES-!
NICE LITTLE CATCH, EH? THEY HAD NAMES, TOO!--- LIKE KREETIN, ZEP, WELDUN ---BRAVO---
DO YOU KNOW WHY THEY'RE DEAD?--- EH? THEY WEREN'T LIKE US CLEAN-CUT TYPES! THEY WERE DIFFERENT!
WHA-! HAIR! YOU BROKE ONE OF GRANNY'S RULES FOR MALE TROOPERS!
YE-E-E-S-S-S-S------ YOU MIGHT BE CAPABLE OF ANYTHING-! ---LIKE VISITING HIMON, PERHAPS---
18

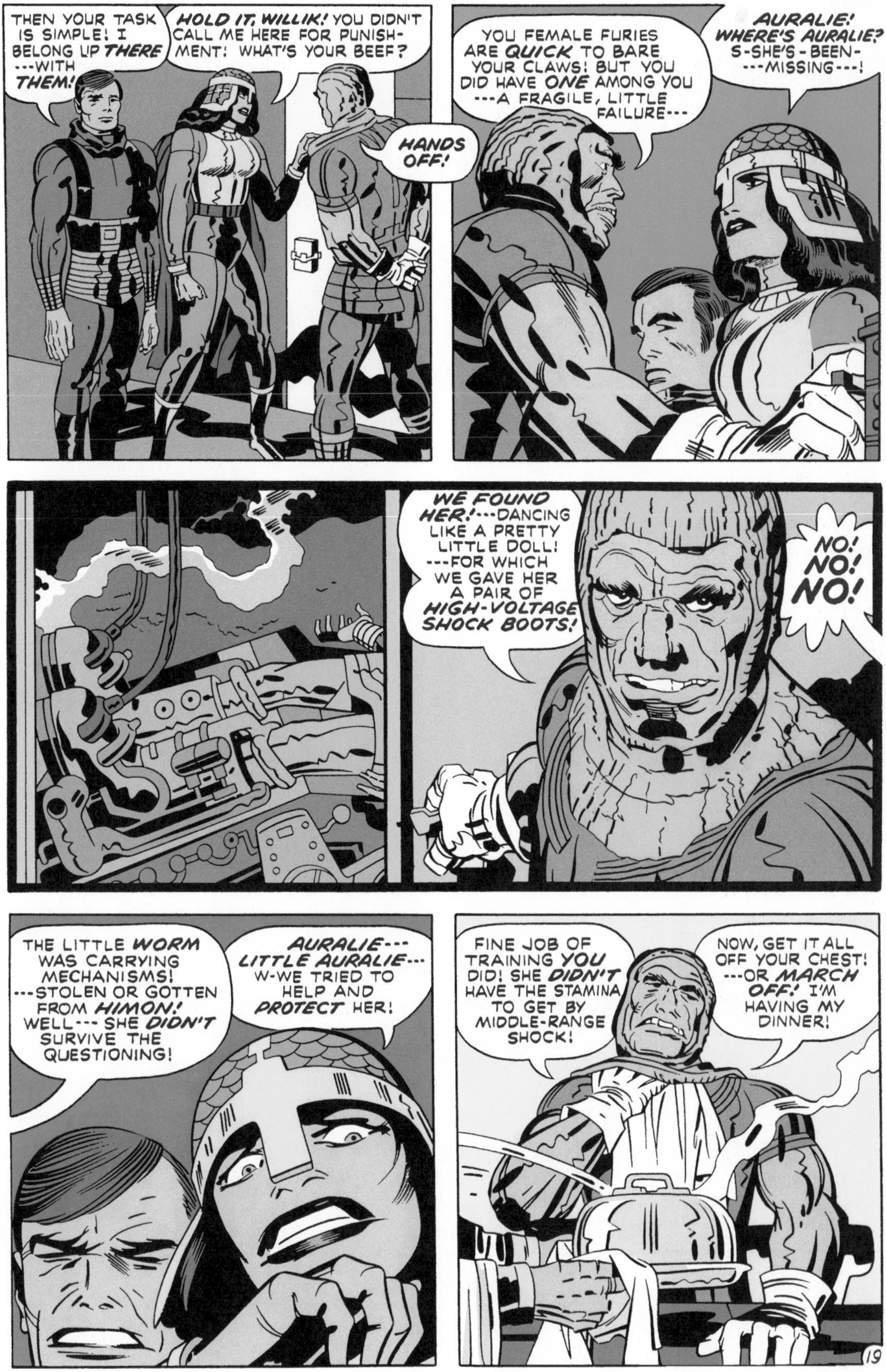
THEN YOUR TASK IS SIMPLE! I BELONG UP THERE ---WITH THEM!
HOLD IT, WILLIK! YOU DIDN'T CALL ME HERE FOR PUNISHMENT: WHAT'S YOUR BEEF?
HANDS OFF!
YOU FEMALE FURIES ARE QUICK TO BARE YOUR CLAWS! BUT YOU DID HAVE ONE AMONG YOU ---A FRAGILE, LITTLE FAILURE---
AURALIE! WHERE'S AURALIE? S-SHE'S-BEEN- ---MISSING---!
WE FOUND HER!---DANCING LIKE A PRETTY LITTLE DOLL! ---FOR WHICH WE GAVE HER A PAIR OF HIGH-VOLTAGE SHOCK BOOTS!
NO! NO! NO!
THE LITTLE WORM WAS CARRYING MECHANISMS! ---STOLEN OR GOTTEN FROM HIMON! WELL--- SHE DIDN'T SURVIVE THE QUESTIONING!
AURALIE--- LITTLE AURALIE--- W-WE TRIED TO HELP AND PROTECT HER!
FINE JOB OF TRAINING YOU DID! SHE DIDN'T HAVE THE STAMINA TO GET BY MIDDLE-RANGE SHOCK!
NOW, GET IT ALL OFF YOUR CHEST! ---OR MARCH OFF! I'M HAVING MY DINNER!
19

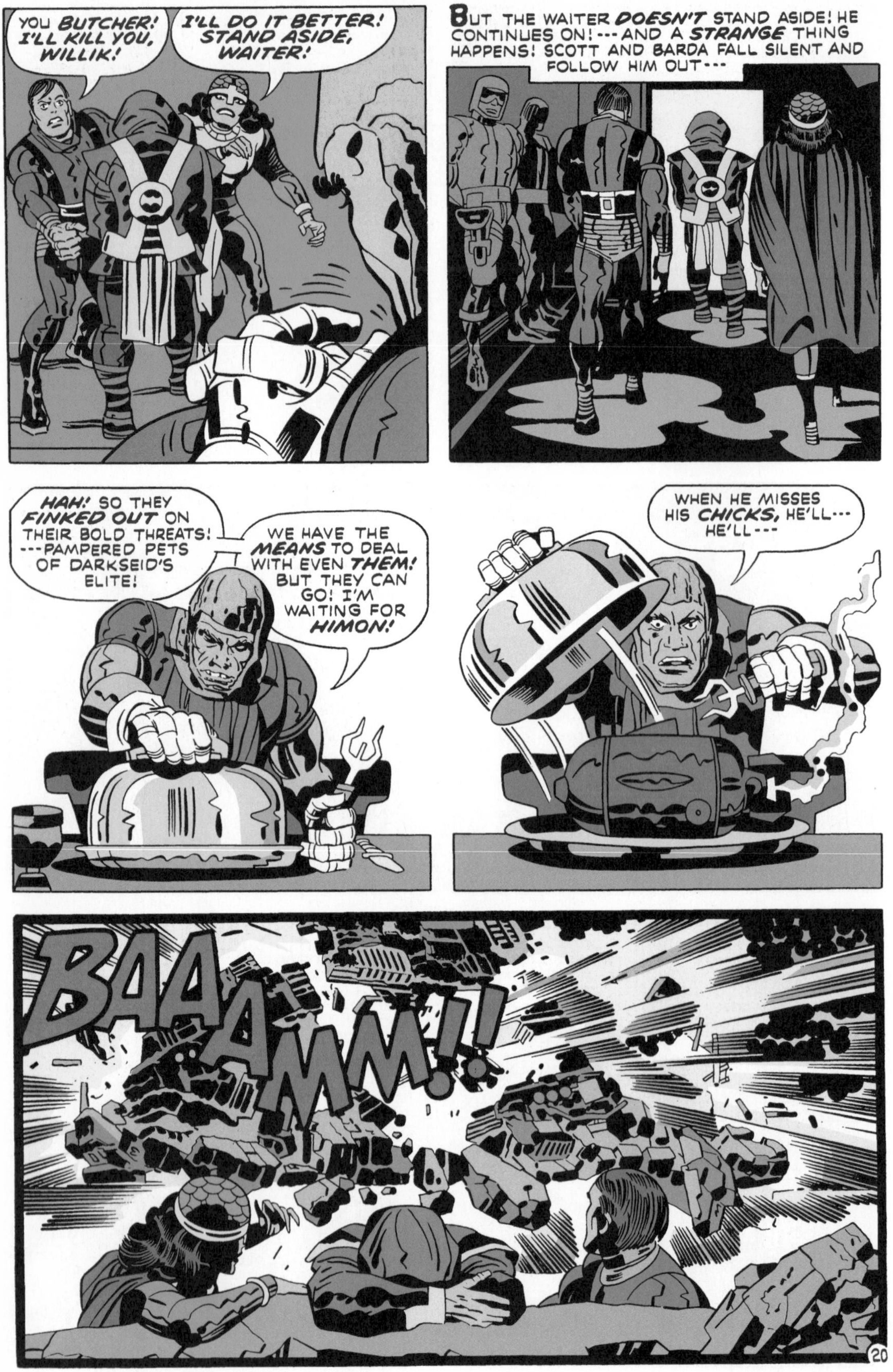
YOU BUTCHER! I'LL KILL YOU, WILLIK!
I'LL DO IT BETTER! STAND ASIDE, WAITER!
BUT THE WAITER DOESN'T STAND ASIDE! HE CONTINUES ON! ---AND A STRANGE THING HAPPENS! SCOTT AND BARDA FALL SILENT AND FOLLOW HIM OUT---
HAH! SO THEY FINKED OUT ON THEIR BOLD THREATS! ---PAMPERED PETS OF DARKSEID'S ELITE!
WE HAVE THE MEANS TO DEAL WITH EVEN THEM! BUT THEY CAN GO! I'M WAITING FOR HIMON!
WHEN HE MISSES HIS CHICKS, HE'LL--- HE'LL---
BAAAMM!!
20

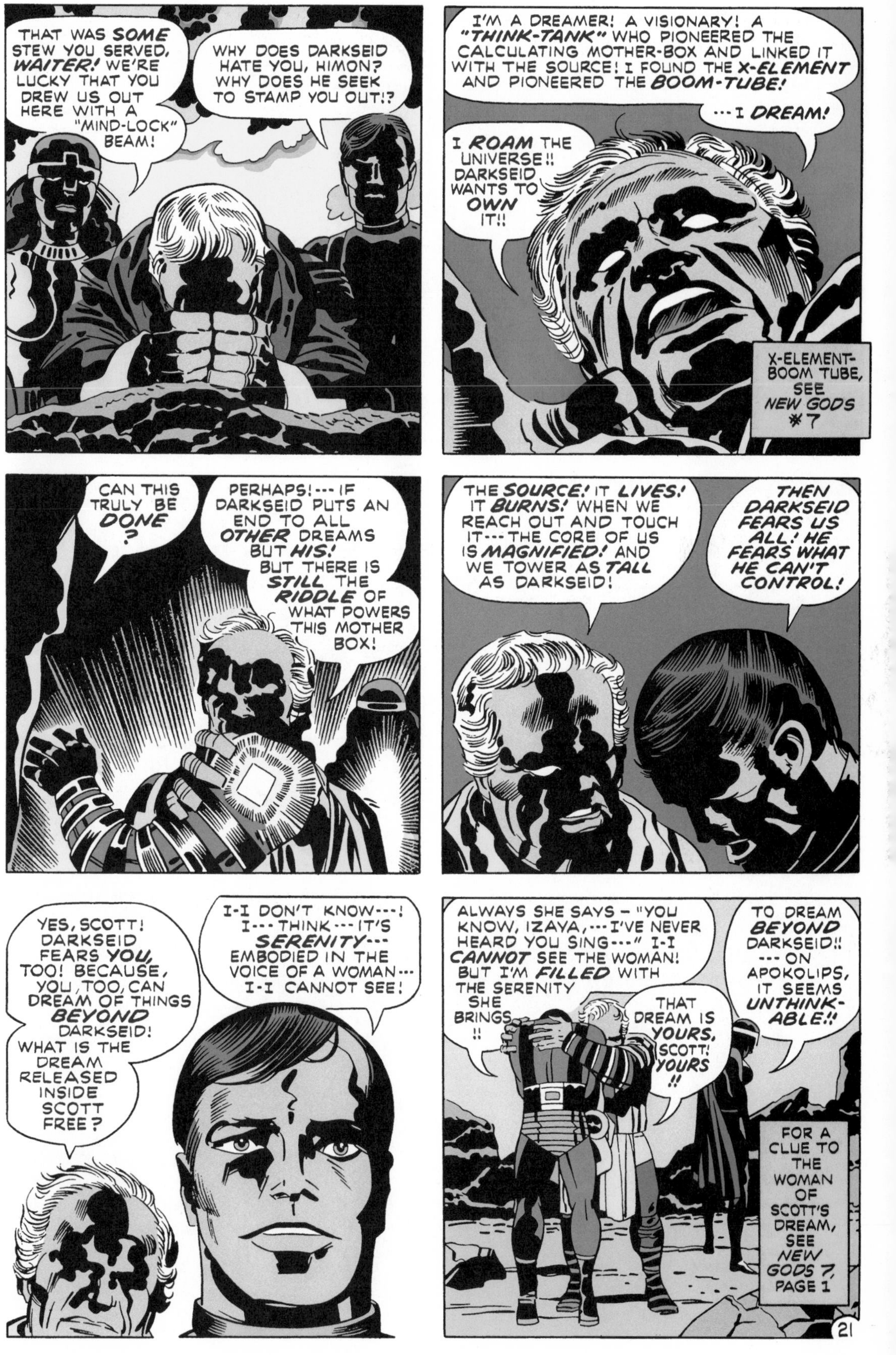
THAT WAS SOME STEW YOU SERVED, WAITER! WE'RE LUCKY THAT YOU DREW US OUT HERE WITH A "MIND-LOCK" BEAM!
WHY DOES DARKSEID HATE YOU, HIMON? WHY DOES HE SEEK TO STAMP YOU OUT!?
I'M A DREAMER! A VISIONARY! A "THINK-TANK" WHO PIONEERED THE CALCULATING MOTHER-BOX AND LINKED IT WITH THE SOURCE! I FOUND THE X-ELEMENT AND PIONEERED THE BOOM-TUBE!
...I DREAM!
I ROAM THE UNIVERSE!! DARKSEID WANTS TO OWN IT!!
X-ELEMENT-BOOM TUBE, SEE NEW GODS #7
CAN THIS TRULY BE DONE?
PERHAPS!---IF DARKSEID PUTS AN END TO ALL OTHER DREAMS BUT HIS! BUT THERE IS STILL THE RIDDLE OF WHAT POWERS THIS MOTHER BOX!
THE SOURCE! IT LIVES! IT BURNS! WHEN WE REACH OUT AND TOUCH IT---THE CORE OF US IS MAGNIFIED! AND WE TOWER AS TALL AS DARKSEID!
THEN DARKSEID FEARS US ALL! HE FEARS WHAT HE CAN'T CONTROL!
YES, SCOTT! DARKSEID FEARS YOU, TOO! BECAUSE, YOU, TOO, CAN DREAM OF THINGS BEYOND DARKSEID! WHAT IS THE DREAM RELEASED INSIDE SCOTT FREE?
I-I DON'T KNOW---! I---THINK---IT'S SERENITY--- EMBODIED IN THE VOICE OF A WOMAN--- I-I CANNOT SEE!
ALWAYS SHE SAYS - "YOU KNOW, IZAYA,---I'VE NEVER HEARD YOU SING---" I-I CANNOT SEE THE WOMAN! BUT I'M FILLED WITH THE SERENITY SHE BRINGS!!
THAT DREAM IS YOURS, SCOTT! YOURS!!
TO DREAM BEYOND DARKSEID!! ---ON APOKOLIPS, IT SEEMS UNTHINKABLE!!
FOR A CLUE TO THE WOMAN OF SCOTT'S DREAM, SEE NEW GODS 7, PAGE 1
21

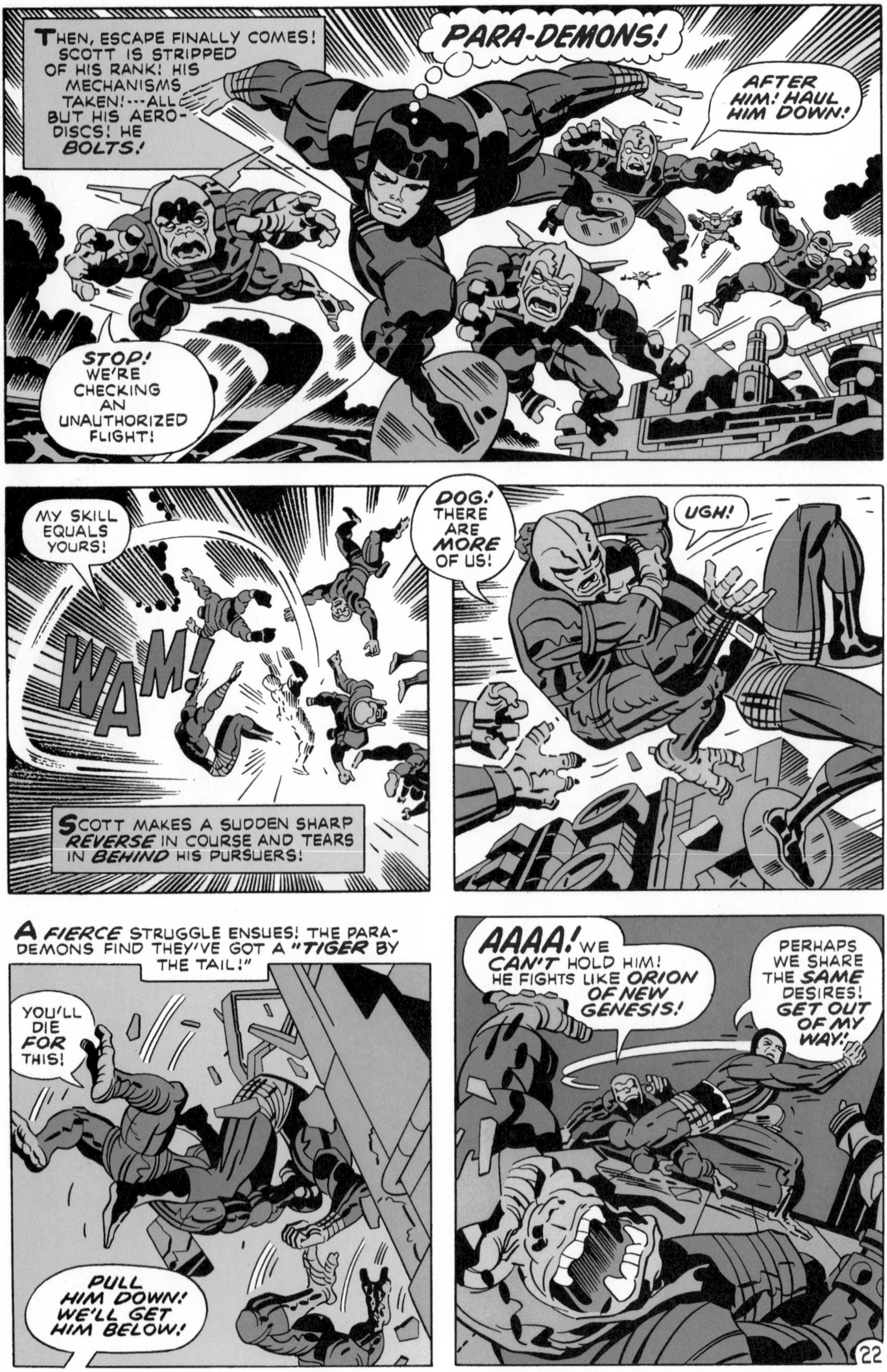
THEN, ESCAPE FINALLY COMES! SCOTT IS STRIPPED OF HIS RANK! HIS MECHANISMS TAKEN!---ALL BUT HIS AERO-DISCS! HE BOLTS!
PARA-DEMONS!
AFTER HIM! HAUL HIM DOWN!
STOP! WE'RE CHECKING AN UNAUTHORIZED FLIGHT!
MY SKILL EQUALS YOURS!
WAM!
SCOTT MAKES A SUDDEN SHARP REVERSE IN COURSE AND TEARS IN BEHIND HIS PURSUERS!
DOG! THERE ARE MORE OF US!
UGH!
A FIERCE STRUGGLE ENSUES! THE PARA-DEMONS FIND THEY'VE GOT A "TIGER BY THE TAIL!"
YOU'LL DIE FOR THIS!
PULL HIM DOWN! WE'LL GET HIM BELOW!
AAAA! WE CAN'T HOLD HIM! HE FIGHTS LIKE ORION OF NEW GENESIS!
PERHAPS WE SHARE THE SAME DESIRES! GET OUT OF MY WAY!
22

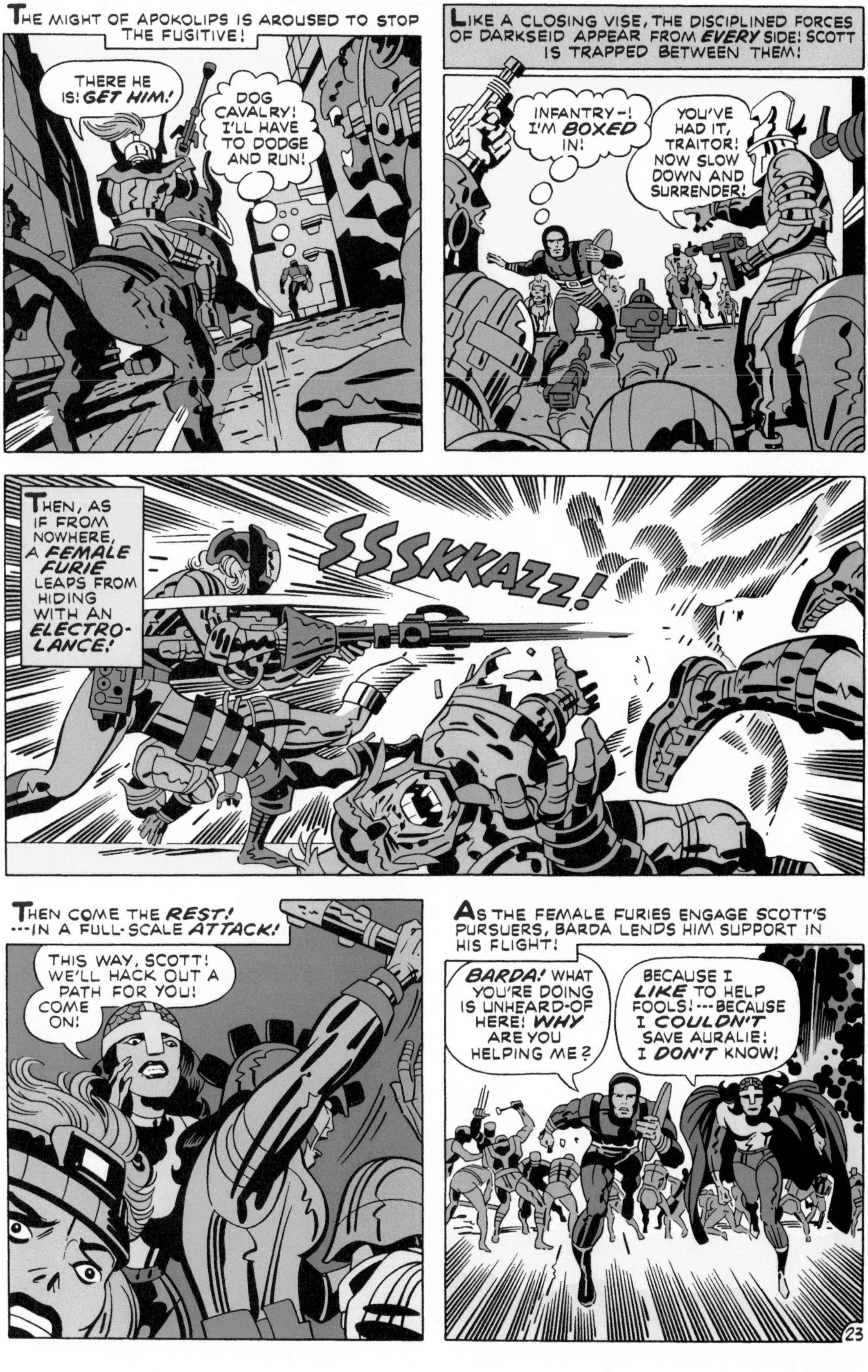
THE MIGHT OF APOKOLIPS IS AROUSED TO STOP THE FUGITIVE!
THERE HE IS! GET HIM!
DOG CAVALRY! I'LL HAVE TO DODGE AND RUN!
LIKE A CLOSING VISE, THE DISCIPLINED FORCES OF DARKSEID APPEAR FROM EVERY SIDE! SCOTT IS TRAPPED BETWEEN THEM!
INFANTRY--! I'M BOXED IN!
YOU'VE HAD IT, TRAITOR! NOW SLOW DOWN AND SURRENDER!
THEN, AS IF FROM NOWHERE, A FEMALE FURIE LEAPS FROM HIDING WITH AN ELECTRO-LANCE!
SSSKKAZZ!
THEN COME THE REST! ---IN A FULL-SCALE ATTACK!
THIS WAY, SCOTT! WE'LL HACK OUT A PATH FOR YOU! COME ON!
AS THE FEMALE FURIES ENGAGE SCOTT'S PURSUERS, BARDA LENDS HIM SUPPORT IN HIS FLIGHT!
BARDA! WHAT YOU'RE DOING IS UNHEARD-OF HERE! WHY ARE YOU HELPING ME?
BECAUSE I LIKE TO HELP FOOLS! ---BECAUSE I COULDN'T SAVE AURALIE! I DON'T KNOW!

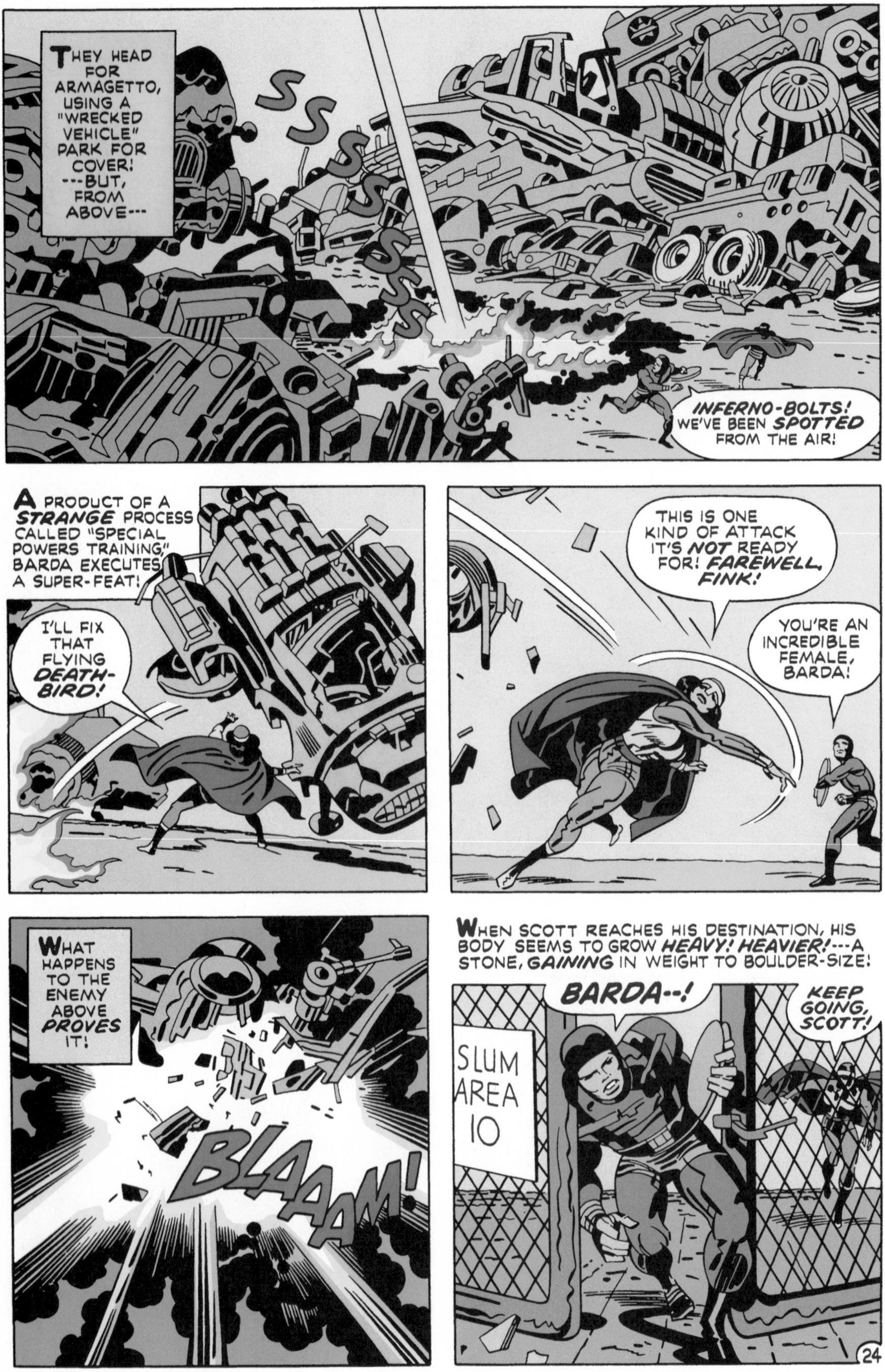
THEY HEAD FOR ARMAGETTO, USING A "WRECKED VEHICLE" PARK FOR COVER! ---BUT, FROM ABOVE---
SSSSSSSSS
INFERNO-BOLTS! WE'VE BEEN SPOTTED FROM THE AIR!
A PRODUCT OF A STRANGE PROCESS CALLED "SPECIAL POWERS TRAINING," BARDA EXECUTES A SUPER-FEAT!
I'LL FIX THAT FLYING DEATH-BIRD!
THIS IS ONE KIND OF ATTACK IT'S NOT READY FOR! FAREWELL, FINK!
YOU'RE AN INCREDIBLE FEMALE, BARDA!
WHAT HAPPENS TO THE ENEMY ABOVE PROVES IT!
BLAAAM!
WHEN SCOTT REACHES HIS DESTINATION, HIS BODY SEEMS TO GROW HEAVY! HEAVIER!---A STONE, GAINING IN WEIGHT TO BOULDER-SIZE!
BARDA--!
KEEP GOING, SCOTT!
SLUM AREA 10

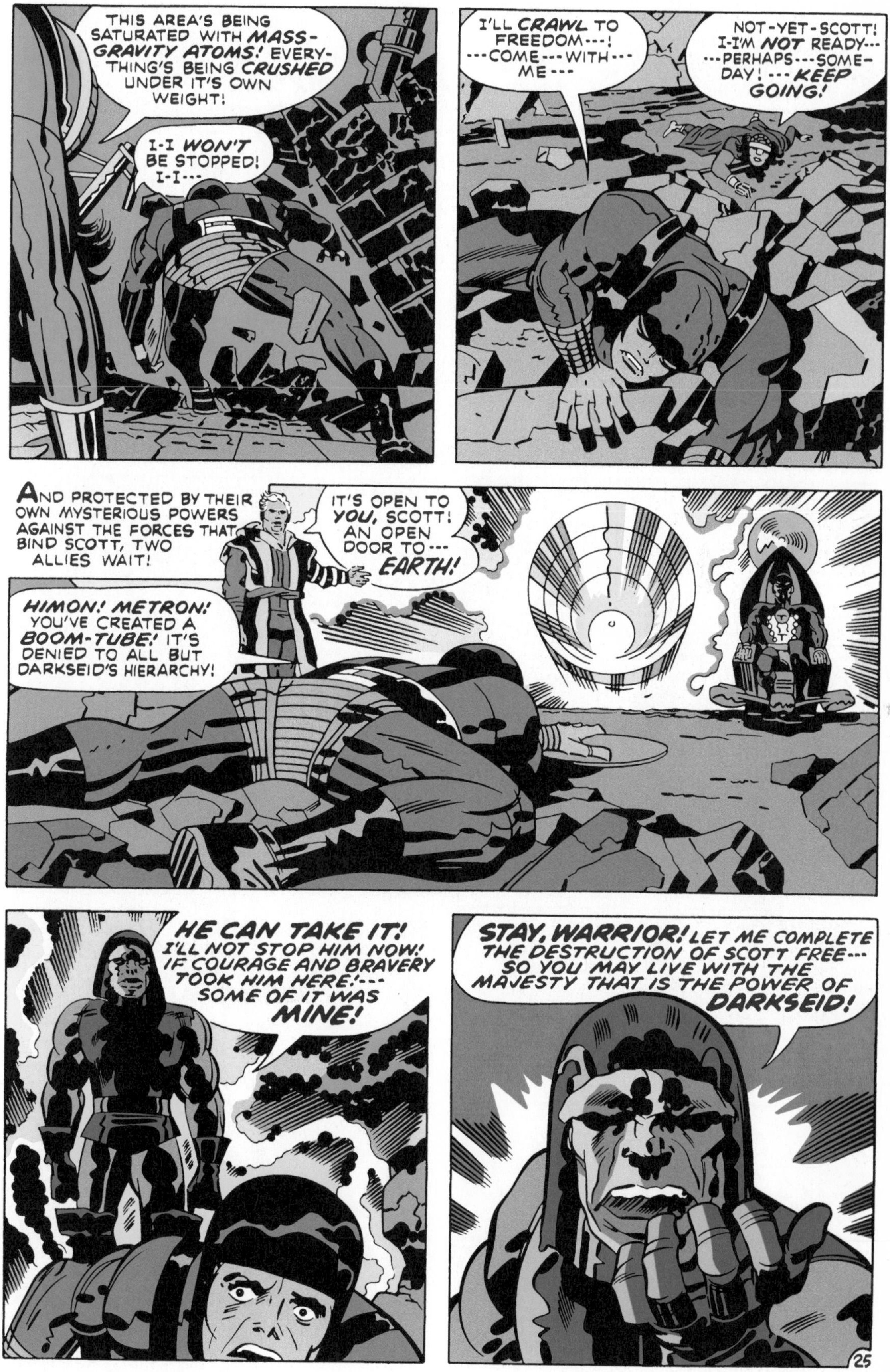
THIS AREA'S BEING SATURATED WITH MASS-GRAVITY ATOMS! EVERYTHING'S BEING CRUSHED UNDER IT'S OWN WEIGHT!
I-I WON'T BE STOPPED! I-I---
I'LL CRAWL TO FREEDOM---! ---COME---WITH---ME---
NOT-YET-SCOTT! I-I'M NOT READY--- ---PERHAPS---SOME-DAY! ---KEEP GOING!
AND PROTECTED BY THEIR OWN MYSTERIOUS POWERS AGAINST THE FORCES THAT BIND SCOTT, TWO ALLIES WAIT!
IT'S OPEN TO YOU, SCOTT! AN OPEN DOOR TO--- EARTH!
HIMON! METRON! YOU'VE CREATED A BOOM-TUBE! IT'S DENIED TO ALL BUT DARKSEID'S HIERARCHY!
HE CAN TAKE IT! I'LL NOT STOP HIM NOW! IF COURAGE AND BRAVERY TOOK HIM HERE!--- SOME OF IT WAS MINE!
STAY, WARRIOR! LET ME COMPLETE THE DESTRUCTION OF SCOTT FREE--- SO YOU MAY LIVE WITH THE MAJESTY THAT IS THE POWER OF DARKSEID!

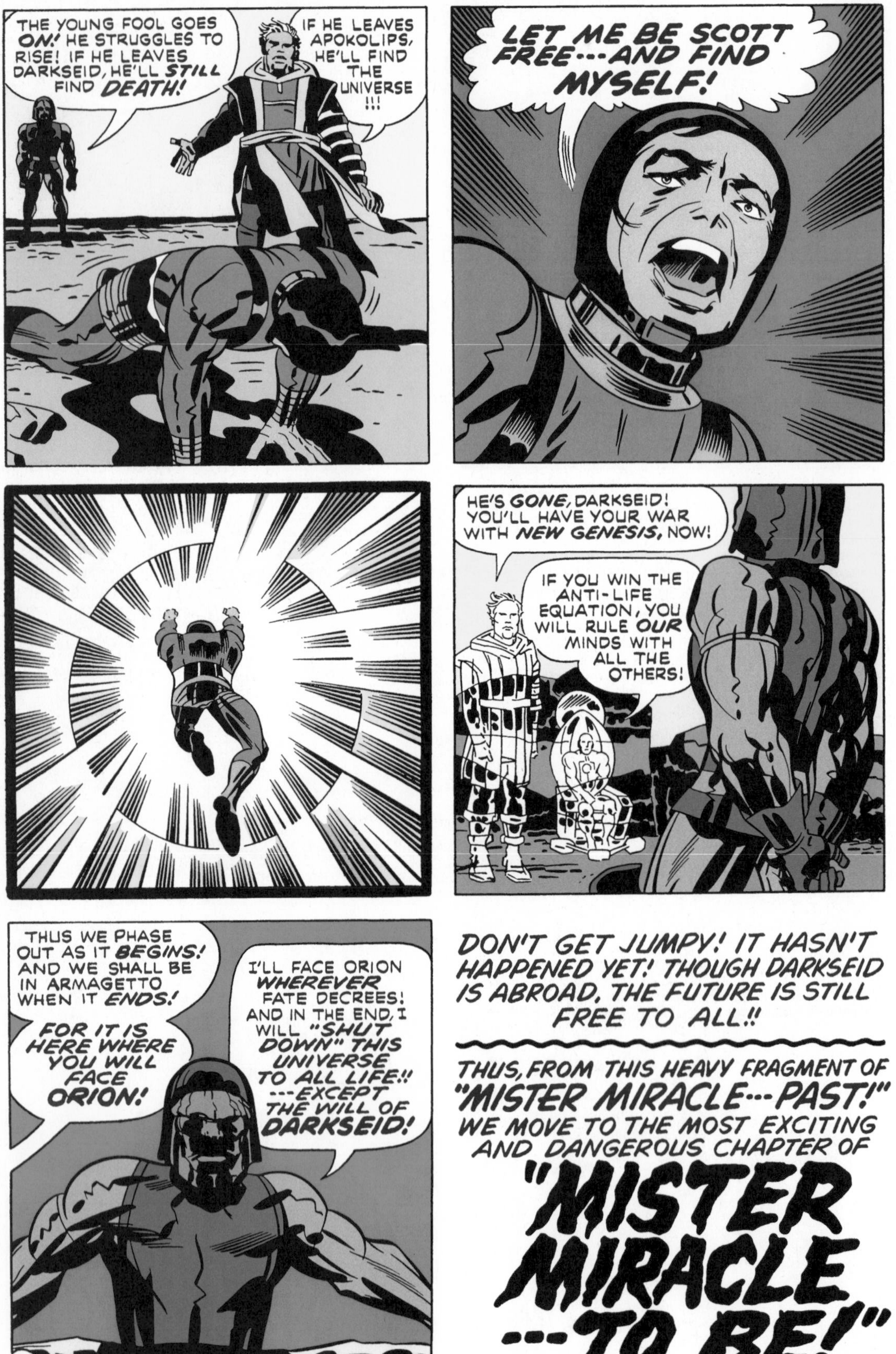
THE YOUNG FOOL GOES ON! HE STRUGGLES TO RISE! IF HE LEAVES DARKSEID, HE'LL STILL FIND DEATH!
IF HE LEAVES APOKOLIPS, HE'LL FIND THE UNIVERSE !!!
LET ME BE SCOTT FREE---AND FIND MYSELF!
HE'S GONE, DARKSEID! YOU'LL HAVE YOUR WAR WITH NEW GENESIS, NOW!
IF YOU WIN THE ANTI-LIFE EQUATION, YOU WILL RULE OUR MINDS WITH ALL THE OTHERS!
THUS WE PHASE OUT AS IT BEGINS! AND WE SHALL BE IN ARMAGETTO WHEN IT ENDS!
FOR IT IS HERE WHERE YOU WILL FACE ORION!
I'LL FACE ORION WHEREVER FATE DECREES! AND IN THE END, I WILL "SHUT DOWN" THIS UNIVERSE TO ALL LIFE!! ---EXCEPT THE WILL OF DARKSEID!
26
DON'T GET JUMPY! IT HASN'T HAPPENED YET! THOUGH DARKSEID IS ABROAD, THE FUTURE IS STILL FREE TO ALL!!
THUS, FROM THIS HEAVY FRAGMENT OF "MISTER MIRACLE---PAST!" WE MOVE TO THE MOST EXCITING AND DANGEROUS CHAPTER OF
"MISTER MIRACLE ---TO BE!"

FEMALE FURIES #1 variant cover
by FRANCESCO MATTINA

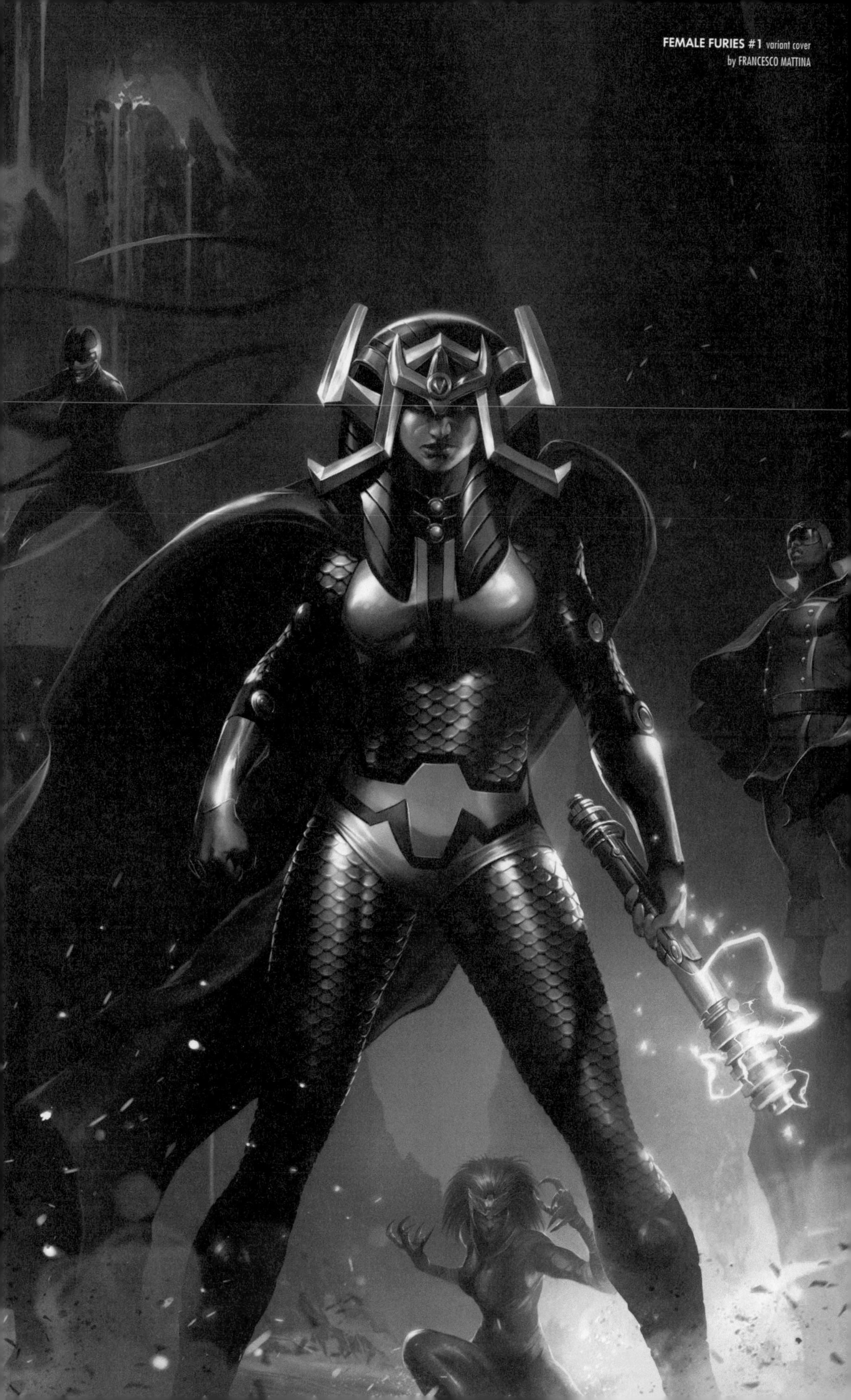

FEMALE FURIES character sketches
by ADRIANA MELO

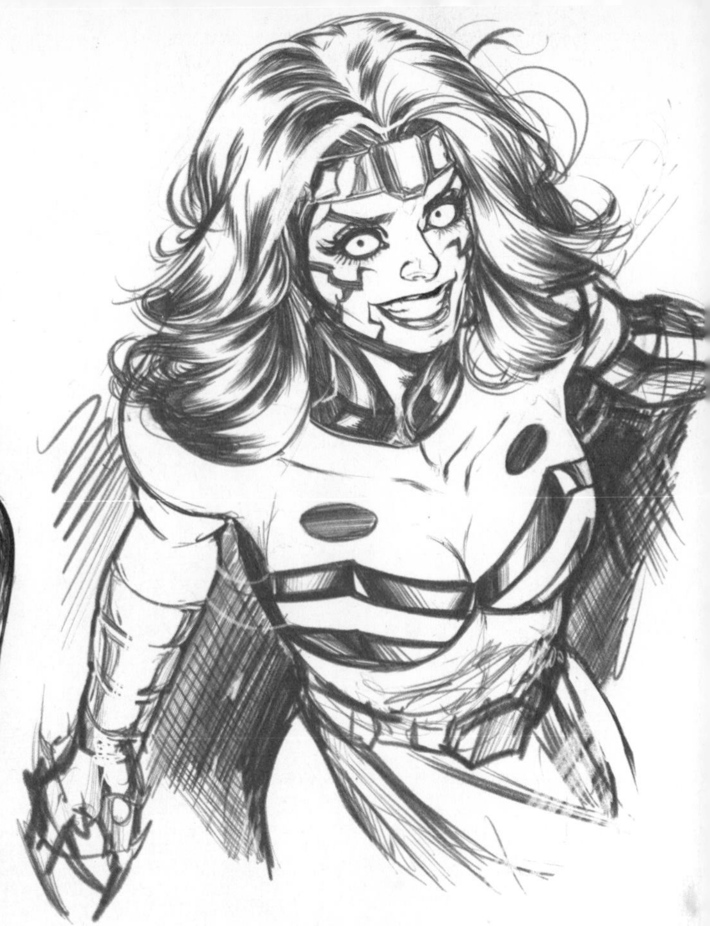

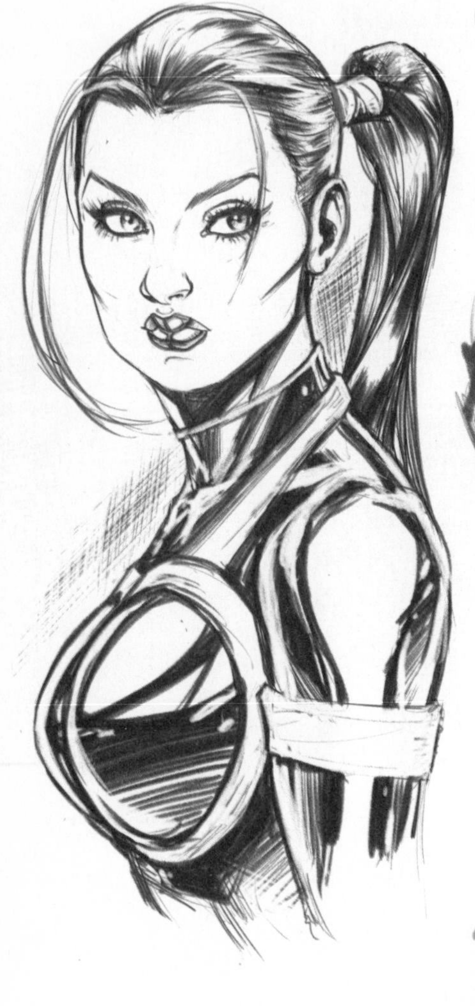

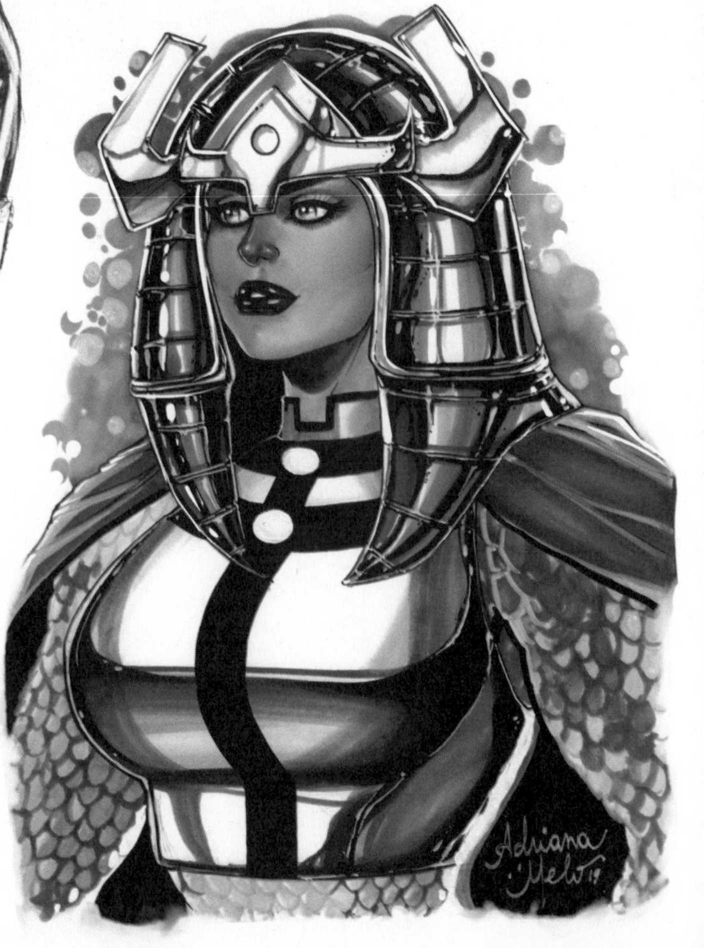
Adriana
Melo 17